ALSO BY PETER EVANS

Good-Bye Baby and Amen
Titles
The Englishman's Daughter

The Life and Times of Aristotle Socrates Onassis

RI

PETER EVANS

Summit Books • New York

10 9 8 7 6 5 4 3 2 1

Library of Congress Cataloging in Publication Data

Evans, Peter, date.
  Ari: the life and times of Aristotle Onassis.

  1. Onassis, Aristotle Socrates, 1906–1975.
2. Merchant marine—Biography.   I. Title.
HE569.05E93 1986   387.5'092'4 [B]   86-3740
ISBN 0-671-46508-2

ACKNOWLEDGMENTS

THIS BOOK, or at least the idea that I should write such a book, began in Paris in the fall of 1967. It was, I later learned, John W. Meyer's suggestion that Ari should tell his own story firsthand—"the way it really was, the whole kit and caboodle"—nobody in his right mind believes the sanitized versions of Ari's life, Meyer told me later—"and I figure people always warm to bad guys who finally level." Ari consulted Costa Gratsos, his wisest and most effective aide, who approved of the idea and persuaded him to go ahead. My debt to Meyer and Gratsos is therefore very great: far too great even to begin to accommodate in the sources and notes section their contributions which run through this entire story. Costa Gratsos's reminiscences gave me a picture of Ari as a young man in Argentina, which would otherwise be lacking. Their help, counsel and encouragement through difficult times convinced me that the concept was realizable. It saddens me that they are now both dead, beyond my sense of obligation and gratitude. I like to think that they would have read this book with satisfaction, and some amusement, if not absolute approval.

It is impossible to write accurately about a man's life without many reliable witnesses, a range of different viewpoints; a biography of this kind stands or falls not only on the willingness of the subject to commit himself totally, or as close to the limit as is humanly tolerable, but also on the cooperation and frankness of others involved in the story. A great number of people went out of their way to assist me. More than three hundred friends, relations, bankers, gofers, politicians, journalists, socialites, lawyers, chauffeurs, celebrities, Onassis executives and former executives—the mightiest and the humblest of the people that were involved— were contacted in preparation for this book. For a variety of personal and professional reasons, and frequently a fusion of both, many of them asked not to be identified. I am grateful to them all.

To none am I more indebted than to Joseph Bolker, Finn Bryde, Alan Campbell-Johnson, Roy Cohn, Geraldine Spreckles Fuller, Wendy Russell Reves, Joan Thring Stafford and Fiona Thyssen-Bornemisza, without whom this book would have been considerably less explicit, and infinitely less well informed. Individual recognition is included in context in the sources and notes.

Within the companies and the family I was treated with fickle cordiality, but I especially value the help of Artemis and Theodore Garofalides, Constantine Konialidis, Mme. Livanos; the trust of Alexander Onassis, and the frankness of the unfailingly patient and friendly Nigel Neilson (whose proposed book on his own remarkable life is one I await with keen interest). Only Christina Onassis proved to be uncooperative. I first met her with her father in Paris in 1968; in the early seventies I was her dinner companion at Fleur Cowles's Albany apartment in London. She was gossipy, relaxed and at the peak of her attractiveness. On October 12, 1982, as I prepared to resume work on *Ari*, I flew to Paris and sent a note to avenue Foch, explaining the purpose of my visit and requesting an interview. The note, as did several others after it, went unanswered. On January 12, 1983, I returned to Paris and had lunch with Hubert Michard-Pellissier, her lawyer and a friend since childhood. I explained the situation and again asked for a meeting with Christina. He suggested that I put my questions in writing; he would talk with Miss Onassis and call me the following day. I sent a list of questions to him later the same afternoon. He did not call the following day nor in the days that followed. He did not return my calls. On January 17, I returned to London accepting the fact that this book would have to be written without Miss Onassis's help.

A great many journalists, writers, and intelligence people were helpful in providing leads and information. In Washington I owe thanks to my former colleague Ross Mark of the *London Daily Express*, not least for introducing me to William A. Lowther, whose finely tuned political instincts and connections within the intelligence community, ability to produce key government documents and memoranda on cue, willingness to ride herd on the bureaucracy to see that my inquiries and requests were not forgotten were above price. I am grateful to the *Toronto Star*'s Bogdan Kipling and his wife for their hospitality during my stay in Washington. I am indebted to Len Deighton for introducing me to at least one intelligence source whose name it would be imprudent to reveal.

In New York I received help from Dudley Freeman, whose prodigious News Service found articles that other agencies and archives said had been lost forever. I am also grateful to Gloria Hammond, whose delitescent digging in the early days of research proved indispensable. I am indebted to Joan Walsh of *Time* magazine; and to Morton Redner; also to Joan and Philip Kingsley. In Florida I had generous help from Brian Wells, who was to have collaborated on Johnny Meyer's autobiography and sent me a copy of the synopsis which contained anecdotes that were new to me, a few of which I have used in these pages with gratitude. In Los Angeles I am grateful to Douglas Thompson and Leslie Salisbury for their assistance. I thank Eve Foreman for her efforts to find the private pictures of her late husband Carl's encounter with Ari. I am fortunate in having as friends William C. Jordan and Lorraine G. Winchester of WCJ Investigative Consultants, Inc.: I thank them for their hospitality during my stay in Los Angeles and also for putting me in touch with their associates in the business, including the splendidly efficient Hal Lipset in San Francisco, who, with a few telephone calls, saved me weeks of legwork. For background to Ari's war years in California, I am grateful to Frank Angel, former FBI bureau chief in Los Angeles. In Boston I thank Walter Conrad, former general manager of the North American operation of Olympic Airways, for foregoing his own plans to write a book about his experiences with Ari to talk to me about them instead; and Ruth and Michael Deeley. I also thank Hélène Gaillet for revealing to me an aspect of Ari in the last days of his life on Skorpios that only she witnessed.

In Paris I was helped by *Newsweek*'s Edward Behr, the *London Standard*'s Sam White, Patrice Habans, Peter Stephens, Lydia Taffouraud, C. L. Sulzberger, Bruno Courtin, Paul Chutkow, Bernard Valery. I am indebted to Jill Ibrahim, my principal researcher in France. Her access to confidential memoranda flowing out of Paris and Monte Carlo during the Ari-Rainier crises was an invaluable source of information and an achievement into which I did not pry. I thank my friends at *Paris Match*, especially the library staff. I thank Yoko Tani for translating the Japanese material. My appreciation also goes to Henry Pessar, who worked with Ingeborg Dedichen on her *mémoires* and gave me the benefit of perceptions that were always astute. I have had valuable advice from members of French intelligence. I am also grateful to Vivienne Wilson Roberts for insights into *le tout Paris,* the beautiful progeny of money old and new. In Monte Carlo I was aided by the background research of Johanna Morris. To the two distinguished Greek journalists, both of whom were important contributors to clandestine publications during the colonels' regime and who translated junta documents for me, and to an able Athens lawyer, I express my gratitude and respect their wishes to remain anonymous. I thank Roger Mainwood of the *Athens News* for his interest and friendly contribution, and Georgio Filandrianos for finding answers to many of my questions. Taki Theodorecopulus gave me useful advice on his fellow countrymen and even better advice on Greek women. In Norway my sincerest gratitude goes to Tore Johannsen, of NRK TV, Oslo, who guided me to Finn Bryde.

In London I thank Eric Clark and Brian Freemantle for their help in the deep waters of international intrigue; and Miles Copeland, former CIA man who knows all the channels; and my unnameable friends in British intelligence. I am especially grateful to Raymond Hawkey who patiently examined the mass of Dedichen albums and explained what made one picture important and another not. The late Willi Frischauer helped me in many important ways: he permitted me to read and compare the statements made by Ari and others in the research and preparation for his biography *Onassis* (New York: Meredith Press, 1968; London: Bodley Head Ltd., 1968); he also provided me with his own memories and views of Ari which, for one reason or another, did not find their way into his own book. I am indebted to Robert Edwards, Michael Evans and Norma Heyman for effecting valuable introductions; and to Lady Carolyn Townshend, for her reminiscences. I learned from listening to the views and anecdotes of Sir John Russell, Brian Morris, Lady Nora Docker, Richard Burton, Alan Brien, Sir Woodrow Wyatt, and Basil Mantzos, head of Olympic Holidays and an old sparring partner of Ari's. I am indebted to Dr. Martin Gilbert, Winston S. Churchill's biographer, for finding time in the middle of his writing to search his papers for material on Ari; and also to Anthony Montague Browne, Sir Winston's former Private Secretary, for answering my queries. The Lady Soames and Mr. Winston Churchill, M.P., showed me similar courtesies, as did Dr. Alan Richardson. I am grateful to Noël Goodwin for his research on Claudia Muzio, and to Nigel Dempster and Sir John Junor for their suggestions. I thank Judith Dagworthy of the Savoy Hotel, and the librarians at the Churchill College Archives Centre, Cambridge; *London Daily Mirror;* London Library; Central Reference Library, Westminster; British Library; British Newspaper Library, Colindale; University of London Library; and the

House of Lords Record Office; Vice-Admiral Julio Zapata, head of the Peruvian Naval Commission in Europe and Naval Attache in London. I am grateful to Simon Wiesenthal of the Jewish Documentation Center in Vienna, who took time to reply to my many inquiries; and also to Deana Cohen at the Simon Wiesenthal Center on the campus of Yeshiva University of Los Angeles.

Many of the interviews in this book were taped, involving months of transcription. Much of this grueling work was done with dedication and reassuring absorption by my secretary, Lisa Jane Pratt. I love her for that and much else. The person who worked longest and most closely with me is Ann Hoffmann, who began as a researcher and became a valued friend. Her enthusiasm and ideas, her calm acceptance of my demands on her time and experience, lightened my task immeasurably. I also record my gratitude to Richard Philpott for his picture research; to my copy editor in New York, Larry Zuckerman; and to my son, Mark, for his help in innumerable ways. In particular I express my affectionate thanks to my friend and literary agent, Ed Victor, who not only put the idea of *Ari* back into my head but hope in my heart throughout the project. For their perceptive comments, patience and consistent encouragement, I owe a great debt to my two editors: Jim Silberman of Summit Books in New York, and Tom Maschler of Jonathan Cape in London. And for watching over me, and this book, from start to finish, I thank my wife, Pamela.

London
December 1985

This one is for
Camilla

PROLOGUE

ALITTLE AFTER eleven o'clock on a January evening in 1968 I received a telephone call at my London home from an American introducing himself as John W. Meyer inviting me to fly to Paris to meet Aristotle Onassis. "We'd like to talk as soon as possible," he said. About what? He wasn't prepared to discuss the matter on the telephone but promised that I would find it interesting—and to my advantage. As soon as possible, it appeared, was the following morning. A ticket was waiting for me at the Air France desk at Heathrow; Meyer would meet me at Orly Airport; I should come prepared to stay overnight; he'd fix a room at the Plaza-Athénée. After I put down the receiver, I called the airline: a first-class ticket had been booked in my name. Twelve o'clock the next day at 88, avenue Foch, I met Ari for the first time. He was more or less the way I had imagined him. A small muscular man in his sixties with an expressive face, his black hair streaked with grey was beginning to thin. His voice, carefully modulated and with the faintly rasping tone of a sixty-a-day cigarette man, or a serious whisky drinker (he was both), had an accent that carried the longing cadence of the exile, which I suspected he knew how to use effectively on women. His eyes were hidden by the dark glasses which were his trademark, but I knew they would be alert, speculating, not without humor. He wore a conservative blue suit with a monogrammed white silk handkerchief in his top pocket. Only his hands surprised me. Dark and hard-looking, to the touch they were as soft as a young girl's. He placed me in a chair facing him across a Louis Quinze desk. His portrait hung on the wall behind him; silver-framed photographs of his children stood side by side on the desk: Christina's features most resembled his own; Alexander looked serious and intelligent. They did not look like happy kids.

He was thinking of "making a book" about his life, Ari came to the point immediately. He was unsure whether it should be an autobiography or an authorized biography, but either way he said he wanted a book "that is a hundred-percenter, exactly how it was." Would I be interested in writing it? I knew that an Onassis biography that had reputedly been written with his blessing, if not his cooperation, was due to be published later that year. Why did he want another? "I was not satisfied with one ship, Mr. Evans, why should I be satisfied with one book?" he replied. I wasn't interested in becoming his hagiographer; I asked him to define the kind of book he had in mind. He started to tell me about his early life, his childhood in Smyrna, now Izmir, the massacre of 1922, his flight to Argentina, where he made his first fortune. After a few minutes he stopped, removed his dark glasses and began slowly polishing the lenses with his silk handkerchief. His eyes, I saw for the first time, were the color of old pennies. "I think it should read like a novel," he said, replacing his glasses. "You've got one hell of a story, Ari. A saga," said Meyer, who had been sitting quietly in a chair by the window. Ari said, "Well, we could make it a goddam thriller, too." Presumably he saw himself as the hero, I said. He could have taken offense, instead of which he said, "No— the villain. Villains always have the best parts." That was a good start, I thought. But I was still curious to know why he had asked me to write the book. We had never met, and as far as I knew we had no mutual friends who might have suggested my name to him. When I mentioned this, he took a letter from his desk and handed it to me. It was from Ari to Jean Paul Getty. It said that he, Ari, was considering writing his life story and could Getty suggest a suitable writer to work on the project with him. Getty had returned Ari's own letter, with my name and telephone number scrawled in the margin. (I was at that time interviewing Getty for a *Cosmopolitan* magazine profile and had spent several days with him in London and at Sutton Place, his estate in Surrey; he was not the sort of man who wasted time on matters that did not directly affect his own interests, and I suspect that mine had simply been the first name that came to mind.)

We lunched at Maxim's. Ari drank Black Label Scotch, and then Dom Perignon champagne, and did most of the talking, although Johnny Meyer was not afraid to lob a few one-liners into the conversation. "Maria used to think you were a Greek God, Ari —now she thinks you're just another goddam Greek," he said when Maria Callas's name was mentioned. Ari laughed, and it sounded genuine as well as guttural; Meyer knew exactly how far he could go with him. (Their friendship went back to Washington in the war years, he had told me in the limousine on the way in from the airport; he described himself as Ari's aide-de-camp.) It was a long lunch. I asked the questions I wanted to ask, and he did not try to evade anything, nor was he perturbed when I explained the kind of personal detail I would expect to go into and the people I'd want to talk to, if we proceeded with the book. There would be no problem: "The unexamined life is not worth living," he said. (Later I learned that the line was from Socrates; the study on his yacht *Christina* was filled with the Greek classics.) After the cognac came, he said: "So what do you make of me so far, Mr. Evans?" I said I thought he had style. "Style, perhaps, but they say I have no class. Fortunately, people with class are usually willing to overlook this flaw because I am very rich. You can't buy class, but you can buy tolerance for its absence." I got the impression that he had prepared for this meeting and I was seeing a performance, although I was sure he could convince anyone of anything when he put his mind to it. Nevertheless, the alchemy of mystery, money and sex held the promise of a remarkable story, and before we left the restaurant that afternoon we had a deal.

We began a series of conversations. I say conversations rather than interviews because I quickly discovered that he did not respond well to formal question-and-answer techniques; his mind did not work in logical patterns. He became angry if he suspected that I had researched before a conversation an incident or some episode in his past I wanted to develop. "It's what deadbeat reporters do when they can't think for themselves," he said, although I realized it was his way of controlling a situation. He was at his best, most recollective and self-analytical, when he was free-associating—preferably over a meal, in a bar, walking the streets late at night in London or Paris. Like all spellbinders, he liked to have an audience; in Paris Johnny Meyer sometimes tagged along, with a pretty girl from Madame Claude's callgirl salon or a showgirl from the Crazy Horse; now and then his son, Alexander, joined us, although he seemed ill at ease listening to Ari's stories, especially when he couldn't tell where an anecdote was leading or what fresh discovery he might make about his father. Theirs was not a comfortable relationship. The man who inspired Ari best was Constantine Gratsos, his oldest and closest friend. They had first met in Buenos Aires in the 1920s, and Gratsos knew more of the hopes, thoughts and sins of Ari than any other man had known. "Costa knows every crime I've ever committed," Ari had introduced him to me. Gratsos also understood how much Ari needed him, and, without either resentment or obsequiousness, remained silent when Ari boasted that he needed no one. "The hungry little Greek," Gratsos called him with affection.*

It was going well. I had access to the right people, and Ari was delivering some breathtaking material; he not only had a good memory for names and faces (especially those with money) but his recall of conversations and emotions, and his evocation of places, were a *tour de force*. Yet he puzzled me. I remembered one of his closest aides—one evening at Regine's—saying, "He is a human Enigma code machine. You press the same key and get different responses every time." "The key to Ari is there is no key," Gratsos had said. Ari had charm, he could be extraordinarily generous, and like most profoundly lonely people he enjoyed the company of children and strangers, but there was a violence in him that was never far from the surface. I knew that he was capable of sadism, especially toward those closest to him, but he was also a man who took delight in siding with underdogs. His humor switched at alarming speed: exhilaration could turn to despair, and not only when he drank. Once when I mentioned Stavros Niarchos—before I knew enough to tread warily around anything to do with his bitterest enemy, brother-in-law and the man who was soon to marry his ex-wife, Tina—he left the room slamming the door so hard that I'd have laid odds that he would never talk to me again. The following day as if nothing had happened he called, inviting me to dinner at Annabel's, his favorite London nightspot. He continued to come and go through the spring and summer months of 1968; I would receive calls to meet him in Paris, where we would talk for a few hours, a few minutes even, and once he failed to find time to talk to me at all after what had seemed to be a most urgent summons. I sat around the Trémoille Hotel for a couple of days and returned to London; he never apologized, never explained. After nine months of working together in this fashion he called and said that the book was off—"or, rather, on ice: now is not the time." He declined to tell me why he had changed his mind, although he realized that I knew enough to guess the reason. On October 20, 1968, he married Jacqueline Bouvier Kennedy.

I did not see or hear from him again for nearly six years. In the spring of 1974 he called and suggested that we meet for a drink at Annabel's. So much had happened in his life since 1968. Alex-

---

* *The hungry little Greek can do anything.—Juvenal.*

ander had been killed. Tina had died. Christina had been married and divorced. Meyer called from P. J. Clarke's saloon in New York and told me to be prepared for a shock when I saw Ari. "He may not have been the best father a boy could ask for, but in his own way he was a loving one," Meyer said. Ari was alone at the bar when I arrived at the nightclub in Berkeley Square, a large glass of Black Label between his soft, hard-looking hands. He made an effort to project his old vitality; but now there was an emptiness at its core, a want of hope. His laugh, his stories, the famous Ari charm, had been used so much over the decades of giving pleasure that their sorcery or whatever it was that made them work had simply given out. He said he had been "a little under the weather" recently but there was nothing the matter that "some R and R won't fix." He was sixty-eight years old, according to the legend; he looked and was older. He lit a cigarette, took a few puffs, stubbed it out, before lighting another. He sipped his drink. He took longer getting to the point than the first time we'd met. "Where were we up to?" he finally asked in an old man's voice— he hated leaving anything unfinished, he added; it was the only explanation he ever gave for the sudden resumption of our conversations. But by the autumn it had become apparent that he did not have long to live, and I suspected that he was talking not for a book he would never see but to find some purpose to his life, an explanation that might set him free. "The rich need something to bank on, too," he said. He rambled, not, as before, amusingly and with a reason, but in confusion; vignettes sharper than recent vicissitudes came into his head from more than half a century ago. Toward the end of 1974 we met for the last time. Almost everything he loved had gone. He was exhausted and had difficulty talking. "You've got one hell of a story, let me tell you," he said when we said good-bye.

He was right. Except for one thing—it needed perspective. And for a long time after he died on March 15, 1975, the silence of the grave gagged the living; people who had talked with his incarnate approval became sepulchrally mute. I kept in touch, and waited. Slowly the doors began to open again. In 1983, the time had come to begin this "one hell of a story."

CHAPTER 1

*Few sons, indeed, are like their fathers.
Generally, they are worse; but just a few
are better.*

HOMER, *Odyssey*

THE CRUCIFIX hung above his cot. Sometimes in the dusk of the Mediterranean evening, sometimes in the small hours of the morning, the symbol of redemption seemed to float off the wall. The dark illusion scared and fascinated the small boy, who was sure that the trick of light was some sort of revelational reproach—every sin, he knew, had its own avenging angel: his grandmother had taught him that.

Since his mother's death, Gethsemane Onassis had been both mother and grandmother to Aristotle Socrates. A small woman with grey hair pulled into a tight hard bun, she was a compulsive churchgoer who decorated the house at Karatass, a coastal suburb of Smyrna (now Izmir), with religious bric-a-brac and souvenirs from her pilgrimages to the Holy Land. The child loved her very much, but some of the things she said frightened him: it was no good hiding beneath the bedclothes—not if you hide yourself away in the midst of the ocean, not in the tallest mountains, will you hide from the punishment of your sins, she would warn him after the smallest disobedience. She believed in God the Father, God the Son and God the Holy Ghost; she believed in heaven and hell, retribution and eternal damnation. She prayed that her grandson would one day become a priest, and every week sent a set of his underclothes to be blessed at St. Friday's, the local Greek Orthodox church where he served as an altar boy and learned the Byzantine psalms by heart.

When Aristotle was born, his father, Socrates Onassis, was

21

twenty-eight years old and already on his way to becoming one of
the wealthiest tobacco merchants and entrepreneurs in Smyrna.
Socrates was the second son of seven children, a Turkish citizen
with a Greek soul, and the richer he got the more Greek he became,
although Turkish would always be his first language. It was a
propitious time for the country's Anatolian Greeks*; their entre-
preneurial skills and administrative talents, vital to the Ottoman
Empire, had earned them privileges and social standing. His Imperial Majesty the Sultan Abdul Hamid II—"Our Lord and Master, the Crown of Ages and the Pride of all Countries, the greatest
of all Caliphs, the Successor of the Apostle of the Universe, the
Victorious Conqueror, the Shadow of God on Earth"—a deeply
wicked man, also known as Abdul the Damned, permitted them
an extraordinary but conditional prosperity. Most Turkish towns
had a thriving Greek quarter with its own hospitals, churches,
schools and legal system. Yet despite the centuries of oppression
and subjugation, the Anatolian Greeks never succumbed to a
ghetto psychopathy.

Socrates was born and raised deep in the interior of Asia
Minor in a village called Moutalasski, and had it not been for
German imperialism he might never have left his birthplace. But
when Germany sent out teams of surveyors and engineers to map
out the Berlin-to-Bagdad railway, a strategic stepping-stone to
India, a British possession, they brought amazing stories of the
quick fortunes being made in Smyrna. Socrates and his younger
brothers Homer, Alexander and Basil took off for the boomtown.
The engineers' tales were no exaggeration: the railroads branching
north and east from Smyrna had opened up the great wealth of
the Ottoman Empire to the West. Tobacco, carpets, cotton, timber,
maize, rye, barley, raisins, figs and coal were pouring through the
port of Smyrna every hour of every day. Socrates wrote home: "A
man would have to be a fool not to make his fortune in this place."

Smyrna was carved up and run by foreigners: the Belgians
controlled the waterworks; most of the carpet, mineral, grain and
dried-fruit business, as well as the city's power, were in the hands
of the British; the tramways and the main quay belonged to the
French; the Americans dominated the tobacco and licorice trades
as well as the oil terminals. It was not an easy town to crash, but
young Socrates had the optimism of youth. A small, short-necked
man with a weathered Levantine complexion and straight black

---

* Anatolia was the name given in the 900s to the part of Western Asia that became
Turkey; it included a substantial area around the city and port of Smyrna, which was
inhabited principally by Greeks.

hair neatly parted on the side of his head, he had dark heavy-lidded eyes that were sharp rather than intelligent, and his thick waxed military-style mustache concealed a curiously thin and feminine mouth. But he relished the challenge of the waterfront. "Never be pessimistic. Pessimism is a sickness you treat like any other sickness," was the philosophy he drummed into his brothers.

For the first two years he worked as a clerk for Bohar Bena-dava, a Jewish merchant. As soon as he had saved enough money, he rented a small warehouse on Port Abri and established an export-import agency dealing in whatever merchandise he could turn around at a profit. The excellence of his goods became recognized throughout Smyrna, and his business increased rapidly. No deal was too small to receive his attention, and within a year he moved into larger premises on the Grand Vizier Hane in the heart of the business district and opened another warehouse at Daragaz Point, a prime site close to the railhead at the pier. Although he lent money, insured cargoes and financed caravans, he was essentially a tobacco trader. His younger brother Alexander, who had moved back into the interior to establish contacts and supplies, returned to Smyrna to manage the Daragaz Point depot.

Soon his clients included some of the most important traders in Smyrna; he had lines of credit from the Imperial Ottoman Bank, the German Deutsche Bank, and the Crédit Lyonnais. It was the age of imagination as well as a time of risk, and there is a hint that while he ran his business affairs successfully he was not always overly scrupulous: rivals spoke of him with that punctilious respect that consists of negatives—he did not bear grudges, he did not break his word, he was not incorrigible.

As their reputations rose, the Onassis brothers gained a place among the finest families of Smyrna; Alexander and Homer became enmeshed in politics, particularly in *Mikrasiatik Ethniki Ameni* (the Asia Minor Defense League), a separatist movement seeking an autonomous Greek area inside Turkey, with Smyrna—with its preponderantly Greek population and as the traditional center of Christianity in Asia Minor—treated as an international zone. But Socrates avoided politics; more of a realist than his brothers, he concentrated his energies on business life, limiting his political involvement to subscriptions to compatriotic societies and nationalistic causes he considered useful and safe.

It was tradition rather than romance that took him back to his village to propose to Penelope Dologlou. The sufficiently pretty daughter of a well-off village elder, Penelope could read and write and make up accounts as well as any man, although the natural turn of her mind was simple, serious and domestic. Both families gave their blessing; it was considered a fine match. The wedding took place in St. Paraskevis's church in Smyrna two months before her seventeenth birthday.

His village-mindedness more than his instinctive prudence probably caused Socrates to move to Karatass, a short ferry ride from Smyrna. Rising from the sea in natural terraces, Karatass was middle class and cosmopolitan, a community in which a mixture of ethnic and religious groups, commercial and trading classes—Armenians, Greeks, Turks, Jews, Moslems, Christians—lived together in almost classic heterogeneity. There were nearly a dozen languages spoken within a few blocks of the Onassis villa, and most families spoke at least two of them.

Very soon almost the whole Onassis clan had moved to Karatass: brothers and sisters, aunts, uncles, cousins. Although he was the second-eldest son, Socrates was the family catalyst, the man who did the thinking and made most of the decisions.

Eleven months after the Smyrna nuptials, Penelope gave birth to their first child, a daughter whom they baptized Artemis, after the Greek goddess of wild animals and the hunt; two years later, probably, although by no means certainly (for he would change the day, the month and the year to suit his purpose), on the morning of January 20, 1900, Aristotle Socrates was born.

The next six years were quietly enriching ones for Socrates and his young family. His capacity for work never faltered, but he became increasingly shut in on himself with an unusual Mediterranean gift for emotional detachment. Obsessed with his own affairs, he seems to have had no more than an obliging interest in Aristo, as Aristotle was fondly called in the family; he never displayed that profound and possessive bond that commonly enters into the soul of a relationship between a Greek father and his only son. Perhaps his aloofness was rooted in a natural abstractedness in matters that were not connected with business, but no matter the root of his failure to express affection, Aristo from an early age felt their distance deeply.

Socrates' business continued to expand, especially his tobacco interests, although it was an uneasy and often dangerous time in Turkey: there had been a bloody revolt in Constantinople, and Sultan Abdul Hamid had been deposed by the Young Turks, many of them educated in Europe and genuinely determined to create a nationalistic Turkey in the Western democratic mold. But in the first elections for the new parliament the boundaries were rigged to all but wipe out the racial-minority representatives, and it was not long before the Young Turks promulgated an ominous policy of Turkey for the Turks.

Following the massacre of hundreds of Armenians at Adana in 1909, a chill of apprehension ran through the Christian population. But for the moment, the Young Turks had higher priorities than the extermination of the racial minorities: Italy had attacked Tripoli and seized Rhodes and nearly a dozen other Turkish islands in the Aegean. Crippling taxes were levied by the Turkish government to finance the war. In 1912, Turkey finally signed the Treaty of Ouchy, ceding Tripoli to the Italians on condition that they withdraw from the occupied islands. But, encouraged by Italy's success, Serbia, Bulgaria, Montenegro and, most alarmingly, Greece, immediately joined forces against Turkey. Socrates quarreled bitterly with his brothers, especially the volatile Alexander, for their open sympathies for the Greek homeland. Angrily he reminded them of the old Turkish saying: "If you don't want hemp round your neck, become a hangman."

It was a dangerous time for the Smyrna Greeks, and although Socrates' discreet wealth and careful connections protected them more than most, tragedy of a more personal nature was soon to strike. In 1912, Penelope Onassis developed an abscess in her kidney. It was not, at first, considered to be very serious, but her condition suddenly worsened; an operation became imperative. Aristo sensed the serious turn of events by his aunts' quiet conversations, which stopped when he appeared; the arrival of grandmother Gethsemane from Moutalasski to take over the running of the house; the mention of his mother's name among those whom Father Euthimion asked the congregation to include in their prayers and in their thoughts; the nuns making a fuss of him when he was taken to visit his mother at the French Hospital on rue Parallèle behind the quay at Smyrna.

A few days after what was thought to have been a successful operation, Penelope suffered an acute failure of her renal function and died within hours. She was thirty-three years old. And so Aristo came under the influence of the holy-minded Gethsemane and a clutch of aunts. There was nothing in all his world so lost to him as his mother's love.

A full-blooded man who needed the body of a woman, Socrates also needed somebody to take care of Artemis and Aristo, and less than six months after their mother's death he had wooed, married and impregnated his second wife, Helen. The birth of Merope was quickly followed by another daughter, Calirrhoë. Aristo, the center of attention in a society of women—small, thin and with a look of extreme fragility that people, when they see it, imagine conveys virtue—was an easy boy to love. It was Uncle Alexander who saved him from becoming a total milksop. He

talked to the boy about hunting and ships, sexual joys and dangerous intimacies, about the world and about a man's place in it. He
was the first man Aristo had ever heard curse and say aloud the
words only whispered in the schoolyard. Alexander did not pa-
tronize him, did not preach at him; it was a relief from grandmother Gethsemane's priest-ridden sermons and conversations,
which were often devotional to the point of unbalance.

Political activist, assertive patriot, Alexander was a fine
talker, although his breath sometimes smelled of ouzo; he could
joke, swear like a trooper, tease and yet always get to the heart of
what really mattered. And politics, so he said, was what mattered
most. Aristo's mind was accessible to the influences of great and
wonderful ideas, and Alexander had an inexhaustible supply.
Aristo listened to his stories with all the attention of a young boy's
fantasy and desire. Alexander was the darling of the family, and
he inculcated in his nephew the power of charm, and also perhaps
the charms of power. He put into his head ideas and concepts that
would shape his whole life. Ideas about passion and revenge, dark
Greek concepts of loyalty and love, and an ancestral sense of defiance that Aristotle Onassis would never shake; no matter how
seemingly sophisticated and civilized he was to become, there
remained deep inside him an atavism that would never be tamed.
"Know of my hatred and my violence and know in your heart that
for your offense I shall avenge myself as I can," he would turn on
an enemy nearly fifty years later, quoting the words of Theognis
but driven by the spirit of Uncle Alexander.

Aristo was enrolled in the church school; he was not a diligent
scholar and consistently got the poorest grades in his class. Several schools later he transferred to the small and expensive Aroni
Academy in Smyrna. There Aristo, fluent in Greek and Turkish,
demonstrated a natural talent for languages, studying English and
German. Since he had no intention of making an academic of his
son, Socrates showed little interest. "Great scholars do not make
good businessmen and are seldom rich. Too much education
might fill his head with ideas above business," he told Helen, who
cared for Aristo's education and might have suspected that his
father was too engrossed in his own affairs to give it sufficient
thought. Aristo's serious learning began when school was finished,
so Socrates said. Every evening, he made his son spend time in his
office, learning the tricks of the trade and acquainting himself
with the atmosphere of business. "Always carry a pencil, Aristo.
Make a note of everything, especially people. If you meet them
again, you will at once know how much time you need give them,
how much attention they're worth." Aristo bought a notebook and

dutifully recorded his impressions, and his secrets. When Helen protested that Aristo should be working at his school lessons, Socrates replied that school could teach him only "how to be a clerkly bourgeois, a servant with an education." He was teaching his son about life, the hard surface where he had to live. Aristo first demonstrated his grasp of economic determinism during a neighborhood fad for miniature windmills—a cotton sail pinned to a balsawood frame—when he became furious with a friend who was hawking the homemade toys at something below the cost of the materials. "Idiot! You haven't even charged for your labor!" he screamed, appalled. "He was a businessman," recalled the unbusinesslike Michael Anastasiades, who became a professor of physics in Athens, "when the rest of us were playing games."

He was sharp and sure of himself in a way that made enemies of many teachers; although others were impressed by him and regarded him with a fondness they could not always explain. He was always willing to argue with adults on their terms; when rebuked he defended himself with a precocious maturity. "Your son has the manners of no class," Mr. Aroni told Socrates, suspending Aristo for a week for goosing a woman teacher. Socrates felt, as most fathers do at some stage in a son's growing up, that he was losing his authority; he turned for help to Michael Avramides. A family friend and neighbour, Avramides was a teacher at Evangheliki, the best school in Smyrna. Founded in 1733, under the protection of the British consulate (the flag of the British merchant navy, the Red Ensign, flew above the school on the monarch's birthday and important British holidays), Evangheliki's first language was English. For Socrates the appeal of Evangheliki lay not in its academic distinction but in its strict codes of discipline. He took Avramides into his confidence over a glass of Masticka brandy on the terrace in Karatass. "My son is driving me to an early grave." He spoke in Turkish, a language he found easier than Greek, although he did not say more than he had to in either tongue. "He has been to so many schools and has managed to get kicked out of them all."

Avramides shook his head. "Young people today want too much fun out of life," he commiserated. But any misgivings he may have had in regard to Aristo were overcome by his admiration for the family, and within a year he got Aristo a place at Evangheliki; it was to be to his eternal regret. "The son was as terrible as the father was kind. He was a really unruly person, a disorderly child, shocking all around him, and disrupting all the other students in the school. I never met such a child. He was the most troublesome one there," he recalled in his memoirs recorded for the Athens Center for Asia Minor Studies shortly before his death in 1961.

"My friend Christos Christou is much too big for his desk," Aristo told Avramides one morning. "Since I'm a little fellow and my desk is one of the large ones, may we stay behind in the lunch break and switch them around?" Permission given, Aristo worked swiftly, rigging wires, intercepting the power circuit. That afternoon, he set off the school's fire alarms. "There was complete chaos until we tracked down what had happened," Avramides recalled, the sense of betrayal still clear in his mind nearly fifty years later. Aristo shrugged off the fifteen-day suspension. "Punishment makes you supple or it makes you hard," he said impenitently. "Either way it's a kind of winning." Said Avramides: "Even when he was young you could see that he was one of those people who would either completely destroy themselves or succeed magnificently."

A keen swimmer, oarsman and water polo player, Aristo joined the Pellos sports club and developed a hard attractive body. Although less than average height, he was proud of his physique, the sensuality of sun-dark skin tightened over bone and muscle, and enjoyed showing off in front of girls. He held the record for the fastest time for swimming to and from the American destroyers that were often moored off the Standard Oil refineries on the north side of the harbor. Scion of a respected family, he was sure that he had all the resources he needed to be a success in a small town: strength, daring, connections—and money. Especially money; money, according to Michael Avramides' testimony, often embezzled from the funds his father had given him to tip school servants. He was usually the one who bought the cigarettes that his gang smoked down at the ferry dock. He brawled ("It's not the size of the dog in the fight, it's the size of the fight in the dog") and lied freely, often for the hell of it, and his lies were always lively and imaginative. He was liked for his shortcomings and indiscretions as much as for his spirit and ready funds; always prepared to take a dare, he was also willing to accept the consequences of his mistakes. A conscious mimic, he could imitate exactly the way Uncle Alexander bit the head off a stogie and set it burning with a strike-anywhere match. He never forgot the sounds and the smells and the tastes of his childhood. In old age, dying in another land, he would remember the small orchestras of mandolins, zithers and guitars playing popular melodies in the cafés; the shunting sounds of the steam engines echoing in the night at Basma Hane on the edge of the Armenian quarter; the smell of almond trees and the freshly baked bread mingling with the perfume of jasmine and mimosa; and the taste of the pastry rich with rose-flavored syrup his stepmother made every Sunday in that far-gone past. "You can smash the vase," he would later reminisce. "But the scent of the flowers never quite goes away."

In 1914, Turkey entered the world war on the side of Germany, and the Moslem Turks turned on the Christian minorities with massive deportation programs and wholesale massacres. The German Gen. Otto Liman von Sanders, a hero who had given the Turkish troops a famous victory at Gallipoli (the disastrous Allied offensive drawn up by First Lord of the Admiralty Winston Churchill), established his headquarters in Smyrna and requisitioned a residence close to the Onassis villa in Karatass. Aware that their administrative and organizational talents were valuable resources, von Sanders tried to win the hearts and minds of the Smyrna Greeks; German officers handed out chocolate and souvenirs to the children. But the Turks misunderstood his motives, and to redeem the relationship with his allies, von Sanders switched tactics. Churches were closed; Aristo and his school friends were made to burn their English-style school caps and wear fezzes and armbands emblazoned with the Turkish star and crescent.

Socrates Onassis preached the gospel of neutrality: "It is many times a blessing, and good business, to see all sides of the question," he said, although it is unlikely that he convinced anyone that pragmatic collaboration was not at the heart of his credo. He boxed his son's ear for refusing to wear the star-and-crescent emblem on his arm. They were difficult times but with a mixture of suppleness, trimming and luck, the family and its fortune survived. When the Armistice was signed in 1918, Turkey was up for grabs. A French force occupied Syria; Italian troops were in Adalia; Arabia had seceded; the British had taken Palestine and placed Mesopotamia under a mandate as the Kingdom of Iraq. And at the Versailles Peace Conference in 1919, Greece sought to annex Thrace, the Dodecanese, northern Epirus—and Smyrna.

But it was Italy's bid to turn the Mediterranean into an "Italian lake" that persuaded President Woodrow Wilson and Prime Minister David Lloyd George to encourage the Greek occupation of Smyrna. Nobody appeared to appreciate the tactlessness of allowing Greek troops to occupy a city much of whose population for centuries had displayed the most vehement Hellenic phobia.

Shortly after seven o'clock on May 15, 1919, Aristo was having his morning swim when he saw the convoy appear on the horizon. I don't believe what I'm seeing, he said aloud to himself. Shielding his eyes from the sun, he counted them slowly: two destroyers, a battleship, five troop carriers and beyond them a line of support ships, every one flying the Greek flag. He swam ashore as fast as he could and joined the thousands of people who were already gathering on the quayside, most of them Anatolian Greeks who were for the first time flaunting their freedom from the Turkish yoke. A Greek band appeared from nowhere, and people began dancing in the streets, and singing Greek songs. Some shouted for *enosis*—unity with Greece. If he had reached out he could have touched the embroidered robes of the Greek Metropolitan, who had come to bless the liberators as they came off the ships with that proprietary cockiness of an occupying force. He got close enough to the ecclesiastical potentate, his grandmother's idol on earth, to notice that his robes were worn and covered with dust. "Viva!" the crowds chanted as the troops marched by. "Viva! viva! viva!"

As the head of the column came level with the barracks where General Ali Nadir Pasha's defeated Turkish infantry corps was confined, a single shot rang out. The Greek troops, young and inexperienced, lost in their new surroundings and believing they were under fire, started firing wildly. Camels that were being assembled for a caravan broke loose, adding to the sudden panic. Aristo fell to the ground, his face pushed into the dust. The beat of galloping hooves mixed up with the screams of the crowd and frenzied commands of officers trying to rally their men filled the air. He crawled into a doorway and kept very still, "like a small bag of flour." Incongruously he thought, "If somebody kicks me they will get blood and not flour on their boots; that will surprise them."

At noon it began to rain, that hard sudden rain that happens in the eastern Mediterranean in May. The rain dispelled the crowds, and as quickly as it had erupted the violence stopped. Aristo stayed still for a long time after the firing had ended; he was unable to move. Today it is called acute environmental reaction; then it was called shell shock. But on his way home he told himself, "I've got balls. I'm a ballsy fellow."

For the next two years Smyrna prospered greatly; the city boomed under the Greek administration. Aristo failed to graduate from Evangheliki; since his passions were physical and not intellectual, nobody was surprised. He went to work in his father's office on the Grand Vizier Hane, and came properly into his manhood. According to his own accounts, the family laundress, a French tutor and even a veiled Turkish wife fell to his "infidel" charms. He was acquainted with Demiri Yolu, the tenderloin district, and was a valued client in at least one whorehouse.

He would have entered confidently, the way he went into most things in his life, that first time at Fahrie's. The smell of body powder and civet was overwhelming, a smell he found extremely agreeable and sought out for the rest of his life, from the whores of Demiri Yolu to the high-class girls of Madame Claude's in Paris. The girls, in their colored silk stockings, fancy underwear and pointed shoes, would have played up to him with more than their usual professional charm, for he carried with him plenty of his father's finest tobacco. He did not mind that the girls did it for money. "One way or another, sweets, that's the way all women do it," one of the girls told him. "If you understand that you'll still get took, but you'll always know you're took. And one day, you'll find out that's a whole damn lot worth knowing, especially if you keep it to yourself."*

After his first transaction in one of the big brass beds at Fahrie's, he hurried back to brag to his mates at the Pellos sports club. Later, as he grew more confident, he would sit around the salon afterward and develop his taste for wine while the girls cooled themselves with little lace fans in the stifling heat and told him how fine he was, and cadged more tobacco to roll their little cigarettes, the best smokes in all of Smyrna. But he would never forget his first time at Fahrie's: "January 1921, that was the year they invented the Thompson machine gun—the year I discovered my own repeater in Demiri Yolu!" he recalled with his fondness for historical detail.

* It was often difficult to trap him into telling the truth, and that was especially so of this period of his life. For example, although he had failed to graduate from the Evangheliki School, he was later to foster the legend that he had turned down an opportunity to go to Oxford: "I had everything prepared, clothes and so on," he told Michael Parkinson on BBC television in 1966. In fact, an attempt to include his name on a registry of Evangheliki graduates, organized by his former classmate Michael Anastasiades, to present to university entrance boards in the absence of records lost in the Smyrna holocaust, failed when headmaster Elie Lithoxoos struck it firmly from the affidavit.

CHAPTER 2

Men must endure whatever ills the gods may send.

SOPHOCLES

ALTHOUGH the ordinary flow of life had been resumed, the summer of 1922 burned down on a land that knew some fresh calamity was waiting. But for the moment, Aristo's mind was on other, more personal, setbacks. He failed to be the *Victor Ludorum* at the summer games of the Pellos club. His pride as well as his confidence was lacerated by the defeat. To him to be champion of champions had been a foregone conclusion. When his uncle Homer, the president of the club, tried to console him with a platitude, Aristo replied rudely. "It's not here that I have to succeed, in this piddling town."

Later that evening, Alexander found him on the beach. "You did fine, boy," he said. Stifling the appearance of distress, Aristo concentrated his attention on a large and beautiful yacht anchored some distance away. He loved yachts, the way many boys loved railway engines. "That's the *Fuad*. It used to belong to the sultan," he said. He would always remember Alexander's response: "In this life the man who takes good care of himself usually gets the best of it." Failure is an attitude, and he was over it now, Aristo told him. They walked on the empty beach together as they had done so often in the past. There's going to be a war, Alexander said, perhaps to put into perspective Aristo's reverses in the games. In the interior, Greek and Turkish soldiers were engaged in bitter and bloody battles, and the Turkish Nationalist Army, under the command of Mustapha Kemal Pasha (who was to become infamous as Ataturk), was having the best of it. It will come to

Smyrna, and it will be a very bad war, Alexander said. Aristo said that he was beginning to understand how uncertain life is. "Then you've learned a lot. The day's not been a complete waste," Alexander told him. He suggested that Aristo apologize to his father for the sharp way he had spoken to Uncle Homer; it had upset his father a lot. Aristo replied: "I disappoint him all the time." He realized it was something he had believed since he could remember. "Sometimes I feel I'm living in the *Klafess*," he said, alluding to the room in the royal palace where the sultan's sons were often incarcerated, lest they should plot to overthrow him. "There are plenty of young men in Smyrna who would be happy at a chance to be in your shoes, Aristo," Alexander reminded him. Aristo promised to apologize.

During that summer of the lost championship, Aristo was summoned to his father's office. All that day, Socrates and his brothers, together with Chrysostomos Konialidis, husband of Maria, their youngest sister, had been locked in conference. There was a smell of cigars in the room when he arrived at the office on the Grand Vizier Hane; the shutters were closed against the late afternoon heat; there was also an indefinable sense of portent. Dressed in a black frock coat cut in the Turkish fashion, a gold watch chain across his stomach, Socrates dominated the conversation. "Your uncle Alexander tells me you must be included in these talks," Socrates said, offering him a cigar; it was the first time he had been invited to smoke in the presence of his father.

Socrates outlined the situation: the Greek army could collapse at any moment. The Turks could take Smyrna within a matter of days. Aristo, lulled by the palmy tranquillity that filled the city, was stunned by the intensity of his father's tone. War still seemed unimaginable. Beautiful women and fashionable men, writers and artists, mixed together in the outdoor cafés and dined at the swanky new Kramer Hotel; people flocked to the theatres and to the movie houses; the expensive shops on rue Franque displayed in their windows the latest fashions from Paris and London; an Italian company had been held over at the Opera House. It was true that Kemal Pasha made no secret of his determination to exterminate the Anatolian Christians. They had all heard the Turkish prayer about infidels—may their wives be widows, their children orphans. And now the Turk had issued a proclamation changing the penalty for murdering a Christian from death to simply punishment. There was no hope for any of them under Nationalist rule, Uncle Homer said quietly; they were all under the domination of events. The youngest of the five brothers, he bore a close resemblance to Socrates, the mouth, the eyes, the coloring; only now his face was sick and drawn. Alexander sat opposite him, looking serious in a way that Aristo had never seen before. Socrates explained that, as fund-raisers and organizers of the Asia Minor Defense League, both Homer and Alexander would be in grave danger if the Turks retook Smyrna. Turkish nationals, they could be executed as traitors. Aristo realized then that the aura of portent in the darkened room pointed to the possibility of death.

That morning, Alexander had received a message from a Defense League fellow-traveler in Trebizond that the entire organization there had been wiped out, its leaders assassinated or hanged; the rest of the town's prominent Greeks had simply disappeared or been packed off to *sevkiats*—deportation camps. "They killed off the Armenians, now it's our turn. Massacres are happening every day, in Amasya, in Merzifon . . . they're not even burying our dead. The bodies are being left to the dogs and the vultures," Alexander said. Aristo could not believe that the Allies would sit by and do nothing. What about the British? What are the Americans doing? "The American High Commissioner, Admiral Bristol, thinks it's in the best interest of the United States to see nothing. They've got their concessions to think about," Alexander answered bitterly. Head of the Inter-Allied Commission of Inquiry on the Smyrna Landings in 1919, which came down heavily on the Greeks, Adm. Mark L. Bristol was no friend of the Asia Minor Defense League. "To me it is a calamity to let the Greeks have anything in this part of the world," he had told a colleague in a private letter leaked to the league. "The Greek is about the worst race in the Near East."

Governments must do business with whoever is the boss, Socrates pointed out philosophically; he was anxious not to be drawn into a political argument with Alexander. Aristo realized how clearly the attitude of the family stemmed from his father: *his* ideas, *his* principles and ways of doing things, *his* will outweighed everything. Homer was persuaded to leave for Athens immediately. Alexander would not budge: he was not prepared to spend the rest of his life looking for new hiding places, he said. With a shock Aristo realized that the look on his favorite uncle's face was the look of a man who knew that his death was at hand.

On August 26, Kemal Pasha's Nationalist Army broke through the Greek lines at Afyon Karahisar, two hundred miles east of Smyrna; six days later, the Greeks abandoned Usak, 125 miles east of Smyrna. The steady trickle of refugees became a flood. Armenians, Jews, Christians and Ottoman Greeks, their possessions

packed on ox-carts, horses and camels, were joined by thousands
of Greek troops, the spent and wounded of a defeated army. Within
days the population of Smyrna had doubled to more than seven
hundred thousand people. Aristo remembered the harrowing
scene. Streets teemed with abandoned animals, wounded soldiers;
stretcher cases waited on sidewalks jammed with trunks, pieces
of furniture, sewing machines, pushcarts, crates and bundles: the
debris of defeat. People haggled and fought for places on departing
boats; it didn't matter where they were going, just so long as they
sailed before the Turks arrived.

On the afternoon of Friday, September 8, his father took Aristo
to the office for the last time. They burnt what few books Socrates
kept together with some Defense League pamphlets and documents belonging to Alexander, who had finally been persuaded to
leave the city for Kasaba, a village 750 miles to the east. Removing
the personal things, photographs, Penelope's Bible translated into
Turkish but printed with Greek characters, they closed the office
and started home. Before they had even left the *bedesten*, the Oriental market at the heart of the merchant district, a stranger
stopped them to repeat the latest rumor: Kemal Pasha had warned
the League of Nations that he could not be held responsible for
the consequences when his troops retook the city. By the time
they reached Karatass they had heard the story many times. The
panic was absolute. Peddlers were doing brisk business selling
fezzes and yashmaks at hugely inflated prices. "Bad times always
bring out the scoundrels, or make men such," Socrates told
his son.

They had nothing to fear. Socrates had kept clear of politics,
and he had many good Turkish friends. Homer and Alexander had
left the city; his sister Maria and her husband, Chrysostomos Konialidis, with one of their children, had gone to stay in Akhisar, a
safe town in the north. Socrates spoke with confidence, as he always did. In the evening, grandmother Gethsemane read to them
her favorite passage from Ecclesiastes. Her voice was strong. The
language was Turkish, the only language she knew.

> To every thing there is a season, and a time to every
> purpose under the heaven:
> A time to be born, and a time to die; a time to plant,
> and a time to pluck up that which is planted;
> A time to kill, and a time to heal; a time to break
> down, and a time to build up;
> A time to weep, and a time to laugh, a time to mourn,
> and a time to dance . . .

As she read from the old family Bible, sitting upright on the divan covered with Kurdish rugs, behind her low table of fretted wood inlaid with mother-of-pearl, amid his father's European furniture, the oleographs and phonograph, Aristo realized how unreal she seemed to him. Born in the middle of another century, she belonged to a past and a world he did not know, yet his father, his uncles and sisters all had come from her; she is the source, the lifeblood that had made the family what it is today, he thought. Its wealth and its future come out of her. She was a constant factor in their daily lives.

> *A time to love, and a time to hate; a time of war, and*
> *a time of peace.*

"Thank you, Momma," Socrates said. "If we remember those words we shall have no cause to fear." He glanced at his son, and in that glance they recognized and shared their doubts. Aristo had never felt closer to his father than he did at that moment, and had never loved him more.

An advance guard of the Fourth Turkish Cavalry regiment, dressed in black and carrying drawn scimitars, entered Smyrna shortly before eight o'clock on the morning of Saturday, the ninth of September. There was no opposition, and by nightfall the city was taken. An eerie silence filled the streets of Karatass. Gethsemane kept Helen and the girls occupied in the kitchen making *pilau* and sweetmeats done with almonds and pistachio nuts; and knowing how it always made them laugh, she showed the girls again the old Turkish paysanne trick of fanning the charcoal fire with a turkey's feathered wing. She still moved with the tread of a woman in the habit of going barefoot.

On the third morning, Monday the eleventh, Aristo awoke to the noise of somebody beating on their door. The visitor was an Armenian who pleaded for food. As he ate, he spoke of the horrifying things that were happening on the streets of Smyrna; he himself had seen a mob of Moslems tearing Metropolitan Chrysostomos to pieces in front of a barbershop, cutting off his nose, his ears and his hands with the barber's straight-edged razors, then gouging out his eyes with knives and sticks. Socrates told him to hold his tongue, to finish his meal and go. The Armenian's silence, the eating sounds of a hungry man, intensified the unnatural atmosphere. Later, Gethsemane made everybody kneel and pray for the soul of the metropolitan—and for the souls of his assassins! Aristo balked at the idea of praying for the people who had murdered the priest he had seen blessing the Greek soldiers three years before. We must always forgive the weak, his grandmother told him: "We must yield ourselves to God." Socrates refused to believe the Armenian's story. He must be deranged, he said. The harbor was full of Allied ships—in addition to the American destroyers *Simpson, Edsall, Lawrence* and *Litchfield*, there were cruisers and battleships from Britain, Italy and France. The Turks would not dare step out of line while they were there.

In the late afternoon of Wednesday the thirteenth, a pall of smoke appeared over the Armenian quarter. "They're torching the town, Aristo," his father said quietly. The Armenian had been telling the truth. They were burning the evidence. Driven by the *imbat*, the wind from the southwest which blows until sunset, the fire moved inexorably toward the Greek quarter. With nightfall came the holocaust. Flames lit up the sky, appearing, as fire does at night, to plunge from above, illuminating the earth with molten cinders. From the hillside of Karatass, the fire had the sound of distant thunder. All night long they watched the city burn, the sky glowing like a cursed ruby.

The Turkish patrols arrived in motorcars decorated with olive branches. By midday, soldiers filled the streets, and officers began house-to-house questioning. "Socrates Onassis, tobacco merchant?" asked the lieutenant with rotting teeth in a child's face. It would be unwise to expect understanding from such a man. He enquired about Socrates's past, his business. Socrates answered respectfully, with neither meekness nor dangerous dignity. Aristo took in everything, remembered everything: the stale masculine smell of the guard who wore white baggy trousers and crossed bandoliers over his American army field jacket; the sound of soldiers shouting for people to open doors, assuring them that General Kemal had given his word that no one would be harmed.

But in the villa the lieutenant's questions had turned to accusations: Socrates had made payments to Greek compatriot groups during the foreign occupation of Turkey. I have contributed to many charities, he admitted confidently, knowing how circumspect he had been with his subscriptions. He had close connections with known enemies of the state, the lieutenant persisted. Socrates denied it completely. Then the officer broke terrible news in a conversational tone, more frightening than threats. Alexander had been captured in Kasaba. Tried before a Turkish military tribunal and found guilty of activities detrimental to the state, he had been hanged in the public square. His brothers John and Basil were awaiting trial in the interior. It was the first time Aristo had seen his father weep; it was a side of the old man with which he did not know how to deal. "I was too young to understand that all men are weak about something," he was later to recall his feeling of shame. Although the death of his uncle removed the influence which might have impelled him to a political career, Aristo's love and admiration for Alexander would remain with him for the rest of his life and ultimately find expression in the naming of his only son.

Socrates was taken to a concentration camp outside the city; the women were ordered to a *sevkiat* to await deportation to Greece. Helen pleaded to be allowed to take her stepson with them, but the officer refused. Aristo's small stature and youthful features made it possible to plead that he was sixteen—the age he would stick to in his lifelong attempt to convert his past into fiction—though he was at least twenty at this stage. He was a strong-looking boy, the officer said: he would be useful at the villa. The inference that the Turk found him attractive was unmistakable. Between the shock of bereavement and the fear for his family, Aristo felt no anxiety about being cut loose for the first time in his life. That evening, he went into the city in search of familiar things; he connected familiarity with survival. But nothing in his life had prepared him for what he saw.

Ashes swirled from the sky, shrouding heaps of abandoned furniture and the dead who littered the streets. He made his way to his father's warehouse at Daragaz Point; it had been burned to the ground. The office on the Grand Vizier Hane had survived the fire, but Turkish soldiers forbade him to enter the building. He returned to the villa, feeling sickness in his stomach. A few weeks previously, he had had a loving family, security and an assured future. The biggest disappointment of his life had been his failure to make champion of champions. Now his favorite uncle was dead, his father in prison and the rest of his family interned. He knew that he was now a man.

Within a few days a Turkish general decided that the Onassis villa would make a splendid residence for himself. His aide-de-camp told Aristo that he was to be packed off to the deportation camp to join his stepmother and sisters. He was fortunate that he was not yet seventeen since Kemal Pasha had ordered that all male Christians between seventeen and fifty were to be deported into the interior to work in labor gangs. The new ruling ("It was virtually a death sentence," he said later) made Aristo keener still to hide his age; the deportation camp seemed barely more attractive. Was the lieutenant sure that he wanted him to leave immediately? he inquired respectfully, although the sight of the Turk in his grandmother's chair was a violation to him. The villa was not an easy house to run, he explained, borrowing his father's deferential tone. Perhaps he should stay until the lieutenant got the hang of things? He explained the eccentricities of the various utilities, ensuring that his instructions were vague and hard to follow, each injunction creating more questions than it answered; he claimed that he could acquire the latest cylinders for the phonograph, and that he always knew where to find the one man who could fix the undependable plumbing. He led the young officer around the villa, making a small adjustment here, another there, as if the whole place was run on a system of delicate adjustments.

Impressed or perhaps simply amused by Aristo's eagerness, the lieutenant invited him to stay on as his unofficial batman. Never in his own mind did Aristo occupy a servant's position, and within a short time a genuine friendship grew between them. The Turk was not much older than Aristo: perhaps in his midtwenties, Aristo judged; but in his uniform, befrogged and heavy with epaulettes, he seemed a good deal more than that. He had fought with the Turkish First Division at the battle of Afyon Karahisar and had killed many times. He had that pervasive sense of watchfulness of a man who could be lethal with his hands. His eyes a hard blue, his fair hair cut close to his head, he looked almost Prussian. He represented strength and vitality, and for a soldier he had a large view of the world. They were an extraordinary pair; they shared similar expectations and a philosophy that put physical endeavor first and attached to it a sense of duty which was almost childish. By tradition and temperament they became lovers.

The liaison was instructive as well as an emotional adventure for Aristo. Eager to understand everything, his curiosity about the adult world in which he felt himself irreversibly embarked was immense. He spent as much time as he could with the Turk; smoking his thin black cigars (they were far less good than his father's) they talked about everything. He was resolved to acquire knowledge and experience in the same obsessive way he would later set out to acquire his great fortune, and anything else he wanted. One evening he asked the Turk why the powers had not lifted a finger to restrain Kemal Pasha's troops. The Allied warships at Smyrna could have prevented the massacre and the burning of the city if they had intervened; the four American destroyers alone could have stopped Kemal Pasha in his tracks. It was very simple, the Turk told him. The economic forces which shaped the foreign policies of the Allies—Britain, France, Russia, Italy and the United States equally—were anxious not to upset a country that straddled the continental peninsula between Europe and Asia: either as a military highway or as an overland trade route, the country that directly or indirectly controlled this strategic crossroad in Asia

Minor could influence the destiny of half the world. Kemal Pasha knew exactly what the Allies wanted and calculated correctly that as long as he dangled the prize before their eyes he was safe from interference. Although Turkey was not herself a world power, the Turk said with pride, she was in a position to tip the balance of power in any direction she wished. It was one of the key moments in Aristo's education. "I realized that if you have one golden apple, you have the power. You can get away with murder if you have a single apple that somebody else wants," he was later to say to Johnny Meyer.

These cozy days were short-lived, and when the general, who ran the villa along the lines of an Oriental satrapy, demanded more liquor of his aide-de-camp (in defiance of Kemal Pasha's proclaimed prohibition) the order aroused in Aristo the gravest anxiety. If his lover and protector failed to deliver the goods, he would almost certainly get his marching orders, thus abandoning Aristo. Realizing that the best guarantee of his own safety would be to procure a plentiful supply of booze, he threw himself furiously into the task. But his fraternization with the Turks had not gone down well with his father's business associates and the old family friends he was counting on to help. He drew a blank.

A few days later he encountered James Loder Park, an American vice-consul who had been an acquaintance of Alexander's. A graduate of the Harvard Medical School, Park had gone to work for the League of Nations in Syria at the end of the First World War and in 1921 joined the State Department and was posted to Smyrna. A combination public relations man, civil servant and intelligence officer, Park knew enough about Alexander's activities not to be surprised to learn of his execution in Kasaba. He was a good man and kind; in spite of many weeks of overwork and interrupted sleep, he suggested they do the rounds again; people might be more willing to do business with Aristo if he had a Yank in tow. This time Aristo managed to buy a keg of raki and several flasks of gin and whisky. He traded the gin for an Allied *laissez-passer*, which admitted him to the United States zone; the raki and the whisky were turned over to the general, who showed his gratitude by giving Aristo a military pass for the whole city.

If the Onassis family was a small piece in the national trauma that accompanied the sacking of Smyrna, its sacrifice was bloody, and more than bloody. Three of Aristo's uncles were executed, and an aunt, Maria, together with her husband, Chrysostomos Konialidis, and their daughter perished when the Turks set fire to a church in Thyatira in which five hundred Christians were seeking sanctuary. Park succeeded in getting Aristo's stepmother and sisters released from the refugee camp and shipped to Mitilina (the island of Lesbos), from where they would eventually be taken to the Greek mainland. Split up from Helen and the girls, grandmother Gethsemane had disappeared. Socrates awaited trial on charges that still had to be framed.

Aristo, with his military pass, and his known Turkish connections, was able to visit the prison camp almost whenever he wished and soon became a familiar figure to the guards. His easy passage enabled him to smuggle messages from prisoners to relatives and loved ones outside. His father was in a bad way; prisoners were being executed daily. "These people don't waste time with trials. It just becomes your turn," Socrates told his son, urging him to find Sadiq Topal, a Turkish friend who owed him money; for collateral, Topal had handed over to Socrates the deeds to several properties as well as some jewelry. Aristo was instructed to cancel the debt and return the deeds and jewelry to Topal if he would organize a "Turks for Onassis" petition. In the prevailing climate it was not healthy for a Turk to be seen fraternizing with an Anatolian Greek. "You're squeezing my balls," Topal complained when Aristo put the deal to him. "I know, I know," Aristo answered, as if they shared the pain: it was to become a familiar note whenever he had to put pressure on, in business or in some private affair. Within forty-eight hours, over three hundred signatures were presented to the *Konak*, the governor's residence, by a deputation of "concerned Turkish businessmen." Socrates was moved out of death row and the manacles removed from his wrists and ankles; but he was not released.

When Aristo went to collect the collateral, hidden in the cellar at Vizier Hane, he discovered a hoard of Turkish pounds. He told Park about his find and was advised to take the money and get out of the country as quickly as possible. That evening the American arranged with Lieutenant Merrill, a naval intelligence officer, for Aristo to leave on the United States destroyer *Edsall*, which was due to sail the following morning. Aristo paid a final visit to his. father.

It was a difficult meeting. Socrates shared a detention cage with about twenty other prisoners, and there was no privacy and no place to sit inside the cage, except on the filthy floor. Wearing the same clothes he had been taken away in, unshaven and unwashed, he was now a very frightened man. Suffering from dysentery, wracked by nightmares and exhaustion, he seemed unable to comprehend what was happening to him or what Aristo was saying; all reasoning power seemed to have left him. Aristo told him about the money and Park's plan to get him out of the country. He would find his grandmother, Helen and the girls and take care of everything until Socrates was able to join them in Greece. Meanwhile, Topal's committee expected to have Socrates released in no time; he tried to sound confident. To take care of the guards, he slipped a bundle of Turkish bills into his father's shirt. The sum put a valuation on his father's life, and he knew it was a parting that transcended the limits of ordinary farewells. As he kissed his father good-bye, knowing that he might never see him again, he felt a sadness he would remember all his life; he understood his father's suffering, because he could feel it inside himself.

He was stopped at the main gate. He had been seen passing money to his father, a guard told him as he was marched back to the commandant's office. Aristo had met the commandant several times. A small corpulent man who treated the camp as if it were his private domain, the Turk was in no hurry to talk about the money. He stared at Aristo with eyes that seemed to have no depth and no color. "You still don't shave, I like that in a Greek boy," he touched Aristo's face and spoke in a gentle tone that was frightening from such a man. Chilled with fear and revulsion, Aristo asked whether he was under arrest. The Turk responded with a quick smile full of charm and evil pride. He came closer to him. "Just then the phone rang," Ari would recall the moment more than thirty-five years later. "The warden (commandant) answered it and told an officer, 'Keep this boy here till I come back,' and rushed out, leaving the door open."

The unexpected breathing space did nothing to still Aristo's apprehension. He knew that eventually he would be searched—it was astonishing that they had not already made him strip—and they would find the rest of the money and the messages he was smuggling. He could destroy the messages, but he was reluctant to abandon the bank notes he had already bandaged around his body in readiness for his departure the following morning. Perhaps because he was such a familiar figure in the camp and had run errands for the Turks, many of whom knew him by name, his guard did not watch him closely. He strolled out of the room; nobody challenged him as he drifted closer toward the gates, his heart beating fast. He was afraid that he would move too quickly, attract attention; it was with a heroic struggle that he stopped himself from making a run for it. "Getting out of a situation or getting into something, the secret is always to move at the right speed," he said later, recalling his escape.

He found the vice-consul at the Hotel Majestic in the United States Marine zone and told him what had happened. Park was a calm man—only the heat appeared to discomfit him—but the story put him in a difficult position; since Aristo was now technically on the run, he could be accused of aiding a fugitive rather than merely assisting a refugee. He had already made arrangements for Aristo to hitch a ride on the *Edsall* and decided to proceed as planned. The Turks made regular searches in the Allied zones, and meanwhile it was sensible to be prepared; if they showed up, Aristo was to hide in the rolltop desk. Aristo laughed. He'd never thought such things happened in real life.

In the evening the Turks came. They were after a young thug who had been seen entering the United States zone; they claimed he had stolen a large sum of money and raped an Armenian girl. That's terrible, Aristo heard Park answer as he crouched in the suffocating darkness of the Victorian bureau, listening to his pursuers grow warm, then cold, then warm again. Fifty years later this episode remained vivid in his mind. It was, he said, the time he began to test himself against fear. After the soldiers left, Park unlocked the desk and gave him an American sailor blouse to put on. They drove to the harbor, where the *Edsall* was anchored in front of a moviehouse advertising a film called *The Dance of Death*. The vice-consul shook his hand, having accomplished all that he could do for him. "Good luck, young fella," he said.

Twelve hours later, carrying a bag of biscuits, the family savings bandaged to his body, he was rowed ashore to the Aegean island of Lesbos. The halfway house to mainland Greece, the island was gorged with refugees; typhus and dysentery were rife, hundreds were dying of malnutrition; and many were drunk, for when there are vineyards and not enough to eat, wine becomes a kind of feast as well as an escape. He searched the makeshift camps, calling his sisters' names, describing them to strangers, who nodded sympathetically and returned to their own problems. He walked for days across the island, from encampment to encampment, through black firwoods and across parched grasslands; he fixed messages to trees and to the doors of stone huts proclaiming that he was alive and on Lesbos. The family was the center within which he would find his strength and vindication; outside his own circle a man must expect only animosity and distrust, he thought, recalling Uncle Alexander's homily. Hunger made him lightheaded, his eyes had become bright with fever, and he had lost count of time when he finally came across them in an encampment at the foot of the Hill of Olympus—his stepmother, three sisters, aunts and cousins: seventeen frightened women and children. Helen wept inconsolably at the sight of him. And so he stepped into the role he knew he had come to play: he was in charge now, he was the head of the family. That night his sister Artemis read from the Bible, and they prayed for the souls of their murdered loved ones, and for the safe return of Gethsemane and Socrates. After a meal of bread and sardines, he smoked a cigarette that he rolled, then wrapped himself in a blanket; in spite of his exhaustion he could not sleep. He thought about the future; after a time he pulled his head down on his neck and closed his eyes. He awoke with the apocalyptic start that comes when one has worked out a difficult problem in a heavy sleep. And in later years as he looked back, Aristotle Onassis insisted that in that waking moment his spirit was recharged with the vibrancy of revenge, and his feelings changed from utter fatalism to a determination "to kick the shit out of anybody who threatened me or my family ever again." Rage was nothing new to Aristo; using it was.

Resolved to keep the family together, he waited more than a month before he was able to buy deck space for everyone on a Libyan freighter bound for the port of Piraeus. Ten days after his twenty-third birthday he walked on Greek soil for the first time. After a brief internment in a displaced persons camp in the Athens suburb of Piraiki, he moved into rooms above a garage in a low-rent quarter close to the docks; within a week he had made contact with Homer. His uncle came with terrible news. Gethsemane was dead. She had made it to Greece, only to be attacked by a purse thief at the docks. She fought back and fell, striking her head against a post. His grandmother's death crushed Aristo, and if the faith that she had tried so hard to instill in his heart no longer guided his life, it still had command of old habits, and that evening he went into a church and prayed for her eternal soul. Although his prayers were the reprise of a ritual practiced years ago for reasons he no longer believed in, fifty years later he would return to the same church to pray for his dying son.

Homer was the antithesis of his brother Alexander. Alternately pompous and pessimistic, with a streak of caution that some regarded as cowardice, Homer painted a grim picture of their situation: they could kiss good-bye to Smyrna, the warehouse and all the stock, he said, and in Greece they were just *Turkospori* (Turk's sperm). He ignored Aristo's achievement in getting the women and children safely to Athens. Regarding himself as the axiomatic head of the family, at least until Socrates returned, he was shocked when his nephew insisted on being treated as an equal. The tension between them increased during the following weeks and was exacerbated further by Aristo's refusal to surrender the family savings, insisting on paying the bills and controlling the finances himself. There were many stormy ex-

changes between them, but the most serious and recurring argument concerned the question of how to get Socrates out of prison.
Aristo wanted to go the backstairs route, which meant getting to
the right people and using bribes—*mordidita,* "the little bite," on
which government officials grow fat; Homer, who believed in the
forces of propriety and patience, preferred going through legal
channels. Homer's trust in rules and regulations irritated Aristo;
he wished it were Alexander he was dealing with: the best investment will always be the bribe, his uncle had told him many times,
baksheesh is the soundest currency of all. But Homer was not
Alexander, and Aristo was finally forced to take matters into his
own hands. Telling nobody where he was going, he invested in a
new suit, a valise, and took off for Constantinople, then the capital
of Turkey.

The Egyptian liner *Abbazia,* sailing under the British flag with
a British crew, was a small but typical floating palace of the period, and although his ticket gave him no more than his passage
and a bunk on the lower deck, he slipped through the barrier to
the first-class section and saw a world whose splendor stunned
him; he felt not envy but a determination one day to be a part of
that society. He had strolled through the saloons several times,
mingling with the dinner-jacketed men and their expensively
gowned ladies, the small orchestra playing "Ain't We Got Fun,"
before he was spotted by a steward. "Come on, lad, this is no place
for the likes of you. Back to where you belong."

"I belong here," Aristo said.

In Constantinople, he took the underground to the Bursa So-
kagi and checked into a small hotel off the fashionable Istiklal
Caddesi; a good address was important if he were to impress the
people who could pull strings to get his father released. "Officials
on the take like to see that their paymaster knows how to remove
the rubber band," as he would later on define his very precise
sense of corruption. He worked hard, and played hard, especially
in the bars and cafés around Cumhuriyet Caddesi where the *con-
sommatrices* (dancing partners) got to know him well. He created
the impression of one who had traveled widely, and had the funds
and the fancy to travel more widely still, for he not only believed
that his hold over men, and women too, was enhanced by his aura
of substance, but he was beginning to develop habits of secrecy
and personation that transcended the ordinary narcissism and
loneliness of youth. He would be a man who would always be
alone: it was the condition of survival, the reality that was trans-
forming his existence, a fact which would not become discernible
to him until many years had passed.

Exactly who he got to in Constantinople is unclear, but six weeks after his return, his father was safe in Athens. Gratitude was too much to expect from the old man—it would have implied a sense of obligation—but Socrates did not even behave like a man who was pleased to be alive, and free again. Thin and pale, suffering from angina, he lost no time in reasserting his position at the head of the family. He questioned his son closely about the money taken from the safe in Smyrna. Aristo had kept a note of everything: much of the money had gone to looking after the family— boat passages, rent, food, clothing, greasing palms in Lesbos and Athens—but the biggest sum by far, some ten thousand dollars, had gone for his trip and the bribes he had paid for Socrates' release. There were unpleasant accusations of improvidence. Homer, still sore about the way in which Aristo had taken matters into his own hands, criticized him for shelling out so much "without condition of success." A bribe is a bet, Aristo answered back. "You can't place the bet after the horse has come home." Socrates slapped him down. He saw Aristo's behavior in Constantinople as profligate, and in that profligacy he suspected a kind of rebellion, was reminded of his own decline. "You know how it is, people forget quickly. They may have been on the verge of death, but the moment they're safe all the recriminations and curses come pouring out," Aristotle Onassis later said about that confrontation, which he described as his first experience of futility.

Soon life in Athens settled down to a routine. But a sense of injustice hung over him; anxiety about the future added to his misery. Prey to fits of melancholy, unable to admit his disappointment, let alone share it, he became increasingly distant and solitary. He began to sleep by day and to walk and think by night; he found it easier to put some order in his thoughts on his nocturnal ambles. He declined when Socrates invited him to join the tobacco business he was starting up again.

Helen felt the rift between her stepson and Socrates deeply. She had never taken his mother's place, she had never tried to, but she had grown to love Aristo with a pride that was almost maternal and almost sisterly. Anxious to mend fences, she pleaded with him to make the first move toward a rapprochement with his father. "I saved his life, and he behaved like an accountant," Aristo told her. "Thanks is not much to want." He intended to emigrate, he told her. The decision, or at least the sudden avowal of it, he remembered afterward, came as a shock to him. He knew the price of whores and politicians, but he had never earned a proper wage in his life.

Men work out their own destinies, Helen told him when he

had finished his declaration. And encouraged by this hint of collusion, he wasted no more time. He made inquiries about the United States, and discovered that Congress had recently introduced the most rigorous immigration quotas in its history, and immigrants from Turkey were especially unwelcome. His next choice was Buenos Aires, where he had distant relatives. Argentina could not be more alien than Athens. By August, traveling on a Nansen permit, valid for a one-way trip for refugees going to a country of resettlement, and with $250 in his pocket, he set out on the first lap of his journey to South America. Helen and his sisters went to the ship to wave good-bye; Socrates had business elsewhere.

He had a three-week holdover in Naples, and, according to his own self-generated mythology, it was an instructive interlude; not only did he pick up a rudimentary Italian vocabulary, but the unashamed Neapolitan warmth of his middle-aged landlady and her war-widowed daughter improved his spirits considerably. With great reluctance on Monday, August 27, 1923, he boarded the emigrant ship *Tomaso di Savoya*, bound for the Argentine. Packed with a thousand steerage-class Italians accommodated in cargo holds and in between-deck spaces, its squalor was appalling. He quickly picked out the man to bribe and got a bunk in a locker above the propeller shaft tunnel. It was noisy and it was airless, but for the next twenty-five days it would give him privacy and a place in which to think.

As the ship advanced northward along the coast of Italy, the emigrants crowded on the deck to wave good-bye to their homeland. "That's when I saw Monte Carlo for the first time, from the deck of an emigrant ship taking me to a new life," he liked to tell journalists in the good days ahead. He knew it was a neat line, nobody could miss its symbolic significance.

CHAPTER 3

I am a citizen, not of Athens, nor of Greece, but of the whole world.

SOCRATES

IN BUENOS AIRES Aristo was just another loser, one of the thousands of refugees from the eastern fringe of Europe—Armenians, Syrians, Turks and Lebanese—all dismissed as *Turkos*. He moved around: dishwasher, laundry worker, night clerk. "Any kind of job, no qualifications," he petitioned in Spanish, in English and Italian, in factories, shops, bars. For a while he shared a room with a distant cousin and his wife in la Boca, the Italian quarter in the east end of the city. The room was above a dance hall, and between the music and brawling below, and the cadences of passion in the next bed, sleep was hard to come by. Eventually he rented a room of his own on the Avenida Corrientes. He was still small for his age and a muscular torso and strong arms gave the upper part of his body the appearance almost of deformity; but his solemnity, his way of keeping people at a distance, gave him an aura of dignity that women found attractive. Fixing them with his dark, heavy-lidded eyes, he had a way of listening to what they said, of appearing interested in their ideas. But his success with women did not compensate for his failure to find a steady job. He was becoming almost accustomed to failure. Poverty was beginning to make him lethargic, he later recalled. "It's hard to sustain a vitality when you are nearly always hungry."

Watching seagulls diving for garbage on the waterfront one evening, he noticed how quickly the light disappeared; summer would soon be over. He didn't want to spend a winter in Buenos

Aires, jobless, his savings gone. In a bar on the Avenida Costanera, which runs along the riverfront, he met a Scots captain of a freighter named *Socrates*. He said that he was looking for a berth out of Buenos Aires and that since his father's name was Socrates he hoped that was a good omen. Had he been to sea before? He said he had. The captain scratched his nose, peering suspiciously at his brilliantined hair shining like patent leather in the tango-dancer fashion of the time. "Well, I dinna hae to gie ye a lecture, laddie. Thou kens we ship out in three days to Liverpool, where damned devils roar an' yell. See me tomorrow e'en, ye'll be right, wee laddie."

He had made friends with several Greek immigrants, and they talked all the time about making their fortunes in South America. That night in a bar in la Boca he told them the news. They said it was a lousy idea. They were sure they could get him a job as an electrician with them at the British United River Plate Telephone Company, which was taking on extra staff, no experience needed. The boss was a Colonel Smith, a plump bald Englishman with a fondness for biblical proverbs and vintage port, who wore a frock coat and a monocle in his eye. He had spent several years in Salo-nika during the war and talked with fond, maudlin affection about the town. It would be a smart move to claim he was from Salonika, too, his friends said, and it would avoid the *Turko* slur. The *Socrates* sailed without him. When he presented himself for work at the Avellaneda exchange, a suburb of Buenos Aires and one of the most important industrial centers in the country, he was told to produce his identity papers. It was inconvenient but not a serious problem. Since the middle of the nineteenth century, almost six million immigrants, mostly European, had settled in Argentina, and citizenship procedures had become perfunctory. Aristo chased up his earlier application with a *bustarella* (an envelope containing a bribe), repeating the details he had invented for Colonel Smith: born Salonika, Greece, September 21 (the date he had arrived in Buenos Aires), 1900.

The money was good, but the work was repetitious and hum-drum, except for the days he had to work on his knees at the feet of the girls on the switchboard; he found pleasure in imagining the faces and the aware smiles that went with the thighs, the rolled stockings. With plenty of overtime and modest expenses, he was soon comfortably off. He sent money home to Greece, and moved into a room in a boardinghouse on Avenue Esmeralda, not far from the Teatro Colón, the great opera house. He felt conscious that he was a cut above most of his workmates and drinking com-panions. There is plenty of camaraderie but no real communication between us, he confessed in a letter to his sister Artemis. But he knew how to be both gregarious and cagey. "The only time you know what Onassis has got in his hand is when he goes to the can," said one of the Greeks in the poker game in which he very occasionally played.

He let no opportunity to make money pass by. When he discovered that at night the company's switchboards were operated by men and that the pay was better than he was getting as an electrician, he applied to be retrained as an operator. He learned quickly and was sent to the Retiro exchange opposite the Buenos Aires branch of the London store Harrods, on the Calle Florida, the rue Saint Honoré of South America. He started at eleven at night and finished at seven in the morning. He did his best thinking in the small hours. The telephone traffic was minimal, and there was ample time to brush up his Spanish, sleep, read the papers . . . and listen in on calls that sounded interesting. Buenos Aires, three hours earlier than London and two hours behind New York, taught him that the best and most interesting deals were done after the markets had closed. He made notes, studied the financial pages, and very soon had made five hundred dollars on a linseed oil deal and two hundred dollars speculating in hides.

At about this time he heard that the young lieutenant who had protected him and taught him so much had died of diphtheria in the Gallipoli Peninsula. Except for his murdered uncle, the Turk had been the most important attachment in his life. Aristo's mourning was brief; he got very drunk. He woke with no hangover on a bright new day, made, he decided, for living. He was now a man in a hurry. The two hundred dollars he got from the hides deal he invested in a couple of good suits, half a dozen silk shirts, a pair of Italian shoes, a Borsalino hat and a year's subscription to a smart rowing club called l'Aviron—the Oar.

It was the start of an extraordinary double life unguessed at by colleagues at the telephone company and his drinking cronies at the bars in la Boca. His new friends at l'Aviron knew him only as a young man with money, business connections of an unspecified kind, a good address, an untalked-of past and considerable charm. It was a complex, almost schizophrenic existence. A natural performer, throughout his life he was able to adapt his personality with extraordinary ease. Costa Gratsos said, "He had an instinct for knowing the image best calculated to impress a particular person, a particular group . . . he invented the multiple personality; it made him a hard fellow to unravel." When in later years he looked back on those days, Onassis would explain his routine like this: at 7:00 A.M. I'd finish at the exchange, have coffee and a *bizcocho*, or biscuit, at a little café just off the Avenida de

Mayo where the waitresses knew me and treated me swell; I'd sleep for a few hours, then bathe, get dressed and do the rounds, looking up friends, a pretty girl or two, anyone who might be useful! "He always wanted every pretty woman he saw, and a few who were far from pretty, but none of them lasted," Gratsos later recalled.

Not long after he started work at the exchange, as part of his self-improvement program he went to his first opera, *La Bohème*, at the Teatro Colón. Singing Mimi was the Italian soprano Claudia Muzio, who, at thirty-five, was a little past her prime although she had a robust beauty and was said to have had many lovers. Aristo sent her flowers. And more flowers. He sent her so many flowers that even a prima donna had to take notice. He let a week go by before presenting his card at her dressing room. "I expected a much older man," she told him. A week later, he was invited to a reception for her at the Club de Residentes Extranjeros, the oldest and one of the smartest clubs in Argentina. The guest list included some of the most influential people in Buenos Aires. He was determined to become Claudia's lover.

Their first intimate moment occurred within days of that party. He told her that he felt like a chrysalis "waiting for the strength to break the shell." Not every chrysalis becomes a butterfly; they are surrounded by so many enemies, she said: "Being a social butterfly is not an occupation to be considered lightly." But he had no intention of becoming merely a social butterfly. It is no accident that the word chrysalis comes from the Greek word *chrysos* . . . gold, he would later remark.

She knew almost nothing of his life, he never spoke about his family. Claudia's pet name for him was Stranger—after the Club de Residentes Extranjeros, colloquially known as Strangers. The seduction of Claudia Muzio revealed the energy and guile, the sharp eye for social progression, the romanticism, too, which were to be familiar elements in his line of advance. The ease with which he had attached himself to a famous woman pleased and amazed him. He continued to work at the telephone company; a conversation between a Buenos Aires movie distributor and a Paramount executive in New York triggered his next and most important move. Rudolph Valentino's fame was at its height, and the distributor was complaining about Paramount's tough terms for the star's latest movie. "That sonofabitch has 'em hanging on the rafters," the movie salesman insisted. "Eastern schlock is all the cheese, it does the business every time." There was no way Aristo could make anything out of the movie business, but the conversation gave him an idea.

He wrote to his father setting out his plans for introducing

Oriental tobacco to Argentina, emphasizing the Eastern vogue. The local cigarette manufacturers were using mostly Cuban tobacco, a dark leaf that women found too strong. Convinced that he could sell the companies the idea of the milder Turkish leaf that would appeal to women and cash in on the Hollywood sheik rage, he proposed a standard dealership contract, collecting a flat 5 percent commission on the first hundred thousand dollars' worth of tobacco sold, and 7.5 percent thereafter. Socrates did not approve of women who smoked cigarettes and railed against the "new woman." But that was not mentioned now. He read into the letter tones of filial conciliation as well as a commercial invitation, and lost no time in shipping to Buenos Aires several bales of the finest leaf he had.

Aristo knew it was going to be tough breaking into the established markets. After a few tentative orders—amounting to no more than $5,000 in three months, on which his take was $250—business dried up. Unable to get to the senior buyers in the big companies, he found himself dealing with clerks; even his generous use of the *bustarella* got him no further than office managers. "Sometimes to win the whole audience it is better to sing to just one person," Claudia Muzio said to him one evening after listening to his problems.

The first time Juan Gaona saw Aristo, waiting outside his villa in Olivos, he was merely curious. The next morning, seeing him again, he stared coldly. On the third morning, his coldness turned to apprehension, and by the end of the week he began to feel the stirrings of panic. When he could stand the suspense no longer, he told his managing clerk, I want you to find out who he is and what the hell he thinks he's playing at. And two days after that, Aristo was face to face with the director of the third largest tobacco company in Argentina. "Tell me what you propose, Senor Onassis," Gaona said, his formality hiding surprise at Aristo's obvious youth. Kids that age are usually rougher-edged, less sure of themselves, he thought. Gaona was an impenetrable man in whose tanned cadaverous face there were lines carved so deep they remained as white as fishbone, and he did not refer to the extraordinary circumstances of their meeting. Find a Way, or Make One read a small plaque on the paneled wall behind his desk.

Talking quickly, Aristo emphasized the potential of the women's market and the attractions of a milder leaf to meet the demand that was sure to come; he repeated the movie salesman's spiel about the Valentino vogue. "You sing a soft song, Mr. Onassis," Gaona said when he had finished. He placed an order for twenty-five thousand dollars with a promise of further orders if the leaf caught on.

The weeks after that first meeting with Juan Gaona were full of dreams of future fortunes and successes for Aristo. To fulfill as quickly as possible the orders he was sure would follow, he cabled his father to ship further stock immediately and book forward balespace (an arrangement which locks the exporter into a deal but protects him against increases in freight charges while giving him the "benefit of fall," the most favorable shipping terms on offer).

But they had not made the breakthrough they had hoped for, Gaona told him at their next meeting. Women were smoking more, only in private. "It's still thought to be a little shocking for a woman to smoke in public, a fast thing to do." The order would not be repeated. He poured out two glasses of brandy. "To our mistakes," he said. Aristo's hand shook as he lifted the brandy to his mouth.

After he had left Gaona's office that afternoon, he went to a café. By the time he had finished his second coffee he had made up his mind. If he couldn't sell his tobacco to the manufacturers, he would manufacture his own cigarettes. Once the idea was in his head he moved with speed, setting up a two-room office on Paseo Colon on the fringe of the industrial quarter of town. Gold lettering on the window proclaimed: Aristotle Onassis, Oriental Tobacco Importer. Highest Grade Turkish Cigarettes Manufactured from Exclusive Stocks of Genuine Macedonian Leaf. He put every penny he had into the idea and borrowed twenty thousand dollars from the First National City Bank—using his father's bills of lading as collateral. It was a sharp move since legally he held no more than a 5 percent interest in the cargo en route from Athens, and would not collect a penny until the tobacco had been sold.

Several months later he and Gaona met again in the cool brown office with the plaque on the wall: Find a Way, or Make One. "It's nobody's fault. We tried, but it didn't work out," Juan Gaona told him. "Buenos Aires isn't ready for Oriental blends." He felt bad about it all the same, Aristo answered gravely: it was his idea and he'd been wrong. With a mixture of suspicion and confusion, Gaona told him to forget it; offering such an apology wasn't the way men did business. Aristo persisted. "You gave me a break," he said; he wanted to repay the favor. Now that he was in the manufacturing end of the business himself, he was prepared to buy back the Turkish bales at a price, and on credit! Maybe there was a directness of understanding between dealers, maybe

Gaona simply admired Aristo's effrontery, but whatever thoughts
and emotions went through his mind that day, Gaona agreed to
sell what was left of the original Onassis purchase at a very good
price indeed for Aristo.

He hired immigrant pieceworkers to hand-roll his two brands:
Primeros and Osman, both gold-tipped and packaged to appeal to
the rich young girls of Buenos Aires. Sometimes when business
was good he would help out with some hand-rolling himself. But
always at half past six, he took a shower, changed into his best
suit (he could shower and dress in ten minutes), did the rounds of
the cafés, had dinner and visited l'Aviron. At 10:30 sharp, he went
home, changed his clothes and began his night shift. He possessed
an energy that seemed recharged by some inexhaustible power
within himself.

It was an interesting time to be in the tobacco trade in South
America; a tough booming business with at least a spiritual affinity with the rackets, "you almost *had* to play rough," he said later.
More than once he impregnated the bales of rivals with a sulfur-
ated chemical that gave off a smell of rotten eggs when the cigarette was lit. For a short extremely profitable period he produced
a cheap cigarette with the brand name Bis. The venture ended
abruptly when he was sued by the proprietors of a very popular
brand, also called Bis. Aristo protested that he had never heard of
the other Bis; it was like a bootlegger disclaiming all knowledge
of Jack Daniels. He settled out of court for a few thousand dollars.
He was learning fast. He was also beginning to make money,
enough to take on his cousins Costa and Nicos Konialidis, who had
been orphaned in the Smyrna massacre and had followed his trail
to Buenos Aires; enough to quit his job at the telephone exchange.
But it was still not enough to satisfy his thirst for what he was
beginning to call "serious juice." Disappointed in the sales of his
Osman line, he was determined to improve the situation.

In the course of that effort to improve he got his first lesson in
an art that was to play a seminal role in his success, the art of
using important people, and asking favors; especially of his
women. He came directly to the point with Claudia. Would she
smoke his cigarettes in public? She had no illusions about him.
"She liked my survival strength, but she thought I was a conner,"
Onassis later said about her, "and I was I suppose, I needed to
be." * He made his pitch. She smoked privately, and so did thou-

---

* Even his Primero slogan had been copied from the De Reszke packets Claudia had
delivered to her from London: "the cigarette for the few." "Courtesy requires that you
should assume in your friends a taste as good as your own," he had told her the first
time he took her to dinner at the Plaza Hotel. Later he confessed that he had stolen the
line from yet another tobacco slogan.

sands of other women. If she were openly to use his gold-tipped brand, it would be an act of emancipation. "And it would help me a little bit, too, you know!" Any resistance she might have had was overcome by his audacity. It is not known what effect her endorsement had on sales, but he showed his appreciation by sending a bouquet of flowers, and a fifty-tin of Osmans, to her dressing room every day. But the affair was finished. "I hate the opera," he was to say later. "I think I must have a tin ear. No matter how hard I concentrate it still sounds like a bunch of Italian chefs screaming risotto recipes at each other."

Aristo had been two-timing Claudia Muzio with a Russian ballerina who was appearing in Buenos Aires with the Anna Pavlova Company. He had known women before, plenty of women, he would later claim, and nearly all of them older, richer and more experienced than himself, but the ballerina was his own age and the first woman he ever really felt he loved. They fought a lot, knew where each other's nerve ends were; they could rub each other raw when they wanted to, and make up with the passion and heal with the speed of the young. They rode through the night in his recently acquired secondhand Bugatti, driving nowhere in particular, just to be alone together; they enjoyed the sacraments and mysteries of candlelit dinners and precipitous lovemaking by the sea. Sometimes, he told Costa Gratsos, he would take her quickly after her workout, the heat and moisture still on her skin. Sex was to play a key role in his life; his business, his success, his fame, all had their sources in a substratum of sex. "He was a horny bastard," said Gratsos. "But even in bed he'd play his hand for all there was in it." He didn't want to listen to sweet nothings between the sheets, he answered when Gratsos expressed surprise at the choice of one inamorata, a noticeably plain-looking German wife of a shipping rival. "I want to hear sweet somethings—somethings I can use."

When the Pavlova season came to its end in Buenos Aires, his Russian ballerina refused to return to Europe with the company. Pavlova herself came to their apartment and put pressure on Aristo to make his girl change her mind, but he refused. Pavlova told him: "You are a deeply wicked, wicked young man. You don't even know the difference between right and wrong!" There is no right and wrong, he answered, increasingly confident of himself; there is only what is possible.

The ballerina had been introduced to Aristo by Alberto Dodero, who had become a legend in Argentina. The youngest of five sons of an Italian immigrant in Uruguay, he had moved from Montevideo to Buenos Aires and, at the end of World War I, with a credit of ten million dollars, had acquired 148 United States ships,

resold them immediately at a fat profit and bought heavily into
the successful Mihanovich shipping company. Dodero entertained
like a Croesus, charmed like an actor and usually picked up all the
marbles. He was a folk hero to Aristo, who accepted every invitation, remembered everything he uttered: Dodero's asides could
alter a quotation on the Pacific stock exchange, but his frown
could also change a politician's mind—"That is real power,"
Onassis would later say to Johnny Meyer.

With energy and determination Aristo kept in the social swim,
especially with the Dodero crowd. And his constant hustling and
his gift for business were beginning to make him rich. He sold the
brand names Osman and Primeros to one of the major manufacturers and concentrated on his export-import business, developing
his links with Athens and cultivating his corner in the Turkish leaf
market. He was proud of his achievements, and especially of his
aura of self-madeness. "Only God and I can make something out
of nothing," became his regular boast. His exact financial status
at that time continues to thwart inquiry—not because he did not
talk about money but because he had as little consistency about
his bookkeeping as he had about his braggadocio. But by the summer of 1928 his trade with Greece had reached a probable two
million dollars* a year. More certain is the fact that he had come
a long way in a very short time—and that his relationship with
the ballerina was rapidly deteriorating. The quarrels between
them became more violent, and the affair ended abruptly shortly
after they had moved into a permanent suite in the Plaza. She had
tried, but his dreams she could not make her dreams. Her departure hit him hard. In spite of his infidelities, he loved her very
much; he missed her understanding, her company. He would later
claim that, like Cinderella, she left behind only a slipper; but he
was no Prince Charming. Aristo's new friend Costa Gratsos, who
watched him dealing with his hurt with anger and drink, saw that
he simply could not comprehend what had driven her away. "I
reminded him that he hadn't been very kind to her," he later
recalled. "Ari said that he couldn't afford to be kind. 'First I have
to be rich,' he said. He was already a very rich young fellow, but
he knew that he was still at the pupal stage of his fortune. I began
to take him seriously."

Gratsos was a young Greek with a hard-looking face that
belied both his well-to-do background and his intelligence. The
discrepancy between the way he looked and the way his

* $8.25 million in present-day terms: Bank of England Information Division, Septem-
ber 1985.

mind operated usually fooled people. A scion of the Dracoulis shipping family and a graduate of the London School of Economics, he had worked his way to Buenos Aires as an ordinary seaman on one of his uncle's ships. He met Aristo at a party or in a nightclub—afterward they could never remember which —shortly after he arrived in town, and they quickly became friends: they shared many of the same interests, often the same women. Although he would always be ambivalent toward Onassis, torn between admiration and abhorrence at the things he did, Gratsos understood his neuroses and his needs better than almost anyone: "Even when you saw him in a bar or simply walking down the street you knew he was a competitor at something. To be doing a deal was his whole life, the rest was waiting."

One morning in the spring of 1929, he called Aristo at the Plaza at eight o'clock in the morning to read him a short news item he'd spotted in the financial pages: the Greek government, in a bid to force Bulgaria back to the negotiating table in a protracted squabble over tariffs, had announced that import duties on goods from countries with which Greece had no trade agreements were to be increased by 1,000 percent. And Argentina had no trade agreement with Greece. "Merde!" Aristo said after making Gratsos read the item again (he had recently engaged a tutor to improve his French). The Argentinians were bound to retaliate, Gratsos said. "Sure as shit," Aristo agreed, forgetting his lessons, as he calculated what a retaliatory tariff would mean to his business with Greece.

Aristo had already acquired the ability to think big. Later that morning he called Gratsos and announced that he was going to prepare a report for Prime Minister Eleutherios Venizelos, demonstrating the immense harm the proposed duties would have on the Greek economy. It was not a thing he was accustomed to doing, and he wanted Gratsos's help. For the next twenty-four hours, living on black coffee and Madeira cake in Aristo's suite, the two men worked on the memorandum. Aristo provided the inspiration, but it was Gratsos, with his LSE background and shipping knowledge, who supplied the expertise. It was a role he was to play for the rest of his life. They made a formidable team. ("They had the ability to look at any situation from two completely different frames of reference: Costa moving cautiously, rationally, Onassis using his animal cunning, his instincts," an aide later noted.) Gratsos calculated that more than 80 percent of the Greek merchant fleet was employed in carrying cargoes from Europe to Argentina. If the Argentinians

were to impose a retributive increase in port duties for Greek
ships it would devastate the Greek maritime trade. They made
out an impressive case. Aristo decided to take it to Athens
himself.

It was a joyous homecoming. Even his father, who was by
no means blind to the deviousness of some of Aristo's deals, and
was sometimes rather too free in alluding to it, was on the quayside of Piraeus to greet him. Although now clearly far from well
(his angina had reached a stage where he was suffering almost
constant pains in his chest and neck), Socrates insisted on
meeting the ship in spite of his doctor's warning that the
excitement would be bad for him. It is not every day that your
only son, who left on an emigrant ship seven years before,
returns first class, a man and at least a fledgling millionaire. "It
was hard for him to admit it, and he never did in words, but
I know he respected what I'd achieved and the fact that I'd
achieved it my way."

Gratsos's influential Dracoulis connection went to work in
Athens, and within a week the Onassis memorandum was on
Prime Minister Venizelos's desk. The grand old man of Greek politics was impressed and arranged for Aristo to meet his minister
of foreign affairs, Andreas Michalakopoulos, whose aides had
drafted the punitive tax laws.

The minister was standing behind a magnificent Louis Quinze
desk, scowling at a document lying on it, as if it were written in a
language he did not understand, or even recognize. The prime
minister appears to think that your views might be of interest to
my department, he said in the tone of polite boredom politicians
use when they have had a problem dropped into their laps from
above. Deliberately closing the file, he told Aristo to summarize
its contents. But all the time he spoke, Michalakopoulos was par-
ing his fingernails with a paper knife. After a short time, he interrupted. Obviously, "Senor Antoniades" was not a man who
recognized that there are times when a government must flex its
muscles, he said. Now he had matters to which he must attend.
He held out his hand. Aristo stared at the immaculately polished
nails, ignoring the churlishness of the misnomer; he knew that his
ambition was destined to arouse opposition, which his disposition
would exacerbate. "I was told that you are a busy man, Minister.
Now I understand that you are busy only with cleaning your nails.
I can see that this is a perfect place for me to stay away from if I
want to be of any use to Greece." His voice was calm, but the
threat was implicit, and Michalakopoulos knew it. "Senor Onas-

sis," he said, getting the name right, "I hear what you are saying, but these matters do take time. I shall study your report with great interest, you may depend on it."

"I walked out of that office knowing two things I didn't know when I went in." Aristo would remember the occasion well and often. "I knew I had what it takes . . . and that one day I was going to have a Louis Quinze desk!"

Aristo's insolence ensured Michalakopoulos's attention, but it was his lavish hospitality during the following weeks that clinched the minister's friendship. And it was thanks to Michalakopoulos that he returned to Buenos Aires with a brand-new Greek passport, which gave his birthdate as January 20, 1906,* and the title of special envoy (although he had become an Argentine national, as a refugee from Asia Minor he had also been granted Greek citizenship under the Treaty of Lausanne). His instructions were to set the ball rolling for trade talks between the two countries. Meanwhile, Greece would exclude Argentina from its stringent import tariffs. "One hand washes the other," Aristo told Gratsos on his return.

In 1931, the Greek government—nudged by the now readily compliant Andreas Michalakopoulos—recognized Aristo's connections in trade and society, as well as in political circles, with a deputy consularship. It gave him not only status, which he craved, but access to large sums of Western currency at basic exchange rates, which he cashed in on the booming black market. Gratsos disapproved. "I thought it was a dangerous game which could jeopardize his diplomatic benefits," he later explained. The game he was playing was espionage, Aristo hinted. Even allowing for his self-dramatization and proneness to exaggeration, it was not unknown for governments to use their consuls as intelligence agents. It would have been remarkable had the Greeks not attempted to use his connections in intelligence-related matters. The government had a variety of covert ways by which to pay Aristo (especially in a country where most businessmen kept at least two sets of books), and sanctioning his black market activities would have been one way of rewarding his services. There may have been others. A police file on Aristo and his cousin Nicos Konialidis sent from Genoa and concerning an insurance fraud involving the to-

---

* It was vanity that willed him to subtract six years from his age to make his achievements appear even more remarkable; later he would tell his mistress Ingeborg Dedichen that he had taken this opportunity to add six years in order to avoid possible military service in Argentina. "To be honest," he told friends in old age, "I'm not sure how old I am, for even my papers lie."

bacco he was importing from his father in Greece, conveniently disappeared in Athens in 1932.*

Although tobacco was still at the heart of Aristo's fortune, shipping was beginning to interest him more and more. He was fascinated by Gratsos's stories of the money to be made (and lost) at sea, stories of the Dracoulis riches. But it is rare that a man is moved by one motive alone, and his formative years around Piraeus had certainly influenced his thinking. And it also annoyed him that other men were making almost as much money as he was out of his company simply by transporting his tobacco. "Shipping's where the real money is," he said to Gratsos over and over. "And the risk," Gratsos would remind him. It was a discussion they had had many times. "You're doing fine, don't mess with something you know almost nothing about," Gratsos would tell him. Shipping would always be a high-risk business, but it had a compelling attraction for Aristo at that time. The depression had hit shipping hard, and eight-thousand-ton dry-cargo vessels costing five hundred thousand dollars ten years before were going for a song; the snag was not the purchase price but the operating costs —too many ships were chasing too few cargoes. Owners would often lose thousands of dollars on a cargo because it was cheaper than paying for a ship to be laid up. Nevertheless, Aristo would not be deterred. Gratsos was appalled when, against his direst warnings, he bought a seven-thousand-ton freighter he found shipwrecked on the Rio de la Plata. He spent a small fortune refloating the *Maria Protopapas* and putting her into shape. The work was hardly completed when she sank at anchor in Montevideo harbor during a storm. Privately, Gratsos hoped that the experience would "put a stop to his crazy dream." But it merely deferred it.

Shortly after Aristo had become deputy consul, his father died of a heart attack, and he returned to Athens for the funeral; after-

---

* *The U.S. Office of Naval Intelligence described the scam a decade later in a confidential memo to the FBI in January 1943: "The tobacco was sent via Genoa, where it was transshipped. And it appears that ONASSIS hit upon the idea of spraying the bales with salt water during their stay at Genoa, the resultant collections from underwriters for sea damage forming a welcome addition to legitimate trading profits. Insurance Agents were involved and, eventually, an employee gave the game away at a time when Nicolas KONIALIDIS, brother-in-law of subject, was in Genoa, with the result that the latter served a term in jail. The dossier appears to have been sent to Greece from Genoa, but is thought to have been lost owing to a close liaison between ONASSIS and one MICHALAKOPOULOS, a Greek Minister at that time." O.N.I. was not the only branch of U.S. intelligence interested in the details of the life of Aristotle Socrates Onassis, which possibly gives credence to his own innuendos that he had operated at least on the fringes of espionage. According to documents released through the FOI Privacy Office, U.S. Army Intelligence and Security Command also closely monitored his activities and reported directly to "Lt. Col. J. Edgar Hoover."*

ward he toured Europe. In London, then the hub of the maritime world, with an old-established community of Greek shipowners, including Stavros Livanos, André Embiricos, Manuel Kulukundis —a society as suspicious and closed in on itself as any exotic sect —he heard a whisper that the Canadian National Steamship Company was heading for a financial crisis and had ten freighters laid up in the St. Lawrence River that were available at thirty thousand dollars each, a price that was barely above their scrap value. He engaged a marine engineer and took off immediately for Montreal.

For three days in subzero temperatures Aristo clambered over the vessels, pursued by a group of Canadian officials. From first light till dark he inspected engine rooms, boilers, examined bulkheads, crawled on his hands and knees through shaft tunnels and climbed into every store, locker and hold from the bridge to the baseline. He made notes of everything. He was also watching the Canadians, gauging their concern. At night he worked out his sums, subtracting thousands for every anxious glance he had caught the Canadians exchanging. At the end of the third day, he stood on the deck of the *Canadian Miller*, grunted, rubbed his ear, shook his head. He would take six of them, he said, at twenty thousand dollars apiece. It was a hard deal, but he was the only player in town. The Canadians hemmed and hawed, and settled. He was finally in the shipping business. His first act as a shipowner was to rename the *Canadian Miller* and the *Canadian Spinner;* the first two ships of his fleet became the *Onassis Penelope* and *Onassis Socrates*, after his mother and father.

CHAPTER

4

All that we do is done with an eye to something else.
ARISTOTLE, *Nicomachean Ethics*

S HE STOOD with a small group of passengers by the rail of the *Augustus* waving good-bye to friends who had come to wish them bon voyage on their journey from Buenos Aires to Genoa, the last return leg of a fashionable pilgrimage to the Antarctic. He could not take his eyes from her. She looked like Garbo, the razored eyebrows and hollow cheeks, the insolent sensuality and aura of solemn fatality. Becoming aware of the intensity of his gaze, she returned his interest with a rich girl's smile. She liked any sort of singularity in a man, and was instantly curious about her fellow first-class traveler with the piercing dark eyes and pomaded hair. There was something challenging about the way he watched her, and she liked that. She thought he was a mobster of a quiet order, a man whose origins nobody knew anything about, she was to tell him later.

He noticed that among the people who had come to see her off was the millionaire Don Juan Christophersen; and it was to this man that she threw a rose from her bouquet. A woman with her looks and style, her almost cosmic scent of money, had to be worth meeting. That thought was to affect the course of both their lives.

He slipped money to a steward to change his cabin for one closer to hers. For the first few days he kept his distance while making inquiries among the crew, and being free with five-dollar bills. Her name was Ingeborg Dedichen, and she was a familiar figure aboard the *Augustus*. Her companions included Gustav Bull, a leading Norwegian shipowner, and Lars Christensen, the owner of a whaling fleet. The youngest of seven children of Ingevald Martin Bryde, one of the most prominent and respected shipowners in Norway, she had grown up in an enchanted world: Kathrineborg, her home in Sandefjord, built by grandfather Johan Maurits Bryde, was known as the Brydeslottet, or Bryde Castle. Hers was a shipping family through and through; her four brothers had graduated from the naval college in Tjome, founded by grandfather Johan. Her maternal great-grandfather was a romantic poet named Pieter Dass. And her mother, Nanna Sabina, was a Klerck, with bloodlines to the Swedish aristocracy. She had been married twice; her present husband, Hermann Dedichen, was a bridge player and gambler who, having gone through his own fortune at the card tables, had started in on hers. She was making plans to shed Hermann as soon as she returned to Paris, where they lived.

Several days later Aristo spoke to her when they met in the pool. She wore the first two-piece bathing suit he had ever seen, but instead of paying her a compliment, he made a jokey remark about her swimming. The clumsiness of his pass did not surprise her; what did surprise her was that he had made it in Swedish! It was several days before he approached her again. She was stretched out in a sunchair. He asked in English (he had exhausted all his Swedish in the pool) whether she was enjoying the book she was reading. It was *My Life and Hard Times* by James Thurber, and she said it was amusing. He had been acquainted too often with hard times in his life to wish to read about those of others, he said, turning on the charm that impressed everyone who had not had occasion to do business with him. There was that husky, rich quality about his voice which made it almost impossible not to go on listening, although, heavily accented in English, French and German, it was also the voice of a man for whom language would always be a blunt instrument rather than an accomplishment to polish: the efficacy of anything was what counted. It must be too awful to be without money, she said, pleased that they could talk so easily together. He introduced himself. "And I know that you are Mme. Dedichen. We shall become good friends." He seemed very sure of himself, she said. Aristo smiled. With her background she must have heard the old saying that there is no such thing as a fair wind for the mariner who does not know to which port he is bound. It was clear that he meant business. Ingeborg sidestepped his pass. The purser had told her that he was the Greek consul in Buenos Aires, she said. Was he in business also? He replied that he was a shipowner. Oh God! A Greek shipowner, she said, with sudden distaste in her voice. From her earliest years, she had heard her family and friends deplore Greek shipowners, accusing them of all sorts of dirty tricks. It was said around Lloyd's of London that the Greeks always made up the most imaginative myths.

But that evening he was invited to join her table with the Lars Christensens and Gustav Bull, men whose friendship he would one day use. (It was aboard the *Augustus* that he developed the trick of eating before going to a dinner party; later, while the other guests were occupied with their food, he could appear both temperate and irresistible!) He and Ingeborg quickly became close. At night they sat on the deck, telling each other their stories. ("He is much more fascinating in conversations *à deux*," she told the Christensens.) Ingeborg's first husband's sister was a friend of Norway's Queen Maud; they had been to many great parties at the royal palace. They were lovely times, she told him. Why did they end? he asked. I caught my husband in bed with my niece, she said: they made a very beautiful baby together. She smiled as if the conception had made everything fine. And now her second marriage was on the rocks; Dedichen had gone through a great amount of her money, and she was having to sell pieces of jewelry and items from her Paris apartment. She dreaded the idea of returning to France. She permitted him to kiss her goodnight. He was in no hurry to consummate the shipboard romance: not only because an encounter as engaging as this takes on an excitement of its own but because he was only slowly recovering from a venereal disease.

All the bands seemed to be playing Cole Porter songs that year, 1934, but whatever tune they played, Aristo danced the same dance—a slow, fast or medium foxtrot. Why is it that even when you're wearing a tuxedo, you still look like a gangster, Ingeborg teased him the last night of the voyage. Perhaps because he was a gangster, he told her. It was an image that appealed to his sense of romance, and a desire to create his own legend with a mixture of fantasy and tangled truths. "No, you're a pirate," later she was to recall telling him. She had a sharp eye for human foibles. He had impressed her against all the odds, and against her will; and he made her laugh, and she hadn't laughed too much lately.

He had his Cadillac waiting in Genoa, he told her that last evening aboard the *Augustus*. Why didn't they drive to Cannes, Marseilles, Venice . . . any place but Paris? "If I go with you it will cause a great deal of mischief, and I'm not sure that my constitution, let alone my reputation, could withstand even a little scandal just now," she said. He wanted to be with her, and she wanted to be with him, he persisted: it was a waste of time discussing the morality of it. She knew that he was the kind of man who would always sacrifice the interests of others to his private ends, she was to say later; yet there was something compelling about the proposition he was putting to her now, and even in her wariness she was conscious at that moment of something incredibly compassionate in his voice, something almost desperate. In Venice (they took connecting rooms in the Hotel Danieli, according to Ingeborg; a suite at the Gritti Palace, Onassis remembered), his enforced spell of celibacy behind him, they made love for the first time. The lovers' names they gave each other—she was his Mamita (little mother); he was her Mamico—said a lot about the relationship.

They careered about Europe in glamorous style, the best restaurants, the finest hotels, making scenes in public places and making up in private; if the harmony was unreliable, the excitement never faltered. (And empires as well as personal affairs evolve upon the basis of private passions: after a week in Oslo and Sandefjord, Aristo wrote to Costa Gratsos that he had met "everybody worth knowing" in Norwegian shipping.) But many of Ingeborg's friends and relations were appalled by what one of them politely called his "excessive Greek vivacity," and the intensity of her infatuation; they hoped that he was a temporary disturbance, a social climber she would disavow when the penny dropped. At Foyot's in Paris, he summoned waiters taverna fashion with clicking fingers and by hissing like a snake; at Maxim's he sought the attention of the maître d' by tapping his knife against a glass. If Ingeborg had private doubts, she also knew that it was his indifference to what other people thought of him that gave him his energy and his style. But she was happier when they dined in the *cabinets particuliers*, the private rooms for lovers. Later, in a wave of sensual reminiscence, she confessed that neither of her husbands had skin that she liked to stroke as much as Aristo's ("It had an odor, a texture, a warmth and velvet softness which was beyond compare, of which I never tired"); and neither of them excited her as much as he did. Making love, he "liked to lick me between the toes, carefully, like a cat . . . he would embrace every part of my body and cover me with kisses before devoting himself to the feet he adored."

Aristo's active social life did not mean a diminished commitment to making money. After Ingeborg had kicked Hermann Dedichen out of her life, he installed himself in her apartment on the avenue de Villiers and continued his habit of working through the early hours, no matter how late they had celebrated or how much they had drunk. He spent hours placing calls to London, Athens, Buenos Aires. His stamina astonished her, his recuperative powers were extraordinary. Sometimes he worked until it was light and the birds were singing in the trees in the place Malesherbes. When, after several nonstop months together, he had to go to Athens and Argentina, while she was obliged to remain in Paris to deal with legal matters relating to her planned divorce, Ingeborg was glad of the break.

He wrote to her almost every day during his travels, letters of extraordinary length, self-revelation, appalling anguish and juvenility.* Again and again he beseeched her to be faithful: "to be mine 100% . . . say you love me, say you are totally true to me . . . Mamita, my adorable Ingse, never betray my trust even for a moment, never let men flirt with you, you must promise it!" He watched over her like a hawk, fussed like a mother hen: "Tell your nice sister in Oslo not to be nasty to you because it is very bad when sisters are nasty to each other"; when she planned to sell a small intaglio, he warned her about dealers who "always when they see a woman they want to make a victim of her. They are Jews," recording this first implication of his at least skin-deep anti-Semitism, which was to cause him so much trouble in the years ahead. He wanted to know how she spent her time, the people she had seen, where she had dined. His sophomoric tone at first amused her, but his reproaches and suspicions began to trouble her, too. She told Artemis: "It is as if he wants me to have no past, no memories, no stamps in my passport." She became accustomed to telephone calls in the middle of the night, calls prompted by suspicion, melancholy, his growing hypochondria. His letters were filled with pain: "Mamita, it can't go on like this. If you really love me, if you really want my love, you must come at once and marry me." She was still married to Hermann: had he forgotten? she would reply. "You just write nice things, which cost nothing, but you refuse to move, to submit yourself to the slightest inconvenience in order to be with me," he wrote from Athens. She hated Athens. She approved of London, but he claimed that it was too expensive to have her there (although he kept a permanent suite at the Savoy) and yet carried on about the consequences of his sworn celibacy: "Don't you think it's stupid and unjust to be so crazily in love and living apart? Have you any idea how many times I wake up in the morning with my bed wet because I have ejaculated in my sleep? It makes my body feel rotten for the whole day."

* Although they were born the same year he lied to her about his age, preferring the legend in his Greek passport; she may have not been totally convinced: in her annotated copy of Joachim Joesten's biography, Onassis, published in New York in 1963, she scored the 1906 claim with a red question mark.

Like any woman who has failed twice at marriage, she had a highly developed sense of self-preservation, and although she was reluctant to relinquish her claims upon his protection (he was now pretty well keeping her), she needed to maintain at least a vestige of independence; she did not mind that people knew that Onassis was her lover, yet bristled at being regarded as his mistress, her nephew Finn Bryde recalled later. "Deals define his life," she told Costa Gratsos, who understood better than anyone what she meant, and how right she was. Aristo's wheeling and dealing had become an existential need. "Like Achilles," he repeated, beginning to develop a profound consciousness of his Greek ancestry, "I am fighting for nothing but my own glory."

In London, he shared a small backroom office at 101 Leadenhall Street with Pericles Dracoulis, an uncle of Costa Gratsos. It was a difficult and lonely time for him. The pressures of trying to keep tabs on his tobacco empire (still the major source of his wealth, managed in Athens by Uncle Homer, and in Buenos Aires by Cousins Nicos and Constantine Konialidis) and develop his shipping business, were considerable. Sublimating sexual energy in work, he hustled sixteen hours a day, seven days a week, running from office to office, dock to dock, bribing, playing one agent against another, to keep his ships in business. He seldom had lunch, settling for a beer and sandwiches in his office. For despite the appearance of affluence, the suite at the Savoy, his expensive dark blue Paris suits (from Creeds in the rue Royale), the toing and froing between London and Athens, Buenos Aires and Paris, he was making heavy demands on his tobacco money to keep his fledgling shipping venture viable. When Mamita offered to give up her apartment on the avenue de Villiers for a smaller fourth-floor flat in the place de Laborde that had belonged to her cousin Stina, who had married the Comte de Montais, he jumped at the chance to save some money. ("He could be stingy, as well as generous," an aide would later admit. "He couldn't always resist the temptation to chisel a buck or two, even on little things.") When Inge wanted the drawing room paneled to go with her Louis XVI–style furniture he insisted that she use the tapestries from the old apartment, and wrote reprovingly: "We have far more urgent and important necessities." He was always struggling with his duality, even when buying her a piece of jewelry: "Mamita, for me to buy such things must be occasion, so that when I see you wearing them and knowing I got them cheaply, though very nice, gives me more pleasure." Sending a check for sixty pounds at the beginning of 1936, he was still urging her to "be careful with the money . . . you must make economy." He had not been able to join her for a single day that Christmas; he had spent the holiday negotiating a cargo in Antwerp, two hundred miles from Paris. "Mamita, I am sick of worrying about so many problems. I wish I could rest for a while, and be with you," he wrote, adding the familiar plea for her to accept no invitations, except family—"When men discover that you are alone and feeling lonesome they will want you to go to dinner with them . . . please, I beg you, don't go with them."

To save cab fares, and unable to find his way around the London subway system, he frequently walked from his office to the Savoy. Thirty years later he could rattle off the old street names of his regular route: Cornhill, Cheapside, Newgate, Ludgate Hill, Fleet Street, Aldwych, the Strand. The long walk kept him in shape and helped to ward off the great sense of loneliness that he felt in London. In the evenings he read everything about shipping he could lay his hands on, from *Lloyd's List* and *Shipping Gazette* to the *New York Journal of Commerce*. He could recite insurance rates, charter conditions, bunkering arrangements, fuel prices and schedules of every important steamship company in the world. A master of predatory pricing, he could gauge a deal so finely that Gratsos later swore that "he could cut off a competitor's legs a slice at a time."

At the Savoy, he felt for the first time in his life that he existed at the edge of insignificance, was on probation among people who were "so rich and so at ease with their wealth." He spent time at the movies. He enjoyed Conrad Veidt in *King of the Damned* and saw Grace Moore in *Love Me Forever* three times, he wrote Mamita. Some mornings he would rise before it was light and walk across London Bridge to breakfast in one of the dockland cafés in Tooley Street or Rotherhithe Street, where the aroma of frying bread and bacon mingled with the smells of hemp and oil and the hops from brewers' warehouses. It was not nostalgia for the waterfront that drew him to these places but a gravitational pull such as rapacious beauties have for men with secret fortunes. He knew he would pick up scraps of information from the stevedores, tally clerks and seamen who frequented the grease kitchens to help him sniff out what cargoes were around.

Returning to the Savoy one evening, he found a messenger waiting for him in the lobby with disturbing news. The Greek consul in Rotterdam was refusing to clear one of his ships, the *Onassis Penelope*, until a Greek national was found to replace a seaman who had collapsed with appendicitis. The Greek-registered vessel was bound for Copenhagen with her remaining cargo from Buenos Aires; delay would incur costly indemnity payments and lose him his next cargo. He telephoned the consul in Holland

and pleaded with him to relax the regulations; the official was implacable. Aristo worked through the night, rousing agents from their beds, consulting with lawyers, adjusting contracts. The next morning, he flew to Rotterdam and invited the consul to join him for a drink aboard the stranded ship. "My friend," he said with wonderful largess, handing him a small package as they raised their glasses. "You are now aboard a Panamanian ship." The package contained the Greek flag. He had not slept for thirty hours— "but the pleasure of outsmarting authority was worth every minute of it."

In Paris, Ingeborg was enjoying a dalliance with an old Dutch admirer, an orchestral conductor. She had no scruples about such things. The affair was no more than "a little grain of sand" in her life, an episode to assuage *her* loneliness: sexual guilt was excluded from her Nordic sense of accountability. But Aristo sensed something was wrong; three days had elapsed without a line. He wrote to her urgently: "What is the matter, Mamita? You have all day to play bridge, but you can't find ten minutes to write me a few words! I think something must be the matter. Why don't you write to me? You are unjust because I am suffering here working so hard, even with a terrible fever, how can you be like this if you really love me? Why are you so unjust? Do you hate me?" Of course she didn't hate him, she assured him. "Unjust" seems to have become his favorite word, she told a friend. And later she would say, "I remembered reading somewhere that a person had to be very just not to think unjust the behavior of a lover."

Unconvinced by her assurances he called her from the Savoy, although he hated telephone conversations that went through operators (he suspected they were listening on the line, "making fun of my lousy English"), and demanded to know whether she had been unfaithful. She did not want to lie to him, yet she knew that the truth was dangerous. Her frank answers to his shameless questions about her experiences with her previous husbands had triggered terrible jealous rages. Cautiously she answered that she had seen an old friend, but the episode had passed almost beyond recollection. He should not confuse one erotic impulse with love, she said. But he took it badly.

As the industrial nations slowly emerged from the depression and his ships started to show a profit, it was time to make his next move. Coal was still providing 75 percent of the world's energy needs, but it was being superseded by oil; in spite of its massive natural resources, even the United States was on the verge of becoming a net importer of oil; with industrial production growing

at an annual rate of 12 percent, and with rapid growth in the
European military arena, refineries were spreading throughout
the Middle East. Tankers were going to be in demand to move the
oil from the terminal ports in Syria, Libya, Tunisia, Algeria and
Lebanon, to the burgeoning marketplaces around the world.
Aristo figured that the real answer was not more tankers but bigger tankers. Like all Greek shipowners at that time, he was a "dry"
carrier (tobacco, grain, timber), but he had done his sums carefully and calculated that he could cut operating costs substantially
if he were able to increase by two-thirds the size of the standard
nine-thousand-ton tanker. As ideas go, it was not in the same class
as the principle of the constancy of the velocity of light, yet marine
engineers told him exactly what experts had told Einstein about
his theory: it contradicted common sense. They quoted displace-
ment scales, specific gravities, maximum permissible drafts and
loadlines. A fifteen-thousand-ton tanker was impossible. Despite
the resistance, he was convinced that big tankers were the future,
and nothing could dispel the idea from his mind. "You don't fail
till you give up trying," he said when Gratsos suggested that he
forget the whole idea. "A man isn't worth shit if he doesn't try to
tear a hole in the line once in his life."

He needed to find a yard physically capable of building a
tanker of the size he envisaged. A shipping agent named Gustav
Sandstrom whom he had got to know in Buenos Aires recommended him to Ernst Heden, the boss of the Gotaverken shipyards
in Göteborg. Twenty-four hours later he was in Heden's office,
along with Mamita. For apart from the problem of persuading
Heden to commit his yard to such a massive vessel, with all its
technological headaches, Aristo needed considerably more credit
than was normal for Greek owners. The presence of Mamita, a
daughter of the esteemed Brydes of Sandefjord, would do his reputation no harm.

Heden thought the ship was feasible but calculated that it
would cost eight hundred thousand dollars, almost twice the cost
of a nine-thousand-tonner. His suggestion: buy two nine-thou-
sand-tonners. Aristo insisted on the big ship, and for the next three
days the two men discussed terms but could not reach agreement.
Aristo got the influential Lars Christensen, Ingeborg's companion
aboard the *Augustus,* to vouch for him; Ingeborg roped in Anders
Jahre, a brilliant Norwegian lawyer who had organized some of
Scandinavia's most powerful whaling and shipping corporations,
to speak on his behalf. Heden agreed to drop "the Greek clause"
requiring at least 50 percent cash and a maximum five-year credit
line; a significant achievement, it was still not good enough for
Aristo. Important and irreconcilable differences remained when

he finally returned to London. One of the finest pressure players in the business, during the following weeks he bombarded Heden with cables, letters, telephone calls, bit by bit chipping away at the shipbuilder's terms, and his resolve, until they began to resemble the deal he wanted.

Heden was in his office in Gotaverken when his secretary told him that Mr. Onassis wanted to talk to him. "Put him on," Heden said, expecting another long-distance harangue. But Aristo walked into his office, and twenty minutes later the deal was sewn up: A. S. Onassis, Göteborg Ltd. had commissioned the world's first fifteen-thousand-ton tanker for eight hundred thousand dollars, one-quarter of which was to be paid in three stages during construction and the remainder at 4.5 percent interest spread over ten years. He would call her *Ariston*, he said. A play on his own name, it was also Greek for "the best."

Every day he wrote Mamita rambling misspelled letters (*pitty, energie, worrie, hipocrit*) asking for her advice, her views, seeking assurances of her fidelity; anxiety gnawed at his heart constantly. It was the minutiae of his life that most deepened Ingeborg's affection for him: lonely train journeys across Europe ("I would love to fly but there have been so many accidents recently that I don't dare to; yesterday seven people were killed in a crash in Norway"), the hours spent watching bad movies he had already seen to pass the time between meetings.

As his shipping fortunes increased, the tobacco business on which so much had depended was running into trouble. In Athens Homer had allowed the situation to drift alarmingly. Now on the edge of old age (Aristo later put him at around sixty at this time) he appeared totally unaware of the crises and his increasing inability to deal with them. When finally it did get through that he was being deposed and that Aristo intended to create a completely new management team in Athens, he reacted violently, threatening to shoot Aristo and afterward commit suicide. "You are not only a coward but a stupid one," Aristo told him. When Mamita expressed her alarm he assured her: "I know how to defend myself. Anyway, he is just an old, desperate man who has suddenly realized how much he has kiked away. I feel pitty [*sic*] for him because, after all, he is a brother of my father and I shall help him again, but next time just by giving him money and not mixing him in my business." *

Despite the tough talk, the strain was immense. Problems

---

* *It is unlikely that Ari believed that Homer had deliberately robbed him, although in inventing a verb with which to link his uncle's behavior to people he deeply mistrusted, he confirms the depth of his loathing for the old man.*

came at him from all directions. As he was dealing with the crisis in Athens, fretting over every phase of the building of the *Ariston* in Göteborg, keeping tabs on his Buenos Aires operation, constantly switching schedules to collar cargoes at the other end of the world, operating on a margin of nerve to squeeze a profit out of the most unpromising circumstances, his health was beginning to crack. He complained of headaches, pains in his hands and kidneys, sore throats and bronchitis.

Although he was used to sailing close to the wind ("my natural habitat," he said later), his investment in the *Ariston* had put a severe strain on his funds, and he had become more frugal than ever with Mamita; even when he was desperately trying to persuade her to join him in Athens in August 1936, he insisted: "I don't want you to come by train, it costs so terribly much. If you decide to come, it is understood that it will be by boat." Relenting a little ten days later, he agreed to a second-class rail ticket. She hated Athens, the heat and the dust, the nightclubs in which he liked to relax. She could not understand the fever of Hellenism. Her refusal to go to him when he said he was sick, plunged him into despair. "You think I like to be here? I would not exaggerate if I told you that I *hate* Greece more than you do," he claimed, reminding her that it was business that kept him in Athens. He wrote her passionate letters, angry letters, he sent telegrams, he called her on the telephone to apologize for the angry letters. His calls, like his letters, veered to extremes: one moment vowing his eternal love and urging her to have a child by him ("It is so serious and such a great responsibility, Mamita, but if you have the courage let us have one, or at least let us try"), the next attacking her for being a snob because she had accepted an invitation to attend a dinner party at the Danish embassy in Paris, and gleefully pointing out that Denmark had no embassy in Paris, "merely a legation, the same as all the little countries!"

There were the first signs of the manic-depressions that would trouble him on and off for the rest of his life. "My health, Mamita, it is unbelievable. I am thirty years old and already I feel I am falling apart," he wrote, carefully preserving the fiction of his age as well as evoking her maternal instinct. His brother-in-law Dr. Theodore Garofalides confined him to bed for a week during his stay in Athens, in which time he lost fourteen pounds. Ingeborg's natural flirtatiousness played havoc with his peace of mind. He lived in fear that she would betray him again. Her betrayal hurt him so much "that I can't describe the pain to you. It takes away all my enthusiasm for life. My egotism, my *amour propre* never permitted me to tell you these things before, but I have had a lot of time to think during the past few days—mostly my brain is always so busy and worried with business and has no time for personal feelings—and I want you to understand exactly how I feel. What does it mean, after all, that the woman a man loves goes to bed with another man once or a few times? Considering the matter sensibly, it should mean nothing, but it hurts the man terribly, Mamita. I used to laugh about things like that. But since I started to love you I have come to realize what fidelity means. I don't care that you have been married twice, that you have had several adventures, but it makes me crazy to think that you might one day betray me again. It means nothing when I think about your past, before we met. I have no troublesome images of you with your husbands or with your American lover, but I can't get out of my head the pictures of you and the Dutchman in Paris. All the time I have in my mind a kind of dark picture made by your description."

Again he suggested that they should marry as soon as her divorce came through: "Life is so short, Mamita, we have only a few years to enjoy our physical love: my *jeunesse* is not going to last forever." Meanwhile, he said, he had made her joint beneficiary (with his stepmother, Helen) of an insurance policy he had taken out in Buenos Aires in 1933 for three thousand dollars—but pleaded that she must tell him immediately if she should ever betray him again!

During the following months he lost his diplomatic passport (the Greeks decided that he was spending too little time in Argentina to warrant a consularship), had his tonsils removed and underwent an operation to remove several small nodes on the lymphatic glands in his neck. As soon as he felt fit enough he decided to return to Buenos Aires to sort out the problems there.

Mamita agreed to accompany him, but shortly before the ship was due to sail from Naples, she had an acute anxiety attack concerning her reputation: "What will my family think? No one will understand how I can accompany you on such a long trip without being married to you . . . it's madness!" Aristo himself might have planted in her head the seeds of that decision when, suspicious of her social round in Paris, he informed her that he wanted her reputation "to be the highest possible, because I consider a good reputation is a great part of the human happiness. Some people, if they are very, very rich can permit themselves certain negligence to their reputations. Very rich women can be extravagant and will be forgiven because of the power of their money. But when money is normal—or, rather, short—you must care about public opinion and behave within certain limits." But now he resented her sense of propriety. "You gave to hell your reputation in your youth, at the age of twenty—with the American, with others, when you surrendered your virginity—and now that you are a grown-up woman, twice-married, quite independent from your mother, you suddenly start to worry about your reputation and what people will think!"

It says a great deal about their extraordinary relationship, their disastrous inability to understand each other, that she was surprised by his anger—and hurt by his refusal to buy her a coral necklace she had admired shortly after her decision not to accompany him to Buenos Aires. She complained to a friend: "Imagine what it would have cost him to take me to Argentina, yet he would not buy me this miserable little necklace!"

The problems in Buenos Aires were less serious than those Aristo had faced in Athens; the Konialidis brothers were making a better go of things than Homer had, and after a few weeks everything was running to his satisfaction. There were good reasons for his growing optimism in the summer of 1937. He had at the last minute canceled a booking to New York on the Zeppelin *Hindenburg* to go instead to Dax to discuss modifications for the *Ariston* with an architect who was having mudbath treatments for his arthritis. On May 6, the *Hindenburg* flight Aristo should have been on ended in disaster at Lakehurst. "All things go well with the lucky man," he said, but there was something mystical for him in the thought that his skin had been saved in such a fashion. Meanwhile, the president of the Reichsbank and economic dictator of Hitler's Third Reich, Dr. Hjalmar Schacht, had launched a massive program of rearmament. As Europe prepared for the worst, the shipping boom went from strength to strength. It was almost impossible not to make a lot of money if you had the vessels, he was later to say. With his first tanker almost completed in Sweden, and a year's contract already signed with Jean Paul Getty's Tidewater Oil Company to move oil from California to the Mitsuis Corporation in Yokohama, Aristo had decided to order two more tankers, even larger than the *Ariston*.

A few days after his return to Buenos Aires, his old mentor Alberto Dodero invited him to a party to meet Fritz Mandl, the Austrian armaments king, boss of the Hirtenberger munitions works in Vienna. A glamorous high-powered affair, the turnout included leading members of the large German community, show business celebrities (just divorced from Hedy Lamarr, Mandl had a weakness for the company of actresses: the German star Eva May had killed herself when their affair ended), diplomats from three Fascist dictatorships in Europe, and the pro-Nazi Argentine generals Basilio Pertine and Juan Molina. British and American intelligence services took a special interest in the guest list.

Although Mandl boasted of his excellent relationship with the Nazis and had aligned himself as early as 1927 with the Austrian Fascists (Franco and Mussolini were his close personal friends) he was also a Jew. Apparently apprehensive about Hitler's designs on Austria, he had already acquired a cattle ranch and a rice plantation just outside Buenos Aires and, with seven hundred kilos of gold bars deposited in Argentina's Central Bank, was looking around for further investments. Aristo was flattered when he sought him out to ask his advice about shipping. He felt part of a new world of economic brotherhood. A jackdaw always sits near a jackdaw, he boasted to his cousin Costa Konialidis.

Dodero continued to invite Aristo, or Ari, as he called him, to all his parties and to long weekends at his home near Montevideo, across the Rio de la Plata, where a dozen or more house guests, the beautiful people of the day, and especially the beautiful women, for whom Dodero had a keen eye, would sip the finest champagne and brunch on scrambled eggs or *pâté de foie gras* with Périgord truffles flown in fresh from France. Dodero's parties were legendary; sometimes it was daylight before the band played the last dance and waiters began serving breakfast on the lawn. It was a way of life that appealed immensely to Aristo. He took in everything and began, perhaps unconsciously, to model himself on the man he called Don Dodero. He showed up at a nightclub dressed so like his host—the same alligator shoes, the same greased-back hair like Don Ameche's—that Fritz Mandl remarked that he should be "arrested for stealing the identity of another person!"

Ari (Dodero's nickname quickly caught hold and seemed to Aristo to be far more grown-up) continued to write to Mamita almost every day, giving a carefully edited version of what he had been up to and taking care to include the kind of detail with which she was now familiar ("Tomorrow one of my ships will be leaving here for Copenhagen with grain; I get so sad when I think that within thirty days she will be within a few hours' train journey from you yet not be able to sail with her"), a mixture of business news and sentiment. During this trip he again rearranged his life insurance policies—"so that if anything happens to me you will get for the rest of your life at least five hundred krone a month," he explained in the way he had whenever he was discussing money or business with her, as if talking to a child. "I want you to feel safe and not have any worries." It was a thoughtful act, perhaps prompted by his narrow squeak in the *Hindenburg* disaster. It was also a way of assuaging his guilty conscience for whatever fun and games he was up to with Dodero and his gang.

The night before the *Ariston* was launched in June 1938, Ari gave a banquet for 150 guests at the Grand Hotel in Göteborg. A team of Greek cooks joined the Swedish chefs to prepare a feast of Scandinavian and Greek delicacies. Artemis came from Athens with husband Theodore Garofalides; cousin Nicos Konialidis was there from Buenos Aires with his new bride, Merope, Ari's half-sister; the Sandstroms and the Christensens were there, feeling like godfathers (Mme. Sandstrom would have the honor of christening the ship). And the elite of Scandinavian shipping turned out to welcome the largest tanker ever built, and to give the once-over to the hottest name in shipping since Livanos.

Ari wore a stiff shirt, which made him uncomfortable, but he gave a dignified speech thanking everybody who had worked so hard to make the *Ariston* possible. He thanked the designers and the architects, the riveters and the welders; he thanked his sisters for their faith in him, he thanked his cousins and his brother-in-law for being there to share his pride. He expressed his confidence in the future of world trade; no matter that Hitler had just annexed Austria and the Japanese were storming through China. He did not mention Ingeborg at all.

5

The quarreling of lovers is the renewal of love.

TERENCE

GETTING OVER a monumental hangover from Mamita's thirty-ninth birthday party, which began on Friday evening, September 1, and did not end until she stormed back to Paris on Saturday afternoon following a blistering row, Ari was in his suite at the Savoy Hotel when he heard Prime Minister Neville Chamberlain's broadcast announcing that Germany had failed to answer the British government's ultimatum to withdraw its troops from Poland "and that consequently this country is at war with Germany." War was not necessarily a bad thing for a neutral shipowner, of course. Ari had retained both his Argentine and Greek passports bearing their disparate details. His freighters were flying under the flag of Panama; the *Ariston* was registered in Sweden; the *Aristophanes* was on charter under the Norwegian flag. The 17,500-ton *Buenos Aires* was close to completion in Göteborg. To possess three of the world's biggest oil tankers, and to be totally impartial, in a time of war, was not going to damage his prospects at all. As he sipped a Fernet branca (his favorite hangover remedy: a thick, black bitters with quinine in it) that Sunday morning, listening to the querulous tones of the British leader, he appeared to be one of those men toward whom fate has the kindest resolve.

There was a nasty shock in store for him. The Swedes, anxious to establish their neutrality, immediately declared that foreign-owned ships under their flag and built in their yards would be laid up for the duration—including the *Ariston*, docked in Stockholm,

and the *Buenos Aires*, which was in her fitting-out berth in Göteborg and registered under the pro-Axis Argentine flag.

Ari had a lot to think about and went for a long walk. He later
remembered that in Piccadilly the shoeshine man polished his
alligator shoes until he could see his face in them. It was a wan
reflection. Two-thirds of his tanker fleet, 32,500 tons of the finest
tankers in the world, had been taken out of his hands at a stroke.
He worried for the safety of the rest of his fleet. That Sunday
evening he telephoned Mamita in Paris, and after they had made
up, she suggested a meeting with her friend Anders Jahre, the
Norwegian lawyer whose backstairs influence had helped him get
the credit he needed for the *Ariston*. All through the phony war, as
that first bloodless autumn and winter became known in England
(in France they called it *une drôle de guerre*), Ari and Jahre worked
on the problem of how to avoid future seizure of his ships. Overcoming his fear of flying, Ari flew back and forth more than a
dozen times to Oslo, Stockholm, Sandefjord and Göteborg, arranging and rearranging his affairs, adjusting contracts, fine-tuning
terms, switching covenants between companies, between countries, between continents. The strain of the secrecy and urgency of
what he was up to, as well as negotiating the sale of two cargo
ships to the Japanese, again surfaced in ill health. Ulitis (inflam-
mation of the gums), headaches and nosebleeds became regular
torments during the bitter winter months of 1940.

Mamita spent Easter with him in London. On March 25, Bank
Holiday Monday in England, they took off for Oslo to put the
finishing touches to Ari's arrangements. It was a busy trip but a
loving one, for it was clear to them both that time was running
out; the world was changing every day. On April 5, he returned to
London to continue the Japanese negotiations, and Mamita returned to Paris. It was a tearful parting in Oslo. Ari felt it deeply.
A few days earlier, a fortune-teller had warned him that there were
bad times ahead in his love life as well as in his business affairs.
Mamita had anticipated the difficulty of their parting and put
what she felt in a letter which she gave him at the airport. "It's
our destiny," she told him; he wiped a tear from her cheek with
his thumb. He remembered those final moments in the departure
lounge; how they held each other, knowing they might never see
each other again.

Flying across the North Sea to England he read: "I love you
with all my heart. Darling, for my own I am quite all right, but I
feel terribly nervous for you—so I beg you don't consider me actually in any way. I have money, I am safe—please in one way or
other do decide to do what for you is safest and best, we can't in

these times make plans . . . what I must know is that you shelter
yourself from all possible danger. My love, I feel miserable being
away from you in times as these. I envy all those who have the
privileges to be surrounded by their families, husbands and children. Anyhow, I have other privileges for which I thank God sincerely. Whatever happens I shall never stop loving you. For me,
your only duty is to shelter yourself and please telegraph me or
write soonest. God bless you, my darling dearest, and always remember my love is with you always and always. Thousand kisses,
Mamita."

Back in London he thought of "all the sad moments, all the
tears" he had caused her because of his "irregular life." Convinced
he felt a seismic change in his character, he wrote her: "I allowed
myself to be too absorbed in my business interests. I know I lose
my temper. I know I get mad with you. But I do love you. My baby,
you have done so much to please me, to help me, you have always
been so kind to me, you have spoiled me like a child. People talk
about my strength of character, my *volonté* in business. But I have
been a coward where we have been concerned. I always told myself: tomorrow, next month, next year . . . and here we are, after
six years, another separation, another heartbreak. I've been so
blind."

On May 10, Winston Churchill became prime minister, and
Hitler invaded the Low Countries. By the sixteenth the German
armies had broken through on the Meuse and were advancing so
fast that they were expected to reach the outskirts of Paris within
days. Ari urged Ingeborg to leave France at once, but she refused
to believe that Paris would fall and, suffering with a back problem,
was reluctant even to leave their apartment. Ari was also far from
well, and his tone moved quickly from tenderness and concern to
exasperation and self-pity. "Don't you understand that I'm now
having to contemplate the possibility of being left with almost
nothing!" he told her angrily. Financially and physically he was
on a knife edge, he said. Almost all of the Greek shipping community had quit London for New York, where the most lucrative
deals were now being done. "Most of my colleagues are now living
on velvet in safety, even the very stupid ones are making fortunes,"
he complained, stuck in London trying to conclude the Japanese
sale. The negotiations had been dragging on for months. He hated
dealing with the Japanese. But his feelings had nothing to do with
the fact that Tokyo had signed a pact with Nazi Germany, which
had sent shock waves through Washington and Whitehall. Rather
it was their way of doing business; the hard bargaining behind the
gracious guile went against the grain. He didn't like dealing with

men who could think like Orientals and act as sharp as any West-
erner. Perhaps it came too close to home, Ingeborg said later.

"A blood vessel or something has broken in my throat. I can't
talk without the taste of blood in my mouth, and the smell of it in
my nostrils. And all the time I am facing the possibility of not
keeping a dime, of being left penniless because of these adventurers called politicians. All my work of nearly twenty years, all the
sacrifices and the abominable and abnormal living of all those
years, could turn into a great nothing! Most men in my situation
now would give up, Mamita, they would be perfectly understood
if they committed suicide!" she read, but she knew he would never
do that; no matter how bad things got he would never take his
own life. His sense of responsibility toward the few people he
loved, his sisters, his stepmother, Ingeborg herself, all of whom he
more or less kept, was too deep to give him that way out. My
obligations, my sense of duty, my pride, he had once told her, may
be exaggerated, but nature has made me like this. He had become
the dominating force in the family, its decision maker, its deliv-
erer. It was an honor, and he had earned it; she suspected that it
was the proudest achievement in his life.

Stubbornly she stayed on in Paris until June 11 when finally,
with exceptional optimism, she drove to the British embassy to
ask for a visa to London. The ambassador and his staff had fled the
previous evening, leaving the embassy in charge of the gate porter,
still dressed in his top hat and purple frock coat, who was waiting
for an American diplomat to arrive with the official seals putting
the embassy under United States protection.

Obeying Ari's instructions, she had taken her money, papers
and jewelry out of their strongbox in the bank some days earlier;
she loaded everything she could into her car, locked up the apartment, and headed south to join some friends in Bagnères-de-
Bigorre, a small town in Hautes-Pyrénées. The roads were choked
with refugees, troops, ambulances, taxis, horse-drawn carts, people on bicycles and the thousands of government officials who
were being evacuated to the south to administer a government
that no longer existed. It took her five days to reach her destination
forty miles from the Spanish border.

The Germans entered Paris on June 14, and three days later
the American embassy in London advised United States citizens
in Britain to return home as quickly as possible. The French signed
the armistice at Compiègne on June 22, the day Ari got a booking
on the Cunard Line's SS *Samaria* to New York, leaving July 1. He
would have preferred to get out of London sooner—Churchill had
declared that the Battle of Britain was about to begin—and he

could only get a second-class berth, but it was a booking and it was confirmed. "It looked as if things were finally going right for me," he later recalled. The Japanese deal was agreed on (he had even succeeded in getting one of the ships out of Marseilles in the middle of an air raid "uninsured, at tremendous risk"), and both ships were now on their way to the Far East; the remaining paper-work would be done in New York. He had received a telegram from Ingeborg (she had sent nine since leaving Paris on June 11) telling him that she was safe and at the Hotel Tivoli in Bagnères-de-Bigorre. He toyed with the idea of flying to neutral Lisbon and from there making his way up through Spain to Bagnères-de-Bigorre. It would have taken time, but it was possible; in Franco's Spain his Argentine passport would have opened a lot of doors. But finally he decided against it; in Europe's present mood it would have been risky, if not reckless.

The *Samaria,* unarmed and unescorted, zigzagged to avoid marauding U-boats: ships without souls, Ari called them and made no secret of his fear of them. His fear turned to terror when a liner ten miles away was torpedoed and went down in twenty minutes. Among the passengers the panic soon turned to that sense of stupor that exists between danger and deliverance. Black smoke stayed in the sky where the ship had been; ten miles is no distance at all in the middle of the North Atlantic Ocean. Ari stopped sleeping in his cabin, preferring to rest on a divan in the smoking room, close to the lifeboats, clutching his attaché case, which contained his contracts, the deeds to his ships, proof of everything he owned, the evidence of everything he was. His whole future was in that case. Several London Greeks watched his be-havior with disapproving eyes and later told unkind stories about his cowardice, the way he lit his cigarettes with trembling hands, his animated conversation and the agitation in his eyes that made him seem a little mad. He ate almost nothing, his face grew thin-ner; he had the neglected beard of a sick man. The Greeks assured fellow passengers (including Henry Bernstein, the French play-wright who had eight times demonstrated his own kind of courage in duels, the last one fought when he was sixty-two) that Ari was not a "real Greek" but a Smyrnan! He was practically a Turk! But he had never even pretended to be brave, not even in his letters to Mamita, when he could so easily have painted a better picture of himself and his courage.

He arrived in New York on July 10, 1940. Due to what he called "a little technical irregularity" (although his appearance after ten days at sea without once changing his clothes, and with very little sleep, must also have counted against him) immigration officials detained him on Ellis Island for twenty-four hours. "This island out in the harbor should be called Devil's Island," he wrote Ingeborg sixteen days later, his anger and humiliation still burning. "It is worse than a third-class prison. It was made and meant for all kinds of adventurers and dirty European immigrants of the old times, and the personnel have been specially trained to treat such class of people, so now they apply the same installations and personnel for first-class people."

Summoned from Buenos Aires, Nicos Konialidis was waiting in New York. Ari explained the plan he had worked out with Anders Jahre. When Norway was invaded in April 1940, the government fled into exile in London and had commandeered the *Aristophanes*, which had been sailing under the Norwegian flag. Nicos was to fly to Rio de Janeiro and "arrest" the tanker. Unless the Norwegians agreed to pay him a million dollars, the *Aristophanes*, among the largest tankers in the world and playing a critical role in the Allied war effort, would spend the duration of the war in Brazil tied up in a thousand lawsuits, he said. He was clearly unwell as he went through the legal paperwork with his cousin. He hated the heat and humidity in New York, he complained of grippe and a sore throat; his gums were bleeding so much that he continually had to sip salted water.

Konialidis protested that the plan that Ari had devised with such care and cunning was simply impractical. The Norwegian mission had seized hundreds of ships and had never paid out a penny. "They'll squeal but they'll pay," Ari told him, confident that the Allies would not risk losing the tanker "in a legal blitz." The Norwegians squealed, just as he said they would; and they paid, just as he said they would. "They did all they could not to pay me, but as I had a mortgage on the ship and having arrested her in Rio they had finally to pay me . . . so while all the other owners have to submit themselves to the mission's wishes, thanks to my measures, I found myself in a very privileged and unic [*sic*] position which saved me," he wrote Mamita.

He had been worth $8 million in 1939, $37.7 million in present-day terms. Now, after the sale of the ships to Japan and the million he had squeezed out of the mission, he was down to $2.5 million, or $11.78 million in present-day currency. He had taken a bath, but he assured Mamita on August 11, 1940: "Now I don't care very much what will happen. You must agree that when Mamico thinks and studies night and day like I did in Sandefjord and Gotenborg [*sic*], finally the day comes that his efforts are compensated to the astonishment of everybody!"

•   •

"My darling darling love, how can words say my happiness and comfort by knowing that you are *safe* in NY," Mamita answered the first of Ari's cables to reach her at Bagnères-de-Bigorre in Vichy France, the unoccupied zone that the Germans had permitted Marshal Pétain to govern as president. "I hope with all my love that you have not been suffering too much. . . ." It had been a difficult letter for her to write. She still loved him very much, yet she felt a kind of pity for him. He would never be able to relax, he would never be able to enjoy an ordinary life. His ambition made her sad, for it was a kind of greed. Yet his generosity confused her as much as his jealousy. Sometimes the idea of never having to be afraid of him again became so intense that she felt she wanted nothing else. The contradictions made an ominous basis for a future together. They were not new thoughts: she had had them a thousand times.

She wrote: "But darling I don't feel the least bit courageous for starting new travellings even if I could. So please try to understand me, try to have patience a bit longer, maybe soon you will be able to return to Europe . . . I feel too tired and down, and absolutely frightened by the thought to cross the Atlantic now . . . so why in moments like this make me come to you? The separation is hard and sad, but let us be thankful for the good things. What I want now is that this and letters from you may reach their destinations quickly. I love you always with all my heart and thoughts, so please try to make the best out of your daily life, it is the best you can do for me. Always my love, Mamita."

She felt almost reprieved by war.

The Allies needed merchant ships, and almost any vessel would do to haul cargoes across the North Atlantic; combat zone freight rates were at a premium, and war-risk policies often paid for a brand-new vessel when not much more than a rust bucket had been lost. It was a no-lose situation for the shipowners, and Manhattan had become the maypole around which they all danced. Ari became determined to join the party, once he had recovered from the traumas of his Atlantic crossing. He spent ten days in bed, suffered from constipation, ruminated that his good digestion was now only a souvenir and had two healthy teeth removed by a dentist who assured him that they were poisoning his system. He rented a suite on the thirty-seventh floor of the Ritz Towers on Park Avenue. Although he could not contrive an invitation to join the Greek Shipowners New York Committee, the discreet expatriate group that represented the first families of Greek shipping, dominated by the legendary Stavros Livanos, Ari did

move in among the high fliers, a crowd that included another
young Greek full of steam: Stavros Niarchos.

With Ari's tankers taken out of his hands and the rest of his
ships on charter to the Allies or running cargoes in South America
under the flag of Panama, he found himself missing Mamita terribly. He began bombarding her with cables and letters setting out
schemes to get her out of France, including one alarming suggestion that she travel by tanker to Mexico. But now that they had
been driven so far apart by fate, she had made up her mind to
make the break permanent. Through the summer of 1940, in thousands of words in a language foreign to both of them, she tried to
explain her feelings, and in scores of letters and cables Ari expressed his puzzlement, his hurt. He blamed "the complexes" of
her age (her hair was turning grey, she had told him in a recent
letter) for her attitude and wondered "what I must have done to
deserve such a terrible situation which you are creating for me . . .
I shall always belong to you, you have won the right to own me
entirely . . . now that I am through the greatest of my troubles,
now that reasonable hopes of better times are before me, now I
see all the wrong I have done you, I am on the point of losing you
or have your love reduced to a sisterly affection. *Quelle ironie!*"

She read his letters through tears. "Please try in *friendship* to
understand me, please give me your real friendship, please try not
to hurt me, even if in vengeance you would like to do so. If you
would write me kindly, it would help me more than anything else,
but please accept the situation—*Je t'embrasses avec tendresses,*
Mamita."

He did not understand her at all. He did not know why she
laughed or why she cried. He examined himself, exposed his own
guilt, confessed his own failures with almost childlike candor, but
he had no idea about the need she had for an affirmation of her
own existence. So he went on beating his own breast, clutching
his own brow, taking the lion's share even of her sadness. She
wrote him, "I can't go on writing you like this, it is too difficult
and painful for both of us. All that I wish I could tell you seems
hopeless anyhow. If you were here you would perhaps succeed by
your clever way of talking, again to change my ideas. Everything
is so complicated and I will not punish myself to write more." She
understood him as no Greek could and as no other woman ever
would, and her letters were love letters even when she was saying
good-bye. He turned on her all the power of persuasion and of the
magnificent dreams that had carried him from the ashes of
Smyrna to a suite on the thirty-seventh floor of the Ritz Towers in
Manhattan. For Ari to protest was expected by Ingeborg, for she

was taking something away from him, and it was not in his nature to lose, to be deprived of anything he really wanted, and so he fought.

On September 1, 1940, her fortieth birthday; friends brought her flowers and chocolate, and a Jewish family at the Tivoli gave her one kilogram of sugar ("an inestimable gift these days"), but there was no word from Ari. She did her piano practice, and in the evening her singing teacher praised the progress she was making. In spite of her age ("I'm as old as the century," she liked to say) and her back problems, she believed that one day she would be able to sing professionally, to make a living for herself.

The following morning she received a delayed cable from New York wishing her a happy birthday, happiness in the coming years, with apologies for the fight they had had on her birthday the previous year. It was signed, *Amour tendresses Onassis*. It was the first time that he had ever remembered her birthday. "Ah *mon dieu*, how things are complicated, and sad . . . yesterday I cried so much that in spite of the most lovely weather I didn't get out of bed until five in the afternoon," she wrote him on September 3. "And this morning, deeply touched by your letter, I cried again— my eyes hurt, my head aches, my back feels tired . . . but in spite of all this I feel better . . . the very essential thing to me is that I can start to believe again that you not only need me because of habit, but that you really love me and that you do realize it."

The American consul in Marseilles was not impressed with Ingeborg's Argentine proposer and guarantor, named Onassis. While she waited at the Splendide Hotel in Marseilles, Ari fumed in New York. He pulled every string he had: he persuaded a contact in the State Department to cable the reluctant consul vouching for "Mr. Onassis's sufficiency and respectability." He told Ingeborg to impress upon the consul that she would be getting married immediately when she arrived in New York and that they would leave at once for their home in Buenos Aires; he got Hugh Reid, a senior partner of his United States agents, and Gregory Taylor, the owner of the St. Moritz Hotel in New York, to cable their personal guarantees; he sent a cable to the consul offering to deposit immediately "whatever sum you feel is appropriate" in an American bank in Ingeborg's name. But the unexpected problems of getting her out of France and into America made him irrationally angry with Ingeborg herself. "Why do I bother?" he said to Costa Gratsos. "She does nothing but complain because I forget to help her out of a taxi, and I won't even get a 'thank you' for going to all this trouble to save her life! She would prefer a man who never forgets to send her some flowers or a silly little congratulation on her birthday!" Then why did he bother? Gratsos asked. "I think I need her," he answered.

The U.S. consul in Marseilles was eventually persuaded, and Ingeborg arrived in New York on a bright late November morning in 1940 that was crisp with promise.

The romance followed the pattern of any relationship conceived by obsession on one side and capitulation on the other. In New York in the early days it was fine. They were both on their best behavior, anxious to prove that it had not been a mistake. But their laughter should have warned them; they laughed nearly all the time at first. They never ate at home, the hotel suite Ari called home, except at breakfast time. And in restaurants, in the *hauteur* of the Pavillon, amid the diplomats and cream of Dun and Bradstreet intelligentsia, in the Colony, where wealth is implicit, in the rich shadows of El Morocco, already Ari's favorite nightclub, people looked up when they heard their laughter. Some nights he took her to the little places, the Greek and Italian places where the menu is chalked on slate, and to those places with walls hung with photographs of movie stars and where the waiters look like pugilists. They made a striking couple: Ari short and dark, with his look of waterfront toughness, and Ingeborg (or Ingse, as she was now more often called), taller than he was, her blonde hair (no trace of grey now) styled with waves like Carole Lombard's; her looks were frequently compared to Lombard's. Ari sent her to Bergdorf's for gowns, to Maximilian for furs, to Helena Rubinstein for beauty treatments. At forty, her beauty still had a touch of coltishness.

Ari had fallen in with a playboy set in Ingse's absence and was beginning to drink far more than he had in Europe. She had never seen him drunk, or out of control, but sometimes his eyes glistened. And his reasonless jealousy floated to the surface when there was too much alcohol in his system; he became belligerent and quarrelsome after a few drinks, although he usually disguised the unpleasantness until they were alone.

He had not wound down his business activities to anything like the level he had claimed in his letters to her in France. The ships he had sold to Japan had been replaced with vessels he had picked up in South America. His appetite for making money was as big as ever. He had no mind to stop now when the price of ships and freight rates were rising so rapidly as the war in Europe escalated; a cargo ship he snapped up in Buenos Aires for $350,000 was worth three times as much by the time it had reached the Caribbean en route to New York for a refit. Ari got out in Florida with a cool $700,000 profit. He loved the excitement of deals—he could almost feel the flood of adrenaline into his bloodstream at the start of a negotiation. When he was working on a deal, time was without meaning, and sometimes he would go for forty-eight hours on nothing more than coffee and catnaps; he could lie down, fully clothed, and be asleep at once, waking the moment he had to. It was a trick, he told Ingeborg; he never set an alarm clock in his life.

If she felt betrayed as she found herself once again caught up in the meshes of his ambition, there was plenty in their social life to keep her occupied. Although he cared little for art, music or the social pursuits of the countryside, Ari had made an interesting circle of acquaintances—largely through the sudden appearance on the New York scene of his role model, Alberto Dodero. Dodero had bought an estate at Center Island on the north shore of Long Island, an hour's drive from midtown Manhattan. Again Ari became a frequent guest of Don Dodero and his second wife, a former Hollywood starlet named Betty Sunmark, at their weekend soirees. Through the Doderos he met a lot of show business people, as well as the simply rich and influential, including Otto Preminger, Ludwig Bemelmans, Spyros Skouras and a very pretty long-haired actress named Constance Keane, whom he dated a few times, slipping Ingse's leash. "It wasn't an affair, and it wasn't innocent," he said later. They did the rounds together, the Copacabana, the Stork Club, the Monte Carlo, 21, Versailles on East Fiftieth Street, and the inevitable El Morocco, or Elmo's. She was about twenty years old, and after Ingeborg she felt like a child to him and left him with no profound impression, except the satisfaction of a conquest. He did not miss her when she went out to Hollywood.

Ari enjoyed his weekends at Center Island and when, in the spring of 1941, his insurance broker, Cecil Stewart, invited him to use a cottage on the grounds of his home on the island, he accepted eagerly. Ingse saw the cottage, known as Foster House after its previous owners, as a chance to give her life a purpose. Within a month she had redecorated the whole place. She rummaged through thrift shops, attended auctions; off the back of a Salvation Army collection truck she bought a sofa, which she recovered in lime-green cotton for the drawing room. Touched by her industry, economy and sense of style (he still thought that class was something you bought at Tiffany's, a friend later remarked) Ari renamed the house Mamita Cottage. They hired a French couple, Antoine and Louise, to look after them; they also had a chauffeur for the Cadillac, an Italian named Carmine.

Ingse was a fine hostess, and very soon Mamita Cottage became a popular weekend rendezvous. Ari loved to give barbecues and invite his drinking cronies over for all-night poker sessions, although he usually preferred to kibitz. He became a fine waterskier, an art that had eluded him completely in Europe. That first summer in the States, the summer of '41, was the best time for Mamita; she was probably happier than she would ever be again. Ari hadn't stopped running, but he was no longer rootless, no longer a nomad. He was beginning to enjoy his wealth, although he still didn't look rich: "I had no idea he was such a wealthy fellow," Otto Preminger would recall. "He looked as if he slept in his suits." Perhaps because of Ingse's sense of class, even the Establishment Greeks, the Embiricos and Livanos families, who had been at pains to keep Ari at arm's length for so long, began dropping in for drinks. Another frequent visitor was Stavros Niarchos. With his second wife, Melpomene, he had bought a house not far away at Lloyd Neck. Like Ari, Niarchos was considered something of a parvenu by the old-school Greek shipowners. Their exclusion initially created a bond between the two men; but their need to become accepted, their need to flaunt their success, turned into a fatal contest.

When Greek meets Greek, they open a restaurant, was an old gag in New York. But now when Greeks met they usually talked about the war: how long would it last? They were all making a great deal of money out of it, but nobody felt bad about that. War is history, and history is simply an expression of divine providence, they said, so how could it be wrong to use it? But Ari did worry about the war. His family had decided to remain in Athens when the Germans invaded, and now there were stories in the newspapers of people fainting from hunger in the streets. He had heard that raisins and dried figs, which had become the staples of the Greek diet, were being commandeered and shipped to Germany. On Thanksgiving Day—they had invited about twenty American friends to dinner—he suddenly left the table without a word.

Ingse found him by the shore. "My grandmother would say a prayer now," he told her. She asked whether he wanted to pray. He said, "Prayers change nothing. Life is fixed."

"You don't want freedom, Ari, because you have that, you want license," Ingeborg told him when he returned to Mamita Cottage, compelled to confession after a weekend in New York. It was a few days after Pearl Harbor. He was almost forty-two years old. He felt that time was running out on him; he had worked hard all his life, and now he wanted to have some fun before it was too late. He was asking for nothing less than her permission to play around. It was a concept that she found hard to accept. He certainly knew how to steal up on the blind side of a person, she said. He insisted that nothing had changed; he still loved her. But you just want to sleep with other women? she asked. "I want to see other people," he replied with that way he had of saying everything yet always concealing something. And you want us to continue exactly as we are? she asked with a sense of apprehension that might have been deeper than fear itself. Had he changed his mind about marrying her? He said he kept thinking about those frogs in Aesop who had a great thirst but would not jump into the well in case they could not get out again. She didn't want him to jump into any wells on her account, she told him.

It was at about this time that he first met Geraldine Spreckles. He would tell her thirty years later, "You were smoking a cigarette and wearing the biggest diamond I'd ever seen outside of a museum. I thought you were the most beautiful woman in the world." She said that the diamond probably had something to do with it and smiled the smile that had turned his life upside down. Merely walking down a staircase she was a sensation, remembered Costa Gratsos, who had introduced them. The heiress to a sugar fortune, she wanted to be an actress (and had a contract with Warner Brothers), rode motorbikes very fast, loved nightclubs, burned money and drove men crazy. But Gratsos felt she was not for Ari. "It's a free country, I can have what I want." It was Ari's favorite comeback, and he rolled his thumb across the tips of his fingers like a Levantine dealer, a gesture he would make only in the presence of a man like Gratsos, who knew him so well and would understand the humor and self-knowledge expressed in that familiar mime.

Geraldine wasn't simply another WASP heiress. Her father had been killed in an automobile accident when she was a baby, and her mother had married a Turk. Geraldine had spent most of her childhood in Constantinople and spoke perfect Turkish, a language she had learned before she could speak English. Her mother had reaped not a penny from her husband's estate, and Geraldine knew what it was like to be poor before she collected her inheritance when she was twenty. Gratsos would later recall seeing on Ari's face a picture of triumph when he made this discovery. Such affinities went against all the odds: it has to be fate, he insisted and pursued her harder still.

Ari fascinated Geraldine. His sharp mind, his complexity and *joie de vivre*, his ego, the stories he told, the sheer energy of the man impressed her tremendously. He made her laugh. He was outrageous ("not being found out was the same to him as telling the truth"), a games-player, a stirrer; he could be positively evil: "the troubles he caused—and then put right with a roar of laughter," she would recall. She had never met anyone like him. "It was an extraordinary thing about Ari that almost immediately you had the impression of knowing him extremely well. He seemed so open, so easy to fathom, and yet the longer you knew him the more you realized how difficult it was to pin him down; trying to cotton on to those twists and turns of mind that make you feel you understand a person was an impossible business." She was intrigued by the conflicting stories of his life, the little lies ("He never seemed very proud of his Smyrna past") but always defended him when her friends put him down. He called her Mamasita. When he discovered that she adored Russian music he got their mutual friend, Sasha de Seversky, to make a list of the best Russian restaurants in New York and took her to every one. They drank champagne and vodka, dined on Beluga caviar and blinis. "We argued and fought all the time. I loved to argue, I was one of the best," she said later.

But twenty-two years old, Geraldine woke up one morning and took off for California.

California, Ari decided, was a good place to be. But first he returned to Buenos Aires to finish some business. Applying for a re-entry visa to the United States, he stated that he was born in Salonika, Greece, on September 21, 1900. He gave his nationality as Argentine and was in possession of a valid Argentine passport, number 701014, issued by the Buenos Aires police department and valid for two years. He gave his legal address as Reconquiesta 336, Buenos Aires, and his address in the States as the Ritz Towers, 57 Park Avenue, New York City. On May 8, 1942, the State Department approved the visa. He closed down his tobacco operation in Buenos Aires and at the beginning of June flew to Los Angeles "to concentrate on my shipping interests and to be close to my friends," he said. Two of his new tankers, the *Calirrhoë* and the *Gulf Queen*, bought from Gulf Oil, were working out of San Pedro under charter to the United States government. Costa Gratsos had been appointed Greek maritime consul in San Francisco; and Spyros Skouras had been made president of 20th Century Fox in Hollywood (and chairman of the Greek War Relief Fund); Otto Preminger, Gloria Swanson, Ludwig Bemelmans, Alberto Dodero, and former British diplomat Sir Charles Mendl and his wife, an American ex-actress, Elsie de Wolfe, and many more of his drinking chums from New York were now on the West Coast. He took a suite at the Beverly Hills Hotel and was already sufficiently recognized to merit a pink registration card, the color code for the hotel's most important guests.

Geraldine Spreckles had become a nurse's aide, sharing a Malibu beach house with a group of girlfriends (they kept their horses at the nearby Riviera Country Club), and was not pleased by Ari's appearance in California. She pleaded with him to go away and leave her alone, but he continued to turn up with steaks and caviar, inviting himself to the regular weekend house parties. Geraldine recalls: "I told him that he was not my type, and he asked what was my type. I said that I wanted a nice clean-cut American boy." He named her recent date, a young United States Air Force flier: "Is he your type?" Geraldine conceded that he fitted the bill. One week later, Ari arrived on her doorstep with the flier dead drunk in his arms. Dropping him at her feet, he said: "Here's your clean-cut all-American boy!"

Gratsos was appalled when he heard what Ari had done. "He really thought by humiliating the opposition he could impress a girl like Geraldine. 'You know nothing in hell about women, Ari,' I told him." He advised him to forget Geraldine Spreckles. "He was having a very nice time screwing all those little starlets, he was just wasting his time with a girl who probably had him at the top of her S.O.B. list after what he did to her boyfriend."

Ari became a model Hollywood playboy, and worked assiduously to promote himself as a great lover. He dated Paulette Goddard and the French sex star Simone Simon. He had a discreet fling with Gloria Swanson. When Constance Keane called him at the Beverly Hills Hotel he could barely remember her face. But her voice on the telephone rekindled fond memories of their dates in New York, and he suggested dinner. When they met he discovered that she wasn't Constance Keane anymore. She had become Veronica Lake.

They dined at Romanoff's, danced at the Mocambo. Miss Lake got very drunk. Ari took her home—to Geraldine Spreckles's apartment at the beach. He put the peekaboo star in Miss Spreckles's bed, and waited for Miss Spreckles to return home. Miss Spreckles was not amused. "I told him that I considered it the most reprehensible display of bad manners I'd ever seen in my life," she was to recall forty years later. "He thought it was funny, but it was also to show me that he could always get another pretty girl. Crikey, he used to make me so mad."

She can't hold her liquor, he explained as they stared down at the famous star, who was beginning to snore gently. "Not like you, Mamasita. You can see anyone out," he said. His attempts to gain her attention usually made Geraldine laugh in the end. "We started stepping out again. It was a very proper romance, apart from hanging around nightclubs. Frankly, every time I went out with him it would be an all-night thing, and if I couldn't stand it I simply went home." They had never been to bed together. Geraldine understood the Levantine mentality: "Ari wanted me to be his wife, not his mistress. He treated me with enormous respect." Most of the time, they were accompanied (chaperoned would be overstating it, although it amounted to the same thing) by Ludwig Bemelmans.

Sasha de Seversky strongly disapproved of Ari's intentions. "You don't want to marry Geraldine," he accused him one evening in the Polo Lounge. "You want to marry the Four Hundred!" Ari replied that there was "safety in numbers!" Seversky liked Ari and disapproved only of his intentions. The next time Ari asked Geraldine to marry him ("It was a frequent request, he pestered me constantly") she said yes.

Ari flew to New York on July 16 to break the news to Mamita. In Washington on that day, J. Edgar Hoover was writing a personal and confidential letter to Adm. Emory S. Land, head of the War Shipping Administration, which controlled civilian shipping movements during the emergency. It consisted of only a dozen lines. Delivered by special messenger, it said this:

My dear Admiral,

Information has been received from a confidential source that Mr. Aristotle Onassis, who is reportedly part owner of the tankers "Calliroy" and "Antiope," was scheduled to depart for the United States on Thursday June 18, 1942, by Pan American Clipper from Buenos Aires, Argentina. According to the informant, the purpose of Onassis' visit is to continue the negotiations for the sale of these two tankers to the War Shipping Administration.

The informant advised that there is no information available indicating Mr. Onassis has any other motive for making a trip to the United States, but it was reported that he has expressed sentiments inimical to the United States war effort, and that his activities and movements while in the United States should be carefully scrutinized.

Sincerely yours,

John Edgar Hoover

Sooner or later Ari was bound to come to the attention of the FBI. His closeness to Fritz Mandl (whose remarkable success in getting his fortune out of Austria in 1938 still intrigued Allied intelligence), and to many other pro-German Argentinians, would have seen to that. In California, he had fallen in with the right-wing crowd that surrounded Lady Mendl—some of whom, Otto Preminger was convinced, were "out-and-out Nazis" and even "Nazi agents." And Ari had done nothing to suggest that his loyalties were in the right place; he had almost come to blows with Spyros Skouras for refusing to contribute to the Greek War Relief Fund. "I've seen what happens to men who get involved in political causes." "You're just another jumped-up shit from Smyrna." Skouras resorted to the old racial slur. "I've always resisted the temptation to be the nice guy," Ari answered; he wouldn't even give to Mamita's collection to buy food parcels for Norwegian sailors.

She was there to meet him when he came through the gates at LaGuardia on that Thursday afternoon. A small civilian in a crumpled suit, he stood out among the men in uniforms. They drove directly to Center Island. Ingeborg gossiped happily. She told him that Stavros and Melpomene Niarchos had had a fearful fight, and Melpo, depressed by her husband's infidelities, had apparently taken a massive overdose; but when the ambulance came she had winked at Ingeborg. She just wanted to throw a scare into Stavros. Ingeborg did not like Niarchos, perhaps because she was fond of Melpo and felt that he treated her unkindly, or perhaps because she foresaw the rivalry and feuds between the two men, the day when they would contest every piece of turf, compete to own the biggest yachts and possess the most desirable women in the world. Although he came from an upper-class family, a cut above the Onassis clan, Niarchos's vanity and affected way of talking (probably meant to sound very English, it came out so plummy that people occasionally thought he had a speech defect) made Ingse's hackles rise. "Watch his eyes, watch his eyes," she constantly warned Ari. Her apprehension was understandable. She had read enough Greek drama to know that deep jealousies between Greeks could be resolved only by the shedding of blood, sometimes among friends, even among the closest relatives. And although Ari and Niarchos had their separate lives, their unrelated backgrounds, they also had much in common and shared so many strengths and weaknesses, so many goals and ambitions, that they might have been brothers.

Ingeborg knew that Ari had returned to New York for a purpose; what it was she could not guess. He had moved into the room next to hers, the room that had been kept only for appearance's sake in the beginning. He remained morose and silent for most of that long weekend at Mamita Cottage. The day he was to return to California, he told her his plans. She was still recovering from the shock some days later when she received a check for two hundred thousand dollars. The note with which it came was affectionate and short, and signed Mamico. In a popular phrase of the day, she was getting the big kiss-off.

On November 13, 1942, the United States embassy in Buenos Aires sent a special dispatch to Washington reporting that they had "information that Onassis possessed fascist ideas and was considered shrewd and unscrupulous." An FBI espionage investigation was begun immediately by the Los Angeles Field Division.

Shortly after this, Sasha de Seversky called Ari and told him that it was important that they meet. Getting ready to go to a screening at the Warner studio in Burbank, Ari suggested a drink at the Sportsmen's Lodge on Ventura Boulevard at Coldwater Canyon, halfway between the Beverly Hills Hotel and the studio. He imagined that de Seversky wanted to discuss Geraldine, whom he adored as a father. Ari respected him a lot, and trusted him completely.* After they had ordered drinks, de Seversky said that he "had come into possession" of reports that caused him concern, Ari recalled. "I think they must have been FBI, but I never got a look at them, so I don't know. But they claimed that I was a shyster and a Fascist. The Fascist shit was mostly innuendo, making a lot out of my friendships with Mandl and some people in Buenos Aires. They covered a lot of ground. They were certainly thorough. There was even stuff in there about insurance claims that went back years and which they said weren't on the up and up."

De Seversky was also anxious about Geraldine, for he had learned too that Ari was trying to get her to invest in a tanker to be operated by him. "She'll probably double her money the moment the first contract is signed," Ari assured him, just as he had assured Geraldine. It was a relief to de Seversky when she decided not to get involved. "I heard afterward that he did these deals with many ships, have other people put money into ships which he would run, but I just didn't trust him," Geraldine later confessed.

---

* Educated at the Imperial Naval Academy and the Military School of Aviation in Russia, Maj. Alexander P. de Seversky had lost his right leg when he was shot down in a dogfight over the Gulf of Riga in the First World War. Sent to Washington as a naval attaché, he had decided to remain in the United States after the Revolution. In 1935 he designed the P-35 fighter, the prototype of the P-47 Thunderbolt, and later worked on the first automatic synchronous bombsight.

A few days after the meeting in the Sportsmen's Lodge, Gratsos confirmed to Ari that he was under surveillance by the FBI. Now running the Greek government's fifteen Liberty ships, prefabricated by America to reinforce the North Atlantic convoys, Gratsos had a reliable pipeline to Washington. Anyone moving regularly between the Argentine and the United States was sure to attract attention, Gratsos told him: Buenos Aires was "running alive with Abwehr agents," and the River Plate was a safe haven for Nazi battleships; Ari still felt he was being "picked on . . . persecuted." He eventually contacted Johnny Meyer, who worked for Howard Hughes and had exceptional connections in Washington. If only some of the things said of him were true, Meyer was a man with dangerous secrets inside him. Sometimes mistaken for a well-groomed gangster, the kind of New York hood who did business between the wars, he liked to think of himself as a superior troubleshooter, the ultimate fixer. Those who met him remembered him as a man with many amusing and scandalous stories about the famous people he knew and had worked for. Ari had met him through Seversky, who said that "Meyer knows everybody, and has the [expense account] receipts to prove it!" Meyer's main business was to ensure that the government didn't forget Hughes's aircraft plants when they were handing out defense contracts. "I don't know where all the bodies are buried," he liked to sum up his *modus operandi*. "But I do know where most of them are sleeping—and that's even better."

Ari explained his problem to Meyer. "He said that somebody was trying to destroy him, and he wanted me to find out who it was." Meyer got back to him in a week with a couple of leads. Spyros Skouras had recently been in Washington talking to the State Department about the Greek War Relief Fund. He was known to have made some harsh remarks about Ari. Meyer had also heard that somebody in the Greek embassy had sent a hostile report on Ari to the FBI. There was no doubt in Ari's mind who that somebody was: Stavros Niarchos, who had joined the Greek navy, was assistant to the naval attaché in the Greek embassy.

All these worries were suddenly eclipsed when shortly before they were to have been married in San Francisco, Geraldine Spreckles called the whole thing off. She had never said that she loved him, she explained with the remarkable directness that beautiful rich girls frequently possess. She told him: "You pestered me so. I felt cornered. You can't start a marriage from a corner, Ari, we're not pugilists, we're proper people." Not long afterward, she wed her cousin. It was a short-lived marriage, and shortly after it ended she married Andrew Fuller. Ari returned to New York, and Mamita.

•   •

Chastened by Geraldine's rejection, ashamed of the way he had treated Ingeborg, and grateful that she had not cashed her kiss-off check, he became especially attentive. He bought a Steinway grand for the Ritz Towers apartment she had moved into on the thirty-fifth floor, two floors below his. She was more than ever in love with him; the next few months were filled with moments she would cling to for the rest of her life. Ezio Pinza at the Met; Lena Horne at the Savoy-Plaza Café Lounge. He enjoyed listening to Ingeborg playing the piano; she taught him to play a piece from Bach's "Inventions"; later, at Katina Paxinou's party for Arthur Rubinstein, he modestly allowed himself to be persuaded to demonstrate his own prowess at the keyboard, playing the only piece of music he had ever learned in his life. Impressed with how well he had done (he had practiced in secret for months) and the guile with which he had carried it off, Ingeborg teased him: "I had no idea you were so passionate about music." He was a man of many passions, he said: "It is a truth that excuses all my wickednesses and all my cruelties."

He continued to commute between Los Angeles and New York. Ingeborg knew that he was still seeing other women, sending them hard-to-get luxuries that he brought in on his ships (Geraldine continued to get jars of caviar until Andrew Fuller found out and told Ari to stop). Ari's women cost Mamita a lot in lost sleep and jealousy. But the girl he met in Stavros Livanos's suite at the Plaza Hotel in the spring of 1943 did not disturb her. Athina Livanos was fourteen years old, a child, and Ari had displayed no interest in "green fruit"—or what would later be called nymphets. Tina had broken her leg in a riding fall and hobbled into her father's suite on crutches to be introduced. Ari, afraid to admit how strongly attracted he was, simply wrote in his notebook: Saturday, April 17, 1943. 7 P.M.

Ingse had changed a lot since Bagnères-de-Bigorre. She wished she were married to Ari now, but marriage was no longer talked about. Even when he called her from Los Angeles, and told her how much he loved her and how much he needed her, marriage was never mentioned. He too had changed. His drinking, while not out of control, was becoming excessive. After an evening of poker and steady drinking at a friend's house on Lloyd Neck he and Ingse had returned to Mamita Cottage on their Chris-Craft motorboat, and he attacked her. He continued to beat her for a long time, and just as she felt he would not stop until he had knocked her unconscious, he curled up on the floor and slept like a child. What had she done to make him so angry? She had worn a pair of plaid trousers that displeased him, he said the following day. He was filled with remorse and pleaded for forgiveness. But a few weeks later he beat her again. It was the beginning of a new pattern in their relationship. He confessed to a sexual pleasure in the violence and taunted her with stories of how his rough stuff excited many of his girlfriends and how good it was to make love afterward. All Greek men beat their women: he who loves well beats well, he said.

She moved out of the Ritz Towers to an apartment on East Fifty-first Street. But their affair and the cycle of drunken beatings and tearful recriminations continued. Ingse's indiscretion in Paris had stayed in his mind, acquiring a disproportionate importance, and although he continued to give her expensive gifts and profess his love, he could neither be faithful nor trust her ever again. The smallest thing could set him off. "It was a real sickness: he would seek an opportunity, waiting patiently for the most futile of pretexts in order to justify his excesses," Ingeborg recalled. Feeling unwell at a dinner party they were giving at the Pavillon, she allowed herself to be taken home by a Yugoslavian shipowner because Ari could not leave his guests. The man very correctly returned at once to the party, which had moved on to the El Morocco, or Elmo's. Later that night Ari paid her a visit. This time even he was appalled by the damage he caused. Her face was battered, one of her eyes had been pulped to "black butter"; her body was swollen and bruised, and her left hand had been paralyzed from warding off his kicks and fists. Early next morning, he bundled her into the Cadillac and drove to Mamita Cottage where, dismissing the servants, he watched over her until the injuries healed. But his behavior was no secret to Ingeborg's friends, nor was it a surprise. "A Greek who had spent so much time in Argentina—what could you expect?" said a New York girlfriend. "He was raised in two of the most machismo environments in the world. Machismo is all about the subjugation of women. Greeks and dagos treat their women like dirt." Ingeborg's doctor was not fooled by the explanations and excuses she gave for her injuries and tried to persuade her to sue Ari "after a horrible beating-up Ari had made me suffer for no reason," she would later write to an Onassis aide in Paris.

When she returned to New York, after the last and most brutal beating, she and Ari discussed the situation, and what it could lead to. She warned him that he might one day go too far and kill her. He swore that he loved her, and again they talked about having a child together, although Ingeborg was almost forty-four years old. She liked to hear Ari talk of their future together, but now, as she listened to his plans, her resignation turned to despair. When he left that night, she tried to kill herself with Nembutal. He returned and discovered her just in time. With the help of Dorothy Stewart, the wife of his broker and Inge's best friend, he revived her in baths of cold water and with mugs of black coffee. He could not understand why she had tried to "do this cruel thing to me." She was human, her understanding was finite, she answered; she had no real wiles, she could act only in accordance with her feelings. She would never call him Mamico again.

When the war ended, Ingeborg was another casualty, better off than some, worse off than others. She still had an excellent figure, but the grief and the uncertainty of the past five years had left their mark. She could no longer look at herself in the mirror with satisfaction. Ari was in his prime. Three of his ships chartered to the United States Maritime Commission were each earning him some $250,000 a year; his tankers were free to leave their Scandinavian berths in which they had been impounded since 1940. Of the 450 Greek ships that had been engaged in the war, 360 of them had gone down with many thousands of lives; Onassis had not lost a single ship and not one seaman.

He could relax now, Ingeborg said, pleased for him that he had come out of it so well. "Money doesn't excuse a man from hard work, it just absolves him from some particular kind of hard work," he said. He had a lot of plans. Ingeborg knew they did not include her. Even the little sign Mamita Cottage had been removed from the front of the house on Center Island, where he now often entertained without her. She tried to fall in love with somebody else. In her forthright way, she wrote him: "From now on, you can no longer count on me. In spite of your continual infidelities, I have never once betrayed you; I've had enough, I take back my freedom, I don't wish to spend my life subject to your caprices, believing your false promises. . . ."

His response was passionate, possessive, hurt and empty . . . an old song-and-dance man going through a routine he has gone through many times before. Ingeborg fell for it as she always had, as she always would. And so their affair drifted dismally on.

6

*Laws are like spider's webs. If some poor
weak creature comes up against them, it
is caught; but a bigger one can break
through and get away.*

SOLON

ARI'S RULING PASSION was business;
he could look at nothing except in terms of its commercial value,
and when he looked at Athina Livanos he knew that he was not
only looking at a very valuable prize, but a very beautiful investment. If that is love, then Ari was in love; deeply, anxiously, determinedly in love. He loved her golden hair, her small, delicate face
and flawless teeth. Her eyes, filled with the brown and golden
colors of autumn, had a mischievous quality, unexpected in so
sweetly sensible a face. She did not look remotely Greek. Born a
British subject, she had become a United States citizen during the
war by an act of Congress, and now her clothes, her gestures, the
way she held herself, were extraordinarily American. Only her
voice remained stunningly British.

Athina, or Tina, as her friends and family called her, almost
certainly knew what he was thinking: the commercial thoughts as
well as the carnal ones. He was cut from the same rock as her
father; if she married Ari, she guessed that she would be delivering
herself from one master to another. The thought would not have
disturbed her, for like all Greek girls of her class she had been bred
for marriage; and like the English aristocracy, she had been
trained for a certain milieu, a milieu she loved so much she was
not even curious to discover what lay beyond it. Born in Kensing-
ton, London, on March 19, 1929, the closest she ever got to depri-
vation, she once remarked, was when her elder sister Eugénie took
junior prize with Dawn Luscombe, as "the Bisto kids, a hungry-

looking pair" (a popular billboard of the time) at the Heathfield School fancy dress dance on All Saints Day in 1938.

Tina started at Heathfield at the beginning of the fall term 1939, in the lower fourth, a class consisting only of Tina, Sheila Rohll and Bridget Cronin. Eugénie was in the grade above, a larger group redolent with the names of the British upper class—Curzon, Villiers, Boscawen, Hubbard. In her third term at Heathfield (motto: the work of each for weal of all) Tina won an enameled blue bow for achievement. Besides the usual subjects, she studied dressmaking and household accounts, played lacrosse and tennis. She was happy there; the Report Book for the summer of 1940 records: "Tina has done a very good term's work. She has made an excellent head of form and is most willing and helpful. We are pleased that she has gained her blue bow."

Having seen their names carved on one of the chapel pews, a Heathfield tradition, the sisters left Heathfield in the summer of 1940 for the Villa Maria convent in Montreal, where they remained for a year before Tina moved to a boarding school in Greenwich, Connecticut, and Eugénie enrolled in Miss Hewitt's Classes, the New York finishing school for young ladies.

Tina already had a family-approved fondness for John Vatis, a boy close to her own age and a member of "a top pedigree" shipping family (the hierarchy of prestige among Greek shipping dynasties includes a keen awareness of the pedigree as well as the fortune of each family), when she became aware of Ari's interest. There followed for Tina a period of considerable fascination while Ari hung around their house at Oyster Bay, putting on an impressive show of youthful activities: swimming, water-skiing, riding very fast on his bicycle. Watching his antics and realizing that they were not done to impress *her*, Eugénie observed that he looked like "a gymnastic gargoyle."

At an exquisitely impressionable age, but understanding the power of remaining aloof, Tina handled him with coquettish silence; even pretending not to comprehend when he trailed a streamer behind his speedboat with the letters T.I.L.Y. (Tina I Love You). She listened to his stories about himself ("All anybody will ever really know about Ari's early days," she perceptively confided to Eugénie, "will be what he chooses to tell them"); played word games ("If I were a ship what sort of ship would I be?" "A tanker," she answered. "A destroyer," he said and roared with laughter. "I *am* a destroyer!"); and they went for lingering walks across the Long Island shore. He seemed very foreign to her English-educated mind; listening to him talking about his past, she was reminded of Oriental storytellers in the marketplace. She never knew what to believe, what to dismiss; the mystery at his core excited her girlish imagination.

While still in the throes of divorcing Melpo, Niarchos expressed his interest in Tina to her father and got extremely short shrift. Determined not to make a similar mistake, Ari took his time; he made a point of being nice to both the Livanos girls, and also ingratiating himself with their mother, Arietta. He invited the family over to his house for Sunday lunches and barbecues, and for rides in his motorboat. It was all directed at Tina, and Tina knew it. When he finally asked for her hand, Stavros Livanos was furious. It was not that he objected to Ari as a son-in-law (a Livanos-Onassis shipping alliance had its attractions), but that he should have asked for the wrong daughter. Sisters marry strictly in order of seniority, he reminded Ari. "Your daughters aren't ships, Mr. Livanos, you don't dispose of the first of the line first," Ari said, shedding years of sycophancy in a single sentence. A man must observe the rules in life, Livanos told him. "The rules are there are no rules," Ari answered back.

Livanos was convinced that Ari would climb down and accept Eugénie; for once in his life it did not work out the way he had planned. And one year later he gave in. He said that it was because he could no longer go on seeing Tina looking so unhappy; he was also reassured by the now-divorced Niarchos's interest in Eugénie. For Livanos, an archconservative loathing any kind of personal publicity, Onassis and Niarchos were not exactly the sons-in-law he would have chosen in a perfect world. The thought of drawing together three of the world's largest private fleets in the same family was a great comfort to him.

Ari did not allow himself to be totally preoccupied with romantic matters, however. In 1946, Congress passed the Ship Sales Act, making Liberty ships available to Allied operators who had their government's blessing. On offer at $550,000—$125,000 down, the balance payable over seven years at an interest rate of 3 percent—the ships were a steal. The Greek government authorized the Union of Greek Shipowners to act as its agent. Dominated by those rich and powerful owners who had moved to New York at the outbreak of war, the union decided that one hundred ships would be sufficient for their needs. But when Ari ordered thirteen he was told that none was available. Livanos got the dozen he wanted. Ari fumed and raged; the union ignored him. Manuel Kulukundis, who had set up the union in the 1920s, made no bones about it—Ari had never been in the running. The union was concerned with Greek shipping, and Ari's ships flew the Pan-

amanian flag, he said. It was the same story when the United
States Maritime Commission offered Greece seven T2 tankers. Ari
applied directly to the Greek government for all seven; Athens
insisted on dealing through the union, and again he was frozen
out. He hated the ruling cadre of aging Greeks as much as he
admired their world, and he would make them pay for every ton
of shipping they had denied him. He would take vengeance upon
them in business, and in much more personal ways.

On December 28, 1946, Ari and Tina were married. Tina was
seventeen years old, Ari was forty-six. The wedding was ritually
reported in the society columns of the *New York Times:*

ATHINA LIVANOS BRIDE
Wed in Greek Cathedral Here to Aristo S. Onassis

Miss Athina Livanos, daughter of Mr. and Mrs. Stavros
George Livanos of the Plaza Hotel, this city, and London,
England, was married yesterday afternoon in the Greek
Orthodox Cathedral to Aristo S. Onassis of this city and
Oyster Bay, L.I., son of the late Socrates Onassis and the
late Mrs. Penelope Onassis, of Athens, Greece. The cere-
mony was performed by Archbishop Athenagoros with the
assistance of Father Euthimion.
The bride had a sister, Miss Eugénie Livanos, as maid of
honor. Bridesmaids were Misses Nancy Harris, Andree
Maitland, Janet Bethel and Joan Durand, all of this city.
Beatrice Ammidown and Cornelia Embiricos were flower
girls. Andre Embiricos was best man. A reception was
given in the Terrace Room of the Plaza.

Winning Tina Livanos was much more than the fulfillment of
a dream. In Ari's mind it was the settlement of a score he had
against his father-in-law and the rest of the Greek Establishment,
who had robbed him of his share of the spoils of victory. "You've
got your revenge now," Gratsos told him the day of the wedding.
The Terrace Room of the Plaza was filled with many of the men
who had done their best to put him down and called him "the
parachutist"—"he dropped on us out of the blue." He replied, "It's
not enough, Costa. I'm looking to beat the shit out of these sons of
bitches. I'm at *war* with these gorillas." Gratsos looked around the
room filled with beautifully gowned women and men in morning
suits with white carnations. "It's a very *civilized* way to conduct a
war," he said dryly. Ari told him not to be taken in. "We *never* stop
trying to nail each other's asses to the floor. It's just that once in a

while, to please the ladies, we go down the line pretending to be civilized."

Among Livanos's wedding gifts was one of his Liberty ships, with a four-hundred-thousand-dollar mortgage still attached. Later, the old man added a Sutton Square town house on the East River, deeded to the Tina Realty Corporation. (Now back in Paris, Ingeborg, with a thirty-five-thousand-dollar payoff and a five-hundred-dollar monthly allowance, got a cable from Ari complaining that she was the only friend from whom he had not received a wedding gift!)

Mr. and Mrs. Onassis spent their first night in a suite at the Plaza. When a forty-six-year-old man marries a seventeen-year-old girl there is almost certain to be an element of suspense, a certain precariousness about the occasion. The only surprise Ari acknowledged was that they were occupying the bridal suite, and it was perfectly legal.

They embarked on a leisurely honeymoon, taking a houseboat through the inland waterways to Florida, then a slow boat to Buenos Aires. ("My father never walks. You never run," Tina told him.) Letting bygones be bygones, they were greeted in Buenos Aires by Spyros Skouras, who entertained them lavishly; Fritz Mandl turned up and gave a huge reception for them at the Plaza. Alberto Dodero invited them to Montevideo, where they met Eva Perón. Dodero had been an early supporter of the Peróns; he wore replicas of their profiles in his gold cufflinks, gave them diamonds and Rolls-Royces. The Perón government returned the favor with shipping contracts, loans to buy more ships and a lot more besides.

The sudden arrival of Mandl and Eva Perón at Bet Alba, Dodero's palatial home on the Rio de la Plata, was no coincidence. Despite appearances, Dodero was running into deep trouble and needed new capital—a regular requirement for a man who thought nothing of taking over Maxim's in Paris for a party, or giving a dinner for fifty guests with gold monogrammed cigarette cases for the men and a diamond for every woman. He had once tried to get Ingeborg to persuade Ari to invest in his Rio Plata Navigation Company. She had refused, claiming, not entirely truthfully, that she never involved herself in Ari's business affairs.

Virtually codictator of Argentina (her popularity with the masses had helped to elect her husband Juan Perón president in 1946), Eva Perón used all her charms to promote Dodero's cause. "I assure you, Argentina has not one economic difficulty of any consequence. Economically we could become the greatest nation in the world." Here was a golden opportunity for Mandl and Ari to team up with Dodero, she said, to weld one corporate identity with a man who already had a special place in the president's plans as well as in his heart! Mandl took the bait. Ari said he wanted to think about it. "If Mandl, Don Alberto and I were to have amalgamated, it would have created a very large corporation indeed. But who would have controlled it? And would the Peróns have been able to keep their hands off such a prize? The risk was just too big," he said later.

Two months to the day after they were wed, the couple returned to 16 Sutton Square, a cul-de-sac off Sutton Place in New York City. Tina at once set about decorating their new home with period French furniture, black marble floors, rich tapestries and fine paintings, including a Renoir; Ari set about business. Although he now had an office at 80 Broad Street, managed by Nicolas Cokkinis, he did much of his work at Sutton Square, often initiating deals and contacts at the large parties he and Tina liked to throw, mixing show business stars with bankers and lawyers, artists and musicians with Wall Street brokers and shipping kings. They spent lavishly, conspicuously. Still only eighteen years old, Tina quickly established herself as the busiest, the youngest and most beautiful hostess in New York. "I'm so happy," she told Ari, she told her friends, she told everyone in her stunningly English voice, which still sounded closer to the classroom than the salon. "I'm so *perfectly* happy."

Always prepared to play his hand for all it was worth, and often for more, Ari signed charters to carry coal to South America, France and Germany in sixteen Liberty ships he did not have. He took the contracts to the First National City Bank, which had been providing him with small loans since his first tobacco venture in Buenos Aires, and asked for a loan to buy the ships. The bank came up with half of the money. The terms were tougher than the terms the other New York Greeks had got from the United States government; he could live with that and be in profit within a couple of years.

He still wanted to get his hands on the T2 tankers, which, at $1.5 million each, were an incredible bargain. While prepared, without asking too many questions, to unload the Liberty ships, which were laid up at government expense, unwanted by American operators, the Maritime Commission insisted that the sixteen-thousand-ton tankers, capable of carrying six million gallons of oil and of considerable strategic significance, be sold only to citizens of the United States. Ari tried his best to get around the exclusion clause. He got Constantine Konialidis, now a Uruguayan citizen, to apply for a single T2. When the application was turned down on September 12, 1947 ("It is felt that a sale to a noncitizen for Panamanian flag operation would remove the vessel from effective control of the United States"), Ari had an idea.

"What I'm interested in is the *use* of these tankers not the *ownership*," he outlined his idea to the New York law firm of Lord, Day and Lord, one of whose senior advisers was Herbert Brownell, Jr. Ari would establish a corporation, fronted by a group of highly respected Americans, in which he'd keep for himself a percentage of stock, a fraction short of control. Several other Greek shipowners had spotted the possibilities of this ruse, including Niarchos and Kulukundis, and the lawyers were already of the opinion that it was at least technically legal. Moreover, they knew that provided there was a reputable American board, and the vessels were to be purchased for cash, the commission's legal division made no inquiries at all into the question of actual control of a corporation, even if the applicant admitted that almost all of the capital investment came from foreign interests.

Ari flew to Washington to talk to Joseph H. Rosenbaum, a senior partner in the law firm of Goodwin, Rosenbaum, Meacham & Bailen. Rosenbaum and Robert W. Dudley, an associate in Rosenbaum's firm and a brother-in-law of former Congressman Joseph E. Casey, specialized in handling clients who sought to obtain surplus vessels from the Maritime Commission; they had dealt with Konialidis's unsuccessful bid for a T2. Now Ari told them how he wanted things done. Within two weeks, the United States Petroleum Carriers, Inc., had been set up as a United States corporation with an authorized capital stock of one thousand shares. Six hundred shares of this stock were issued to a trio of front men, Robert L. Berenson, Robert W. Dudley and Adm. H. L. Bowen, all of whom were United States citizens. Four hundred shares remained unissued.

On December 30, 1947, the Maritime Commission approved the sale of four T2 tankers to the United States Petroleum Carriers, Inc. Almost immediately, Dudley paid Admiral Bowen $7,500 for his 250 shares, doubling Dudley's holdings. One week later, Robert Berenson bought Dudley's shares for $125,000 (original cost $1,000) and on the same day, the Sociedad Industrial Maritime Financiera Ariona, Panama, S.A., owned by Aristotle S. Onassis and Nicholas and Constantine Konialidis, purchased the remaining 400 shares of the authorized stock. During the following six months, the same Panamanian corporation acquired an additional 90 shares of stock from Berenson, giving them a total of 490 shares, or a 49 percent interest in the corporation. At the same time, Berenson reduced his own personal holdings to 48 percent by sell-

ing 10 shares to each of three American citizens closely tied to Ari
—Clifford N. Carver, who had worked for him during a short-lived
whaling venture in California; Nicolas Cokkinis, who was running
his New York office; and Arne C. Storen, a naval architect and
friend. From the point of view of voting stock control, Cokkinis
(who had been naturalized a United States citizen ten days before
acquiring his USPC stock), Carver and Storen held the balance of
power; in a dispute between Berenson and the Onassis-Konialidis
team, any one of the three could put the foreign interests in the
driver's seat.

Niarchos (who became Ari's brother-in-law at the end of 1947
when he took Eugénie for his third wife), and several other Greek
shipowners had pulled off similar coups. Even Niarchos's success
could not spoil Ari's high spirits as he took off for a well-earned
vacation with Tina to the south of France. Not only did he have
his T2 tankers (and the hard winter of 1947 had precipitated a
United States fuel crisis, which sent tanker freight rates shooting
up) but he was negotiating a spectacular forty-million-dollar loan
with the Metropolitan Life Insurance Company in New York to
build a brand-new generation of supertankers.

Mixing with the kind of people she liked best, the society that
was the source of her pleasure and of Ari's progress, Tina was in
her element in Monte Carlo. Like all true socialites, her strength
was artifice. She was enthusiastic when they met up with Eva
Perón and Alberto Dodero at the Hotel de Paris. A less innocent
mind, a more worldly woman, might have been apprehensive
about letting a man like Ari too near a woman like Eva Perón.
With their similar backgrounds—born poor in a pampa village
outside Buenos Aires in 1919 (revised to 1923 after her husband
came to power), Eva had used sex to make her way up in the
world, and now flaunted her wealth—they must have understood
many things about each other. Ari confided to Dodero his keenness
to meet Eva in more informal circumstances. It was a conversation between old friends, between men of the world. Accompanying Eva on a state-and-pleasure swing around Europe, Don
Alberto said it could be arranged. An indefatigable charity worker,
Eva levied tribute from everyone for the Eva Perón Foundation,
he said. Ten thousand dollars should do the trick.

Eva received him at her villa at Santa Margherita on the Italian Riviera. ("You move right along, don't you?" he remembered
her telling him.) Afterward she made scrambled eggs. They were
the most expensive scrambled eggs he'd ever eaten in his life, he
told Meyer; he'd tasted better. And after Dodero's ships, airline
and most of his properties had been nationalized by the Peróns for

a mere three million dollars, Dodero (who still had a comfortable fortune tucked away in Uruguay) said: "The president did to me what I fixed for Onassis to do to his wife!"

Ari had plenty to celebrate in the spring of 1948. On April 30, at the Harkness Pavilion, a private clinic in New York City, Tina gave birth to a boy. He was named Alexander, after Ari's murdered uncle. Ari's first American tanker, *Olympic Games*, was launched at Bethlehem Steel's Sparrow Point shipyards in Baltimore; four more were under construction. "Five tankers—and the only time I had to put my hand in my pocket was to scratch my balls," he told an English friend. His drinking was still heavy, and he had developed a taste for Gibsons (1.5 ounces gin, light dash French vermouth, stirred with ice and served in a chilled glass, with a cocktail onion); it had not slowed him down, nor had it impaired his ability to finance his ships with other people's money. OPM, he called the formula. And just as he had signed to ship coal in ships he did not have, so he had done deals to carry oil in tankers that weren't even built, a fact that gave rise to doubts about the morality, if not the legality, of his methods. But if his ethical composition was less than perfect—and "he lived from sleight of hand to mouth," in the words of a former aide—OPM continued to work for him impeccably. The oil majors, including Mobil, Socony and Texaco, preferred to sign long-term fixed-rate charters with Ari rather than have the headaches of building and operating their own tanker fleets, which would have had to fly the American flag and pay American wages and taxes. Their charters were as good as gold at the banks. And sailing under the Panamanian flag, with low operating costs and no taxes, Ari was able to make a profit on every shipment, and the tanker was paid for at the end of a single sixty-month charter.

The "Golden Greek," the headline writers were beginning to call him. Yet he had not won the respect of the people whose respect he wanted most; in the eyes of the Greek Establishment he was still a Smyrnan upstart. "They even claim that I dye my hair black for dates and grey for business meetings," he said. He invented many of the best stories about himself. The press loved him. He still looked like a man who could take care of himself in a back-alley brawl, and his rags-to-riches saga was what the public wanted to read about; and the richer he became the humbler he made his beginnings. By any calibration he was good copy, and he had the politician's gift for feeling the pulse of the press; although newsmen knew he was capable of bursts of anger that made aides walk softly around him, they only wrote about his charm, his generosity, his relaxed style. His love affair with the media was not entirely motivated by ego. "His image sanctioned his sharp deals," said Meyer. In copy terms, how he made his money was less important than how he spent it, and with whom. "We knew Ari was an asshole in a lot of ways, but that wasn't important. He was a celebrity. Celebrities are short-lived phenomena. You use them the best way you can," admitted a Paris gossip writer. Gratsos, who was now regarded as Ari's house intellectual, cautioned him about the amount of publicity he was getting. Too much exposure in society columns is not good for the image of a serious businessman, he said. Ari answered: "That's just the *myth*. The more people read about the myth, the less they'll know about the man. Costa, old sport, I'm really a very private person."

The "old sport" made Gratsos wonder if he realized just how much he had been influenced by Tina and her friends. That imbibed English expression, uttered with his Levantine inflection, seemed only to emphasize his foreignness. Tina often told her friends that he reminded her of "a rehabilitated savage" who had acquired a veneer of respectability that was "not deep enough to make him plausible." She could always surprise Gratsos with her perspicacity.

Meanwhile, the competition between Ari and Stavros Niarchos kept pace with their success. Ari built a twenty-eight-thousand-ton tanker; Niarchos built two. Less visible than Ari, and certainly less mythologized, Niarchos troubled his brother-in-law in all kinds of ways. Ari was jealous of his succession of anonymous but always stunning mistresses; he envied him his dandy's elegance, and railed against "that damned Continental air of his." Ari could not wear even the finest suit for more than a morning without looking like a displaced person. They were opposites in every way: "Niarchos exuded the *ennui* of the very rich; Onassis had a pauper's *joie de vivre*," an American oil executive summed up the difference between them.

Yet the rivalry, which fueled each other's ambition and made friends smile, had its darker side. Both men expected their wives to be loyal in every way, sharing prejudices and enemies, grudges and desires. Each man judged the allegiance of their friends by their abhorrence of the other. Ari even forbade Tina to attend Eugénie's wedding to Niarchos. The alienation caused the sisters a lot of pain; Ari saw nothing wrong in his demands. According to a former employee in London, "He considered forgiveness a weakness and détente a defeat. He needed adversaries. He would have been lost without an enemy to hate . . . sometimes the enemy had to be drawn from the closest circle of his own family."

On December 11, 1950, their second child, a girl, was born in

New York. She was named Christina. They had been married seventeen days less than four years. Tina, twenty-one years old, beautiful and immensely rich, convinced that whomsoever she needed must need her more, did not suspect that her life had reached a turning point. Her marriage, in the sense that she and Ari had always been together, traveled together, lived always under the same róof and shared the same friends, was over. The transition was imperceptible, and almost unavoidable, given his need to be always a jump ahead of the game, and her interest in her own social milieu.

In addition to their home on Sutton Square they now had a house in Montevideo; a permanent suite at the Plaza in Buenos Aires; a villa by the sea outside Athens; an apartment on avenue Foch in Paris; and a villa they had rented in the south of France, Château de la Croë, which stood amid twenty-five acres of the finest countryside of Cap d'Antibes, had forty-two rooms and a staff not quite as large as Buckingham Palace's: the duke of Windsor had lived there before them. Tina thought it was divine, although even she might have been taken aback by its size. A millionaire must always live a little beyond his means to maintain his credibility, Ari told friends with the insouciance of a man who knows it is not beyond his means at all. He was not pleased when Niarchos took a similarly grandiose place along the coast. "I think Stavros is suffering from an identity crisis. He hates me because he has no original ideas of his own," he complained. Tina said she thought that Stavros was in love with her. If she had tried very hard, she could not have thought of a more disturbing idea to have planted in her husband's head.

Father Socrates Onassis relished the challenge of the waterfront.
Mother Penelope: there was nothing in all Aristo's world so lost to him as her love.

A keen swimmer, oarsman and water polo player, Aristo enjoyed showing off in front of girls.

Claudia Muzio, the prima donna who taught Aristo an important lesson in life.

Ingeborg Dedichen and her lover, who was now known as Ari, on the maiden voyage of his first tanker, the *Ariston*, in 1938; his stamina astonished her.

Ingeborg and Ari's sister Artemis simply adore Ari but his new brother-in-law, Theodore Garofalides, is asking for more. On a tour of Italy, c. 1937.

With sexual guilt excluded from her own Nordic sense of accountability, Ingeborg teased Ari about his jealous rages . . . and threatened reprisals.

Ram—or devil? Theodore flourishes a pair of horns above Ari's head.

FIVE PHOTOS: COLLECTION OF INGEBORG DEDICHEN

Ari relaxes with his sisters Artemis and Callirhoë at their home in Glyfada in 1938.

The tourist: Ari with sister Merope and her husband, Nicos Konialidis, after attending a rodeo in Salinas, California, in 1938.

The drag artist: *left*, Ari wears Ingeborg's clothes for a private prank in the thirties; and *right*, slips into something a little more comfortable to amuse his guests aboard the *Christina* twenty-five years later.

Macho man: Ari poses for Ingeborg in the south of France.

Diplomatic man: he was appointed deputy Greek consul in Buenos Aires—was the game he was playing espionage?

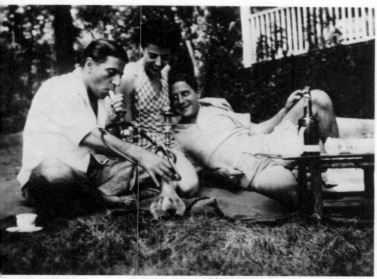

Ari, with Melpomene and Stavros Niarchos on Long Island in 1942, relaxes with a hookah—but it was no pipe of peace.

The respectable young businessman: New York, 1941—J. Edgar Hoover wasn't impressed.

Veronica Lake: they dined at Romanoff's, danced at the Mocambo . . . Miss Lake got very drunk, but Ari took her to the wrong bed.

Geraldine Spreckles: heiress to a sugar fortune. Ari thought she was the most beautiful woman in the world. After a very proper romance, she stood him up at the altar.

Gloria Swanson: a lady whose favors both Ari and Joseph Kennedy once enjoyed.

"From now on," Ingeborg wrote Ari at war's end, "you can no longer count on me . . . I take back my freedom."

"Once in a while, to please the ladies, we go down the line, pretending to be civilized." So Ari summed up his glitzy wedding reception in the Terrace Room of the Plaza. He seemed very foreign to his bride's English-educated mind. Seated on the left is Tina's sister, Eugénie, and Stavros Niarchos, with Tina's father, Stavros Livanos, standing behind.

Stavros Niarchos with Eugénie and Tina—the sisters he married, and buried.

The *Christina* sailing off Monte Carlo. It cost Ari more than $4,000,000 to convert the $50,000, 322-foot Canadian frigate to what ex-king Farouk called "the last word in opulence," and another guest described as "the crystallization of Ari's charm."

If the taste level of the *Christina* was, at the time, dubious and sometimes vulgar—bar stools covered with white whale foreskin: "Madame, you are sitting on the largest penis in the world," Ari informed Greta Garbo—it was never cheap.

DESMOND O'NEILL
REX FEATURES/SIPA

Christina and her brother, Alexander (seen here aged three and six), lived in a charmed world of pampered neglect, their parents' affection scrawled in postcards from distant places and wrapped in secondhand hugs from passing friends and strangers.

Opposite, Christina was Daddy's little girl . . .

. . . but was Tina secretly ashamed of her?

The family that skis together: Ari with Alexander, Tina and Christina pose outside their Swiss villa.

Ari and Tina dancing cheek to cheek in London, although they both recognized that their life together increasingly lacked meaning for them.

Ari with King Saud: their deal became a crisis issue in Washington.

Robert Aime Maheu: the private eye who collected a $5,000 advance to do a job for Stavros Niarchos—to scupper the Saudi deal.

Proud of her power to pander and terrorize, the old society fixer Elsa Maxwell dines with the patriarchal Stavros Livanos in Monte Carlo.

Ari takes Churchill for a ride—but was it also a betrayal of trust?

LONDON EXPRESS/PICTORIAL PARADE

At the feet of the master: J. Paul Getty and Ari.

Opposite, publicity shots: Ari striking a victory pose in front of the casino, and with a model of one of his tankers in his Monte Carlo headquarters. If he had not been quite so useful, he might have been a perfect person for Prince Rainier to cut dead.

CHAPTER 7

No man ever became a villain all at once.

JUVENAL

WHEN THE AMERICAN yards became too expensive for his liking, Ari went to explore the Hamburg scene. The second biggest city of Germany, where great ships had been built for a thousand years, was a ruin. "It was impossible to see how anyone could ever build ships there again, the town was a disaster area," he later recalled. The 1945 Potsdam Agreement prohibited the Germans from building any ship over fifteen thousand tons ("goddam toys," he now dismissed ships the size of his first big tanker); but Costa Gratsos had insisted he go, convinced that it was only a matter of time before the cold war transformed West Germany from a defeated enemy into a valuable ally. "Then the Potsdam restrictions will be out of the window."

Accompanied by Tina and his German adviser, Dr. Kurt Reiter, Ari inspected the yards and assessed the situation. At first he was bored and offhand and often made no secret of his wish to get back to his hotel, or the fact that he would prefer to go for a drink. Then something happened. "He telephoned me one night from the Atlantic Hotel, very excited but very sober," Gratsos remembered. "He had recognized the incredible resources of renewal in that town; he sensed the economic miracle before anyone. He said, 'We've got to find a way around that goddam agreement because these people are willing to break their balls to do us a job.' I didn't see any way round the agreement except by being patient, but I told him I'd think about it."

Ari started to take the shipyard owners seriously, although

many of the meetings took place in Ehmke's restaurant in the Gansemarkt, and sometimes in Tarantella, a nightclub where Ari claimed to have introduced the Gibson to Hamburg. He disliked offices—"Gratsos was a clean-desk executive; Ari was a no-desk executive," explained an aide—offices were too somber. He said that the best deals, like the best sex, came out of exuberance. He was drinking heavily, and the conservative German industrialists found him difficult to deal with, although they played up to him, and he knew it; he traded on their adversity, and they knew it. Tina later told friends that she did not like the side of Ari she saw in Germany.

About a week after Ari had called urging him to find a way round the Potsdam Agreement, Gratsos turned up in Hamburg "looking like the cat that had eaten the canary," remembered Tina. How did Ari feel about getting back into whaling? he asked. (They had dabbled in the business together in California during the war; Ari had called it "gambling at its most elemental.") After thinking for a moment, Ari said: "I ask you about tankers, and you talk to me about whales. One of us has to be crazy." But there was a connection. As well as being prohibited from building big ships, Germany had been outlawed by the Allies from redeveloping its prewar whaling fleets. So not only was there a gap in a very lucrative market, but Gratsos had discovered that the Potsdam Agreement put no limit on conversion work. Ari could use the German yards to convert an eighteen-thousand-ton tanker into a floating factory ship. "And when the building restrictions are lifted you'll be inside ready to go." Ari, Gratsos later recalled, began to grin. "He simply said, 'That's beautiful,' and the next day we got started."

In a befuddling nest of deals, the factory ship *Olympic Challenger* (formerly the T2 tanker *Herman F. Whiton*), financed by a corporation controlled by an Argentinian citizen and affiliated to American Pacific Tankers Inc. in New York, was transferred to a company registered in Panama and run by the Olympic Whaling Company in Montevideo, Uruguay. Significantly, neither Panama nor Uruguay had signed the 1946 Washington Convention, which had decreed a maximum quota of sixteen thousand whales a season. The *Challenger*'s seventeen catcher ships flew Honduran and Panamanian flags, although the commander and most of the 519 seamen were German. The expedition manager was the Norwegian-born Lars Andersen, said by many whalers to be one of the greatest harpoonists of all time. A Nazi collaborator (he stood trial after the war and was fined $160,000), he was advising Juan Perón on Argentina's whaling fleet when Ari caught up with him in Buenos Aires. "He's tough, expensive, unpleasant and an unscrupulous sonofabitch," Ari told Gratsos. "Just like me—only with a harpoon!"

Gratsos's hunch had been right. On April 2, 1951, restrictions on German shipbuilding were lifted; within weeks Ari had finalized a massive one-hundred-million-dollar loan to build eighteen tankers (including two forty-five-thousand tonners) at yards in Hamburg and Kiel. Celebrating at 21, Gratsos gently reminded him of the size of his commitments. "I hope you're not crowding your canvas," he said. If Ari had been a painter, Tina cut in, he would have painted the largest murals the world has ever seen.

Meanwhile, his activities continued to arouse official interest: "A new and amazingly prolific source of capital has appeared in this area in the person of one A. Onassis," Hamburg's United States consul Halleck L. Rose pouched a confidential dispatch to the State Department on January 21, 1952. "In the past two years [he] has ordered ten large ships, founded a successful whaling company, and offered to buy two Federally owned shipyards which together form the largest shipbuilding combine in Western Germany. Despite the extent of his activities, very little is known about this gentleman locally except that he can produce bank references indicating a dollar worth in eight figures. He is said to be of Greek birth and American citizenship, but during his visits to Hamburg has never approached either the Citizenship or Visa Sections of this office."

Ari believed that, like war in the mid-nineteenth century, when generals and their ladies had picnicked on a Sebastopol hillside to watch the charge of the Light Brigade, whaling was a spectator sport, and as he sipped hot toddies with his guests, the gunners made use of their grenade harpoons with a terrible diligence. A broad cloak of blood extended over the surface of the sea. The *Olympic Challenger* was the first factory ship to use a helicopter to seek out its prey; it hovered surreally in the air like a hawk. Some of his guests had been to fiestas in Rio and to grand balls in Venice; none of them had been to anything like this. Only Ari, it was agreed, would think of organizing a whale hunt in the Antarctic Ocean. The men were invited to try their skill with the harpoon gun. "I think he simply wanted them to feel the blood on their hands and share the guilt," Gratsos said later.

In addition to Tina, Kurt Reiter and Nicolas Cokkinis, the party included Frederick Pratt, a director of Socony Oil, and his wife; marine broker Marshal Dodge and his wife; and Mr. and Mrs.

Walter Saunders. Saunders was the legal adviser of Metropolitan Life, which had put up the money for the fleet, including the four million dollars it had taken to convert the *Olympic Challenger*. The expedition started sixteen days before the season opened and would go on killing for seventeen days after it closed. People like the Pratts and the Dodges put much store in playing by the rules, Tina reminded her husband; she always cautioned him when she felt that he had gone too far in some way that might work against their social standing. He told her that he did play by the rules; his rules. He laughed at her scolding. They were at their closest aboard the *Challenger;* Ari did not hide the fact that he was aroused by the spectacle of cruelty; "For Tina I'm sure the hunt evoked a pleasurable psychic high," said a close woman companion. Later Ari talked of the "predatory satisfaction" the warmth of Tina's body gave him beneath the soft white crêpe nightgowns she always wore aboard the *Challenger*.

Each evening while his guests dined off the finest porcelain china, attended by white-gloved waiters, he would be hard at work in the wireless room. Most of the traffic was between the *Olympic Challenger* and Paris. For hiding behind the usual maze of Panamanian companies, he was quietly buying up all the shares he could get his hands on in the Société des Bains de Mer et Cercle des Etrangers (Sea Bathing Society and Foreigners Club, SBM for short), which owned an Edwardian pile of real estate in Monte Carlo, including the casino, the yacht club, the Hotel de Paris and about one-third of the principality's 375 acres. Situated between the ports of Marseilles and Genoa, between the oil fields of the Middle East and the consumer markets of Europe and North America, Monte Carlo was a perfect base for his operations. The climate pleased him, the social life met with Tina's approval and it was tax-free. But his attempts to rent the abandoned club had got nowhere, and nobody tried to hide the reason why: he was not considered by the SBM board in Monaco to be a suitable person to encourage.

In exactly forty-eight minutes at the annual meeting in the summer of 1953, he took control of the SBM; within a week, his staffers had moved into the Old Sporting Club on the avenue d'Ostende. No general ever stood atop a conquered rampart with more pride than Ari when he stepped onto the balcony and looked out; almost everything he saw was his. He was fifty-three years old (or forty-seven, according to his press releases), and it was exactly thirty years since, as an emigrant on his way to Argentina, he had first seen the lights of Monte Carlo from the deck of the *Tomaso di Savoya*.

Prince Rainier of Monaco welcomed the takeover with its promise of new blood and money. With his royal veto over SBM decisions, he had nothing to fear. His tiny principality on the Mediterranean littoral, which had built its reputation in another time, when archdukes and famous courtesans roamed the Riviera, had been in deep decline for years. Onassis, who took it for granted that the business side of Monaco was to be left to him to run, would bring in his rich friends, the roulette wheels would soon be spinning again, and Monte Carlo would become something more than a sepia photograph in Edwardian picture albums, a fond aside in aristocratic memoirs.

In Washington, Ari's progress was being watched more closely than usual. J. Edgar Hoover memoed Assistant Attorney General Warren Burger that the bureau had learned that "Onassis's agent, one Charles Simon, was elected General Manager of the Société on June 29, 1953, and Onassis, therefore, except for the prince of Monaco, whom the French regard as an inconsequential person whose only real interest is in a reliable source of funds for his pleasures, may be regarded as the real ruler of Monaco."

The summer of '53 was the most satisfying of Ari's life. In Hamburg, he launched the *Tina Onassis*. Not yet three years old, Christina broke the champagne across its hull; Alexander pressed the button that sent the biggest tanker in the world (forty-five thousand tons, six million dollars to build) sliding down the slipway into the waters of the Elbe. At the Howaldt Werke in Kiel, preparations to convert the Canadian frigate *Stormont* to a private yacht for himself were well under way, although the plans changed from day to day as the designs became more and more grandiose. It would be called *Christina*.

Ari was celebrating his Monaco takeover with his French bankers at the Café de l'Opéra in Paris when he heard that Niarchos had been indicted for violations of the Ship Sales Act of 1946 by the Justice Department in Washington. Accused of circumventing the act to get control of tankers prohibited from sale to foreigners, his entire American operation was threatened; if found guilty, he faced a stiff prison sentence. "Onassis couldn't give a sou about Niarchos's troubles, but he was worried about the terms of the indictment. It was not to be unsealed until Niarchos returned to the States. He was convinced that it was a trick to put pressure on Niarchos to cooperate on other investigations," recalled one of the bankers who was lunching with him that day. Ari had cause for concern since his own deals were identical to Niarchos's; they had even used some of the same people in Washington. There was not much that Stavros Niarchos did not know about the business of Aristotle Socrates Onassis. It was not compassion that filled Ari's breast when he said, "I don't like to think of Stavros's goose stewing in the States."

On October 22, Hoover informed his New York bureau that warrants for the arrest of Ari, Nicolas Cokkinis and Robert L. Berenson had been issued based on a secret indictment returned by a federal grand jury in the District of Columbia on October 13: "The New York Office should immediately ascertain through discreet inquiries the exact whereabouts of these three individuals. Every effort should be made to determine through confidential sources the future itinerary of these three persons. Any information developed by the New York Office regarding their present whereabouts should be promptly communicated to the Bureau and the Washington Field Office. No arrests shall be made without prior Bureau authority." Attached to the director's memorandum was an instruction from department attorney Allen J. Krause that he "did not desire Robert L. Berenson to be arrested in the event that he entered this country by himself . . . by arresting Berenson it would be necessary to open the secret indictment thereby putting Onassis and Cokkinis on notice and thereafter they would never enter this country knowing that an indictment was outstanding against them."

Ari spent most of the summer in the south of France, commuting between Monte Carlo and the Château de la Croë. In Monte Carlo he stayed at the Hotel de Paris while decorators put the finishing touches to a *pied-à-terre* above his Olympic Maritime offices. Taking over the SBM had brought him worldwide fame. He was more than just another rich Greek; he was established in the public consciousness as larger than life. His wealth was documented, people recognized him in the street and asked for his autograph; women approached to stare, to touch, as if he were a movie star. Journalists reported his recipes for success ("If you do not have money, borrow; do not ask for small amounts, borrow a lot of money but pay it back on the due date") and invented stories about his extravagances. "My vocation is to be rich and even the world-wide victory of communism would not alter that," he proclaimed. He took to dark glasses, and engaged a public relations man; headline writers dubbed him the king of Monaco (a tabloid ennoblement that did not amuse the prince). He acted surprised by the extent of his new fame, but every week his press cuttings were collected and read to him by a secretary. And now when he spoke his words had a faintly imperious sound. "I love this country, but it is a legend which is in decline. I will do my business, and I will do yours, too," he told the citizens of Monaco. "I'll build,

I'll embellish, I'll renovate. The new administration of the SBM will give Monte Carlo a new grandeur. I will help it."

He was dining with Tina at the Carlton Hotel in Cannes one evening in August when Spyridon Catapodis came over to say hello. Tina had no great liking for Catapodis ("tacky" is how she described him) and was plainly displeased when Ari invited him to sit with them. The two men had first met in London in the thirties. Catapodis had been a school friend of Costa Gratsos's in Ithaca; the rest of his background, like so many of his deals, was obscure. A fat man, not much taller than Ari, he smelled of feminine scents and talked rapidly with exquisite gestures. Like many fat men he was light on his feet, and boasted about his dancing skills. Tina knew that he had an unsavory sexual reputation, although she wasn't sure what his interests were. She had seen him with beautiful women, and she had seen him with beautiful young men. He had once owned a few tramp steamers, operating in the eastern Mediterranean between Alexandria and Russia's Black Sea ports. Essentially he was a middleman and a fixer. He was also a compulsive gambler. Tina knew that he had done a few favors for Ari in the past, but not, she thought, much more than getting a hotel suite in places where there were no hotel suites to be had.

She underrated his usefulness to Ari. One deal Catapodis had set up (to supply the Iraqi government with a fleet of Liberty ships and tankers) collapsed only after a coup d'état in Bagdad had iced his contacts. Over drinks they lamented the loss of the Iraqi contract. As they mused over what might have been, Ari grew restless. Up to his eyes in projects, he still missed the excitement of beginning a new deal; stimulated as he was by high stakes, an Iraqi-type package had an especially strong appeal for him at that moment: when he embarked on his massive tanker-building program, it was based on projections that world demand for oil would increase at 8 percent a year. This had proved too optimistic. Freight rates had collapsed; several of his tankers were already laid up; and he was looking for buyers for others still under construction. He suggested that they try to resurrect the Iraqi deal somewhere else in the Arab world.

No one will ever know for sure what was agreed between these two men. What is beyond doubt is that each of them planned to make a killing; at that level they understood each other very well. Yet when they parted that night, Catapodis was convinced that Ari had commissioned him to set up a deal for which he would receive a piece of the action (a figure of one million dollars a year tax-free he felt sure had been mentioned); Ari was equally convinced that Catapodis would collect his rewards from the Arabs.

About a week later in a suite at the Hotel Martinez in Cannes, Catapodis outlined to Mohammed Abdullah and Ali Alireza the concept of a Saudi Arabian tanker fleet, to be provided and run by Onassis. Close to the powerful finance minister Sheikh Abdullah Al Suleiman Al Hamdan, the brothers monopolized the Saudi shipping industry, controlled the port of Jiddah, and held the Lincoln automobile franchise for the kingdom. They were not easy men to impress. Catapodis made much play of the national aspirations of the Arabs. He still had to sweeten the pot. ("You'd be amazed how many desert flowers have to be sprinkled," he told Ari.) According to Catapodis the Alirezas wanted 125,000 pounds when the contracts were signed plus a further 75,000 pounds the day the first Onassis tanker left a Saudi port under the deal. An annual "commission" of 50,000 pounds would be paid into a Swiss account for as long as the deal remained operative, plus 100 pounds for each Onassis tanker cleared from a Saudi port.

On this understanding, the Alirezas would get negotiations started with Sheikh Abdullah Al Suleiman Al Hamdan. It was not an easy deal to put together. The backstairs of Saudi politics are "dark, slippery and well-worn," Catapodis said later. The death of old King Abdul Aziz Ibn Saud and labor unrest in the oil fields had complicated matters even more. Catapodis was proud of his achievement when he briefed Ari in November 1953. "Here's your lemon, my friend," he would recall telling him. "All you've got to do is squeeze it."

The profits were potentially massive, the global implications enormous. If he succeeded, Ari would become richer and more powerful than some nations. It was vital that the deal be concluded swiftly: ARAMCO, the consortium dominated by four major American companies—Standard Oil Company of California, Mobil, Exxon and Texaco—had a treaty with the Saudis, which included the right to transportation as well as exploration and production concessions, signed in 1933 and to last until the year 2000. Ari did not underrate the furor that would ensue when it was discovered what he was up to. He said, "I was about to stick my finger into the American pie"—a pie that a State Department official had once called "the richest material prize in history."

It was what he would later call "the biggest dry-throat deal of my life." He could not sleep, his head ached all the time, his gums bled. In the middle of November he flew to Dusseldorf to ask Dr. Hjalmar Schacht to lead his negotiating team. Schacht, the former president of Hitler's Reichsbank, had been acquitted of war crimes at Nuremberg in 1946—"you can't hang a banker," cynics were saying even before the trial began—but was later found guilty by a German denazification court. "The swastika brushed from his sleeve," he was released from jail in 1948 and now specialized in advising countries in the Moslem world. In January 1953 the West German magazine *Der Spiegel* called him the "medicine man of high finance" and reported that he was being "worshipped almost mystically" throughout the Middle East. Ari was convinced that he was the man to cut through the intricacies of desert kingdom diplomacy. In less than an hour in Schacht's office at Schadow-platz 14 the two men had reached a perfect understanding.

Ari omitted to tell Catapodis about Schacht, and when Cata-podis discovered that the German was involved in talks "with high Saudi personages" in Geneva (including finance minister Sheikh Suleiman) he suspected that Ari was trying to squeeze him out of the deal and attempting to avoid the "commissions" promised to the Alireza brothers.

Ari was sleeping off a hangover after a heavy night at Maxim's when Catapodis burst into his bedroom on avenue Foch. He must have been shaken by the sight of Catapodis's taurean bulk looming above him, grabbing the lapels of his silk pyjamas, their faces inches apart. "You dumbfuck, you no-good Smyrna shit, you'll screw up the whole deal. We'll both climb out of this tub of tits sucking our thumbs." The tirade lasted several minutes. All the household came running; nobody quite knew how to react, so no-body attempted to intervene. Ari finally calmed him down, as-suaged his fears. Later, he made light of the grotesque episode ("There isn't anything that spoils one's day more than being awoken by an aggrieved Greek with bad breath") but it rankled and humiliated him deeply; eventually, he denied it ever hap-pened.

By the end of December, Schacht had drawn up a draft agree-ment that satisfied the Saudis and contained all the ingredients that exhilarated Ari: guile, audacity, imagination. Known simply as the Jiddah Agreement, its existence still a closely guarded se-cret, it called for Ari to supply five hundred thousand tons of tanker shipping toward the establishment of the Saudi Arabian Maritime Company, or SAMCO. Headquartered in Jiddah, but ex-empted from Saudi taxes, the fleet would fly the national flag, its officers drawn from a Saudi maritime college to be established and funded by Ari. The company would get priority rights on the shipment of Arabian oil, with a guaranteed 10 percent (or a mini-mum of four million tons) of the country's annual output. Al-though tankers owned and registered in the name of ARAMCO's parent companies on or before December 31, 1953, would not be affected by the deal, Ari would be free to take over from ARAMCO ships as and when they became obsolete. "A carnival of grab," a prominent London shipping broker called the arrangement that within a decade would give Ari a strategic monopoly on the transport of more than forty-five million tons of Saudi oil a year.

On January 18, 1954, Ari and Tina arrived in Jiddah aboard the *Tina Onassis*. Nicolas Cokkinis and Spyridon Catapodis (convinced that he was still part of the deal) had arrived by air a couple of days earlier to make sure that everything was in good order. The agreement was signed in Finance Minister Suleiman's villa on January 20 without a hitch. It was Ari's forty-eighth birthday (according to his Greek passport), a double celebration. Official photographs were taken. Ari and Tina were feted by the Saudis; there were picnics by the Red Sea, and banquets attended by senior members of the royal family. Tina was taken to tea at the palace of King Saud's four queens. The king presented Ari with two Arab ponies and a pair of gold-sheathed scimitars.

But still nobody had disclosed the sensational terms of the agreement to ARAMCO and the rest of the world. Who would tell the oil men? The agreement, signed by Sheikh Suleiman on behalf of the government, had not yet been implemented by royal decree, and until the king's signature was on the contract Ari knew that he had nothing. He suggested that they keep the deal "inside the family" until after the royal implementation. Keen to distance himself from the deal, now that the *ad volorem* had been settled, Suleiman offered to leave the timing and the handling of the announcement to Ari.

8

It is wretched to be found out.

HORACE

Avenue Foch glistened in the late January rain. Ari paced his study, his shoulders hunched. He went to the window and stared out, swaying a little on the balls of his feet, a familiar stance that reminded Randolph Churchill of "a bantam-weight watching which way his opponent is going to move." Gratsos knew it wasn't nerves that made him restless. Anger, not nerves, energized Ari. He had been living with the sealed indictment pending against him since October. Every time one of his ships put into a United States port, it was seized, a letter of attachment posted on its bridge by a United States marshal. To the ordinary person, being indicted by a federal grand jury would be a disgrace. But Ari ordered his life by a different set of rules, and by his own standards he had done nothing of which he needed to be ashamed. He made an impatient movement with his hands and shoulders. "Indictment or not, I am proud of what I have done," he told Gratsos, who would later incorporate the line in the "defense paper" he drafted for Ari to present to the Justice Department. It was just bad timing. The Saudi Arabian deal had still to be ratified by the king, and the last thing he wanted was a public brawl with the United States government.

"He was especially mad about Brownell," who had become attorney general, Gratsos recalled. "Seven years earlier, he [Herbert Brownell, Jr.] had been one of the lawyers in the firm that examined and approved his plan for getting the surplus ships. Ari said to me, 'Now this same guy wants to get me for criminal fraud

120

for taking his advice. How can he do that? How can the bastard get away with that?' " Although he believed that "law is a mystery where logic ends and blind chance begins," Gratsos had a talent for unraveling and defining the thoughts and weaknesses of others and suggested that Brownell couldn't be "feeling too comfortable" about the situation. He urged Ari to go eyeball to eyeball with the attorney general. "He can hardly be relishing the prospect of being called to the stand to have some smartass lawyer work him over about the advice and opinions he was dealing out before he became attorney general." He encouraged Ari to return to the States and force the Justice Department to unseal the indictment. "Let's find out exactly what's in there, because whatever Brownell and his people know about you, you certainly know plenty about Brownell." He regarded it as "a stabilizing division of intelligence."

Onassis complained that "the Justice Department is full of life's smart guys"; he reminded Gratsos that his lawyers didn't want him to go anywhere near the States. Niarchos was getting the same advice from his legal people and was sitting tight in London. Gratsos answered, "Brownell was a lawyer too and look what happened when you took his advice!" More than a dozen of his ships had already been seized and their revenues impounded; the problem had to be resolved soon. Returning now, he would have an edge, Gratsos argued: "the Justice Department won't be expecting you, and Brownell won't want you." On February 1, 1954, Ari passed unchallenged through customs and passport control at Idlewild International. On Thursday, February 4, he sent a wire to the attorney general:

> I wish to inform you that having arrived from Europe on Monday night I place myself at your disposal during my visit in this country for any information you or your department might care to have.

He could have saved his money. Hoover's men had already reported that he was back in town. "[He] was traveling via an Argentine passport and upon arrival indicated that he intended to stay in this country for two months and that his address during this period would be Central American Steamship Agency, 655 Madison Avenue, New York, New York," Hoover informed Assistant Attorney General Warren Olney III. The bench warrant for Ari's arrest was dispatched to the United States Marshal for the Southern District of New York "for appropriate service."

Convinced by the medicinal illusion of his second Gibson that he had called Brownell's bluff, Ari was lunching at the Colony on

Friday, February 5, when a federal marshal informed him that he was under arrest. "He said that he hoped he hadn't spoiled my meal. I told him that I wasn't too happy about his timing. The Colony isn't exactly the kind of place where a fellow expects to have to keep his guard up," was how Ari recalled the occasion. Not even Colony boss Gene Cavallero, who was tossing his special salad for Onassis, knew what was happening. Ari accompanied the marshal ("He looked more like a salesman for Abercrombie & Fitch than a lawman") to the foyer, where he was permitted to call his lawyer, Edward J. Ross. Ross talked to the marshal and made an offer to deliver his client to the district court in Washington first thing Monday morning. "I guess there's nothing stopping you from going back in there and enjoying your lunch," the marshal said when Ross's offer had been agreed to by the sheriff's office. Ari had lost his appetite. "It was a very civilized bust," he later said; he knew that Brownell had won the first round.

When the indictment was unsealed that weekend, Ari learned for the first time that he was being charged on seven civil counts plus a charge of criminal conspiracy to defraud the United States government; nine individuals and six corporations were named. "Well, what's the ransom going to be?" he demanded after his legal team had studied the situation. Eliot Bailen, a young attorney who had quit the Washington law firm that put together the deal to become Ari's personal counselor, spelled out the possible consequences: imprisonment for up to five years, or a ten-thousand-dollar fine, or both. "For a man as busy as you, Mr. Onassis, I'm surprised you found the time to make so many enemies," Ed Ross told him. Ari replied, "I know, and it's really starting to trouble me."

There was one light moment that weekend. As his legal team went through the indictments line by line and the scale of the problem became increasingly apparent ("Justice seemed to have all the answers before they'd asked us a single question," said Gratsos), Ari asked: "Do we know who'll run the federal case against me?" The Admiral, Ross told him, alluding to Warren Burger, the assistant attorney general and the future chief justice of the United States. "He's seized so many of your ships, he's known at Justice as the Admiral."

Ari's mood changed constantly: "from ranting self-pity to an almost benumbed kind of calm," a lawyer at Center Island recalled that weekend. He dictated, and was persuaded to abandon, at least half a dozen statements before a one-thousand-word press release was finalized. It was an interesting document, described by one aide as "a mixture of a chairman's report and the unrepentant ravings of a killer on his way to the chair." The lawyers tried to persuade him to "cut out the cloying sentiment and stick to a short dignified announcement that he would answer all the charges in the proper place." He asked Gratsos for his opinion. "I have to go along with these gentlemen," his oldest ally told him, pointing out that it was just a press release, not Parnassus. He replied: "Shit, Costa, this is propaganda," and told them to release it the following morning.

The statement detailed how he had returned to the United States voluntarily the moment he learned that "several sealed indictments had been obtained by the Department of Justice in which I might have been included." His wife and two children were American citizens, and his good name in America meant a great deal to him. His relationships with American businessmen and with the government were a source of pride to him. Shortly after World War II, it had been his good fortune to have been able to prevent the closure of one of the finest American shipyards (the Bethlehem Yards at Sparrows Point) by placing with them an order for the first fleet of supertankers. "At the outbreak of the Korean War I offered unconditionally my entire foreign fleet, together with my whaling fleet, and also my personal services and resources, to the United States Navy for the duration of the emergency—an offer which I believe was made by no other shipowner, and for which I was officially thanked by the Navy."

The paragraphs relating to the actual deals were an extraordinary amalgam of revelation and misinformation. "The simple facts are these," he declared, and proceeded to outline a situation that was anything but simple. "United States Petroleum Carriers, Inc., an American corporation, was organized in 1947 by a group of American citizens to purchase and operate vessels. Sometime later, a foreign corporation, which I represent, was offered by the American group and acquired a 49 percent stock interest in the American company, as permitted by the shipping laws." With the shipping know-how, funds and collateral provided by the foreign company he claimed to "represent," USPC bought more than twenty vessels over a period of three years. "The company and its subsidiaries derived gross revenues of over $50 million and an operating profit of over $20 million . . . this successful shipping operation was at all times beneficially owned and controlled by American citizens owning 51 percent of the stock."

Wearing a dark blue suit, blue shirt, black tie and a black overcoat, early Monday morning he flew to Washington and presented himself to United States District Attorney Leo Rover. "I understand it's showdown time," he said. Rover summoned a marshal to make the formal arrest. Fingerprinted, documented, mug shots taken, he was put in a holding pen with petty thieves, male prostitutes and a group of Puerto Ricans charged with shooting up Congress the previous day. Although his captivity lasted no more than forty minutes, it shook him badly, rekindling memories of his father's imprisonment. The arrest took him out of the social columns and financial pages and put him smack on the front page of newspapers around the world. Newsmen noted a distinct pallor beneath his customary tan when before Justice Bolitha J. Laws in United States District Court he pleaded not guilty to all eight counts. Released on a ten-thousand-dollar bond, he was directed not to leave the United States.

In London meanwhile Niarchos had heard a whisper of the Jiddah Agreement. (With the high-living Spyros Catapodis back on the Riviera celebrating his coup, it was extraordinary that Ari ever imagined that he could keep the deal quiet.) Among the leading carriers of Saudi oil not transported in ARAMCO vessels, Niarchos knew he could quickly be squeezed out of that lucrative market. But it was more than that. Although Ari had lovers he trusted with his secrets, and relatives he trusted with his companies, Niarchos alone shared his dreams. It was inevitable that he should see the deal as a new dimension in their private struggle. No history meant more to them than the history of Greece, with its sense of pride and ambition, where valor and esteem rests on achievement and possessions. Their father-in-law had once said that shipping was a kind of blood sport. Stavros Niarchos knew the time had come to spill some blood.

Robert Aime Maheu had been in business on his own account for only a matter of months when he was offered a five-thousand-dollar advance to do a job for Stavros Niarchos; five thousand dollars was a lot of money for a private investigator who normally got fifty dollars a day, plus expenses. What exactly did Mr. Niarchos want done for five thousand dollars? Maheu asked the English lawyer sitting in his small office at 917 15th Street, N.W., in Washington, D.C. The lawyer outlined the broad concept of Onassis's deal with the Saudis and the threat it posed to America's foreign interests. "Mr. Niarchos would like you to scupper that contract. He wants a monkey wrench thrown into the works, Mr. Maheu." His client wanted Maheu to use his Washington connections to see that the reverberations of the Jiddah Agreement were felt "all the way up to the top."

It was Maheu's first big assignment in the shamus business ("I didn't get rich overnight," he has said, "but I did very well"). Thirty-seven years old, a man whom people remember for his charm, Maheu had quit the FBI in 1947 to go into the dairy business. He had remained a great admirer of Hoover's, always remembering to send him a birthday greeting ("Those of us who truly comprehend the insidious forces which you have consistently and are continuing to combat," read one birthday message, "thank the Good Lord that He has blessed you with so many years of physical and mental health. We pray that He may continue to do so"), and when the dairy company went sour two years later, the much-blessed director got him a job with the Small Defense Plants Administration in Washington. In 1954 he launched Robert A. Maheu Associates. Later, as chief executive of Howard Hughes's Las Vegas operation (where, as a devout Roman Catholic, he surprised associates by reciting grace before working lunches), he preferred to remember it as a management consultancy business, although most of the associates, like Maheu himself, were ex-FBI and intelligence agents; from the beginning the CIA was picking up the tab for his office expenses with a five-hundred-dollar monthly retainer. Along the way, he produced a pornographic movie for the CIA, purporting to show Indonesia's President Sukarno capering with a blonde; later he was the company's middleman in the recruitment of underworld figure Johnny Rosselli in the plot to assassinate Fidel Castro.

It is unlikely that Niarchos approached Maheu with management consultancy in mind. And shortly after his London lawyer left Maheu's office, a messenger delivered photographs of Ari and a detailed dossier on him, his business affairs and his key employees.

About two weeks after Ari's arrest in Washington, details of the Jiddah Agreement—garbled, incomplete but effective—were leaked to a Rome newspaper funded by the CIA through Maheu himself. Rome was the center of the CIA's covert political action program; under William Colby, later a director of the agency, one of the station's high-priority objectives was to match the sophisticated Soviet technique of placing damaging or mischievous stories in foreign publications to be picked up and replayed throughout the world.

Predictably, ARAMCO expressed its consternation to the Saudi government; shipowners everywhere issued vehement protests. In London, Stavros Niarchos launched a less covert assault on his brother-in-law, engaging Alan Campbell-Johnson, a veteran public relations man (Lord Mountbatten's wartime aide and his press attaché when he became India's viceroy in the last days of the raj), to get the deal raised in Parliament, convinced that his animus for Ari would find a political echo. His instructions were brief: "I want Onassis brought to heel."

Campbell-Johnson, who had twice stood as a Liberal parlia-

mentary candidate, "recognized that national interests were involved," and set up a meeting between Niarchos and Jo Grimond,
then chief whip and soon to become leader of the Liberal party, to
get questions raised in the House. Although Campbell-Johnson
thought that Niarchos was a "miserable man with no inner élan,"
he was convinced that he was "acting more in sorrow than in
anger" and that his efforts to sabotage the Saudi deal were intended to "curb Onassis's excesses, not to destroy the man."

Niarchos's attempts to stir up trouble in London came as no
surprise to Ari. When Gratsos had predicted on the day Ari returned from Jiddah with Suleiman's signature that Stavros was
certain to try "some kind of spoiling operation," he replied, "He'll
be looking out for his own ass. We can't squeal about that." Only
Tina, who had remained fond of her brother-in-law (she knew that
her affection for Niarchos incited her husband's jealousy) was unprepared by what she saw as an act of treachery in the family.
"Relationships, like principles, are forgotten when they threaten
profits," Ari told her.

"As the Jiddah details started leaking out, people were staggered by the scope of the deal," Gratsos said. "I told Ari that
neither Livanos nor Niarchos could believe what he had done.
'Guys like that can never believe what exceeds their own imagination,' he told me." Yet he was still unaware of the extent of the
firepower ranged against him; privately, Gratsos thought that he
had been "visionary but ill prepared."

Maheu lost no time in getting a wiretap in Ari's New York
offices on Madison Avenue; the apartment on avenue Foch was
also bugged. He hired military-economic analysts to delineate and
project the implications of the Jiddah Agreement to Vice-President
Richard M. Nixon, and to the National Security Council. It was
inevitable that the agreement would seriously undermine United
States influence in the Middle East. Iran's attempt to nationalize
the Anglo-Persian Oil Company (later BP) in 1951 foundered on
the fact that it did not have its own tanker fleet with which to
withstand the boycott imposed by the multinational oil companies; the Jiddah Agreement would get round any future multinational strictures and destabilize the entire Arab world. This was
the thrust of the case Maheu put to Richard Nixon.

Nixon had sat on the Senate Permanent Subcommittee on
Investigations, which spent months unraveling the complex and
intricate facts involved in the surplus tanker deals. He knew a
great deal about Ari and his ways of doing things. Maheu must
have found the vice-president's apocalyptic vision of Ari and the
Jiddah Agreement reassuring. Exactly what these two men said to

each other during the briefing sessions on Capitol Hill was not put into memos or minutes. Maheu was a man who wanted very little in writing.* What is known is that Maheu believed passionately that the solution to what they both perceived as a threat was the destruction of Ari's credibility. And Nixon seems to have given him the encouragement to go in hot pursuit. John Gerritty, a Maheu operative who attended at least one briefing on the Hill, was impressed by the vice-president's enthusiasm for the chase. ("Nixon gave us the whole bit . . . this was a top-secret, highly sensitive national security matter, and that if we took the assignment and got caught—well, the government couldn't be of any help. They'd deny all involvement.") It is never easy to know in politics where national interest ends and the defense of big business begins, but since an important Nixon function was to raise campaign funds for the Republicans, the effect the Onassis-Saudi deal would have on the bountiful oil companies must have been an effective element in his thinking.

Maheu's move to embroil the vice-president was brilliant. For Nixon was extremely close to CIA boss Allen Dulles, and their friendship went back to 1947, when they had toured Europe together on the Herter Commission investigating the effectiveness of the Marshall Plan. Through Allen, Nixon got close to his older brother, John Foster Dulles. The Nixons and Janet and John Foster Dulles became frequent dinner companions in Georgetown à quatre. Foster Dulles was at the height of his powers, a secretary of state so omnipotent that few leaders in the Western bloc would have even dared to dream about making a move of any external significance without first consulting him. Through Nixon, Maheu had thrown the hooks into the highest echelons of State and the CIA. And catastrophes quickly began proliferating for Aristotle Socrates Onassis.

In Monte Carlo Ari was getting ready for dinner when Costa Gratsos called from New York to tell him that the *Daily News* had got hold of a copy of Hoover's letter to the War Shipping Administration branding him anti-American. Gratsos read a copy of the twelve-year-old letter supplied by the New York paper, which wanted a quote from Ari. "What I have to say they wouldn't print

---

* During his $17.5 million defamation suit against Howard Hughes's Summa Corporation in 1975, Maheu was challenged to produce his billings to Niarchos. He said that although he had met Niarchos in London, New York, Washington, Rome, Beirut and Athens, he never submitted billings but asked during the period of the assignment for additional money for expenses—money that was always placed immediately in his bank account.

even in that rag," Ari swore, and continued for several minutes a
diatribe against the press and Hoover. Not thrown by an anger
different only in expression from his own, Gratsos told him that
he thought it would be sensible to make some reply to the charge.
"It wasn't going to go away. I'd already talked to John Meyer. It
was the sort of thing he could often take care of with a couple of
phone calls. This time there was nothing he could do. He said that
the *News* was 'working the other side of the street,' " Gratsos recalled.

Ari was bitter toward the Americans ("I even have to get the
court's permission to leave their goddam country . . . they want to
hang me out to dry"), and Gratsos was anxious not to get side-
tracked by his me-against-them ethos. Ari blamed Niarchos. There
is now little doubt that it was Maheu who had leaked the damaging Hoover letter to the paper. Gratsos suspected that Niarchos
("full of old scores and new ways of settling them") was involved
somewhere. Neither Niarchos nor Ari was ever totally beyond suspicion: they plotted against each other out of habit and sometimes
out of pure divertissement. He again asked how Ari wanted the
situation handled. "If I'm pushed against the wall, I'm going to
defend myself," he answered. "I'm in the *total* business. I win any
way I have to."

At the beginning of April 1954, he returned to Jiddah for an
audience with King Saud. Among several amendments made to
the agreement was a clause stipulating that "A. S. Onassis shall
have the right to combine the company whose head office will be
in Saudi Arabia with one or more of the companies a majority of
whose shares are directly owned by himself or by members of his
family of Greek origin, provided that Jews have no direct or indi-
rect interest in any of these companies and the company shall not
deal with Israel." Ari, who had urged his mistress to beware of
Jews, and of being "kiked," felt no qualms of conscience in accepting this as a commercial sop; and although he would later defend
it as a Saudi demand, the wording of the clause had been drafted
by Hjalmar Schacht and approved by Ari at Schadowplatz 14
several weeks before the Saudis raised the issue.

Formally ratified by King Saud on May 18, the Jiddah Agreement became a crisis issue in Washington. John Foster Dulles was
kept constantly in touch with bulletins from his State Department
advisers as well as from ARAMCO and the CIA. The situation
called for kid-glove diplomacy. United States ambassador George
Wadsworth warned of the Saudis' national pride in the proposed
fleet: "High Saudi circles," he cabled, "obviously lack background
experience to really appreciate questions of principle involved and

to their shrewd trader mind it follows that if the foreigner cries he must be hurt financially and they gain in corresponding measure." After personally delivering a strongly worded communiqué to King Saud, drawing attention to the potential threat the fleet posed to United States interests (the king's eyesight was extremely weak, and the protest was read to him by his brother Prince Faisal), Wadsworth related that the king replied "with some heat and, I thought, irritation, not with me but rather, I surmise, because the whole matter was distasteful to him."

Ari hurried back to the United States to put his own case to the State Department, protesting that the Jiddah Agreement was a shotgun wedding. Although he had tried to limit his involvement, the Saudis were determined to establish a national fleet, and either he signed on their terms or lost the deal, he said. "There is stirring a new ideology of political and economic emancipation in all countries . . . sooner or later all the oil-producing countries of the Middle East are bound to set up their own tanker fleets," he argued. "That deal was on the table for almost a year, just waiting for somebody to pick it up," he asserted. "It was like watching a loaded gun lying around, anybody could have grabbed it. I finally went for it before somebody else got there and had me up against the wall." Observed a Middle East Desk official, "He gave the impression of being a man in a tight spot." But the oilmen declined to buy his version of events. When his tankers arrived at ARAMCO's Saudi terminals they would be turned away, he was told. "They're putting me through the wringer. I caught them with their pants down, and that's something they can't forgive," he said after getting ARAMCO's tough answer.

He'd been made to feel dispensable, and Gratsos wondered "whether he had ever been confronted with his own dispensability before." Aware that he was fighting for his very survival in a geopolitical game, Gratsos told him: "You're in the front line. The front line is a dangerous place to be." He had had misgivings about the Saudi deal and the nature of the people involved; he'd always suspected that it would come apart in Ari's hands "the minute anyone even looked at it too hard."

May was a bad month for Ari, culminating in a scene at Nice airport that did nothing to ease his mind, or help his reputation. Five months earlier, while checking some detail in his contract, setting out his payments on the Saudi deal, Spyridon Catapodis's heart had lurched. Onassis's signature, he later claimed, had faded to nothingness. "It was as if it had never existed." He again confronted Ari at avenue Foch, accompanied by Leon "Lou" Turrou. Turrou was a useful man to have along. A former FBI agent and intelligence colonel, he had quit the army after the war and joined the CIA, working out of a Paul Getty proprietory (a company accommodating CIA operatives) in Paris; his relationship to Catapodis was vague, although the Greek introduced him as his "confidential adviser." His presence inside 88, avenue Foch at about the time Maheu got a bug planted in the apartment suggests that he might also have been Maheu's man.*

Ari said that the contract must have been signed with an ink of inferior quality! Although Catapodis walked away with a check for twenty-five thousand dollars, Ari somehow succeeded in holding on to the original contract, and in spite of all his efforts Catapodis had been unable to retrieve it or catch up with Ari again. Until their encounter at Nice International in May. He grabbed Ari by the throat, pushed him down on his knees, and proceeded to throttle him. "You're not even a true Greek!" Catapodis screamed, his face bloated with rage and cognac. "You're nothing but a goddam *Turk!*" And spitting in his face, he walked away. A crowded departure lounge is not a good place to have a private quarrel; within hours it was the talk of the Riviera.

Consternation grew among Ari's aides as the pressure mounted. News of his close association with Hjalmar Schacht was followed by the disclosure of the anti-Semitic clause in the Jiddah Agreement. It was also at this time that his links with the former Austrian armaments king Mandl and Fascist dictator Juan Perón were uncovered. Recalled an Onassis executive in Monte Carlo, "It looked bad. We were dealing with Jews every day. The American Jewish lobby had already told the oil companies to stop dealing with us. I could see the backlash hurting the whole operation." His people in Germany advised him against inviting Alfried Krupp von Bohlen und Halbach (head of the House of Krupp, which had stuck by Hitler to the end) to the launching of *Olympic Cloud* in Bremen. "We pointed out that it would be Krupp's first official public appearance since serving six years in prison as a Nazi war criminal; it was going to attract attention," remembered an aide. "I don't know whether he was being bloody-minded or resigned, but he insisted that the invitation stand." One of his people in New York recalls hearing him say, "I don't think one more Nazi here or there is going to make much difference to my reputation now."

On June 12 he was back in Paris relaxing at the bar in Maxim's when he was told that Niarchos was having lunch in a private

---

* *Maheu testified that "after consulting with the agency, he arranged for a listening device to be placed" in Onassis's apartment. Congressional Document O.C. 1975.*

room with *New York Times* reporter C. L. Sulzberger. What do you think Stavros is plotting now? he was asked. My downfall, he answered amiably; with a few Gibsons inside him he enjoyed his role as bad boy on the block.

Upstairs (in a room designed more for seduction thàn for business, Sulzberger recalled later) Niarchos was doing exactly that. Between paranoid outbursts that he was being spied upon, repeatedly going to the door to check that nobody was listening (the fourth time he pulled open the door, he *did* catch a waiter "standing right outside with flapping ears"), he told Sulzberger that Ari had bought up Monte Carlo for chicken feed—"only a few million dollars"—in order to "bribe and subvert" businessmen and politicians who were getting free rides in the principality. "Niarchos seemed to resent this and thought it highly immoral." It was not long before he got around to the Saudi deal. It was "highly unorthodox and was upsetting all standard business practices," he complained and emphasized that he "was not affected and had more business on hand than he could possibly carry out for some years to come." He told Sulzberger that he was talking to him only because he knew he would be interested in "the morals of the situation." He handed the *Times* man a thick envelope, bulging with papers purporting to reveal the murky depths of Ari's dealings. Glancing through it, Sulzberger thought it was slender stuff ("It seemed to comprise mostly newspaper clippings and other public material," he noted in his diary) and expressed surprise that Niarchos relied on such meager intelligence in his business affairs. Niarchos was explaining that there were other documents, which he would supply, when the maître d' informed him that Ari was downstairs and would like to have a word. Sulzberger snorted with laughter. "For God's sake, invite him up because he must have had agents hearing every word you've been saying," he told his host pleasantly. Niarchos did not think that was a very good idea and went downstairs to talk to him. "After all," he shrugged when he returned, "he is my brother-in-law, and he heard I was here so he just wanted to say hello." He looked, Sulzberger thought, rather flushed.

A few days later, Tina called from St. Moritz to tell Ari that she had broken her leg; her accident-proneness puzzled her. ("If life is rich, I suppose one cannot expect that it should also be safe," she told a friend.) She simply couldn't understand how it had happened, she said. "I wasn't even *moving*. One moment I was standing there, a perfectly fit lady, and the next moment I was sitting on the ground with a horribly broken leg." When she coquettishly reminded Ari that her leg had been in plaster the first time they met, he told her that she was not a little girl anymore. Would she be able to go to Hamburg for the launch of his latest tanker? he asked, as if waiting to pounce on some fresh capriciousness in her nature. She assured him that she would be there. "I'm already practically running amok with boredom, my dear."

She had had a busy year, watching over the interior designs for the *Christina*, skiing, so many parties. She lived in isolation from Ari's needs and problems. She adored the social caravanserai: in Paris for the Collections, in London for Ascot, in New York for the Met. It was already June, and she could count on one hand how many whole weeks she had spent with Ari that year; just as she had learned to live in his shadow, so she had learned to live with his absence. They had been married eight years. Although she had become an exquisite flirt, and loved to be surrounded by admirers, she knew how to be discreet. The most assiduous of her present admirers was Venezuelan oil millionaire Renaldito Herrera. Ari seemed not to mind her social life, her tête-à-tête dinners with handsome young skiers and the kind of men who gravitate toward rich and beautiful women. She was the quintessential socialite: "That's what she does best," he said. He had grown up a great deal since Ingeborg, when his days and dreams away from her were filled with jealousy and suspicion. Unlike Ingeborg, Tina had always been his, a possession, a chattel, a very Greek wife.

Nevertheless, she did not hide her displeasure when he told her that his new tanker (hitherto known only as Baunummer 883, or Building Number 883) would not now be named after Alexander. The biggest tanker in the world—two thousand tons heavier than the *Tina Onassis*—was now to be named in honor of King Saud I. It was to be the flagship of the Saudi fleet, and he wanted the world and ARAMCO to know it. Over 120,000 Germans, including some of the biggest names in West German business, industry and society, attended the ceremony at the Howaldt-Hamburg yard. It was, thought Gratsos uneasily, "like a scalp dance around ARAMCO." Princess Anne-Marie von Bismarck broke a bottle of holy water from the sacred Zamzam wells of Mecca across the hull (the bottle, lacking the pressure of shaken champagne, alcohol being strictly forbidden by the Riyadh delegation, broke only on the third attempt) and *Al Malik Saud Al-Awal* slid down the slipway into history. What were you thinking when she slid into the water, Ari? a friend asked. "I was thinking, 'Up your ass, ARAMCO,' " he said.

On the Hegelian principle that quantity becomes quality, Allen Dulles had built an impressive case against Ari. On Thursday, July 1, the American spymaster sent his brother, the secretary of state, a CIA briefing which traced the background to the Jiddah Agreement. The tone from the start was inimical toward Ari. "We believe it was a case of a smart Greek selling the SAG [Saudi Arabian government] a bill of goods and the prestige-hungry Arabs jumping at the deal." Few had jumped with more enthusiasm than Sheikh Abdullah Suleiman, the minister of finance, who "pocketed approximately US 100 thousand in return for his signature," reported a Middle East agent. Although the Saudis were becoming "more cantankerous and difficult we do not believe they dreamt up this arrangement," the briefing continued. "Onassis apparently has some mighty plans to monopolize the tanker industry by playing the same theme to Kuwait, Iran and Iraq." It was suggested that the maiden voyage of the *Al Malik* was arranged to satisfy "the ego of the SAG and King Saud and possibly to influence other Near East countries to sign similar agreements with Onassis."

It was State Department strategy that American oil operations should be used as an "instrument of foreign policy in the Middle East," and Foster Dulles was determined to break the agreement. However, the crisis had laid bare disturbing ambiguities in the original ARAMCO deal with the Saudis. In a confidential memorandum State Department legal adviser Bob Metzger had raised questions about the wisdom of arbitrarily challenging a contract not quite so ironclad as it might have appeared when it was signed in 1933. The Saudis had granted the oil combine the right to "explore, prospect, drill for, extract, treat, manufacture, transport, deal with, carry away and export petroleum." But exactly what did "export" mean? queried Metzger with painstaking attention to legal detail and justification. Webster's dictionary defined it as "to carry or send abroad"—but which? "If it means to carry abroad, the right might encompass the exclusive right to carry by whatever means the company chooses. If, on the other hand, it means to send abroad, this right does not necessarily carry with it the exclusive determination by which the oil is to be physically carried." It was a delicate point, and Metzger admitted that he was by no means certain the company would lose in international arbitration. "On the other hand," he added didactically, "I am not confident that they would win."

A hard-line architect of American foreign policy, Dulles made it clear that he would back the oil companies to the hilt in any showdown, even though he knew that ARAMCO's decision to boycott the Onassis-Saudi tankers could result in the Arabs' nationalizing the whole shebang. On July 16, he cabled Ambassador Wadsworth a vigorous and uncompromising briefing:

From practical business viewpoint US believes Saudi Government would run grave danger substantial loss by implementation Onassis agreement. Financial benefits to Saudi government bound to be infinitesimal compared potential loss oil royalties. Loss of markets for only one million barrels of oil would roughly cancel contemplated annual financial benefits. If contract implemented resentment and resistance on part many oil buyers likely impair ARAMCO production, income and hence Saudi royalties to much greater extent. There is increasing evidence that resistance will be tremendous. From dollars and cents viewpoint Saudi government appears to have been seriously misled.

Newly appointed to the Saudi post, Wadsworth was about to earn his keep. He knew that the "dollars and cents" remark was out-and-out rough stuff since the "oil buyers" were simply the men who ran ARAMCO. And if there was still any doubt in his mind, it must have been dispelled by the FYI (for your eyes only) coda:

It looks to us from here as if this issue may produce critical point in our relations with Saudi Arabia and might lead to situation similar to that in Iran in 1950 and 1951. Judging by tone of Saudi communications to ARAMCO it would seem quite possible that King would declare ARAMCO concession nationalized on being confronted with clear-cut, flat refusal of company to deal with Onassis. King's decision to take such drastic step might be based on mistaken impression that he could find others to exploit and sell oil for him and that by dispensing with American collaboration he can make himself hero of the Arab world.

On the other hand, it seems possible King is engaged in a species of bluff, encouraged by past successes in wringing concessions from ARAMCO and past acquiescence by USG in such concessions. If King has decided to dispense with American companies we should of course utilize every means to make him and his advisers realize disastrous effect this would have on his position, his government, and country.

The secretary of state directed Wadsworth to ask the king and his advisers to consider what their situation might be after "even one year" without oil revenues! And, more ominously, to bear in mind what had happened to Iran's Dr. Mossadeq when he nationalized Iran's oil industry. (He was toppled, in a CIA-assisted coup, in favor of the young Shah Muhammad Reza Pahlevi.) Dulles was convinced that the king, apprised of "the facts," would have second thoughts about the Onassis connection and reconcile his passion for independence with a sense of realism. He also suspected that Ari, feeling the heat from ARAMCO, with many of his tankers laid up as he found himself being squeezed out of more and more of his regular contracts with other oil companies around the world, had already lost his appetite for the great Saudi adventure and was "probably anxious to squirm out."

Although Foster Dulles maintained a moralistic public stance in his conduct of United States foreign affairs, his brother was prepared to "fight fire with fire" in an imperfect world. It was not without some significance, perhaps, that although Wadsworth was told to point out the universal disapproval of Saudi Arabia's blatant abrogation of ARAMCO's concession, he was not to make too much of this aspect since "resolution Onassis matter may not, repeat not, depend primarily on legalities involved." Shortly after this message to Riyadh, Robert Maheu flew to London for talks with Niarchos.

The two men met in the shipowner's suite at Claridge's. It was a long meeting, which began with kippers at breakfast and ended over a bottle of cognac in the early hours of the following day. Niarchos said that he regretted the alienation the deal had caused in the family; *alienation* was a word he used a lot, recalled one of his aides at the session: "The grief and tragedies it causes transcend time and change history," he told them. Alan Campbell-Johnson later recalled: "Onassis was like a younger brother going beyond the family compact to play the game; they were rivals within an agreed market, and the danger of the Saudi deal was that it destroyed the agreed market. Niarchos took the view that it was inimical as much to Onassis's interests as it was to his own." During the grueling session at Claridge's a great deal of time was spent considering the Catapodis incident. "Stavros was convinced it was something on which we should capitalize; he wanted to clobber Ari with it; the question was how we could turn it to our advantage," said an aide.

On September 27 at the British consulate in Nice, Catapodis swore a sixteen-page affidavit—"the gospel according to Saint Spyridon," Gratsos called it—accompanied by more than thirty exhibits: letters, memos, cables and photographs of himself, Ari and Tina, Nicolas Cokkinis and his wife, Suleiman and Alireza, taken during the celebrations at Jiddah. Even if only partly true

("I have my truth and Onassis has his," Catapodis told a friend), it was a blow to Ari's badly mauled reputation. Catapodis's accusations, picturing Ari as an unscrupulous wheeler-dealer who signed contracts with disappearing ink, were bound to sow suspicion and distrust within the Saudi ranks; he itemized graft to palace aides including a $350,000 rakeoff to Finance Minister Suleiman. Bribes are a fact of life in desert kingdoms; it was the tenor rather than the details of the affidavit that worried Ari most: he was out for himself and didn't give a damn about the Americans or the Saudis was the underlying message on every page. Even after the agreement had been signed, he was still looking to do a deal with ARAMCO "whereby he would get either a large amount of money or some other valuable concessions in return for canceling his agreement with the Saudi Arabian government," claimed Catapodis. When he "vigorously objected" to this ploy, Ari allegedly replied that he "did not care very much to do business with the Arabs" and that was why he had insisted that a no-penalty clause for nonperformance of the agreement be incorporated in the contract.

Maybe Catapodis was scared of the political repercussions, as he claimed; maybe he did advise Ari against such a vast international intrigue and warned him not to mess with ARAMCO, as he claimed; and perhaps Ari had imperialist impulses—"He told me that he knew exactly what he was doing, and that he felt confident that, in the end, he would play an important role in the development of the natural resources in Saudi Arabia, which ultimately, would make him the richest and most powerful man in the world." And maybe Bob Maheu believed every word of it when he took a copy of the affidavit to Niarchos.

It was clear that Niarchos tasted victory as he read the document aboard the *Creole*, his sleek black-hulled schooner anchored off Athens. Although some of Catapodis's claims were hard to swallow, others had the ring of truth. Ari had shown his wariness of getting into bed with governments when he turned down Eva Perón's proposal to join up with Mandl and Dodero; he knew that once his Saudi Arabian Maritime Company had trained Saudis to run the show there would be nothing to stop the Arabs from grabbing the lot, just as the Perón regime had grabbed Dodero's empire in 1949. "The probability is that Catapodis was nailing it on the line when he claimed that Ari had signed the deal knowing that the Yanks would never buy it, but with that gun at their heads, would be forced to do a deal increasing his market share of ARAMCO's tanker contracts," says a London shipping analyst who knew Ari well.

Niarchos agreed that Maheu should take the affidavit to Saudi Arabia and acquaint the king with its contents. Only there was a problem, and it was an ominous one: the Saudis would grant entry visas; applications for exit visas could be made only in Jiddah, and were issued at the king's convenience. Since some of the most powerful men in Saudi Arabia were named in the affidavit, Maheu was not disposed to hanging around the city once he had delivered a copy to the royal palace. To smooth his path to the palace, he took along Karl Twitchell, the American geologist who had helped bring together the American oil companies and King Ibn Saud in 1933 and was still a respected and trusted figure in Saudi Arabia. Although he had both CIA and State Department approval, neither would overtly support the operation; he was, he would later claim, permitted to communicate with Niarchos through United States intelligence channels.*

A few days after his arrival, Maheu was invited to "make a presentation" to the king's confidential advisers—at the villa of finance minister Sheikh Abdullah al Suleiman. The Saudis listened politely, sipping coffee; their faces wore expressions to which he had no key. Their silence disturbed him; it was the silence that comes after a whistle has been blown. Afterward, he was told that he would be contacted the following day at his hotel.

It did not especially trouble the king that his ministers were on the take. His regime was already "riddled with corruption and racked with scandals that were the talk of the Middle East."† In fact, Maheu's mission suited his purpose perfectly. His appointment of Mohammed Abdullah Alireza as minister of commerce had upset many members of the House of Saud (with some five hundred princes in direct line, family consensus was always a constraining factor); there had been murmurs of dissent in the corridors of the palaces of Riyadh. And although he resented the State Department's interference in Saudi's sovereign affairs, Dulles's strictures had caused him to think hard. Since the Catapodis affidavit conveniently named both Alireza and Suleiman, his chief negotiator in the Onassis deal, he could kill two birds with one stone. Maheu was encouraged to leak the Catapodis affidavit to the European press. "Europeans take the matter of baksheesh more seriously than we do, and we shall feel constrained to respect their Western sensibilities," explained a palace aide, hand-

* *Niarchos's affinity with the CIA is known to be close: the agency regards him as "a useful and willing informant," claims Brian Freemantle in* CIA: The "Honorable" Company, *New York: Stein and Day, 1984.*
† Power Play, *Leonard Mosley, Random House, New York, 1973.*

ing the American his exit visa and a reservation on the next flight to London.

In October, Ari was summoned to Riyadh by the king and told that Suleiman was out. He was a man of the old politics ("as was proved by his having been caught," Ari later recalled) and had no role in modern Saudi Arabia. "The future blots out the past," the king said and declared that there were many things in the Jiddah Agreement which displeased him and were causing unpleasant-nesses between his country and its longtime business partner and friend ARAMCO. He wanted "a just peace," and unless Ari was willing and able to renegotiate the agreement directly with ARAMCO, the case must go to arbitration, he said. Meanwhile, the chairman of the board and his executives were already in Jiddah and prepared to discuss the situation with him immediately. Ari was shaken by this development. With Suleiman gone and the king's appetite for the agreement no longer what it was he had no hole card. He still tried to make a deal. He would abandon the monopolistic clauses if ARAMCO guaranteed that a fixed percent-age of Saudi oil would be carried by his tankers. The Americans had him on the run.

"ARAMCO has yielded nothing in substance or in principle and has gained valuable Royal assurance that, whatever be result arbitration, Saudi-ARAMCO relations will continue on basis full cooperation," Ambassador Wadsworth cabled the State Depart-ment that evening, adding in a seizure of undiplomatic candor: "Onassis, when finally pinned down on rates issue, has weaseled and outsmarted himself."

9

The fox knows many things—the hedge-hog one big one.

ARCHILOCHUS

KILLED ALMOST only blue whales today," a German factory hand aboard the *Olympic Challenger* wrote in his diary on September 7, 1954, a month before the open season, off the west coast of South America. "Woe if this leaks out." Whaling was Bruno Schlaghecke's living, yet the greed of the expedition, the killing of so many small sperm whales, many of which had not even grown teeth, made him feel "inwardly dumb and empty." On October 22, he wrote: "Shreds of meat from the 124 whales killed yesterday are still lying on the deck. Scarcely one of them was full grown. Unaffected and in cold blood everything is killed that comes before the gun."

The slaughter meant nothing to Ari except in terms of profits and adventure. He never questioned the ethics of the expedition; the whales were there for the taking. It was merely a matter of beating the opposition and grabbing as many as possible. His first expedition in 1950 had netted "a very nice" $4.2 million. "Whaling is the biggest dice game in the world," he said, ignoring the fact that he was playing with loaded dice. The Norwegians suspected Hjalmar Schacht's hand behind his success. It was Schacht who had created the German fleet in 1936 when he compelled the Anglo-Dutch Unilever group, the world's biggest single buyer of whale oil, to finance the building of the Nazi fleet by blocking the company's German profits and threatening an exemplary reduction of its margarine quota. His involvement in Ari's Saudi scheme

139

did nothing to allay suspicions that the ex-Nazi was also his whaling majordomo.

The suspicion that surrounded Ari was augmented by the controversy and complexity of his activities. "ARAMCO, Monaco, Warren Burger, Catapodis, King Saud . . . he had so many problems, I think he found a simple primitive hairy-chested kind of satisfaction in his whaling expeditions," an aide said later on. The season of 1954 also presented a new dimension of risk. At the Santiago Conference on the Exploitation and Conservation of the Maritime Species in the South Pacific, Peru had extended its territorial waters to two hundred miles, within which it would exercise "military, administrative and physical jurisdiction." The United States, Britain and Norway were among the maritime nations that protested; apart from a few shouting matches with United States tuna fishers that had strayed inside the area, it seemed unlikely that it would ever be seriously defended by the Peruvians.

While his fleet was still making its way through the Panama Canal toward the South Pacific, the Peruvian press launched a vitriolic campaign against "Onassis the whaling pirate." The leading Lima newspaper *La Nacion* warned that his planned proximity to Peruvian waters must not go unpunished: "If he persists he must be brought to book and his ships must be seized." Gratsos feared that the attack was less than spontaneous. "Washington was gunning for him, and we'd had a taste of what the CIA was capable of. He had upset powerful people." However, Ari's ships were sailing under the Panamanian flag, and Panama was a protégé of the United States; Washington regarded the Canal Zone as its own backyard. "None of those dagos are going to mess with Panama because it would be like pissing on Uncle Sam's shoes," he said. "And, of course, he was right, although I still thought he had to move carefully down there, and take plenty of cover," Gratsos recalled. In spite of his outward confidence, Ari did take notice of Gratsos's warning, and a few days later ordered Captain Wilhelm Reichert, a former German navy officer commanding the *Olympic Challenger* and her sixteen killer ships to keep outside the two-hundred-mile limit, the richest grounds, where he had planned to hunt until the Antarctic season opened in January.

"Today production surpassed 60,000 barrels, an output never before recorded," the compulsive diarist Schlaghecke noted on October 31. "More whales are continually coming in, sperm whales, blue whales, fin, humpback. . . ." More than 50 percent of the blue whales caught, and 96.4 percent of the sperm whales, were under the permitted minimum size; and the total catch of 580 baleen whales had been taken from inside an international protection zone. "This time nothing will stop them," wrote Bruno Schlaghecke.

President Manuel Odria was attending a cocktail party on November 15 with members of his cabinet and the Peruvian naval chief of staff, Adm. Guillermo Tirado, at the Palacio de Gobierno in Lima when he was informed of a Hamburg newspaper claim that the Onassis fleet was violating the two-hundred-mile limit and that the German seamen were treating "with amusement and contempt" the Peruvian naval presence in the area. Within hours, four of the killer ships were boarded by Peruvian marines and ordered to Paita, north of Lima. In the early hours of the following morning aboard the factory ship (380 miles off the coast, it would later be claimed, although since its log book and charts had been dumped overboard in a weighted bag, nobody will ever be sure), Reichert was astonished when a Peruvian bomber appeared overhead and ordered him to head for Lima. He signaled full steam ahead for the open sea. Machine-gun fire raked the deck and a warning stick of bombs exploded across his bow. "We are being bombed and strafed by Peruvian planes," the *Olympic Challenger* radioed company headquarters in Panama before surrendering to a boarding party from the destroyer *Aguirre*.

In Paris four days later, Spyridon Catapodis called a press conference at the Hotel George V to announce that he had filed suit in criminal court charging that "by various fraudulent maneuvers" Aristotle Onassis had swindled him out of two hundred thousand dollars in commissions and his share of the spoils of the Jiddah Agreement. Ari dismissed him as "a peddler of deals" who was being used as a front by a scourge of powerful rivals to discredit his name and reputation: "These accusations are a part of the propaganda that has been going on ever since the [Jiddah] agreement was published, with the sole purpose of jeopardizing the agreement," he said in New York. Disappearing ink, indeed! How could anyone believe such rubbish? Yet people did.

In the Federal District Court of New York on November 23, the Justice Department filed suit against Ari and nine associates, including his sister Merope Konialidis, a board member of one of the indicted companies, for twenty million dollars, the calculated earnings from sixteen United States surplus ships, which had allegedly been acquired unlawfully. For the first time, he started to take seriously Gratsos's conviction that Washington and Peru were acting in alliance. Ari said with a kind of incensed pride, "It's got to be some kind of record for two countries to declare war on one man."

Five of his ships had been seized and four hundred of his seamen were imprisoned in Peru; the rest of his fleet had fled back to Balboa, Panama. Yet those who knew him well and who saw him in those days were puzzled by his reaction to the crisis. There was "a calmness about him that is often the prerogative of a good poker player or somebody with a secret," thought Graham Stanford, who would later write an authorized but heavily bowdlerized version of Ari's life for the *News of the World*, Britain's most popular Sunday newspaper. Ari did have a secret: he was being bombed all the way to the bank. He had protected his whaling fleet with a palisade of policies against all possible hazards, including a war-risk clause covering seizure for a sum of up to fifteen million dollars. He had also insured against any interruption of the expedition to the tune of thirty thousand dollars a day; a third policy insured against loss should his fleet fail to reach the Antarctic before the opening of the season. Taking the risk, Lloyd's of London laid off a mere 10 percent in the United States and foreign markets. "The view was taken that nobody down there would go as far as to attack a ship flying the Panamanian flag, knowing Washington's policy toward Panama. It was a very bad misjudgment by us and a very good one by Mr. Onassis," a Lloyd's underwriter later admitted.

The Peruvian attack caused a seismic shift in public opinion: one week after being damned in Paris as a big-time swindler, and indicted in New York by the Justice Department, Ari found himself an almost heroic figure. In London, *The Times* pondered: "Other shipping interests may well be grateful to Mr. Onassis for involuntarily bringing to a head a situation against which most of the major maritime powers have already made vehement protest. ... Whether this [Panamanian] flag is the oriflamme of the freedom of the seas, as Mr. Onassis maintains, or is indistinguishable from the Jolly Roger, which is the Peruvian view, depends at the moment on whose eye is set to the telescope."

He summoned Tina to London to be by his side. He knew that her presence gave him a touch of class, although they both recognized that their life together increasingly lacked meaning for them. "I'm simply part of the background, a spear carrier in Ari's latest drama," she explained her presence in London to friends. A lot of women in her position would not have been so pliant; she seemed to have no vanity at all in this sense. Or perhaps her hubris was in her detachment, her ability neither to sanction nor spurn him. "My role was simply to be around, like an expensive scent," she later told Lady Carolyn Townshend in a tone that had no complaint in it. She was there when he gave a press conference in his suite at Claridge's (the Claridge, as he would always call it) to condemn Peru's "tropical madness." The press treated him like a movie star, or a celebrity who might shortly be in jail.

• •

The complexity and multiplicity of the war being waged against Ari had escalated to a pitch where it was impossible to break down its individual components. On December 14, the day after a fine of fifty-seven million Peruvian soles, about $2.9 million, had been paid by Olympic Whaling in Lima, the check signed by Ari, the cash donated by Lloyd's, he begged off everything and with Tina and the children flew to the south of France, and their first Christmas aboard the *Christina*. He knew that his dream of creating a Saudi-Onassis superfleet was over. The row with ARAMCO was going to arbitration in Zurich in the new year, but that was a formality; he had been forced to recognize the limits of the possible: "I played for high stakes and lost." He had made up his mind to diversify out of his tanker base; his acquisition of Monte Carlo was a start. While his mind had been almost completely on the Saudi deal, Monaco had been mentioned only peripherally. Now he would turn that "sorry-ass town into something very tasty." As they toasted in 1955 at the New Year's Eve ball at the Hotel de Paris, Gratsos said to him: "It was some year, wasn't it, though?" After a long silence, Ari grinned. "It had its moments," he said.

There was not a single quality that His Serene Highness Prince Rainier III and Aristotle Socrates Onassis had in common. "If he had not been quite so useful, Onassis might have been a perfect person for the prince to cut dead," a Rainier equerry recalled. Rainier, who had succeeded to the throne of Monaco in 1949, at the age of twenty-seven, had a vain look; his appearance hid a genuine shyness. Educated in England (Stowe) and Switzerland (Le Rosey), he had joined the French army in 1944 and won the croix de guerre. Although he was a fine athlete with a weakness for fast cars, he was also indecisive, suspicious and a man with few friends. With a civil list of a mere $150,000 a year, he was always in need of funds to maintain his expensive tastes, and those of the pretty French actress Gisèle Pascal.

In contrast Ari was a gregarious, ambitious man; a man physically past his best yet still intimidatingly sure of himself. ("I can hold my own in any rough-and-tumble they can think up," Ari had told Rainier during the difficult times in 1954.) Rainier's initial enthusiasm for Ari had waned, perhaps because he sensed in Ari's arrogance a narcissism as regnant as his own. The constant newspaper references to him as the uncrowned king of Monte Carlo, and the power behind the throne, niggled the imperial pride. But if the honeymoon was brief, it was also productive. Three new floors and a spectacular penthouse restaurant were to be started at the renovated Hotel de Paris; a concrete floor was to be laid in the deepened harbor; thousands of tons of golden sand had been ordered to dress up the meager beaches.

Never far from the surface, though always denied in their early attempts at statesmanship, the friction between the two men was complicated by what seemed to be an extraordinary reversal of their expected roles: the prince wanted to turn Monte Carlo into a Las Vegas–style operation; Ari wanted to restore its lost glory and to create a sanctuary for the rich. No bigger than some Hollywood backlots he had known, Monte Carlo was simply a piece of real estate that he wanted to develop to the hilt with the finest hotels and the most luxurious apartment blocks. He had little time for the casino side of his investment; he considered "that kind of gambling" immoral. "Really, Mr. Onassis," complained Rainier, "I don't need you to tell *me* what is moral or immoral." And Ari replied, "If you're going to be a woman of ill repute and make no money, you might as well be an honest woman."

They got along best when they left each other alone; leaving each other alone was the one thing they could not do. Ari felt fettered by a feudal management, a board dominated by Rainier men he called "the corporate warlords." Yet despite his power of veto, the prince knew that some of his own people regarded him increasingly as the throne behind the power, and instanced the way Ari expressed himself in language that often lacked delicacy and respect ("You must be confusing me with somebody who gives a shit," he once interrupted Monaco's minister of finance). Yet somehow the mismatch worked. The chronic postwar losses were halted; in 1955 the SBM paid a dividend for the first time since World War II.

Monte Carlo, Ari was fond of saying, will always be prosperous so long as there are three thousand rich men in the world. Having discovered the pull of show business friendships through his youthful fling with Claudia Muzio, he began personally enticing many of those three thousand names to Monte Carlo. Although the prince set no store by actors, he could not help but be impressed by the new sense of excitement and glamor they brought to the principality. Although he might not have known the word, he understood the value of "hype." Ari's parties, especially his parties aboard the *Christina*, "were as compulsive as Gatsby's," said Hollywood mogul Darryl Zanuck, a frequent guest. It was nothing unusual to see on his yacht as many as a dozen international celebrities as well as royalty. When earnings are no longer estimable, it is the excesses of the very rich that finally impinge on the imagination: the Shah's greed; Getty's frugality; Howard Hughes's hiddenness. And Ari's showmanship.

Nowhere was he more auspicious than when he was aboard his yacht. It had cost him over four million dollars to convert the fifty-thousand-dollar 322-foot Canadian frigate to what ex-king Farouk called "the last word in opulence," and another guest described as "the crystallization of Ari's charm." If the taste level of the *Christina* was at times dubious (Marcel Vertes' frescoes of the seasons on the dining-room panels depicted the family in allegorical scenes: Tina ice skating, Alexander and Christina picnicking on a summer's lawn) and sometimes vulgar (bar stools covered with white whale foreskin: "Madame, you are now sitting on the largest penis in the world," Ari informed Greta Garbo), it was never cheap. Modern technology (radar, forty-two-line telephone and telex system, air-conditioning plant, operating theatre and X-ray machine, electronic temperature control to ensure that the water in the swimming pool, the floor of which could be raised to deck level for dancing, and which was decorated with mosaic scenes from Greek mythology, remained a refreshing ten degrees below air temperature) threaded the ship like a nerve system. In addition to his own four-room suite on the bridgedeck, with its sunken blue Siena marble bathtub (a replica of one built for a Minoan king) and Venetian mirrored walls, there were nine luxury suites, each named after a Greek island (Ithaca being the one usually reserved for his very special guests of honor and occupied variously by Garbo, Callas and Jackie Kennedy). "I don't think there is a man or woman on earth who would not be seduced by the sheer shameless narcissism of this boat," said Richard Burton. "I've found that to be so," Ari replied. He had always been drawn to big names. "Celebrities are important to Ari," Tina told a friend. "All his fantasies are connected with them." Sometimes he liked to surprise a guest with a piece of information, an unexpected insight to their world. Margot Fonteyn, the wife of Roberto "Tito" Arias, his Panamanian lawyer, found him charming and a perfect host yet must have had grave reservations about any man who "never went to the theatre or ballet" and preferred to discuss business with her husband in nightclubs at two o'clock in the morning. She was stunned when one evening he began talking knowledgeably about *élévations* and *entrechats, fouettés* and *sur les pointes. Giselle* was his favorite ballet. He had seen Pavlova dance it in Buenos Aires when he was a young man, he said. His eye had been caught by one of the dancers in her company. He did not elaborate.

Monday, June 27, 1955, was a summer's night like any other in Monte Carlo. *A Prize of Gold* was playing at the open-air moviehouse; the roulette wheels were spinning in the casino; people lingered over their drinks at sidewalk cafés. The *Christina* bobbed gently in the harbor, although Ari was in New York; Rainier was incommunicado at his villa near Saint-Jean Cap Ferrat, recovering from an appendectomy. Neither man knew that a catastrophe was imminent. At 10:30 P.M. in a small rectangular room in a building close to the royal palace, Minister of Finance Arthur Crovetto revealed that the principality was on the verge of bankruptcy. The head of one of the oldest families in Monaco, the director of Rainier's cabinet, he knew the moment he began his statement to the urgently convened National Council that his career was finished.

Government funds had traditionally been invested in thirteen banks throughout the state. But for two years, he admitted, one bank alone had been entrusted with the Treasury's deposits: the Société Monegasque de Banque et de Métaux Précieux (Monaco Banking and Precious Metals Company) established in 1949 by Constantine Liambey. Liambey had speculated massively in a television company with Monaco's money—and Crovetto's approval. The company ran into trouble; Crovetto poured a further 900 million Treasury francs into the kitty; in three days on the Paris Bourse the shares tumbled from 33,000 francs to 16,000. The members of the National Council listened to Crovetto's tale with astonishment. No more than a consultative assembly (eighteen leading businessmen elected by the principality's six hundred male voters), the council was openly ignored by the prince and his cabinet. Now Crovetto was pleading with them for 330 million francs to avert the collapse of the state.

They would cover the debt, but the price was high: Crovetto would have to go, along with the rest of Rainier's cabinet and entourage. Rainier resisted fiercely. People could hear the screams in the street outside his villa, reported *Paris Match*. "A hundred years ago, it would not have been their resignations we would be demanding but their heads," the distinguished biologist and vice-president of the council Auguste Medicin told the prince. Although it fell short of usurpation, the council's terms crimped the prince's style. His principality almost bust, his closest advisers removed from office, Rainier was in a pretty mess. "Now who needs lessons in what's moral!" Ari said when he got the news in New York. Yet the crisis was as much his as it was Rainier's. For Monaco needed more than an infusion of cash. He told Gratsos: "They want new blood, not more bucks. Rainier's got to stop worrying about getting his dick wet all the time and find himself a princess to liven up the place."

At the beginning of July, with Tina and some dozen guests, he set off aboard the *Christina* on a cruise to Venice. On Saturday, July 16, returning from a spell at an Italian health spa, Ingeborg Dedichen wrote in her diary: ". . . Venice—Lido horrible—dreadfully hot—depressed, no hotel—'Christina' passed in! Ari walked up deck—could have called—feeling awful—wrote letter—depressed, dined and returned—ah! ah! ah!" And the following day, in the city in which they had first made love twenty-two years before, she wrote poignantly: "No news Ari!—not realy [*sic*] surprised. . . ." Although she could not have known it then, this was to be the last time she would ever see him.

Ari's refusal to acknowledge her note was unkind, a Paris friend who was on the cruise said later. "But his life was fraught with problems enough. He was working doubly hard, worrying about the Monaco crisis, entertaining his guests." Certainly, Mamita's unexpected presence in Venice at that time—a lonely, middle-aged lady who had given him so much, knew so much—disturbed his conscience. "We were to have spent four or five days in Venice, but we left early and very suddenly," remembered a guest. Although Ingeborg's Venice letter has not survived, it is likely to have been similar to a great many she would write, reminding him of all they had been to each other, his promises to always take care of her, and pleading for an increase in her monthly allowance.

In spite of the rueful episode in Venice, Ari returned to Monte Carlo refreshed and with an exciting idea, but first he had several matters with which he had to deal. Among the pressing problems (according to Sir Lionel Heald, the British lawyer counseling him in the ARAMCO dispute) was the question of his own public image. The day he returned to Monaco he sent for Nigel Neilson, a public relations man recommended by the distinguished jurist. A New Zealander, Neilson had had an extraordinary career. He'd been an actor, singer and soldier. In Syria he rode in the last cavalry charge in history; in World War II he fought with the crack Special Air Service and won the Military Cross for gallantry. He was now an account executive (Cheese Bureau, London Stock Exchange) with the J. Walter Thompson organization in London. "He asked me to tell him how I thought he was seen by the public. Before I could answer he held up his hand. 'I'm forgetting my manners. You are my guest. I must not embarrass you. I will tell you what *I* think people say about me. They say I'm a Greek shit with too much money. Am I correct?' I told him that was about the size of it," Neilson later recalled their first meeting. Ari wore white slacks, short-sleeved blue shirt, white-and-tan shoes, and dark sunglasses with heavy black frames. He was smaller than he appeared to be in newspaper photographs; Neilson thought it might be his office ("a cross between a museum and a war room") in the

Old Sporting Club, which made him seem less than average height. The walls were hung with gilt-framed paintings of Onassis tankers; behind his desk a magnetic map showed the disposition of his fleet around the world. "People have very sinister ideas about you," Neilson told him in a voice that had directness as well as humor. Six weeks later, he quit J. Walter Thompson and became Ari's public relations chief.

Neilson was left in no doubt as to what was expected of him. "Boycotted by the Americans over the ARAMCO business (half of his fleet was now idle) Ari had turned his attention to the British companies. Heald told me, 'Your job will be to bring him into the fold, make him persona grata to our people.' " Neilson had fortuitous connections. Through his brother's wife he had a line to Basil Jackson, chairman of British Petroleum. Why, he asked Jackson when the meeting was effected, didn't BP charter Onassis's tankers? Jackson came back to him a few days later: "I've spoken to my directors, and they've all said quite frankly we can't deal with this sort of person." Has any one of them met him personally? Neilson asked. Two of them have, said Jackson. "I asked whether if I were to arrange an invitation to lunch with Ari on his yacht in the south of France, would Jackson accept, so he could judge the man for himself? He said he'd love to."

A few days after Neilson began cleaning up his reputation in London, Ari invited Father Tucker to lunch aboard the *Christina*. It was to be a delicate meeting—a four-eyes session, Ari called it —for Rainier's Vatican-trained chaplain was no admirer of Ari and regarded him as a "claim-jumper, anxious to plant the Panamanian flag atop the palace." However, they shared a similar concern over the bleak state of the Monaco economy; and were both conscious of the fact that if there were no direct male heir to the succession, under the Treaty of Protection the principality would come directly under French rule—including French taxes, French bureaucracy, French military service. Although Rainier was a healthy thirty-three, and enjoying his bachelorhood, what if he were to have an accident? Even now he was somewhere in the Mediterranean, showing no inclination to return: the bank scandal was still a touchy subject in Monaco.

The sixty-three-year-old vinegary American who moved about his parish on a motor scooter and relaxed afternoons on the beach in a clerical-black bathing suit was as at home with martinis as matins, and after a few Gibsons Ari broached the subject he had been thinking about since the Venice cruise. He said he thought that the prince's "symbolic value would accrue wonderfully" if he had a princess. People would sleep more easily in their beds if he were wed, he added. "When God made time, He made plenty of it," the priest replied. "Although he did praise my concern for the people," Ari later recalled the conversation. "I told him that when my time came to go to heaven, I didn't expect to stand on line. I could see he was interested in the marriage business. We talked about this and that. Sip sip. He came back to the subject, saying how difficult it was for Rainier to find a suitable bride [Tucker had more than pastoral clout at court: he had greased the skids, and Gisèle Pascal slid out of favor]. I suggested he look in his own country: an American princess would be romantic and visionary —the way Americans like their dreams. I thought perhaps Marilyn Monroe." Exactly what was said after that is uncertain, although there is no question that Ari felt that he had been given at least a tacit nod, if not Tucker's blessing, to sound out Monroe's feelings about little princes.

When she had married Joe DiMaggio (the baseball idol whom Spyros Skouras had told Ari he resembled physically) Ari had cabled Skouras: "Would like to be in DiMaggio's bed tonight." That marriage was over, and she was seeing Arthur Miller. But what chance would a playwright stand against a prince? "Beautiful women cannot bear moderation," Ari once said. "They need an inexhaustible supply of excess." Only Skouras didn't want to get involved; he had enough problems with Marilyn's professional life without getting mixed up in her private affairs. Her last three pictures had grossed 20th Century Fox twenty-five million dollars; stockholders were demanding that the studio get her into another movie fast. She was in New York, refusing to return to Hollywood until she got a new deal.

Ari called Georges Schlee. The Russian entrepreneur, the lover and mentor of Greta Garbo, had performed some useful services for Ari before. He had organized the invitations and free villas when Ari wanted to decorate Monte Carlo with people who would give it a touch of class. It was Schlee who had introduced Ari to Garbo. Schlee outlined the idea to Gardner ("Mike") Cowles, Jr., the founder-publisher of *Look* magazine and a friend of Monroe's; Cowles relayed the proposition to the star. She was intrigued. A meeting was arranged at Cowles's farmhouse in Connecticut, close to where she was living with Arthur Miller. Schlee and Cowles discussed the proposal with her around the pool. It aroused her keenest attention. She asked two questions, the publisher later recalled. Is he rich? Is he handsome? Cowles had a suspicion that she didn't even know where Monaco was. He asked whether she thought the prince would *want* to marry her. "Give me two days with him, and of course he'll want to marry me," she replied with all the assurance of a lady whose name would always appear above the title. Looks like business at first sight, Schlee reported back. Before the plan got any further, Rainier revealed that he intended to marry another movie actress: Miss Grace Kelly. With her chiseled beauty and subtle sensuality, she was the absolute antithesis of Monroe. She looked as if she had stepped straight out of the Philadelphia Social Register, but her father, John B. Kelly, the son of a farm boy from County Mayo, had been a hod carrier and brick layer before becoming a millionaire contractor. Although Grace had been a movie actress for less than half a dozen years—eleven films, two Academy Award nominations, one Oscar—she had assured her place in Hollywood history with her performance in Alfred Hitchcock's *To Catch a Thief*, in which she was cast as a coolly elegant heiress obsessed by a Riviera jewel thief, played by Cary Grant.

As Ari watched from the *Christina* the entrance of Grace Kelly (trailed by five private detectives, twenty MGM executives, seventy-three relatives, bridesmaids, hangers-on and the world's press), he turned to a friend and said: "A prince and a movie queen. It's pure fantasy." It was not a dismissive remark. He understood perfectly that a town like Monte Carlo needs fantasies, the way Detroit needs engines and Iowa needs corn. Socialites and jewel thieves, movie stars and gate-crashers, princelings and con-men were converging on the Riviera playground. Sirens screamed, Klaxons honked. On the palace ramparts cannons fired a twenty-one-gun salute, fireboats sent up sprays of water. A quayside band played "Love and Marriage" as Ari's private plane blitzed the harbor with thousands of red and white carnations. "But what I remember most vividly," a guest aboard the *Christina* on that April morning in 1956 later said, "was Tina in her English voice reciting a little poem she'd probably learned during her Heathfield days. A couple of lines I remember were, 'Life is a journey: on we go/Through many a scene of joy and woe.' " Ari had certainly had his own moments of joy and woe in the past months.

At the International Whaling Commission meeting in Moscow, the Japanese had delivered a telling attack on Ari's illegal killing methods. He dismissed it as a collection of rumor, innuendo and lies invented by jealous rivals, and appeared to have ridden out the storm when in January the *Norwegian Whaling Gazette* published irrefutable proof of the Japanese charges. Together with reports from the *Olympic Challenger*'s chemist and chief engineer, they produced affidavits sworn by seven crewmen; logbooks, kill tables, photographs and personal diaries added weight to accusations of ecological butchery and cover-ups by bribed Panamanian inspectors. It was clear that his fleet had inflicted massive damage on whale stocks. The Norwegians got a court order to seize sixty-three hundred tons of whale oil discharged in Hamburg by one of his tankers; the *Olympic Challenger* and her cargo were impounded in Rotterdam. "Let's get out," he told Gratsos after the courts had blocked a slippery transfer of the detained factory ship to another of his companies. He had been preparing the ground since the Peruvian raid, and, at the end of March, Gratsos flew to Tokyo for talks with the Kyokuyo Hogei Kaisha Whaling Company. Twenty-four hours later he placed a call to Ari in Monte Carlo. It was two o'clock in the morning, and he was in a nightclub off the Ginza when the call came through. He told Ari that he had done a deal for $8.5 million. It was several million more than Ari had expected. He could hear the music in the background. "Where the hell are you, Costa?" he demanded. Gratsos said he was celebrating. Ari said, "You're drunk." Gratsos confessed he was getting there. Ari's whaling adventure, born in a Hamburg bar, was buried in a Tokyo nightclub.

Meanwhile, the Catapodis case, dismissed in Paris for lack of evidence, had moved to New York. Ari was in a confident mood: "There isn't a country in the world with any pretense of justice, in which such an accusation, supported by such evidence, will not be laughed out of court." At the pretrial hearing he set about raising the suspicion of criminal conspiracy. Catapodis was only too willing to confirm his affinity with Stavros Niarchos, whom he described as "a friend and neighbor." But Niarchos was anxious to keep his distance from the man Ari had branded "a peddler of deals"; a man who was not above a little pimping for his rich Arab friends. The south of France is a village, Niarchos retorted: "You see people a lot. You may see Catapodis in the casino. If I used to go to the casino every night, he may have been there. On the other hand, we never had any serious discussion. Nowadays a lot of people say he's my friend, and that depends on what you call a friend. In my theory, the definition of friendship is entirely different and his frame of mind may be different. By being only your compatriot, being of the same race, he may have called me a friend. As far as I was concerned, he was not my friend. I want to put it that way."

Closely questioned by Ari's attorney, Charles Tuttle, Niarchos agreed that his company had hired Maheu in connection with the Saudi deal and that before taking off on his mission to Jiddah, the Washington investigator had given Niarchos a copy of the Catapodis affidavit. It was clear that Catapodis's case was in trouble.

But before Tuttle could move in for the kill, Niarchos announced
that serious security matters were involved: "The whole thing is
coming down to a wall," he said, "and I would like to be clarified
by Washington whether I'm going to answer these questions or
not." Four days later, Spyridon Catapodis abandoned the action.

Although he had won, Ari also knew that he had been outsmarted. His deepest suspicions had been confirmed, and there
was nothing he could do about it. He said, "Never before in the
history of business was so much power combined to fight and
destroy an individual." While the psychic and financial cost of the
Jiddah Agreement was high, there was a hint that having reminded him who was boss, the oil majors were prepared to call a
truce. ARAMCO affiliate Socony-Vacuum Oil Company chartered
the *Al-Malik Saud Al-Awal* to carry oil from its Persian Gulf terminal to Philadelphia. (This piece of the action was what he had
always wanted, but the charter had also polished off his plan to
file an antitrust suit against ARAMCO.) And shortly after Nigel
Neilson had cajoled the BP board into meeting him ("I hear you
chaps have got something against me," Ari came to the point at
the lunch in a private suite at the Savoy. "I'd like to know exactly
why you think I'm such a bad hat"), the British oil giant chartered
its first Onassis tanker.

In Washington the horse-trading with Warren Burger came to
a sudden end. "I'm not going to back down, Mr. Burger. I'll litigate
for the rest of my life if I have to because I know I'm going to win,"
he had warned the assistant attorney general at the outset. And
now, in return for guilty pleas on the part of his corporations, and
a press statement from Justice "all dressed up to look like a federal
scalp," the criminal charges against him were dropped. Ari convinced himself that he had won at least a moral victory over
Burger, a man whom he disliked profoundly. The evening the
terms were agreed on, Ari, surrounded by his aides, as platitudi-
nous as a Greek chorus, dined at Harvey's restaurant in Washington. Across the room sat J. Edgar Hoover and Clyde Tolson.
Restrained by Gratsos from going across to their table and "ripping into them," he settled for a cold-eyed stare. "This is a dumb
town. In England I would have been knighted for what I did. Here
the bastards indict me," he said. A great deal of his corporate maze
had been exposed by Burger's investigation (forty agents had been
assigned to the case) and Gratsos feared that Ari's notoriety
"would attract unwelcome interest" from government agencies in
other countries. "I don't give a rat's ass," Ari almost shouted, his
eyes on Hoover. "The best deals never stand up to moral scrutiny.
Every businessman and politician in the world knows that." A
longtime aide said later, "Ari could tough it out with the best, but

I don't think he ever lost the psychological scars from that war with Washington."

In a memorandum dated January 4, 1956, Burger thanked Hoover for the FBI's "splendid cooperation and excellent work in investigating the complicated financial and business arrangements involved" and set out a summary of the settlement:

> Under the terms of the settlement agreement, the government will receive $7,000,000, which will include the payment of $6,600,000 in cash and the release by the Onassis interests of claims approximating $400,000. An additional sum of approximately $500,000 will be paid to make up arrears in principal and interest on outstanding Maritime Administration mortgages against some of the vessels and to bring payments on the mortgages to a current status. The settlement agreement also requires the domestic corporations which own the vessels to be reorganized in such manner as the Department deems necessary to insure American citizen ownership and control of the vessels.

Ari assigned 75 percent of the stock in Victory Carriers, United States Petroleum Carriers, Western Tankers and the Trafalgar Steamship Company to his American-born children, Christina and Alexander, and their interests were put into a trust controlled by Grace National Bank of New York until they were twenty-one. He retained the remaining 25 percent interest through Ariona, a Panamanian corporation. As soon as the trust was established, taking advantage of the Maritime Administration's "trade-out and build program," permitting shipowners to deregister existing United States flag carriers in return for new building commitments, fourteen of its twenty-one United States–registered ships were transferred to a flag of convenience. In return, the trust undertook to build three new tankers in United States yards, and orders were placed with Bethlehem Steel.

The fine was to be paid in installments over five years. According to one Washington lawyer it was "all done with mirrors— some computing jugglery designed to make Justice look good." Certainly that is what Ari wanted the world to believe, as his ego could not have it any other way, but privately he accepted defeat: "Pay the man the two dollars," he closed the episode dismissively. His visits to the States were to become fewer and briefer.

Tina's presence in Monte Carlo in the spring of 1956 had been unusual. Spring meant England: spring in England, summer in the Mediterranean, autumn in America, winter in Switzerland, partying nearly every night. Her predictable patterns and Ari's erratic wandering disguised the fact that they had decided to live

apart from one another, except for the occasions when they acted
as happy host and hostess: a simple deception since they often had
no more than a passing acquaintance with their guests ("I like to
surround myself with nice guys who didn't finish last," Ari had
once summed up his ideal dinner companions).

Their pragmatic concept of marriage certainly predated the
afternoon in 1957 Tina caught Ari in bed at the Château de la Croë
with Jeanne Rhinelander, an old American school friend of hers
who lived in nearby Grasse. It was the end of the château ("Something as bad as bad can be spoiled that lovely house"), which
Niarchos promptly bought for Eugénie, and the beginning of the
end of her marriage. "He never gave me my due in his life," she
told Lady Carolyn Townshend. "He never recognized my contribution to his life." The marriage had been a mistake, made when
she was very young and when she acted almost entirely under the
influence of a determined mother, she told friends. And she would
remark when not entirely sober: "Like Mark Anthony, Ari is a
colossal child, capable of conquering the world, incapable of re-
sisting a pleasure." She knew before the Rhinelander episode that
he slept with other women. She could always guess which women,
she claimed. And she often knew when, she said.

She had inherited from her father an acquisitive temperament
("With the anticipation of a party, a dress or a simple diamond to
occupy her, Tina is happy," Ari said), and now in revenge took
from life whatever pleasures it held out to her. Her affairs were
numerous. "Her susceptibility to handsome men was second only
to her susceptibility to extremely handsome men," said a friend.
Yet she told a French actor whom she had taken up with some
ardor, "The lack of happiness in my life, is hidden by a great deal
of pleasure." Ari's conjectures became certain when he received
an extremely detailed dossier of a week she had spent with a lover
in Rio de Janeiro. Yet the wound of infidelity had been not to his
heart, but to his self-esteem. Now into his fifties, drinking hard, he
was filled with all the anxieties of male menopause. It was loneliness that was gaining on him now. "We are just two vulnerable
people, Johnny, we're just two grown-up kids with damaged illusions," he told Meyer shortly after the Château de la Croë drama.
"The terrible things people who are married, who profess to love
each other and have children together, do to each other." Meyer
felt that Ari's vulnerability was exposed by this situation, as by no
other. "I said, 'Shit, Ari, you didn't marry her for the qualities you
look for in a nun.' I was sorry for both of them. Her indiscretions
were understandable, they were of no real significance. For both
their sakes, I didn't want to see the marriage go out the window."

But the course of events could not be changed. Moreover,

there were signs that Ari was still prey to the alarming outbursts of psychotic behavior that had first surfaced with Ingeborg in New York. An eyewitness to one of his fits of violence was Alan Brien. Just down from Oxford, embarking on a journalistic career, he had been invited to stay at the Château de la Croë to write an article on Ari for the now-extinct English magazine *Illustrated*. The assignment had been set up by Randolph Churchill in order to enable Brien to ghost a profile he himself had been commissioned to write for *Life*. Ari and Randolph had established a close relationship, and used it to their mutual advantage. "There were obvious difficulties in Randolph asking Onassis questions as an equal, there was a certain amount of protocol involved between them, whereas I was just the unknown hack who could ask whatever," recalls Brien.

Unable to sleep on his second night at the château, in the early hours he went downstairs to the library to find a book to read. Returning to his room, he heard the sounds of physical violence coming from Onassis's suite. He recognized Ari's voice, screaming, "You whore, you whore," and Tina sobbing uncontrollably. The door to the suite was ajar, and Brien could see shadows on the wall—"a man hitting out, the shape of a woman covering up." It would have been a delicate moment for any guest, but it was especially so for a young man who knew that his presence was tolerated only as a favor to Randolph. "But humanity overrides all things, I suppose. I knew that I was going to have to stop it," Brien recalls his dilemma. "I was about to enter—I'd decided to go in and say, 'You can throw me out of your house tonight if you like, but I cannot stand by and allow you to beat up a woman'— when they threw their arms around each other and began kissing passionately. They moved into the bedroom, and clearly they went off to bed to fuck. I've never forgotten that scene, the menacing shadows . . . it was like an Orson Welles movie; even the château could have been modeled after Kane's Xanadu."

At twenty-seven, the mother of two children, Tina's body still possessed an adolescent svelteness. Her new McIndoe nose ("a little like Pinocchio's," she thought) acquired at the London Clinic after a car accident in Switzerland, gave her the *gamine* look that was coming into fashion. Although privately amusing and capricious, she could also be distant and guarded, as if cheated of some early trust and determined never to be taken in again. "She had a sort of fear of losing her soigné air in front of strangers," a girlfriend said of her public image. It was a useful defense against the snubs of the Monacan society matrons who found her position not so grand as she herself imagined it to be. Society was her passion, and her place in it was secure enough in London, Paris and New

York; only Monaco was not big enough for both her and Princess
Grace. The principality became "the dead zone—it is where one
day we will find we buried our marriage," she told Ari a long time
before they finally did.

But even when she knew that they would never have a good
life together again, Tina wanted to see Ari established in the eyes
of the people she most admired and never ceased to encourage his
social climbing. "If you want to be esteemed, you must mix with
estimable people," she told him many times. Now on Monday
evening, January 16, 1956, on his journey to La Pausa, millionaire
publisher Emery Reves's villa in Roquebrune, high on the moun-
tainside above Cap Martin, Ari reflected with satisfaction how
galled Rainier would be when he discovered that he was about to
meet the most famous Englishman in the world: Sir Winston
Churchill.

Churchill was Ari's big fish. He had been after him for years.
Now, through his friendship with the statesman's son, Randolph,
he had finally got an invitation to dine with the great man at the
villa that the duke of Westminster had built for his mistress Coco
Chanel in the twenties. (Ari treasured such details.) Born in Hun-
gary, Emery Reves had known Churchill since the 1930s when he
had handled the syndication rights of many of his articles. After
the war, he acquired the foreign rights to Churchill's war memoirs
and his *History of the English-Speaking Peoples,* making a great
deal of money for his client and also for himself. La Pausa was
filled with one of the finest impressionist art collections anywhere
in the world in private hands. It included nine Renoirs, four Cé-
zannes and three Degases, together with a display of porcelain, old
glass, furniture and fifteenth-century Spanish rugs that few mu-
seums could match. Churchill, with a team of secretaries, butler,
Scotland Yard detective, and occasionally members of his family,
was a regular houseguest.

The mistress of La Pausa was Wendy Russell, a stunningly
beautiful woman, a former New York model, many years younger
than Reves, whose wife she would become. She was astonished by
Ari's appearance. He looked, she recalled, "absolutely dreadful, in
an ill-fitting suit, clutching a bouquet of long-stemmed roses almost as big as himself." (Not the correct thing to do at all: he
should have sent the flowers either in advance or the following
day; as it was, the butler did not know what he should do with
them. Later Miss Russell told him to give them to the servants.)
When they shook hands she felt that his palm was very wet. "He
said, 'I'm a nervous wreck, Mrs. Reves.' I said, 'I am not Mrs.
Reves. I am Wendy Russell. You may call me Wendy.' " She led
him into the salon. "He took a couple of drinks rather quickly"

before Churchill arrived. Churchill was depressed; his wife, Clementine, was in the hospital. Egged on by Randolph and Churchill's private secretary, Anthony Montague Browne, a frequent visitor to the *Christina*, Wendy Russell had decided that Ari might be just the person to snap "the Former Naval Party" (his wartime code name) out of his black mood. She might also have been influenced by the warm profile of Onassis that Randolph had written for the *London Evening Standard:* "As well as Greek, he speaks fluent Spanish, French and English . . . he is a born orator with a poetic sense . . . just as his listener is caught by the spell, he will suddenly bring the whole edifice tumbling down by a deliberate piece of comic bathos." Ari had gone out of his way to ingratiate himself with Randolph, and like almost every other journalist who wrote about him at that time, Randolph had succumbed to his generous hospitality; he made him sound cute, a charming host and companion.* "Randolph seemed to miss the hint of hoodlum, the rough customer, behind those black lenses," said his sister Sarah, who suspected that Ari preferred dark glasses because "he dislikes eye contact." Later she also expressed "grave doubts about any man who wears white shoes with black patches—corespondent's shoes."

The evening did not begin well. Ari greeted the great man with a display of Levantine servility ("He wanted to kiss Sir Winston's hand, used exaggerated grand words," Wendy Russell remembered it afterward—" 'I'm so very honored,' etcetera, etcetera") that annoyed Churchill and embarrassed the other guests. Ari drank quite a lot. There was no evidence of his poetic sense. He seemed to laugh at almost everything, even at serious things: a growling yet curiously hollow laugh that disturbed his hostess. Unfortunately, during a discussion about the Mediterranean island of Cyprus, governed by the British since World War I, and being torn apart by an underground Greek Cypriot terrorist campaign to unite the island with Greece, he vehemently supported the cause of the insurgents, who were blessed and financed by the black-bearded Archbishop Makarios, head of the Greek Orthodox church on the island.† It was a viewpoint calculated to make Churchill, aware of the strategic importance of Britain's military bases on the island, and bitter about the murder of so many British soldiers, very angry indeed.

When he left that night, and Churchill had made it clear that he wanted him to leave, Ari knew that he had done just about

---

* *Randolph was not completely starry-eyed about Ari. "He's a Turk," he told Alan Brien. "He pretends he's a Greek because that was the side to be on."*
† *When the militant archbishop was released from his enforced exile on the Seychelles Islands, Ari sent the* Olympic Thunder *to bear him home in triumph.*

everything wrong. "I have made a fool of myself. I am really sorry," he apologized to Wendy Russell. But his look of total dejection, his apocalyptic tone, touched a nerve of compassion in her. "When are you coming back for dinner?" It was more of an invitation than a question; he stared at her, not knowing what to say. "Why don't you ask us down to the boat?" she suggested kindly, understanding that Churchill was a man who inspired awe. "Would you come?" he asked. It would be the gravest of ill manners not to, she assured him.

Returning to the library, she found Churchill in a rage. "What a bloody fool, what an ass. . . ." It was a delicate moment. "Darling sir," she said, conscious that the decision to invite Ari had been a serious error of judgment (she should never have trusted Randolph; nobody else did), "don't you see, he was saying those things on purpose, to put you in a rage, to rile you up . . . look at you, darling sir, you haven't been this pepped up for a very long time!"

With a worldly eye, Emery Reves saw, as Miss Russell had failed to see, the guile of Ari; he was convinced that "the Greek's earthy exuberance," his "manner of appearing terribly uneducated and naive about social things" was "one big act from beginning to end." He berated Wendy for being taken in. How could she possibly imagine such a man was sincere? He suspected that Ari had debts all over the world. Hungarians have a saying that if you borrow enough, he reminded her, you can always go on borrowing because people won't dare not lend you more money in case the bubble bursts. He was convinced that this was how Ari operated. When the invitation to the *Christina* arrived, they all accepted on condition that there would be no press, a rule that was strictly observed at La Pausa. Nevertheless, when Ari came down the gangway to greet "the biggest fish he had netted so far" ("Oh, my dear, dear friend, welcome, welcome aboard") a swarm of photographers and newsmen were there to get their pictures and file their stories, touching off the legend of a remarkable friendship. Churchill, who had difficulty getting up the gangplank, was visibly upset by the presence of so many cameras. To Emery Reves it was a betrayal of trust for which he never forgave Ari, although the perfectly chilled Dom Perignon and bowls of caviar secured Churchill's immediate absolution. Ari knelt at his feet and spoon-fed him as one would a small child. His entrée to Churchill had come faster and more easily than he had ever thought possible.

CHAPTER 10

*Our country is the country in which we
fare the best.*

ARISTOPHANES

Socially Ari's utmost hopes were realized. He had taken possession of that curious milieu on which he had set his sights. The combination of savvy, charm and mystery that had made him such an effective tycoon had also established him as one of society's most fascinating new celebrities. But he was a celebrity with a lot of problems. Certainly when Rainier returned from his honeymoon "with the posturing spirit of a crusader," although his attitude was picturesque and pleased the people, Ari knew that it meant trouble ahead. The obsequiousness with which Monegasques treated the prince was not one of Ari's accomplishments; only in the most formal situations would he call him Prince Rainier, preferring plain Rainier. Among his own staff Ari pointedly referred to him as Mr. Grimaldi, his family name.* And his stake in SBM gave some credence to his claim that he, rather than Rainier, was the dominant force in the principality. Their polarized positions on Monaco's direction and identity had hardened, and their last meeting before the royal wedding had been their most acrimonious. Ari accused him of avarice. "He won't be satisfied until Monte Carlo is nothing but hotels, tourists and tax shelters from one end to the other." And Rainier told him,

---

* Ari was extremely conscious of titles and rank. He would show visitors to the Château de la Croë a notice in the elevator that had been put up when the duke and duchess of Windsor lived there. Commanding the servants to be silent and never to venture outside their quarters unless summoned, it was signed Her Royal Highness. "Look at that!" he said to the English journalist Alan Brien. "It says Her Royal Highness. She isn't Her Royal Highness at all. The title has never been given. In France she puts on airs."

159

"Mr. Onassis, you were badly brought up. Your money has brought you everything except an education." The situation had not been improved by Ari's newly proclaimed friendship with Churchill. The prince was still sore at the English. The precedent set by the Court of St. James's in dispatching to the Monacan nuptials only a modest representative from its diplomatic service, had inclined all the other European royal houses to a similarly cool response. Egypt's ex-King Farouk had been the most distinguished representative of outside royalty to attend the royal wedding. Yet Ari seemed almost to relish their fights. It defined his sense of being alive; "He lived by instinct and instinct is unrelenting," said one of his French bankers.

But for the moment, Rainier was the least of his worries. The rapprochement with the oil companies had not resulted in the big upturn in charters he had anticipated, and more than half his heavily mortgaged fleet remained idle. Only Costa Gratsos was safe enough to be trusted with his deep anxieties; only his oldest friend knew how much he was hurting. And privately he feared that Ari's instinct for business had finally let him down. "Ari's nose for a deal, when he got it right, was so perfect" that Gratsos (whose own genius came out of scholarship and calculation) thought of him as "a kind of magician." Only now it seemed as if his big trick had gone badly wrong. He needed a miracle to save him. Ironically, the miracle worker turned out to be John Foster Dulles.

On the morning of July 19, 1956, the secretary of state informed the Egyptian ambassador to Washington, Dr. Ahmed Hussein, that, exasperated with President Gamal Abdel Nasser's provocative flirtation with the Soviets, the United States government had decided to withdraw its backing for the Aswan High Dam. A few hours after this decision was announced, Randolph Churchill was on the telephone to Ari, predicting that as a reprisal Nasser would try to nationalize the Suez Canal, the West's lifeline to the East. And Prime Minister Anthony Eden ("the Jerk Eden," Randolph called him) could not let the Egyptians seize the canal without a fight. It was obvious that if there was going to be trouble in the Near East, oil supplies for Europe and the United States would be forced to go around the Cape of Good Hope, a journey twice as long as the Canal route.

Randolph Churchill drank too much and repeated the most scurrilous gossip. Although Ari frequently enjoyed his bibulous company (on one occasion they turned up for a television interview in London so drunk that the producer simply pretended to film their conversation), found his social connections useful and his well-informed prittle-prattle amusing, "Randolph had become a bit of a nuisance: there was no getting rid of him," remembers Nigel Neilson. Nevertheless, Ari listened carefully to what he said. When the Suez war exploded on two fronts in October 1956, an Anglo-French attack against the canal itself and an Israeli thrust across the Sinai Peninsula, Ari was the only major independent shipowner with the best part of his fleet available and deployed to cash in on the rush for vessels to carry oil around the cape. The oil companies that had conspired to squeeze him out of existence ("to zero volume," as a State Department aide later admitted), now fought each other to charter his tankers, forcing up the spot market rate from four dollars a ton to more than sixty dollars.

Ari began making money on a scale unimaginable even in his own grandiose dreams. "Fortune is always on the side of the largest tankers," he had often insisted, and now he was proving it, making a profit of two million dollars on a one-way charter from the Persian Gulf to Europe. The war was brief, but with the canal blocked with wrecked ships, twice as many tankers were needed simply to maintain Western Europe's basic supply of crude oil on the journey around Africa. "The oil companies set out to destroy Ari and in the process made him one of the richest men in the world," said Costa Konialidis. Yet as the Worldscale Index (a kind of Dow Jones barometer of shipping rates) climbed from 220 to a record high of 460, Ari remained peculiarly blind to the fact that the boom could not last forever. By the end of the year, Gratsos was begging him to get out of the spot market and take some of the safer, less lucrative time charters the oil companies were offering. It was hard to convince a man who had made between seventy-five and eighty million dollars on the spot market in less than six months to walk away from the table. "I'm hot, Costa, I'm in front of the parade. I've got the touch, I don't even have to breathe hard. Why the hell should we crap out now?" he argued, his smile full of abrupt violence.

He was convinced that the canal would stay closed for a very long time, possibly years. Alerted by Gratsos, the trustees of Victory Carriers in New York, appointed by the Justice Department under the terms of the settlement, took the initiative and early in 1957 chartered a dozen tankers to Esso on a thirty-nine-month contract. "Ari hit the roof when he found out," remembers a former VC executive. "Costa stayed very calm. I heard him say, 'Tell me about it in three months, Ari.' He had a lot of style as well as all the savvy in the world." The canal reopened in April 1957. The Worldscale Index plummeted through the 100 barrier. "You read it right. I read it wrong," Ari admitted to Gratsos privately. It was not much of an apology to a man who had saved him millions.

He would dismiss the post-Suez slump "as all part of the

game." In vigorous early middle age, he was convinced that his
best years were still to come; he was constantly looking for new
challenges, new battles to fight. And the most recent pie into
which he had stuck his thumb was TAE, the Greek national airline.
He had pulled out no plums. Prime Minister Constantine Karamanlis, whose right-wing National Radical Union party had come
to power in the 1956 elections, determined to harness the wealth
and know-how of the shipping expatriates, had encouraged Ari to
take over the small (twelve DC-3s, one DC-4) loss-making airline
for a mere two million dollars; Niarchos got the contract to build
a major shipyard at Skaramanga on the outskirts of Athens, a deal
Ari very much wanted for himself. "I sometimes feel I'm only kept
going by hatred for that sonofabitch Stavros," he admitted to
Gratsos the morning he learned that his brother-in-law had landed
the shipyard. Still, Skaramanga was a minor disappointment
compared with the prize of owning a national airline—which he
promptly renamed Olympic Airways. Hiding his jubilation, he
proceeded to squeeze, chivy and prize some extraordinarily generous concessions out of a government desperately anxious to encourage more rich expatriates to invest in Greek industry. Told
about what to expect, Karamanlis had ignored the warnings. He
wanted Greece to have a successful airline of international repute,
and Ari was the man who could deliver the goods. But he had
never dealt with anyone quite like him before. In bargains struck
behind closed doors, Ari racked up concession after concession:
compensation by the government for any losses incurred by unofficial strikes; compensation for losses on transatlantic flights; the
right to export profits; exemption from landing fees in Greece; the
right to import capital goods without paying customs duty; a call
on government loans of up to $3.5 million at a fixed interest rate
of 2.5 percent; complete exemption from corporate taxes; a total
ban on transatlantic charters by other airlines. His original
twenty-year monopoly of Greek civil aviation, including the handling and refueling of all foreign airlines, was extended to the year
2006.

They were painful negotiations for the politicians, who
quickly discovered that out of the imbroglios and chaos that Ari
seemed to prefer to straight businesslike negotiation, Ari always
emerged on top. He could change in a moment from an "irresistible cheerfulness to an inexplicable anger." Resistance to his demands merely strengthened his obduracy. " 'What's in it for me?'
That's the only question he ever seems to consider worthwhile
asking," a government negotiator complained. Karamanlis dismissed his behavior as a cost of doing business.

But running a shipping company is not the same thing as

running a passenger airline. And while he was making demands in Athens, he was seeking all the help he could get in Paris. "I want you to help me get Olympic Airways off the ground," he went straight down the line with Francis ("Tom") Fabre, an old New York acquaintance who ran the French airline UTA. A soft-spoken man with a deceptively absent-minded air and a fondness for English tweeds, Tom Fabre had known Ari only as a playboy. This was the first time he had encountered the serious side of the man, and he was impressed. "Two years from now, you leave," Ari told him. "I won't need you any longer. That's the deal. Are you in or out?" The directness of the proposal, even the brusqueness with which it was put, amused the Frenchman. And the idea of trying to turn Olympic into an international operation was a challenge that appealed to his own ego. Also, he figured correctly, two years would test the limits of any business relationship with a man like Ari.

In June 1957 Olympic's international operations began with a twice-weekly London-Paris-Athens-Nicosia-Beirut service, its aging prop-driven fleet boosted by three DC-6Bs chartered from Fabre's UTA, which also provided the technical and administrative backup systems. Two years to the day when Fabre and Ari had shaken hands on the deal in UTA's Paris office, the Frenchman withdrew. "He was very smart, but street smart," Fabre later said. "If he'd had a formal education he'd have been tied hand and foot by its rules . . . he cut through conventional ethics, he wasn't bound by petty legalities and moralities."

Olympic was not a happy airline. Ari tired of it quickly. Nevertheless, his pride would not permit him to let it go, although he constantly threatened to do so, usually to wring further concessions out of Karamanlis, whose faith in him as a financial catalyst remained resolute. "The louder Ari squeals, the tighter he holds the reins," complained Niarchos, who very much wanted to get his own hands on Olympic. The company staggered from crisis to crisis, with no organizational chain of command, no integrated direction, no investment strategy. In a decade of substantial expansion in international aviation its revenues remained almost stagnant. But Aristotle Onassis was the only private citizen in the world who could claim that he owned a national airline.

He lived high, even for a town like Monte Carlo. "When you are worth $300 million you don't begin selling your cars and sacking your servants for economies of a few thousand . . . it is meaningless," he told reporters anxious to discover how he was coping with the post-Suez shipping recession. The *Christina* was still the favorite rendezvous of the rich and famous. Churchill and Garbo were among those who regularly dined aboard his yacht, which continued to dominate the Riviera harbor. The young senator from Massachusetts, John F. Kennedy, and his beautiful wife, Jacqueline, were invited to a cocktail party to meet Churchill. The invitation had been the idea of Winston, who had known Joe Kennedy when he was United States ambassador in London in 1940. Although his early fondness for the old man turned sour after he had suggested that Britain could not win against the Nazis and had tried so hard to keep the United States out of the war, Churchill had heard interesting things about his son. He told Ari: "They tell me he is presidential timber; I should like to meet this presidential timber."

He does not look like an embryo president, Ari thought as he welcomed Jack Kennedy aboard, warning him not to outstay his welcome: "I must ask you to leave by seven-thirty. Sir Winston dines sharp at eight-fifteen." He believed he could see below the surface of most men, and Kennedy did not seem to him to be a man headed for the White House. He liked the look of Jacqueline much more. He noticed everything about her. She was wearing a simple white dress, the hem raised to just cover the knees, cut in the trapeze line that Saint Laurent had recently brought in. She was hatless, and the evening breeze caught her short dark hair. She had a withdrawn quality that wasn't shyness and wasn't boredom either. He admired the way she yielded to her husband rather than be eclipsed by him. He was surprised to hear her speaking perfectly to French guests in their own language. Her accomplishments as well as her good looks and her youth were obviously an asset to Kennedy in his public life as well as in his private one. Ari proved that he had looked upon her with no careless eye when later he told Gratsos: "There's something damned *willful* about her, there's something provocative about that lady. She's got a carnal soul." (She also had a teasing wit. The meeting with Churchill had not been a success; the old man had been in one of his gaga moods. "Maybe he thought you were a waiter, Jack," she later told her dinner-jacketed husband.) Ari and Gratsos continued constantly to give each other good advice on the dangers of womanizing, and as frequently to confess their lapses. She's too young for you, Costa said, sensing the complexity and depth of Ari's interest. Jacqueline was four months younger than Tina.

In the summer of 1958 a series of incidents kept Ari in the news. The tanker recession had lasted longer and cut more deeply than anyone had thought possible. He was forced to cancel orders for new vessels—including the three tankers which were to have been built by Bethlehem Steel as a *quid pro quo* for transferring fourteen of his American trust's vessels to the Liberian flag under the United States Maritime Administration's "trade-out and build" program. He also imposed a 20 percent wage cut on his remaining seamen. It was an unpropitious time to have a high social profile. Unlike most wealthy people, he was always willing to contribute to the discussion of his personal fortune. In May on the BBC television program "Panorama," in an interview filmed aboard the *Christina* (the cameras lingering on the fireplace inlaid with lapis lazuli at a cost of five dollars a square inch, bar hand-rails made of the finest whale-tooth ivory engraved with scenes from the *Iliad* and the *Odyssey*, the rare ikons, and the staircase with marble balustrades) he explained why he had been com-pelled to cut his seamen's pay: "After telling the officers and crew our intention of laying up the vessels they volunteered to contrib-ute to any possible saving in order to enable the vessel to carry on for a while with the hope that things would improve, and we tried it . . . but in spite of that cutting back we had to go home and lay up," he told Woodrow Wyatt. It was a tough interview; Ari felt he gave a good account of himself.* Wyatt had pressed him hard on why he sailed his ships under flags of convenience. "Because Li-beria and Panama gives us what the British flag used to give before two wars, in other words free enterprise, initiative, no restrictions . . . while flags of convenience exist so you will either have to make yourself convenient or dispose of the convenient flag," he an-swered. "Unsmiling, he spoke vehemently, sometimes almost an-grily," reported the *Daily Telegraph* next morning.

At about this time Ari was subpoenaed to appear as a witness before a congressional subcommittee inquiry into the state of the United States merchant marine. A leading member of the commit-tee was Herbert Zelenko, a New York Democrat who made no secret of his intense dislike for shipowners who operated under flags of convenience. "I remember telling Ari that Zelenko was boasting that he had enough on him to change the color of his suit for three to five years," Meyer said later. "Ari told me, 'He's got nothing that can't be squared away with eight million dollars'" (the penalty payment if the trust failed to build the ships promised under the "trade-out and build" program). Ari had already admit-ted that he wanted to renege on the deal: "Why don't you just take the money and we kiss each other good-bye?" he told Maritime Administrator Clarence Morse, who was pressing him hard for a

---

* "He was quite a civilized man, although he very much wanted everybody to see the gold taps in his bathrooms. But he had charm. Charm is being interested in you, I suppose. He was obviously a tough egg. I wouldn't want to have got involved with him in business. I think he had the ability to always get the upper hand," Sir Woodrow Wyatt later recalled.

start date. It was the wrong approach. Morse wanted work in American yards, not compensation in his books. And both men knew that eight million dollars would have been a steal; the vessels transferred to the Liberian flag in 1956 had already earned the trust some twenty-five million dollars.

But there was probably more surprise than wile in Ari's attitude. He said, "If those ships had remained under the American flag, they would have been laid up. They would have been too damned expensive to operate. I just did the smart thing. You can't put a guy on trial for being smart." Some people in Washington thought he was too smart. Again it was left to Gratsos to lay it on the line. "Zelenko's not the only one who thinks you made too much money on that deal to rat on the building commitment," he told him. Ari was unrepentant. How could anyone make too much money? Making money is the American dream, he said. Anyway, conditions had changed. "It's a fluctuating world, and I have to fluctuate with it or go under. Morse and everybody else knows that it'd cost three times as much to build those tankers in the States as it'd cost in Europe or Japan. I don't call eight million dollars ratting on a deal." It had not crossed his mind that they might see it differently in Washington.

From day one it was clear that the House subcommittee was going to put his feet to the fire. Chairman Herbert Bonner actually smashed a carafe of water banging his gavel so hard ("We'll run this hearing!") when Ari attempted to interrupt another witness, suggesting that what he had to say would take "just ten minutes." Herbert Zelenko, a man who was not ashamed to admit that he was "a little sentimental about jobs for Americans," was determined to prove that Ari controlled the trust and that he and he alone was responsible for ratting on the pledges to United States shipbuilders. Ari decided that the best way to deflect Zelenko's attack was to establish the distinction between paternal concern (he had a legal 25 percent stake in the trust through the Panamanian corporation Ariona) and control. In the speech he had prepared on the plane to Washington, he anticipated Zelenko's jingoism:

> Yes, I have an interest over and above my twenty-five percent share in the trust, and this is a God-made interest and there is no law or constitution by man-made law that can interfere with or change in any way whatsoever that God-made interest. By that I mean, Mr. Zelenko, I happen to be the father of those two children [Christina and Alexander], and no matter what laws you can put, that one is made by God. I belong to those children and those chil-

dren belong to me. Therefore, yes, I have a great, great
interest.

Zelenko did not feel like exchanging paternal profundities
with this man. He said, "Let me ask you this. You have been in
business all your life?"

"I think so."

"I believe you are quite familiar with it. Would you say that
the man who controls the purse controls the business?"

"In other words, money talks?" Ari was never above showing
off, even before a congressional inquiry. "That is what you mean?"

"You know what I mean." Zelenko knew all the euphemisms
for power. He was a lawyer, and there was nothing he enjoyed
more than cross-examining smart-alecky witnesses: they always
tripped themselves up in the end. "I guess you can take it in a
number of languages." Money did not always talk, Ari said. He
could offer thirty thousand examples, he said. Take banks: "Do
you want anybody more than a bank to apply the proverb, 'Money
talks?' If a bank gives me fifty million dollars, payable over a
period of ten or fifteen years, tomorrow what say does that bank
have with me? Nothing, as long as I am not in default. They have
fifty million dollars of their money in my hands, but as long as I
am not in default, what say can that bank have? Their money
doesn't talk at all. It talks as much as a fish. I can give you examples like that until tomorrow morning." Zelenko said he would
settle for more straightforward answers. Ari said that straightforward answers were dangerous things; he could cut his own throat
with straightforward answers. Zelenko replied that in his case he
didn't think it was a possibility. "There is always time for that to
happen, Mr. Zelenko, so one has to be a little wary also." Ari felt
in control. Zelenko was a smart guy, but he was asking the wrong
questions.

Zelenko shifted his attack. He wanted to know about Ariona.
How much stock did Ari own in the Panamanian company? Ari
couldn't be exact; he thought he owned about 85 percent. Was it
in his own name? Whether it was in his own name or through
another corporation whose stock was in his name was a detail that
he could not answer. He said that Zelenko was asking very technical questions, involving some seventy complexly structured corporations, it was impossible to remember all the details. It was
possible that the shares might have been in the name of someone
else, he conceded, rattled for the first time in the four-hour roast-
ing. "But I am telling you if it is someone else, I own that someone
else."

That must have been music to Herbert Zelenko's ears. "I own

that someone else," said everything Zelenko wanted to hear. It had the very whiff of self-indictment; it exposed Ari's reach and his strength. "Onassis slowly began to smile this small apologetic kind of smile, as if he had suddenly realized how damaging that boast was," recalled a reporter who covered the hearings. Zelenko was smart enough to end it there. He thanked Ari for being so cooperative. Smart-alecky witnesses never let him down. "I own that someone else." Zelenko was sure he had him dead to rights. Only Zelenko was wrong. The committee bought Ari's assurance that the trust was substantially independent and that the post-Suez recession, aggravated by the United States government's decision to restrict oil imports, had made the cancellation of the shipbuilding program unavoidable. "Looks like you just walked off with the game," Meyer congratulated him afterward. "It's not in my nature to lose," Ari answered.

Although things continued to go badly between Ari and Tina, and the problems were affecting her health (life aboard the *Christina*, reported the *London Evening Standard*, had caused her to have "a form of nervous breakdown"), she remained staunchly supportive in his business dealings. In the spring of 1959, a series of palace maneuvers unseated Ari's man from the helm of SBM. The revolution, reported Sam White in the *Standard*, left Rainier "the unchallenged master of all he surveys in his principality." As from this week, wrote White, "It can be said that Mr. Onassis's power in the affairs of the casino is at an end. This power, based on his 42 percent shareholdings in the company, was exercised through an administrator appointed by him and primarily responsible to him. Now this administrator, M. Charles Simon, has resigned in circumstances which have given unconcealed satisfaction to both the palace and the French. Both have made it clear that never again can there be an Onassis man appointed to this key post." According to White, the prince had summoned Ari to the palace to complain that the Hotel de Paris rebuilding program was behind schedule and alarmingly over budget. He blamed Ari's interference. "Mr. Onassis denied that he had interfered. Unfortunately, M. Simon was unable to support him in this denial and resigned in protest."

Tina rushed to her husband's defense. In a handwritten note on April 15, she pleaded with Lord Beaverbrook (who owned the *Standard*) to ensure that White in future "got the true facts before writing." (Although she also complained that "this man deliberately twists any facts concerning us so that they appear detrimental.") Ari's relationship with the prince was most cordial, she insisted. And Charles Simon had been asked by Ari to resign "for the simple reason he was getting fed up with him." And while not denying White's story that she had suffered a kind of nervous breakdown, she added: "I have the greatest fun in my life when I am on the yacht, as you have seen yourself."

A man who loved making mischief, Beaverbrook was delighted that White's article had hit the spot; he would do nothing to discourage his Paris correspondent from filing copy that might displease Ari. For Beaverbrook was among many of Churchill's friends who resented the way Ari appeared to have wormed his way into Churchill's inner circle. But he did genuinely like Tina, and replied kindly, although not entirely truthfully, on April 20:

> Dear Madame Onassis,
>
> I am very distressed by your letter.
>
> The *Evening Standard* will always present you in a favorable light. And indeed it would be impossible for the Paper to take any other course.
>
> I am far, far from London for ten months of the year. The papers are not really under my control. I still have the right to vote the majority of shares and to that extent I am responsible. But my son is conducting the business now and I am sending him a copy of your letter and my reply.
>
> And with all good wishes and great admiration.
>
> I am,
>
> Yours ever,
>
> (signed) Max Beaverbrook

Ari dismissed Beaverbrook's reply as "barony bullshit—he promises nothing, admits nothing. His newspapers will go on crucifying me and this Canadian son of a bitch will go on washing his hands of the whole business." He knew that his friendship with Churchill was the cause of the Beaverbrook newspapers' "animosity" toward him. But Ari never missed a chance to rub salt into the wound, and at the end of a prolonged newspaper strike in England that summer he emphasized his increasing closeness to Churchill. "Together with Lady Churchill and Sir Winston we all send our heartiest congratulations and greetings," he cabled the press baron. "We all hope now the strike is over you could fly to Athens, and our plane would bring you on board within less than one hour." Beaverbrook—"tied and bound and fenced in by duties"—was unable to accept.

CHAPTER 11

*If a woman tricks herself out in finery
when her husband is away, you may
write her down no faithful wife.*

EURIPIDES

EITHER TINA nor Ari took parenthood personally. To be international nomads, to appear and go away again, sometimes for months, often separately, did not seem to them unkind. Christina and Alexander lived in a charmed world of pampered neglect, their parents' affection scrawled in postcards from distant places and wrapped in secondhand hugs from passing friends and strangers. Assigned to the care of nannies, secretaries and private tutors, often left to eat their meals in solitude or with servants, yet occasionally invited to lunch with some of the most famous people in the world, to gawk at Cary Grant or converse with Churchill ("One lunch with Sir Winston," Ari told his son, "will teach you more than three years at Oxford"), their existence was not like any ordinary childhood. The *Christina* did not kindle a sense of reality, nor did it encourage self-restraint. In one spectacular temper tantrum, Alexander smashed every window of the Château de la Croë, costing thousands of dollars.

He was six years old when Alan Brien met him. Brien considered him "a ghastly little creature, very brattish." Ari took him to see Alexander's apartment in the château. "He opened one wardrobe. There were fifty suits in there. Military uniforms, sailor suits, yachting outfits. He said, 'What do you think? Do I spoil the boy?' I said I thought he did. I said it must be terrible to have so much so young, to be denied the excitement of expectation." With an abruptness which surprised Brien, Ari answered: "Yes, that's what I think." Walking in the grounds the following morning, Brien was almost knocked down when Alexander drove his gasoline-driven racing car straight at him. When Ari heard about the incident, he said: "It's only a toy." Brien answered angrily, "A toy traveling at twenty miles an hour." Twenty-five, Ari corrected him. "That's enough to cripple me for life," Brien said. Ari laughed and shook his head.

Alexander had never been to school and had no friends of his own age, and although he was not academically gifted, he had a knowledge of cars and engines that impressed even Fiat's Gianni Agnelli. For his tenth birthday, his father, whom he both admired and feared, gave him a Chris-Craft speedboat, which he souped up and serviced entirely himself. His closest companions were found among the staff: "Chauffeurs and servants were his confidants," recalls an Onassis staffer. "In spite of everything, he grew up to be a pretty nice kid." His relationship with his sister was cool. She was not a communicative child; her shyness was often misconstrued as disdain and put people off; for a brief period she declined to speak to anyone at all. Tina consulted child psychologists in Zurich, who told her it was simply an attention-seeking silence that is often associated with insecure, overprotected children. It was a typical Tina overreaction, said a family friend. "Most mothers would have said, 'The cat's got her tongue' and been patient. Tina had to make a big thing about it. She loved expensive things, including expensive explanations. Christina found her voice again in good time." She was never left alone in a room in all her girlhood; maids, bodyguards and governesses watched over her; everything she did was reported to Ari. She had her father's Levantine complexion and hair ("black as a raven's wing," he would say), and her eyes had that kind of darkness indissolubly associated with holy pictures. Slightly plump and often clumsy, she was not a pretty child, and although her father called her *Chryso mou* ("my golden one"), at least one close friend of the family believed that Tina may have been "almost ashamed of having produced such a child . . . I don't think it was given to her to love her daughter." Christina lived in a world of her own within the world of her father. She saw everything, and felt the pain. "I've been a woman since I was nine years old," she later snapped at an elderly adviser who she felt was patronizing her. She was nine years old when her parents divorced.

For about a year before that, an air of alternate anger and armistice filled the atmosphere whenever their parents were together. Alexander and Christina felt both caught up in the mood that had entered into the family and left on the sidelines, as their parents quarreled elliptically, spitefully. "I think it's beastly that we still sleep together," one close friend recalls Tina, a little tipsy, saying at a dinner party, as if she were talking about other people whose manners she found wanting. "It makes me feel soiled." Ari answered like a man exchanging condolences: "We are all soiled. We live in a soiled society." Tina did not object to infidelity discreetly done. She had forsaken her rights to demur. Only Ari's new adventure broke the rules. He had fallen in love with Maria Callas.

A tyrannous prima donna as unloved by colleagues as she was worshipped by audiences, Callas's fame went beyond the world of opera. She was born Maria Anna Sofia Cecilia Kalogeropoulos on December 3, 1923, in Manhattan's Flower Fifth Avenue Hospital, three months after her parents arrived from Athens. A registered pharmacist, her father, George Kalogeropoulos (he changed the family name to Callas in 1926, about the time Maria was christened in the Greek Orthodox Cathedral on East Seventy-fourth Street), lost his business and much of his will in the crash of '29. Although Maria was myopic, overweight and reclusive, she did have an exceptional voice; encouraged by her mother, Evangelia, she began winning radio amateur contests, investing the prize money in opera librettos and singing lessons, dreaming of musical grandeur. When she was fourteen, she returned on a visit to Athens and got caught up in World War II.

A scholarship to the National Conservatory was followed by starring roles with the Athens Opera Company. Life in Greece under the Axis was hard; people were starving, and when Maria sang for German troops she would gratefully accept their gifts of groceries. It was less an act of collaboration than of survival. Maria was not a popular member of the company, and when the war ended, her "fraternizing" recitals were made the excuse to terminate her contract. She returned to New York and was out of work for two years until in 1947 she was invited to sing *La Gioconda* (four performances, sixty-three dollars a performance; no travel or accommodation expenses) at the Verona Festival. And it was there that she met Giovanni Battista Meneghini. A round, sawed-off man with thinning sleeked-back hair, he was known as a ladies' man, and had an income from the family building business and a dozen brick factories to support his reputation. "I knew he was *it* five minutes after I first met him," she remembered the moment some years later. (In his 1981 autobiography, Meneghini's recall is more prosaic: "We arose from the table and it was at this moment that I experienced my first genuine feelings toward Maria Callas. When she was seated she didn't seem that large, even though she was solid and well set, but when she stood up, I was moved to pity. Her lower extremities were deformed. Her ankles were swollen to the size of calves. She moved awkwardly and with effort.")

She was convinced that Verona was her last throw. If she failed there, she told him, there would be no future for her in opera. He became an unstinting patron, picking up her hotel bills, paying for her voice lessons, taking her to the best restaurants. A lover had never entered her life before. And in fifty-three years he had experienced no greater absorption of self into some other being than Maria Callas. His family and friends felt that he was making a fool of himself and spoke of Maria with profound resentment; her family, equally concerned about her deepening relationship with a man thirty years older than herself, pleaded with her to end the affair. In April 1949 they were married in Meneghini's parish church in Verona. No one attended from her family, or his. Shortly afterward, he sold his factories, invested in property, and applied his business acumen and all his energies to her career. Her personal impresario and only agent, her minder and mentor, a shrewd manipulator of circumstances and tough negotiator of deals, he did a fine job. In 1956 she returned to New York in triumph, svelte, assured, unassailable, the hottest, most tempestuous soprano in the whole world. "All was summer," Meneghini liked to repeat the line in a John Donne poem. Maybe he was possessed of clairvoyancy, or maybe he just did not know the line that came next, "And yet how soon a fall of the leaf!"

Maria met Ari for the first time in 1957 at a ball the American society hostess and gossip columnist Elsa Maxwell threw for her in Venice. Afterward she and Meneghini had breakfast aboard the *Christina*, which was anchored in a lagoon outside the Grand Canal. Later neither would recall feeling anything deeper than polite interest in each other: "There was a natural curiosity there; after all, we were the two most famous living Greeks in the world!" Ari told Spyros Skouras. Ari had always been attracted to success, to people who were the best in their world and whose friendships would add luster to his own name. And although he could never refuse a chance of a conquest ("I approach every woman as a potential mistress," he often bragged), a year went by before he made a move to develop the Venice encounter. "I think what dragged his ass was the dread of being invited to sit through an entire opera," said Meyer.

Not until December 19, 1958, would she get the first intimations of his interest. It was the day of her Paris debut at the Théâtre de l'Opéra, a gala performance to be followed by a supper dance in aid of the Légion d'honneur. Everybody who was anybody in France would be there: President René Coty, the duke and duchess of Windsor, Brigitte Bardot, Charlie Chaplin, Jean Cocteau, the Rothschilds and the Ali Khan, Françoise Sagan and Juliette Greco. On the morning of her performance he sent flowers to her hotel. Throughout the day baskets of roses arrived with messages of good luck and admiration written in Greek but with no clue as to the identity of the sender; only the final delivery contained the signature, Aristotle Onassis. And just as he had impressed Claudia Muzio in Buenos Aires some thirty-five years before, so he impressed and tantalized Maria Callas in Paris. A jealous Meneghini was furious. It was the first time anything like this had happened in their marriage. For the flowers were not the familiar tributes to her artistry, conferred with propriety and innocence; the manner of their bestowal had excited too much pleasure and too much curiosity in a woman who had conquered the world.

That year Ari and Tina spent their first Christmas apart. Now photographed with Venezuelan millionaire Renaldito Herrera more often than with her husband, Tina flew to New York ostensibly to be with her sister, Eugénie, who was having a baby. Ari was dismayed by her renewed closeness to "the Niarchos woman," as he called his sister-in-law. He told reporters questioning the Yuletide separation that he had important business in Monte Carlo. Tina had grown to detest Monte Carlo. "The place has become so paralyzingly vulgar," she told her friends, and her friends were no longer Ari's friends.

At Contessa Castelbarco's annual Venice ball, which launched the summer season of 1959, they met—Tina and Ari, Maria and Meneghini. It was apparent from the start that Callas adored Ari's virile authority. This was the best time of her life ("diva divana," Elsa Maxwell had called her, "prima donna of the world"), everything was fine for her, and everything would improve. It is not hard to imagine Tina's feelings as she watched her husband move in on Callas with all his charm and all his guile. Driven by the imperatives of middle age, he was a man in a hurry, demanding life to yield up quickly its remaining pleasures. Yet there must also have existed in the mind of Maria an impatience for complete self-surrender, a lack of judgment. For these two remarkable people, made each to excite the other, were also made perfectly for the other's hell.

Although Tina was one of the youngest and most beautiful women present, in a gown by Jean Desses (the designer who had dressed all Ari's women since the days when Ingeborg shared his bed and worked on his sense of style), wearing jewels of priceless value, she must have been conscious, more than at any time in their relationship, of the truth of a line of Ari's: "My women do not attain the best happiness of women." When Meneghini put his face close to hers and asked in an anxious tone what kind of man her husband was, she told him: "He requires space in the world.

Without space he wreaks damage on things and on people." You don't look damaged, Meneghini answered with his own small share of charm. But what she thought, what she felt, were eclipsed in the fragility of her smile as she watched Ari and Maria dancing together in that ballroom of Contessa Castelbarco's magnificent palace.

Ari was almost but not quite Maria's height, and she would remember to wear flatter shoes in future. Although mostly she would remember "our hands, the textures of our skin, so pleasing to each other's touch." It must have been an extraordinary moment, that moment when she first accepted that her happiness was no longer entirely in her own keeping. Ari did not ever want the party to stop, and Tina had grown accustomed to his habit of "going on somewhere," but when he invited Maria back to the *Christina* for scrambled eggs and champagne Meneghini would have none of it. Maria had to leave the following day for a concert in Madrid. Ari suggested that they join them on a summer cruise. Callas had a crowded schedule. She would be thinking of them on their beautiful yacht when she opened in *Medea* at Covent Garden in June, she said, as they prepared to part that night. Ari vowed to be there.

"Meneghini's pissed off with the way he thinks you're climbing on Maria's bandwagon," Johnny Meyer told Ari the day Maria Callas was to open in *Medea*. It was the London opera event of the year, and Meyer had spent weeks buying up tickets on the black market for the fifty friends Ari had invited to Covent Garden. Afterward, Maria was to be the guest of honor at a supper party he had arranged at the Dorchester for 170 guests. "I warned Ari that Meneghini was making noises about giving the party the go-by," Meyer remembered later. "He said, 'Meneghini's an undertaker.' He was sure Callas'd be there. He'd gotten a hell of a cast list: the Churchills (but not Sir Winston), Gary Cooper, a whole coachload of royals. It was obvious to everybody that he was making a play for Callas, and he didn't deny it. I remember when one of his people suggested it as a kind of joke he just said, 'I hear Meneghini likes a little spare pussy now and then. Anyway, he's not servicing the account, so what the hell.' "

Tina knew that Callas was not like the rest of Ari's women. ("He talked about her too much; he never talked about the others," she later told a friend.) They were close in ways that Tina, for whom luxury had been familiar from the day she was born, could never understand. They shared experiences she could never possess. Both had known the severities of war, both had overcome great difficulties to achieve riches and extraordinary fame. They behave like strangers in a foreign land who have fallen in love with each other's past, Tina remarked at the Dorchester party. Maria Callas, born in New York, an Italian citizen, was the only woman who could make Tina, born in London, an American citizen, feel less than European.

Callas had taken a dozen curtain calls and arrived at the party at 1:00 A.M., to be greeted by spontaneous applause from the guests gathered in the candlelit ballroom. Ari did not try to hide his obsession with her. When she mentioned that she regretted nobody played tango music anymore, he told the musicians to play nothing but tangos for the rest of the evening (a whim that taxed the repertoire of the Hungarian orchestra and the imagination of the dancers). Only Tina seemed subdued. "I sometimes wish," she told a society columnist as they watched Ari pursuing Callas around the floor, "we could stay in one place and wait for the opera to come to us instead of us having to go to the opera."

It was after three o'clock when Callas left the party, closely followed by both Ari and Meneghini. In the foyer she was caught by photographers in a foreshadowing trilateral embrace, her husband on one side, Ari on the other. "I will never forget the warm smell of her furs as we kissed goodnight," Ari would recall the moment.

Her London engagement ended at the end of June, and after concerts in Amsterdam and Brussels she returned to her Italian villa in Sirmione on the shores of Lake Garda. On July 16, Ari telephoned the villa and pressed his invitation for her and her husband to join him aboard the *Christina*. According to the Meneghini memoirs, Callas was reluctant to go and told their housekeeper to inform Ari, "We are absolutely not here." He continued to call and finally she gave in. Her husband says he assured her, "This invitation comes at just the right time. The doctor recommended sea air. They say the Greek's yacht is very comfortable. Let's give it a try. If you don't like it, we can return home at the first port."

Only Maria and Ari had settled the matter weeks before in several secret rendezvouses during her London engagement, when they had become lovers. "Maybe her reluctance to join the cruise was simply a desire to tease Ari, or perhaps it was part of a performance cooked up to reassure Meneghini," says a former Onassis aide who knew about their illicit trysts in a London mews cottage. Certainly by the time she got to Amsterdam she had not only cuckolded Meneghini but was planning to put her duplicity onto a regular basis. The fee for her concert at the Holland Festival was not to be paid into the usual Callas-Meneghini Swiss account, but was to be kept in escrow until she could make new banking arrangements. In Milan, she spent millions of lire on what looked suspiciously like a trousseau. To Meneghini her purchases seemed out of character; he had never seen her so interested in lingerie before.

On July 21, they flew to Nice, took a taxi to Monte Carlo and booked into the Hotel Hermitage. That evening they dined at the Hotel de Paris with Ari, Tina and Elsa Maxwell. Maxwell had not been invited on the cruise, an omission that deeply wounded the old society fixer; she felt they owed it to her for bringing them together at the Venice ball in 1957. And in an insidious valedictory note delivered to Callas before the dinner, Maxwell made it plain that she knew the score, *exactly*. Suggesting that Maria was now taking the place of Garbo ("now too old") aboard the *Christina*, Maxwell urged her to "*take* everything . . . and *give* all that you can bring yourself to give."

It was an uncomfortable evening. The gravest apprehensions were fastened on Maxwell as she harped on Ari's sexuality, telling Tina that she was a most fortunate woman to be married to such a brilliant man. Rich husbands, Maxwell said, proud of her power to pander and terrorize, are always exciting—and dangerous. Rich husbands always roam, she said, looking from Tina to Callas, and finally resting her tiny gimlet eyes on Ari herself. Meneghini, who spoke no English and very poor French, understood perfectly what was going on; he despised Maxwell and her spiteful innuendos. He felt that her own moldering virginity (she boasted that she had never had a sexual experience in her life) made her obsession with the sex lives of her friends faintly obscene. At the end of the evening, Tina kissed Maxwell on the cheek and said, "You know, Elsa, my dear, there really isn't a lot of difference between being married to a moderately rich man and a very rich man . . . if only you could understand that, you'd be a much smarter person."

The *Christina* moved out of Monte Carlo just before midnight on the evening of July 22. In addition to the Churchills (and Sir Winston's pet canary, Toby), the Meneghini-Callases, Ari and Tina, its passenger list included Churchill's daughter, Diana Sandys; his doctor, Lord Moran; his private secretary, Anthony Montague Browne, and his wife, Nonie; Umberto Agnelli of Fiat; Artemis and her husband, Dr. Theodore Garofalides.* In the presence of such worldly company—Churchill, Callas, Onassis, Agnelli: people with one-name recognition—Meneghini might have felt a dull man who, without his wife, would not be counted for anything very much; at any rate, he reacted by withdrawing into an instinctive melancholy interrupted only by speculative attempts during

---

* To everyone's relief, since Lord Moran was "rather past it," Garofalides traveled medically equipped, remembers Lady Sargant, the former Nonie Montague Browne.

dinner to engage Montague Browne's attractive wife, Nonie, in games of footsie beneath the table.

Ari relished the sexual competitiveness that yachts and beautiful women engendered, and life aboard the *Christina* had a constant undercurrent of "jealousy and intrigue—it was part of its excitement," said a frequent woman guest. For the first few days, as they cruised through the Mediterranean toward the Aegean, nothing happened to ruffle the appearance of strict propriety. Yet, like Meneghini's footplay, things were stirring beneath the smooth surface of normality and order. In Portofino they visited nightclubs; in Capri, Gracie Fields, the popular Lancashire music hall star of the 1930s, was invited to dine aboard, and afterward sang some of her most famous songs for Sir Winston. Ari continued to dote on Churchill. They played word games together. "If you were an animal, what animal would you be?" Ari asked. "A tiger," growled the grand old man. "And you, Ari, what animal would you choose to be?" "Your canary, Toby," answered Ari. As guests became companions and companions became cliques, mutual observation and mutual speculation were unavoidable, but not even to the eyes of people shrewd in the aesthetics of conspiracy did Callas behave like a woman who was having an affair with her host. If recent deceits, and the deceits still to come, troubled her conscience, she did not show it. "Maria and Battista seem very close," Nonie Montague Browne noted in her diary.

In spite of appearances, Meneghini (Meningitis, Tina called him privately) was not happy and wanted to leave the cruise on July 25 in Capri; Callas insisted it would be ungracious to disembark so soon. He was not a good sailor and spent much of the cruise confined to their stateroom. On July 26 he was too unwell to go up on deck to see Stromboli smoking; he was still confined to his quarters on the twenty-eighth when they sailed through the Gulf of Corinth and put ashore for a tour of Delphi. Cut off by language, temperament and his queasy stomach, his resentment simmered; and in spite of the salutary presence of the Churchills, his imagination inflamed by the sight of sunbathing women, he began to suspect all kinds of debaucheries and bacchanalia. He sneered at Ari's dark hairy torso, likening it to a gorilla's, and unkindly compared his wife's body to Tina's. Tina's body was a model's body, and she possessed an awareness of the fact that was almost shameless.

By the time they got to Chios, Meneghini had given up trying to hide his displeasure. "It was sad to see the marriage disintegrating, the tenderness fade," Nonie Montague Browne observed in diary notes. "Tina continued to be a sparkling hostess, but one was aware of the well controlled tension—I seemed to be the Pig in the Middle." Tina and Maria both regarded her as a friend and confidante. And although she continued to brush Callas's shining long brown hair (it was one of Maria's favorite pastimes, a way of relaxing and gossiping and forgetting her problems as well as putting off the Bellini score she had brought to study) Nonie learned to "keep my mouth shut"—and her feet well out of Battista's reach under the table!

Still the atmosphere of uncertain calm continued. The Greek prime minister, Constantine Karamanlis, and his wife came to lunch; the British ambassador to Greece, Sir Roger Allen, paid a visit. "Onassis was boasting about the beautiful thin wine glasses he had, which he said if squeezed would change shape," Nonie Montague Browne remembered the occasion. "Diana Sandys tried it with hers—not only did the glass break, but red wine squirted all over the ambassador's white dinner jacket. The jacket was immediately whisked away to be dry-cleaned and the ambassador draped in Lady Churchill's fur stole. And very quickly Onassis popped his own glass—to put Diana at ease—though he took care to do it with his water glass and not one of the expensive wine glasses. The ambassador later went home in an impeccable white jacket." Churchill continued to cast his giant shadow of withered grandeur and Ari's deference to the great man was deep and genuine.* Ari displayed his prowess on waterskis; Maria made shortsheeted beds for everyone (except, of course, the Churchills) and Nonie, who helped her with the mischief, ruefully noted in her diary: "Did not go down well!"

On August 4, the *Christina* dropped anchor at the old port of Smyrna. It was an emotional return for Ari. He took his guests on a tour of the city, describing to them, and especially to Callas, the way it had been when he was a child, before the great fire, and before the earthquake. He took them to Karatass, where his home had been, to the places in which he had played as a boy, to where his father's offices and warehouses had stood, and to the graveyard where his mother lay buried.

After "the Former Naval Party" had retired that evening, Ari persuaded Meneghini and Callas to accompany him back into

---

* *Less genuine was his El Greco in the* Christina's *saloon; only to the connoisseur, Emery Reves, who challenged its authenticity, did he admit that he let people think it was an original: "If people wish to believe it to be genuine, why spoil their pleasure!" Onassis possessed two "El Grecos"*—Boy Lighting a Candle, *as well as* Madonna Supported by an Angel, *the painting Reves challenged aboard the* Christina. *Both are considered by Harold E. Wethey* (El Greco and his School, 2 vols., Princeton University Press, 1962) *to be of dubious origin. Dismissing another painting as "a dubious work, unrelated to El Greco in any way," Wethey adds: "The same comment applies to the* Madonna Supported by an Angel *located on the yacht* Christina of A. S. Onassis." *(Vol. 2, p. 192.)*

town to visit the less salubrious places of his youth. Although he
frequently tampered with his origins in interviews with the press
and in conversations with friends, he was straight with Callas. He
led them through the old tenderloin district, telling the stories of
his nights in the big brass beds in the cathouses in Demiri Yolu.
He told them about the Turkish whore who had given him wisdom
as well as sex ("One way or another, sweets, all ladies do it for the
money"). Money and sex intertwine at some point in every society,
he said. He got very drunk. "We made merry all night in the
company of dealers, prostitutes and assorted sinister characters,"
Meneghini said afterward. It was five in the morning before they
returned to the *Christina*. It was a mistake for Ari to have got so
drunk. Meneghini was jubilant. "He was tighter than a goat. He
couldn't stand up, he couldn't talk," he crowed, coming alive for
the first time on the whole trip. It was the highlight of the cruise
for Giovanni Battista Meneghini. It may have been one of the last
truly happy moments of his life.

The following day, Ari apologized to both of them. And to
Callas he said in Greek, "When dealing with the wicked, the gods
first deprive them of their senses." Are you wicked? she asked, also
in Greek. Most men are knaves, he told her in a language that they
knew excluded Meneghini. They had not made love since the end
of June in London when, according to Ari's own braggadocio, she
performed the act of fellatio on him in the back of his Rolls-Royce
as they drove down Park Lane. Now, as they cruised up the Dar-
danelles toward Istanbul, it was August 5, and perhaps the absti-
nence was beginning to tell on both of them.

Once the heart of Byzantium, the soul of the Ottoman Empire,
few cities have played so violent or sentient a role in the history of
intrigue as Istanbul. Still known as Constantinople by Orthodox
Greeks, it was to play a critical part in the drama of Ari and Maria.
On the morning of August 6, while at anchor on the Bosporus, the
Christina was visited by Patriarch Athenagoras. Although invited
aboard to meet Churchill, the patriarch ended up bestowing blessings upon the lovers as they knelt side by side on the varnished
deck. "The world's finest singer and the most famous mariner of
the modern world, a modern Ulysses," he called them and offered
prayers for the honors they had brought to Greece. Afterward, all
the non-Greeks, including Meneghini, but excluding the Churchills, were sent ashore while the patriarch was entertained at
lunch.*

---

* Artemis, Ari's "little sister," fond of Tina, disturbed by the sun deck liturgy and the
unmistakable undercurrent aboard the Christina, was "a bit too outspoken" at this
lunch for Ari's liking. Reluctant to cause a scene, he had a telegram brought to her saying she was wanted in her room, where she was confined until the patriarch had left.

That evening a party was arranged at the Istanbul Hilton. Meneghini, still distressed by the Byzantine ceremony that had taken place aboard the *Christina* that morning (he could not rid from his mind the feeling that a kind of marriage rite had been performed), weakened by seasickness, was in no mood for another long night with Ari. Callas seemed more attractive and elated than he had seen her for a long time. She danced almost all the evening, and almost always with Ari. When a man marries a woman twenty-eight years younger than himself he must be tolerant of such moments. He had made all the calculations: when I'm seventy, she will be forty-two; when I'm old, she will still be young. In the past she had chided him for his rueful lifetables. Only now when he suggested that they slip away, she declined to leave with him. "I'm enjoying myself," she said, her loverlike attention to him gone. "You do whatever you want—oh, and Titta, don't touch the air conditioning, you know what it does to my throat." It was as public a dismissal as he had ever known. Later he would say he wanted to smash things the way he had seen Ari smash plates in the waterfront cafés the night in Smyrna. But it was not his nature. Later he told opprobrious stories about the cruise and the people on it. In Istanbul, pointing to the filth in the harbor water, he had complained to the *Christina*'s captain, "We're floating in shit." He relished the captain's reply: "The real shit is that which exists on board." Telling the story was Meneghini's way of smashing plates.

The change in Callas's affections toward him was so abrupt that the surprise almost exceeded the pain. When they had set out on that cruise their relationship seemed to be as fine as at any time in the dozen years they had been together. Meneghini felt in control, and in spite of his customary sourness and bad temper, even in spite of Elsa Maxwell's malevolent bodings, he felt no cause to doubt his wife's loyalty. There had been no disturbance in the rhythm of their lives, no warning look, no alerting tone. "Yet if she had changed toward him slowly, bit by bit, day by day, if he had known that he was in trouble with his marriage, he might have suffered more," said a family friend. But now the stress was on, and what had begun as a secret affair in London had suddenly become in Istanbul a subject for gossip writers and speculation.

And so he waited for Callas to return from the party. At sixty-three, he found no satisfaction in romantic despair. She came back in the early hours and told him what he must already have guessed. She had fallen in love with Ari.

During the days that followed as the *Christina* sailed in the shadow of Mount Athos and on toward Delos and Mykonos, the tension spread among the rest of the company. Only Churchill seemed unaware of the situation, continuing to enjoy lunchtime sing-songs with Ari ("Daisy, Daisy" was a favorite number) and, more rarely, a game of bezique or some serious conversation. "Ari loved to talk of fundamental things, especially late at night," said a frequent *Christina* guest, "of ethics and conscience, power and freedom, virtue and honor, love and death." Lord Moran, like Nonie, kept a diary. One entry is especially revealing. Churchill and Ari had been discussing a Washington scandal that had ended with the resignation of Eisenhower aide Sherman Adams following accusations that he had received gifts (including a vicuña coat, which was to give its name to the affair) to intercede for industrialist Bernard Goldfine in his dealings with government agencies. The president had been prepared to ride out the storm. Churchill strongly disapproved: "You must either wallop a man or vindicate him." Ari, who would never trust a man who refused a bribe, replied: "You must let your nearest and dearest go to hell when they are no longer any use to you." It was a perfect summary of the advice he had been feeding Callas.

Ari and Callas continued openly to seek one another's company and no one else's. For Callas, her love possessed all the poignancy, force and impetuosity of the first passionate physical affair of her life; for Ari there was the satisfaction of a man past his prime ("I used to think how terrible it was to be half a century old knowing that nothing better is ever going to happen to me: how wrong I was," he later reflected) on winning the heart and the mind of the world's greatest prima donna. On August 9 the yacht arrived in Athens. Artemis and Theodore gave a party at their home in Glyfada. Again, the lovers barely left each other's side, Callas watching him with heavily made-up eyes ("he reminded her, she said, of a gigolo, no longer young, but still predatory, still sexy, still stalking," a friend remembered). On her wrist she wore a single gold bracelet. Inscribed on the inside were the initials TMWL: To Maria With Love.

Meneghini went back to the yacht at four o'clock in the morning and went straight to bed. Callas did not return to their stateroom until after 9:00 A.M. They began to quarrel, their voices— especially her voice—reverberating with embarrassing clarity in the fragile quietness of the morning after. He was too possessive, too dull, a bourgeois; he had no poise, spoke no languages, was out of his depth in this cosmopolitan company. He behaved more like her keeper ("a peevish attendant," were her words) than her husband. She was ungrateful, inconsiderate, shameless. He had brought her from *nothing*, and she was repaying him by behaving like "that greedy little Greek's plaything." Not much remained hidden from their fellow guests, nor from the crew. A steward opened a book offering five to two against their finishing the cruise together.

Had matters been left to Ari the affair might have gone on until it died of natural causes. His affairs were mostly temporary; Cartier baubles were a common parting gift. However, in the early hours of August 12, unable to sleep, Tina went for a stroll and saw her husband and Callas making love in the saloon. She walked away and woke Meneghini and told him what was happening. "I could see by his face that he was beyond doing a thing about it," she later told a lover. Trapped in capricious alliance, they exchanged the small confessions of commiseration. She was "almost completely naked," the Italian recounted the moment with a suggestion of a sexual conquest, although it is unlikely that she had troubled to inspire in the man she had dubbed Meningitis more interest than she could handle. It will blow over, he said, clinging to the hope that it was simply a shipboard romance. It seemed inconceivable to him that his marriage had gone so badly wrong: how many times had they "knelt together and thanked God" for their happiness, and prayed for things to stay just as they were. If Maria no longer considered her marriage a moral obligation, he was convinced that she would never disavow their sacred ties. Tina was more realistic, and tougher. "He has taken her away from you, Battista," she told him. Her own marriage was over; it no longer mattered to her. She was genuinely sorry for Meneghini, and "also poor Maria . . . she'll learn soon enough what kind of man he is." (He was "a brutal drunk," he recalled Tina's exact words in his memoirs, suspecting that she intended him to pass the message to Maria to "open her eyes.")

On August 13 the *Christina* returned to Monte Carlo, and Callas and Meneghini hastily disembarked. That evening they were back in their apartment in Milan. Meneghini's hope that things would return to normal was quickly abandoned. Callas ended the prolonged silence of those whom something troubles deeply by musing openly about a separation. "I sometimes wonder how different our lives would be if we were no longer together." Meneghini said he didn't even want to think about it. Callas insisted: "I *have* to think about it. You are not immortal, Battista. The day will come when I will have to sing alone."

Meanwhile, Stavros Livanos had flown to the south of France to discover for himself "what Ari thinks he's playing at." The European scandal sheets were filled with stories about his burgeoning friendship with Callas. Ari told his father-in-law to go to hell. "I'm fifty-four years old, I'm richer than you are, and I have never been this happy in my life. Don't tell me how to run my affairs,"

was how Ari remembered the conversation. The next day the
Christina embarked for Venice with Tina and the children. Ari
knew that he was a man with a problem that wasn't going to go
away.

At Maria's suggestion, Meneghini returned to Sirmione while
she remained at their Milan town house; she needed "to be alone,
to work out my feelings." On Friday, August 14, Ari flew to Milan
in his private Piaggio aircraft. The first evening they avoided the
paparazzi, perhaps because the last place the press expected them
to surface was in Maria's hometown. He wanted her to leave Meneghini immediately. "He's an old guy, imagine how it will be for
you a few years from now!" he pressed her. The following morning
she called Meneghini and asked him to return to Milan at once so
that "we can work out a civilized solution to this whole mess."

It was an extraordinary meeting, closer to a boardroom discussion than a confrontation between a deceived husband, the
unfaithful wife and her lover. Ari did most of the talking—"he
talked like a man with a compulsion," Meneghini later told a
friend, "as if afraid that if he let up even for a minute everything
would crumble." Meneghini said that he had no experience in
these matters and asked, "How am I supposed to behave?" Ari
said that they had to ensure that Callas "was hurt and embarrassed least of all." Meneghini said he would go along with whatever was best for Maria ("How could I win against the modern
Ulysses?" he later harped back to the patriarch's blessing in Istanbul); he would arrange with his attorney in Turin to begin working
out the details of a separation. "I'll make it easy for you both.
Which is a damn sight more than you've done for Tina and me."
They talked long into the night. Ari saw no effrontery in outlining
his plans to build an opera house for Callas in Monte Carlo. He
drank a great deal of whisky yet seemed to stay sober, frequently
interrupting his diatribe to call New York or London. Callas loved
to watch him in action. His power and his sexuality were indivis-
ible. It seemed unbelievable to her that he was only nine years
younger than her husband. His brushed-back hair was still thick,
although there was grey in it now. There was a look she liked of
"ruffian strength" in his body. It was almost four o'clock in the
morning, the Milan sky streaked with light, when Meneghini went
to bed in the guest room, leaving his wife and her lover alone. At
thirty-six, she was "behaving like a little goose, a teenager with
stars in her eyes." He rose after a few hours, had breakfast alone,
and was back in Sirmione before she awoke.

During the following days public interest in the affair grew
till no one would have believed it could grow further. The lovers

could not outfox the paparazzi for long and were photographed entering the Hotel Principe e Savoia in Milan; it was a delicate hour to be seen going hand in hand into a hotel: too late for dinner and too early for breakfast. In Venice, Tina was reported dancing cheek to cheek with Count Brando d'Adda at Elsa Maxwell's annual ball. She did not act like a woman in the throes of an emotional crisis; yet it was clear that a juicy social scandal was in the making. Both Meneghini and Ari were drawn into indiscreet remarks. "This man has billions. I am being gutted by this man. What am I supposed to do? What *can* I do?" Meneghini began asking friends, overawed by the trespass against him. Ari tried a lighter touch with reporters. "I am a sailor, and these are things which sometimes happen to a sailor."

Nevertheless, even when everything seemed settled after the confrontation in Milan, the progress of the breakup had its ups and downs. A meeting at Sirmione to discuss Callas's career was doomed to disharmony when both she and Ari arrived late and less than sober. Ari had been drinking whisky steadily during the drive from Milan. Whisky made him garrulous and aggressive; his response to, and tolerance of, alcohol were always unpredictable. He was ecstatic at the thought that he had won Callas, and was now guiding her career. Maria had dressed for dinner in a strapless black chiffon evening gown, as if she were attending a grand ball. But her pearls drew attention to her wrinkled neck (her weight had dropped from 202 to 120 pounds). Ari wore his familiar dark glasses and a dinner jacket, a blend that Meneghini thought gave him "a decadent look." Elaborately grave, Maria seemed almost disconnected from reality; she demanded that a fire be lighted in spite of the warm late summer evening. Absorbed in his own opinions, indifferent to Meneghini's disapproval, unconscious of Maria's tranced air, continuing to drink through dinner and after it, Ari's talk moved from Maria's future to his ambitious schemes for Monte Carlo. The booze and the braggadocio finally broke down Meneghini's resolve to stay calm. The two men began to quarrel: a Greek and an Italian, fueled on alcohol and rivalry, their voices grew louder, their language (Italian, the only language Meneghini knew) got rough. More than anger, Meneghini was driven by a desire to put up a final fight that he could live with. Ari taunted him, "I am bad people but I'm richer than you'll ever be and a better lover than you ever were . . . I do what I want and I take what I want." His wealth was a topic he would not leave alone. He demanded to know how much Meneghini wanted for Maria. "Five million dollars? You've got it. Ten? Take it. Just don't bother us." ("I told him to stick his money up his Greek ass,"

Meneghini later repeated his riposte with satisfaction, although his memoirs are less precise on the exchange: "I replied, 'You are a poor drunk and you turn my stomach. I would like to smash your face in but I won't touch you because you can't even manage to stand up.' ") Perhaps conscious of being more coveted than loved, Maria became hysterical and accused her husband of denying her "this last chance" of happiness. Meneghini cursed them both: "For what you have done to me you will pay over and over again for the rest of your days. You will never know happiness; I pity you because you both will pay in hell for this."

On September 8, Callas made it official with a statement confirming that her marriage was over and that lawyers were working out the details of a settlement. The break had been in the air for some time, she claimed, and the cruise on the *Christina* was merely coincidental. "I am now my own manager. I ask for understanding in this painful personal situation. Between Signor Onassis and myself there exists a profound friendship that dates back some time. I am also in a business connection with him. I have received offers from the Monte Carlo Opera, and there is also a prospect for a film. When I have further things to say, I shall do so at the opportune moment, but I do not intend to call a press conference." Meneghini confirmed the split in a communiqué that acknowledged a "sentimental link" between his wife and Ari; friends felt it was an uncommonly chivalrous way to describe self-confessed adulterers. "I bear no bitterness toward Maria, who honestly told me the truth, but I cannot forgive Onassis," he said.

Reporters caught up with Ari at Harry's Bar in Venice. It is not the best place in which to drink if a man wishes to avoid the press. "Of course, how could I help but be flattered if a woman with the class of Maria Callas falls in love with someone like me? Who wouldn't be?" he said, going some way beyond Callas's claim that nothing more than a profound friendship existed between them.

Although Tina was hurt by the speed with which members of her husband's entourage paid court to Callas, she continued to keep her distance, appearing to ignore the whole business. She took Christina and Alexander and without telling Ari fled to the Livanos family home in Paris. When he tracked her down, she refused to see him. That evening he received a small package containing a gold bracelet inscribed, Saturday, April 17, 1943, 7 p.m. T.I.L.Y. His response was to set off on another Aegean cruise; this time there was only one other passenger aboard the *Christina*— Maria Callas.

At the beginning of October, Meneghini filed suit for a legal separation in Brescia, Italy. His writ of application did not name Ari, referring only to Callas's abrupt transformation from a "loyal and grateful wife" to one whose behavior was "incompatible with elementary decency" following a cruise with "persons who are reckoned the most powerful of our time." The court went through the ritual rigmarole of striving for a reconciliation, but on November 14, after a six-hour settlement hearing, it declared the separation legal. Maria got the Milan townhouse, most of her jewelry and the income from all her recording royalties; Meneghini kept Sirmione, and all their real estate holdings. Eleven days later, Tina filed for divorce in the New York State Supreme Court on the grounds of adultery, the only grounds recognized in New York state at that time, claiming custody of Alexander and Christina. That same evening, newsmen were summoned to her Sutton Square home, and her attorney read from a prepared text:

> It is almost thirteen years since Mr. Onassis and I were married in New York City. Since then he has become one of the world's richest men, but his great wealth has not brought me happiness with him nor, as the world knows, has it brought him happiness with me. After we parted this summer in Venice, I had hoped that Mr. Onassis loved our children enough and respected our privacy sufficiently to meet with me—or, through lawyers, with my lawyers—to straighten out our problems. But that was not to be.
>
> Mr. Onassis knows positively that I want none of his wealth and that I am solely concerned with the welfare of our children.
>
> I deeply regret that Mr. Onassis leaves me no alternative other than a New York suit for divorce.
>
> For my part I will always wish Mr. Onassis well, and I expect that after this action is concluded he will continue to enjoy the kind of life which he apparently desires to live, but in which I have played no real part. I shall have nothing more to say and I hope I shall be left with my children in peace.

Ari was aboard the *Christina* in Monte Carlo when the statement broke in the New York papers; Costa Gratsos read it to him over the telephone. "This stuff's been written by lawyers and scored for Jascha Heifetz," Gratsos said when he came to the end. Ari's advisers suggested it would be "good public relations" if Callas left the yacht for a while; she moved into a suite at the Hotel Hermitage. It fooled nobody, especially not the small army of photographers and reporters that followed them everywhere. But to everybody's surprise Tina eventually cited a "Mrs. J. R.," with whom he was alleged to have engaged in adulterous conduct "by land and sea in the United States, France, Monte Carlo, Greece and Turkey from 1957 up to the present time." Tina had a long memory, as well as detailed dossiers. The mysterious Mrs. J. R. was soon disclosed as her old school friend Jeanne Rhinelander. "I won't give that canary the satisfaction of being named the other woman," she told friends in New York with Livanos pride, and some Livanos shrewdness too. For if she had cited Callas, Ari would have had grounds for a countersuit, claiming that she had been doing a little double time with her own admirers long before Maria Callas came on the scene.

Far from blameless, Mrs. Rhinelander still resented her privacy being violated and threatened to sue Tina for slander. Ari was concerned about his former lover's volatile temperament. He confided to friends that he had already taken her on a couple of cruises "to help her over emotional and drug problems." An action for slander was the last thing he wanted. "Put Jeannie on a witness stand and she is likely to say *anything*," he fretted. He was also anxious to stop Mrs. Rhinelander, a tall beautiful New York divorcée who occasionally appeared in the society pages as Mrs. T. J. Oakley Rhinelander II, from talking to the press. As soon as her identity was revealed he drove to Grasse to persuade her to handle the situation calmly; a few hours later she issued a statement expressing her astonishment that her name had become enmeshed in a scandal in which she claimed she had played no part. "I am an old friend of Mr. and Mrs. Onassis. I am astonished that after so many years of friendship of which everybody knew, here and in the United States, Mrs. Onassis should try to use it as an excuse to obtain her freedom . . . I repeat that I know Mr. Onassis and that I remain a devoted friend."

His own statement to the press was a disappointment to Maria Callas. "I have just heard that my wife has begun divorce proceedings. I am not surprised, the situation has been moving rapidly. But I was not warned. Obviously I shall have to do what she wants and make suitable arrangements." There was something unsettling, irresolute, almost ominous about its tone. Callas had expected much more: she had expected a declaration of his love for her, a public commitment to their future. The pattern of their relationship for the next eight years was cast.

DESMOND O NEILL

Enter Maria Callas.

If recent deceits, and the deceits still to
come, troubled Maria's conscience, she
did not show it as she sipped Dom Perignon and listened to Ari's beguiling
stories.

LONDON EXPRESS/PICTORIAL PARADE

DESMOND O NEILL   AP/LONDON   CAMERA PRESS/PATRICK LICHFIELD

Opposite, three o'clock in the morning and Maria is caught by photographers in a foreshadowing trilateral embrace, her husband on one side, Ari on the other. Ari never forgot the warm smell of her furs.

Jeanne Rhinelander, the "Mrs. J.R." in Tina's divorce suit—Tina refused to give Callas the satisfaction of being named the other woman—threatened to sue for slander, the last thing Ari wanted (they'd had an affair "by land and by sea").

Sixteen months after her divorce, Tina married the Marquess of Blandford, son of the Duke of Marlborough, a kinsman of Churchill, in a Greek Orthodox ceremony in Paris. She was, she told friends, in splendid shape.

This page, Ari was in no hurry to marry Callas, although the crew of the *Christina* treated her as *la patronne*, and Princess Grace and Prince Rainier welcomed her as a suitable successor to Tina.

AP/LONDON

LIAISON/GAMMA

Ari made an effort to get close to Christina and Alexander. It was no secret that they blamed Maria for breaking up their parents' marriage.

Alexander had never been at peace with his father. "I admire him. I also admire Howard Hughes." He thus revealed his ambivalent feelings toward Ari.

Baroness Fiona Thyssen-Bornemisza—Alexander's "mistress, mother and priest confessor."

Ari's heavily mortgaged fleet re-mained idle. Only his closest friend knew how much he was hurting. He needed a miracle to save him.

The last thing in the world Ari wanted was premature disclo-sure of his deepening intimacy with Jackie. Their very incongru-ity was an important element in their being able to hide what was going on for so long.

Opposite, Maria: she went for weeks at a stretch without leaving her apartment.

An aging millionaire in the throes of love is a natural source of concern to his heirs. Alexander and Christina were shattered by the news that Ari and Jackie were to wed.

This page, wedding day: Caroline Kennedy sits on her mother's lap, with Ari at the wheel.

The bride and groom on Skorpios.

CHRIS
Y. C.

In the early days there were signs
of domestic tenderness.

Odysseus had become his alter
ego: to return to his homeland
proclaimed and celebrated had
become a haunting dream.

"The marriage," he told lawyer Roy Cohn, "had gotten down to a monthly presentation of bills."

Ari, Christina and two close friends attend a Venetian Masked Ball.

Ari steps out in Paris with Odile Rodin.

Alexander, the pilot: the plane simply seemed to lose its balance . . . from becoming airborne to impact took little more than fifteen seconds.

The ill-fated Piaggio parked on the beach at Skorpios shortly before the crash. The *Christina* is at anchor in the background.

Christina and Ari attend Alexander's funeral.

Fiona Thyssen-Bornemisza accompanied to the funeral by friends: "The brain defends itself to a degree," she said. "You drink a lot of wine, and take sleeping tablets, but it's the little things that break you in the end."

This page, Christina with Peter Goulandris: Ari considered it to be the perfect match.

With husband number one: Joseph Bolker. "What's wrong with me? Why won't you marry me? Am I not good enough for you?" she demanded to know.

Opposite, with husband number two: Alexander Andreadis. He looked a better bet than Bolker, but she soon discovered that precipitate passion is not the best harbinger of domestic bliss.

With husband number three: Sergei Kauzov. Their affair was uncovered by the French secret service. Was the groom working for the KGB?

With husband number four: Thierry Roussel. They survived the rocky start.

EX FEATURES/SETTIMIO GARRITANO

CAMERA PRESS/BENOIT GYSEMBERGH

CAMERA PRESS/MICHAEL STAFYLAS

Opposite, when Ari's eyelids became too weak to stay open, Christina cut strips of adhesive tape to hold them up and ordered darker lenses for his glasses to hide the tape.

The press watch was an affirmation of what Jackie and Christina already knew in their bones: Ari had returned to Paris for the last time.

This page, it seemed as if there had been a rapprochement between Christina and her father's widow.

Ari's sisters Artemis Garofalides and Calirrhoë Ionnalides share a limousine with Jackie on their way to the funeral on Skorpios, but Jackie had already made a bad mistake in not returning to Paris forty-eight hours earlier.

TWO PHOTOS: REX FEATURES/SIPA

Ari's last journey—and Jackie finds herself a long way back.

CHAPTER **12**

We learn the value of a thing when we have lost it.

SENECA

ARI SPENT the next months absorbed in self-pity and anger. He broke down in Spyros Skouras's suite at Claridge's and "sobbed like a child" after pleading for more than an hour on the telephone with Tina, who was in New York, to change her mind about the divorce. His relationship with Callas had changed dramatically. He was no longer in constant attendance, and his moves became erratic, his absences unexplained. Optimistically Callas blamed his business problems. The post-Suez shipping slump showed no signs of going away, and there wasn't a shipowner in the world who was not hurting.

He was still begging Tina to come back when they met in Paris in April 1960 to discuss the terms of the divorce. Photographed dining together, he encouraged press speculation of a reconciliation. Still, there was no relaxation of that wariness with which divided couples regard each other ("Even in love," Tina would later say, "he could not give himself without bargaining"), and there was no fresh start. She wanted no money for herself, not even her legal fees; financial provisions for Alexander and Christina, of whom they were to have joint custody, were to be guaranteed through the American trust. To pacify her father, who feared that a messy divorce would both harm her and the children and embarrass the Greek shipping establishment, she agreed to drop the New York action with its necessary allegation of adultery. In June, in Alabama, after thirteen extraordinary years, she was granted an uncontested "quickie" divorce on the grounds of men-

189

tal cruelty. In future she would be known as Tina Livanos. She had "no wish and no need" to retain her husband's name; the name Livanos had its own cachet and a lineage infinitely grander than Onassis's. "It is always sad when a marriage and a home break up," Ari told reporters in London. But he was not lonely, and he had no thoughts of remarrying. "There was never any romance between Callas and myself. We are just good friends," he said. It was a humiliating situation for Callas. Yet a sense of resignation settled on her. "I don't want to sing anymore. I want to live just like a normal person, with a family, a home, a dog." She canceled a concert in Belgium at the last moment, claiming that she had lost her voice; her enemies and critics wrote her off.

That summer Ari had a change of heart, becoming as caring and attentive as he had been when they first became lovers in London the previous June. Their favorite rendezvous was the Maona nightclub in Monte Carlo, where gossip writers spied them behaving in the most affectionate fashion. "It is impossible for them to dance cheek to cheek as Miss Callas is slightly taller than Mr. Onassis," reported William Hickey in the *London Daily Express*. "But as they dance she has lowered her head to nibble his ear and he has smiled rapturously." Speculation that marriage was imminent was rife and pleasing to Callas's ears. Nevertheless, when Tina fractured a leg skiing in St. Moritz and was flown to a clinic in England, Ari rushed to her bedside, encouraging fresh rumors that they would remarry. The rumors persisted until, sixteen months after her divorce, Tina married the thirty-five-year-old marquess of Blandford, son of the duke of Marlborough, a kinsman of Churchill, in a Greek Orthodox ceremony in Paris. Never missing an opportunity to irritate Ari, Niarchos laid on his private plane to fly the newlyweds to Greece and the start of their honeymoon, a cruise in the Aegean Sea.

Still Ari was in no hurry to marry Callas, although the crew of the *Christina* treated her in every way as *la patronne*. "The plain fact was the kids hated her. If it hadn't been for the kids, he'd have got it sealed the moment Tina did the Mendelssohn march with the marquess," said Meyer. It was no secret that both Alexander and Christina blamed Maria for breaking up their parents' marriage. They never gave up hope that their mother and father would get back together. Their mother's remarriage had pleased them no more than it had Ari, but in their young eyes it was Callas's presence that was the obstacle to a happy family reunion. In spite of her maternal yearnings, Callas had no way with children, she had no language with which to communicate with the young. ("Endings," she told nine-year-old Christina, attempting to explain the realities and blessings of divorce, "are a kind of accident but also a kind of beginning.") They would not call her Mme. Callas, they could not call her Maria; the result was that for a very long time they did not call her anything at all. Privately Alexander referred to her as the Singer, just as later he would dub his stepmother the Widow. When they talked, there was often a hint of insolence in his tone, which he knew incensed her, although it was always too subtle to justify a complaint to his father; it was a game he played to amuse Christina. They were private and precocious children whose childhood was a paradox: brought up with professional fuss, they had been neglected in private ways no less excessive. Salutes when they boarded the yacht, Alexander would later say, could not compensate for parents who were often absent or, when they were around, were "so absorbed in themselves that they might just as well have not been there." When Callas tried to encourage them with praise and with gifts, the praise was unnoticed and the gifts were left unopened. Christina had the air of a person already disposed to be a law unto herself. There was "something inaccessible in her face" that made Callas ill at ease to be alone with her. "She has the look of a child marked for the nunnery," she told Ari.

Ari would not permit Maria to join the *Christina* when the Churchills were on board, claiming that her presence would "embarrass Winston," who had been genuinely fond of Tina. It brought home to her "how much more she had lost in leaving Meneghini than his devotion," said a family friend. "It's not difficult to be swept off one's feet. Living with the consequences, that's the hard part," she later admitted to her friend Panaghis Vergottis. But in operas she had played heroines who died for love, "and that's something I can understand." As her fortieth birthday came into view, and she recognized that both professionally and privately she was no longer in her best years, she began more and more to believe that Ari had never intended their affair to be more than an adventure sanctioned by Meneghini's weakness and Tina's license. Yet she also knew that if it were to start all over again she would act in exactly the same way.

When she returned triumphantly to Greece to sing *Norma* at the classic Epidaurus theatre he basked in her glory, but he did not appreciate her talent and listened to her performances, when he had to, with polite boredom, and praised her in the same spirit. He wanted her to be a movie star because "a movie star in his book was more important than an opera star," said Meyer. He did everything in his power to persuade producer Carl Foreman to cast her opposite Anthony Quinn in *The Guns of Navarone*. Although he was not convinced of her ability to handle the small but important part, Foreman shrewdly appreciated the box office value of using her in the movie ("you couldn't *buy* that much publicity"). "Give her ten days and if she's no good, okay, dump her, get somebody else—and I'll foot the bill," Ari told the producer after several days of wining and dining aboard the *Christina*. "That could be a great deal of money, Mr. Onassis," Foreman told him. "I've *got* a great deal of money, Mr. Foreman," Ari said. When the role was offered to her, she got cold feet; it went to the Greek stage actress Irene Papas. "I get up every day of my life to *win*," Ari shouted at her when she turned down Foreman's offer. "I don't know why you bother to get up at all."

Their relationship cooled, became passionate, grew cool again. Although they no longer talked in Greek together, as if they were in a conspiracy, they stayed together. He never stopped trying to mold her, to demonstrate his power over her. He got her to wear more black, his favorite color. As if he were ordering some ritual of possession he told Alexandre of Paris to cut off her distinctive mane. According to one fashion writer, her new shorn look took "ten years off her age and deprived her face of its elemental excitement." But still often when she fought him, her passion was elemental enough to drive him back to Athens to his favorite bars to drink ouzo and Greek brandy, and eat from his fingers, and dance to the *bouzouki* music and smash plates until all the anger had gone out of him. Only in Greece, among his own people, could he let himself go. ("In Greece he behaved like a Greek, in England like an Englishman. He had this facility for adaptation. In Greece among Greeks he adopted the conduct of the marketplace," his friend Prof. Yanni Georgakis recalled.)

Callas now often went for months without practicing a note; even Ari appeared to have moved down a gear from the headlong pace of earlier years. He had built up a formidable team to take care of the day-to-day running of his seventy or so corporations around the world. In addition to the ubiquitous Meyer, and Costa Gratsos, his minister without portfolio in New York, he had made Thomas R. Lincoln, the son of Leroy Lincoln, who was president of Metropolitan Life in the days when he got his first major financing there, chief counsel to the organization; his cousin Costa Konialidis was running Olympic Airways; Nicolas Cokkinis, a member of the Embiricos shipping family, watched over Victory Carriers; miscellaneous cousins and lawyers mothered his Monaco interests; Roberto Arias steered his Panamanian corporations; and Nigel Neilson continued to protect his image with the oil giants in London. They all knew that Ari was never far away: he had everybody hearing footsteps, said Meyer. Ari claimed, "After you get to a certain point, money not only ceases to be a problem, it ceases to be important. What matters is to be happy and content."

But what mattered more was to be noticed, to be admired, to be envied. He believed he had achieved everything he wanted when he bought his own island, Skorpios (it is shaped like a scorpion), a perfect expression of feudal opulence in the Ionian Sea. In the beginning, the island was covered with olive trees; he added "all the trees and shrubs of the Bible"—almonds, bramble, pine, oleander, figs. Sometimes he stripped down to his shorts and planted trees himself, sweating in the sun, digging alongside his workers, telling them about the flowers, the fruits and the trees they were planting, stories he remembered from his grandmother . . . the almond tree blooms in the Holy Land as early as January . . . the fig is the first of the fruits to be mentioned in the Bible, it is a beautiful tree for providing shade; to sit beneath one's own fig tree was the Jewish ideal of peace and prosperity . . . when the cone of the pine is cut lengthwise, the mark on its surface resembles the hand of Christ, a sign of His blessing on the tree that sheltered the Virgin Mary when she was in flight with her family from Herod's troops. He was happy then, planting his land.

Among the new crowd surrounding him, the external proof of his social acceptability, and through whom he sought the aggrandizement of himself, were Prince and Princess Stanislas Radziwill. It was not Radziwill's defunct Polish title (Stas ignored the fact that he became plain mister when he became a British subject in 1951) that appealed to Ari so much as the fact that his wife, Lee, was the sister-in-law of the most powerful man in the world: "The guy I didn't ask to stay to dinner." Princess Radziwill, Jacqueline Kennedy's younger sister, was already drifting discreetly apart from her second husband when they got caught up in the Onassis circus in the early months of 1963. At twenty-nine, a high-toned Eastern Seaboard postdebutante (Farmington, three terms at Sarah Lawrence), Lee was a lightning rod for men like Ari. He admired "the way she was at home with wealth, the way she took luxury in her stride." She had been born with a taste for money; there is no higher kind of chic.

Their relationship quickly became close, and although he frequently confessed that he found her a "very sexy woman," and Lee was at a vulnerable stage of her life, it was some while before Callas recognized her as a potential rival (even though Ari had started to treat her more unkindly than ever). At a dinner party when somebody recalled that Puccini had described himself as a passionate seeker of beautiful women and good libretti, he banged the table and roared: "Son of a bitch, just like me! Only I don't give a damn about the libretti!" Friends continued to urge Callas to leave him. "When slight has followed slight, and insult has been added to insult, the love which remains is often illogical, but it is also indestructible," she answered. "It's a kind of madness and nobody chooses to be mad."

She sought solace in her work again, accepting a three-week concert tour in Europe. It was not a success, and it must have recalled to her Luchino Visconti's declaration that her great moment had gone; for Maria, the Italian director was a genius, almost a god, and his opinion preyed on her fragile confidence. ("As a woman she is still young, but as a singer she is not so young, and the voice changes with age," he had said. "Besides, now she is involved with private adventures, which is not good for her.") Yet when the tour ended on June 9, she could not stop herself from hurrying back to Ari, and her destructive private adventures.

The fact of the Onassis-Radziwill liaison surfaced with unexpected suddenness in the United States in the summer of 1963. "Does the ambitious Greek tycoon hope to become the brother-in-law of the American President?" mused the *Washington Post* columnist Drew Pearson. In Milan, Meneghini lost no time musing, assuring reporters that Ari had already dropped Maria for the princess. He always knew, he said, that the affair would have a bad ending. He never abandoned the hope that one day Maria would return to him.

The Pearson item was a double embarrassment to the president in the buildup to the 1964 election campaign. For not only had Ari been indicted by the United States government for fraud, but he was a divorced man already having a highly visible affair with a married opera star. It was almost certainly the Kennedy clout that had succeeded in getting Vatican permission for Lee to wed Radziwill in a Catholic ceremony after her first marriage to publisher Michael Canfield had ended in divorce; and even now, as Pearson publicly pondered her future, the Vatican tribunal was considering annulment of her first marriage by *Sacra Romana Rota*. "Last summer it was Castro and the missile crisis," said one White House aide. "This summer it's Onassis and the marriage crisis."

It was at this time that Jackie gave birth prematurely to her third child, a son, Patrick, who died within hours. Dining with Ari in Athens shortly after returning from the funeral, Lee said that her sister had taken the baby's death very hard. Ari immediately offered to put the *Christina* at her disposal for a recuperative cruise. Lee called Washington then and there. "Tell Jack that Stas and I will chaperone you. It will be perfectly proper and such fun. Oh Jacks," she said, using her sister's childhood nickname, "you can't imagine how terrific Ari's yacht is, and he says we can go anywhere you want. It will do you so much good to get away for a while." Although the president recognized how embarrassing the connection would be likely to prove in the future, Jackie accepted the invitation. Bobby Kennedy tried to salvage something out of the situation. "This business with Lee and Onassis," he said, taking Jackie to one side before she left, "just tell her to cool it, will you?"

The *Christina* was stocked with eight varieties of caviar, the finest vintage wines, and exotic fruits flown in (courtesy of Olympic Airways) from all over the world; the crew sixty-strong buttressed by two hairdressers, three chefs, a Swedish masseuse and a small orchestra for dancing in the evenings. They all set sail at the beginning of October for wherever the First Lady (occupying the principal stateroom, Chios) wished to go. "She's the captain," Ari told the mob of reporters gathered in Piraeus to witness the departure, and inventory the elaborately provisioned yacht. "Mrs. Kennedy's in charge here."

Abandoned in Paris, the first Callas knew of the guest list, and the fact that Ari himself was going to be on the cruise (he had offered to withdraw; Jackie would not hear of it: "How can we possibly go without our host?") was when she read it in the newspapers: the Radziwills; Princess Irene Galitzine, the dress designer; Artemis and Theodore Garofalides; Accardi Gurney, a friend of Lee's; Kennedy's Under Secretary of Commerce Franklin D. Roosevelt, Jr., and his wife, Susan. (Kennedy had little confidence in Lee's credentials as a chaperone and had drafted the Roosevelts to accompany Jackie: "Your presence will add a little respectability to the whole thing.") Ari lay low. To the disappointment of the press, he was nowhere to be seen when the *Christina* anchored first at Lesbos, then at Crete. But when the yacht reached Smyrna, Jackie led the demand that he give them a conducted tour. He quickly shed his shyness, taking her by the hand and showing her the places of his past. Photographs of the First Lady, looking extraordinarily happy and relaxed, strolling with Ari through the backstreets of his birthplace, were wired around the world. In Paris, the pictures on the front pages filled Callas with sadness and longing. ("Four years ago," she told Panaghis Vergottis, "that was me by his side, being beguiled by the story of his life . . . although I'm sure he makes most of it up. Memories demand too much effort.") In Washington, a Republican congressman lambasted the cruise, impugning the propriety of the president's wife and questioning Roosevelt's motives in accepting hospitality from a foreigner who had plenty to gain from the under secretary's influence with the United States Maritime Administration. The president called the *Christina* and advised his wife about the attention the trip was getting. According to Roosevelt, the president did not *order* her to return to Washington, although there can be no doubt what was uppermost in Kennedy's mind throughout their long static-plagued conversation on the radio-telephone. "I think Jackie felt that he was overreacting to the mudslinging of some cheesecloth congressman," said Meyer. "Anyway, it was left that she would return on the seventeenth, as planned."

Whether Lee knew it or not, the cruise was the turning point in her relationship with Ari. Not for the first time had he been close to two sisters, and not for the first time had he jumped in a surprising way. Within days he had become besotted by the First Lady's "sense of vulnerability." And she was beguiled by him. "I've dealt with a lot of people and they haven't all been scouts," he said one evening, conscious of the president's objections to him and feeling a need to explain himself, although Tina had warned him that he revealed himself most in the way he reminisced. "It's impossible for an entrepreneur, a man like me, not to tread on somebody's toes. All profit is an injustice to somebody. I've made a lot of enemies . . . but what the hell!" He dropped his postulant tone. "No excuses. I'm as rich as I know how to be, and rich I know about."

Meanwhile, in Washington, one of those enemies "indicated he would like to have a summary" on Aristotle Socrates Onassis. A lengthy new profile was prepared "from Bufiles and public source data," although there could not have been very much that J. Edgar Hoover did not already know about the man whom he had investigated as a spy and as a criminal and who was now beguiling the president's wife. "Hoover instinctively disliked Ari. He was a great believer in no-smoke-without-fire theories and was convinced that the Greek was getting away with something. At the same time he must have been enjoying the president's discomfort. It was exactly the kind of situation that appealed to his sense of evil," said one of the agents who contributed to the October 16 memorandum on Ari.

On the last night of the cruise, Ari presented the women with expensive gifts. Lee collected three jeweled bracelets; Jackie got a magnificent diamond-and-ruby necklace. In a revealing letter to the president Lee complained: "Ari has showered Jackie with so many presents I can't stand it. All I've got is three dinky little bracelets that Caroline wouldn't even wear to her own birthday party." It was a joke; it was also unfair. ("Your total understanding of women you got from a Van Cleef & Arpels catalogue," Callas had once chided Ari.)

Jackie returned to Washington on October 17, as she had promised. A few evenings later at a private dinner with Ben and Toni Bradlee, two of the president's close social friends (Ben Bradlee was also *Newsweek*'s White House correspondent), Jackie expressed her regret for the awkward publicity the cruise had created, and for the harm it had done to Roosevelt's reputation. But if Washington had returned her to her senses, and with them a promising malleability, she still bravely stood up for Ari, whom she called "an alive and vital person who has come up from nowhere." Kennedy said that Ari would still have to be told that he would not be welcome in the United States until after the 1964 election. Always the politician, always looking for new ways to manipulate people, he knew that Jackie's "guilt feelings" about the whole affair could be turned to his own advantage. "Maybe now you'll come with us to Texas next month," he said. "Sure I will, Jack," she told him.

On November 22, 1963, Ari was in Hamburg for the launching of the *Olympic Chivalry* when he learned of Kennedy's assassination in Dallas. He immediately telephoned Lee at her London home in Buckingham Place. She asked him to accompany her and Stas to Washington for the funeral. He reminded her that he had been warned not to step foot inside America for at least a year. "I don't think that matters very much now," she told him. The following day he received an official invitation from Angier Biddle Duke, chief of protocol, not only to attend the funeral ceremony but also to be a guest at the White House during his stay in Washington. Although he was one of only half a dozen people outside the immediate family to be given this honor his presence went almost unnoticed in the days of shock and mourning that gripped America.

He was surprised by the atmosphere inside the White House. It was the way he had always imagined an Irish wake to be. Men got drunk and sang sentimental songs and told outrageous stories about Jack's adventures, remembering the great coups and the narrow scrapes. Nobody referred to the dead president in the past tense. Ari quickly discovered his role as a kind of court jester. It was a part he had played often for Churchill, and he was prepared to play it again for the Kennedys.

Sunday, November 24: Rose Kennedy dined upstairs with Stas Radziwill; Jacqueline and Lee were served in the sitting room with Robert Kennedy. The rest of the Kennedys ate in the family dining room with their house guests, noted the historian William Manchester: Robert McNamara, the secretary of defense; Phyllis Dillon, the wife of the secretary of the treasury; David Powers, a Kennedy insider since Jack ran for Congress in 1946; and Aristotle Socrates Onassis. After dinner, Ari quickly became the center of interest. Robert Kennedy set the tone, harping on his "mystery man" image, and soon they all joined in the fun. He was teased remorselessly about his yacht (were the bar stools really covered with the scrotum of whales?), his wealth, his airline, his kingdom (Monte Carlo) and his past. The attorney general was especially interested in his past. Ari knew that when people did not like him (and only weeks before Bobby Kennedy had encouraged the president's resolve to keep him out of the United States for a very long time) they never failed to ask about his past. He played out the game. "I have never made the mistake of thinking it is a sin to make money," he said. After a while, Bobby disappeared and later returned with a serious-looking document that required Ari to donate half his fortune to the poor people of Latin America. It was the least he could do, the attorney general told him, since that was where he had made his first million. Ari solemnly signed the outlandish contract, in Greek.

On December 3, he was back in France for Maria's fortieth birthday. The distinct chill between them since her exclusion from Jackie's cruise in October seemed forgotten as they celebrated the occasion with a conspicuous party at Maxim's. "The shepherd, when the spring returns," she told Panaghis Vergottis that evening in Paris, "thinks no more of the cold that is gone." Perhaps it was an act, and certainly he knew that her immense feline pride had been tested to the limit; her new unguarded mood disturbed the old Greek shipowner a lot. He had known Ari since the 1930s, he knew the way his mind worked, and even if he did not precisely foresee Ari's seesaw years between the two women, he knew that his interest in the widow Jacqueline Bouvier Kennedy would not quickly go away. "Maria," he told her gently, "when the spring returns, sometimes that is the best time to think of the cold to come."

Ari's renewed attention could not completely annihilate the hurt and the humiliation he had caused her. And although it had been eighteen months since her last performance in a full-scale production, she told Covent Garden's General Administrator David Webster that she would sing *Tosca* provided it was put into the current season and directed by Franco Zeffirelli. The date was fixed (January 21, 1964) and the contracts signed before she found the courage to tell Ari what she had done. "I need it, Ari. I want to be *me* again." He did not fight her. "It's very short notice," he said.

"Isn't it a risk?" "I'm forty years old, Ari," she answered. "My whole life is a risk."

Life was no safer for aging tycoons. Ari's deteriorating relationship with Rainier had reached a critical phase. The crisis had its genesis in the Quai d'Orsay. More than half the three thousand companies registered in Monaco were French post office box numbers, fronts avoiding French tax. When the principality launched a hard-sell campaign in Paris headed "What Monaco can do for you," de Gaulle began wondering what Monaco could do for him. When Rainer refused to introduce a profits tax to stop the drain, de Gaulle threatened to cut off Monaco's water and power and set up checkpoints on all access roads. Rainier quickly capitulated. Foreign requests to set up shop in Monaco plummeted, and the real estate boom they had triggered fizzled out. Rainier renewed his pressure on Ari to plough his SBM profits into tourist hotels. Ari finally agreed to build a luxury apartment block and two hotels, but wanted guarantees forbidding any rival hotel development. Infuriated by the monopoly clause, Rainier vetoed the whole scheme and went on television attacking the SBM for its "lethargy and bad faith." *Newsweek*'s Elizabeth Peer filed a memo to New York that Ari had "telephonically exploded when asked his reaction to the prince's astonishing public attack, shouting, 'You must be very hard up for news to call me!' He insists speech was no concern of his since Rainier belted SBM rather than naming him. Onassis technically correct, which gives him neat excuse to dodge the issue."

Meanwhile, Callas prepared for her comeback. Her opening night at Covent Garden was a triumph; she immediately signed to sing *Norma* in Paris in May. Ari missed her opening night at the Opéra; he was there for her fourth performance on Saturday, June 6. It was an auspicious date in the French calendar, the twentieth anniversary of the Allied invasion of Normandy, and the array of celebrities (Charlie and Oona Chaplin, Begum Aga Khan, Yves Saint Laurent, Jean-Paul Belmondo, Princess Grace, Jean Seberg, David Niven, Rudolf Bing, socialites and cabinet ministers) turned the occasion into a kind of *fête nationale*. The French notices had been more mixed than for her *Tosca* in London. In Paris her phrasing and timing were off; she struggled on, missing a high note here, fluffing a line there. In the last act, she broke on a high C. It was the signal the anti-Callas claque had been waiting for. Amid the catcalls, she stopped the orchestra and told the conductor to begin again. It was the kind of risk that Callas at her peak would have taken with contempt. Now it was a kind of madness. The sudden silence—"the sort of quiet the mob probably made as the guillotine shivered before its descent," Rudolf Bing recalled—was unreal. She hit the note and held it with perfect control. It was not enough for her hecklers. Fights broke out between those who applauded her courage and those who resented it. There was a time when that kind of incident would have filled her with ferocious pleasure. "As long as I hear them stirring and hissing like snakes out there, I know I'm on top. If I got nothing from my enemies, I'd know I was slipping. I'd know they're not afraid of me any more," she had said seven years before when she was the greatest prima donna in the world. She hated to be pitied, she said when she had the opera world at her feet. She had never pitied anyone.

Ari had never felt prouder of her. Winning meant everything to him, yet it was at the moment when Maria's failure was absolute that he admired her most. "You showed a lot of courage out there tonight," he said. "It was mostly impudence," she told him, perhaps because she could not describe her feelings, nor believe in the force of her will. For the first time the snakes had scared her. The admission was not a small surrender, and he knew that some of the responsibility was his. "I think we need to build some time together," he said as he stepped back into her life. It was their first full summer on Skorpios, and it was the most intimate summer of their relationship.

One of their visitors that summer was Panaghis Vergottis, and a frequent subject of conversation was Maria's investments. By their standards, she was in financial straits. She could not maintain her present life-style without more money, and money that did not depend on her voice. When shipowners discuss investments it inevitably means ships. It was agreed that she should become an owner. (Full of high spirits, they called their enterprise Operation Prima Donna.) On September 2, Vergottis heard in London that a twenty-eight-thousand-ton bulk carrier nearing completion at the shipyard of Astilleros y Talleres del Noroeste in Spain had failed to meet its delivery date, and the owner in New York had used the delay clause in the contract to get out in a falling market. The vessel was available at around $4.2 million. Vergottis made an offer of $3.6 million, 25 percent cash with the balance on mortgage over eight years.

He caught the night flight to Athens. The following morning he called the *Christina* from the Hotel Grande Bretagne and told Ari what he had done. On his way to his family home on the island of Cephalonia he suggested that he call by the yacht to discuss the situation. "We must think about this carefully," Ari told Maria. "Ever since those damned American ships, I have made it a point of principle never to buy a leftover something from *anybody*."

The terms had already been agreed to: Callas would buy a 25

percent holding in the company (Overseas Bulk Carriers, a Liberian corporation formed in New York with a capital stock of one hundred bearer shares*), Vergottis would acquire a 25 percent interest and Ari 50 percent. Ari would make a present of 26 percent of his holding to Maria, guaranteeing her a 51 percent interest in a vessel to be managed by Vergottis. According to Ari the split had been suggested by Vergottis, inspired by his "eagerness to protect her in the event of my death, in regard to heirs, partners, and complications, and so forth." In time, all this would become the stuff of scandal in an English court of law; the only decision now was whether they should go ahead with the Spanish ship if their offer were accepted.

Vergottis arrived the following day, accompanied by Charles Graves, a writer who had written a history of Monte Carlo. Everybody was in a relaxed mood. Ari, whose antipathy toward Rainier had become obsessional, pumped Graves for dirt on the prince and "dared me to eat one of these lamb's eyes which are a sort of Greek hors d'oeuvre," the writer later recalled. It was decided to let Vergottis's offer for the ship stand, and on September 9 the yard made a counteroffer, higher than his $3.6 million although significantly lower than the original asking price. Vergottis cut his offer down to $3 million, and the talks were broken off. A few weeks later, he met Ari in London and told him, "You know that ship is still fooling around. Nobody wants it. Shall we have another try?" Ari told him to offer $3.4 million "and not a penny more. If they come back, fine. If not, forget it." The deal was signed on October 27 on Ari's terms. Three days later the new partners met for a celebration dinner at Maxim's. Although the controlling arrangements in *Artemision II* (as the vessel was now called) had not been put in writing, Operation Prima Donna was toasted as a triumph, and Maria was welcomed into the circle of shipowners. It was a world and a role she relished. She was fascinated by financial talk and listened for hours while Ari and Panaghis analyzed markets and discussed business opportunities.

In spite of her canny teachers and her keen interest in increasing her pile, Maria often made a muddle of business; she got lost in the details. On her maiden voyage to Japan the *Artemision* developed engine problems, which apparently convinced Vergottis that she was "an unlucky ship." On January 8, 1965, over another dinner at Maxim's (Ari was in Athens), he talked her into altering the terms of the partnership by converting her $168,000 invest-

---

* *A share simply made out to "bearer" in which the title passes by delivery, akin to a banknote.*

ment in Overseas Bulk Carriers into a straight loan, paying 6.5 percent interest. She brightened at the prospect of "earning more than she was getting on deposit in Swiss banks at that time." She would, of course, be able to exercise the option on her own twenty-five shares in the company anytime she wished. "As I love you very much," she later recalled his words, "I think this is a better way . . . if, which I doubt, the ship does not do well, you can always pull out, and you have had the interest on your money." She replied: "Thank you, Panaghis, that is very nice of you."

Ari had already transferred twenty-six of his shares in the Liberian company to her; the remaining 24 percent of his stake was shared between four of his nephews. Although, on paper at least, his interest in *Artemision II* and Overseas Bulk Carriers was over, he was far from pleased when Maria talked to him in Athens the following morning. "I could not explain it very well—technically, I cannot explain these things, my Lord," Callas would later tell an English judge, reconstructing the conversation with stilted propriety. "I remember Mr. Onassis's reaction to it. He did not like it, but said, 'Why does Mr. Vergottis do it, because it is useless.' I said, 'Never mind, Mr. Onassis, let us not hurt Mr. Vergottis's feelings. He is doing his best for me. On top of everything I gain the 6.5 percent, so I mean, there was no problem, and when you come over you talk to him about it.' " Yet in spite of Ari's curious reaction to the arrangement, it seemed unlikely that Vergottis was seeking to cheat her; an immensely rich man, he had initiated the deal out of affection for her. There was no rational motive for behavior that would inevitably lose him her friendship, and that of Ari, who had trusted him for thirty years.

Several months went by. Ari continued to slug it out with Rainier, and the question of shares in a one-ship company was not uppermost in his mind. In March, Maria flew to New York for two performances of *Tosca* at the Met, and although the presence of Jackie Kennedy in the audience captured most of the headlines, the audience was enthralled by her performance.* Nevertheless, as the first night of *Norma* at the Opéra in May loomed, a sense of foreboding enveloped her. More and more she began to suspect that the shares Ari had given her in *Artemision* were a kind of payoff—which they were, although he was not yet willing to acknowledge the fact, even to himself. She was unable to shake the bad memories of her last performance at the Opéra a year before.

---

* The critics were not so convinced. "Never an instrument of luscious quality, her soprano last week was a thin and often wobbly echo of the voice that [thrilled] the Met in 1958. Her high notes were shrill and achingly insecure . . . Callas relied almost wholly on dramatic rather than vocal brilliance to carry her through," reported Time magazine (March 26, 1965).

Her anxiety shaded into sheer terror by opening night. Pumped full of vitamins and tranquilizers, she got through the first performance; after that it was downhill all the way. Her dressing room was filled with Ari's flowers, only this time he did not come. By her final night on May 29, another gala occasion, she had gone as far as her spirit would carry her. At the end of the third act she broke down and was carried unconscious to her dressing room. Ninety minutes later, in a kind of stupor, she told the crowd of admirers that had gathered at the stage door, "I know I've let you down. I'm so sorry. I promise you all that one day I shall return to win your forgiveness and justify your love."

She set out for the sanctuary of Skorpios. She wanted another summer of '64. It was not to be. Ari's attitude toward her had never been bloodier. "Most of the time he ignored her utterly, as if she simply wasn't there. Then he'd explode in a terrible rage against her for no reason at all that anyone could fathom," said a friend who was around at that time. Several guests made excuses and left early rather than witness her distress. "Once you knew they always had a good time in bed, even when they fought. Just to look at them you knew that the sex was fine. But now he acted as if he couldn't stand to be near her," said one visitor who got off the island early that summer.

Yet while he appalled and angered many by his treatment of Callas, others continued to see only the attractive and sensitive side of his nature. The death of Sir Winston Churchill at the beginning of 1965 upset him deeply. Although he had used the great statesman for his own ends, he had become genuinely and inordinately fond of him. At the funeral service at St. Paul's he became so visibly distressed (his silk handkerchief was wet with tears long before the service began) that Nonie Montague Browne attempted to calm him with a tranquilizer, which he had difficulty in swallowing. "He was sobbing like a baby," said a senior Foreign Office diplomat, who found the emotional display "a touch vulgar— there is no other word for it." After the service, Nonie, whose husband was accompanying the cortege to Bladon, accepted Ari's invitation to travel in his car. He told the chauffeur to stop at the first pub in the Strand and insisted that they all (including the chauffeur) go in for a brandy. As they talked about the times they had shared with the great man, Nonie reflected "what a real, warm, understanding friend" Ari had turned out to be. When she first met him, in a nightclub in Monte Carlo, ten years earlier, he had "all but ignored" her, concentrating his charm on her husband: he was "head hunting" Churchill, she recalled wryly. Since then she had revised her poor opinion of him. She remembered a trip to Morocco when antique kaftans were brought on board for the guests to try on and buy. The Montague Brownes took one look at the price tags and slipped unobtrusively away. Later Ari said in a surprised voice, "Oh, dear, we've got one too many of these dresses—oh, Nonie, do you think you could possibly wear it?" It was, she thought, typical of his kindness, and sensibility.

Meanwhile, he continued to conduct the war with Rainier from Skorpios. "He behaved like some feudal king who believed that plots against him could more easily be discovered if his palace were set apart and a sharp eye was kept on the comings and goings of his courtiers," said a Paris banker who, in a three-month period "at the height of the battle," was summoned to Skorpios twenty-three times. "If Rainier thought Ari was out of it, holed up in his island citadel, he was wrong. Ari owned the finest intelligence network that money could buy. Rainier didn't take a leak without Ari knowing about it."

Rainier was now running his own show and proving himself a shrewd politician. Yet within forty-eight hours of giving his approval to a plan to create six hundred thousand nontransferable SBM shares in the name of the principality, effectively reducing Ari's 52 percent domination to less than a third, Ari had the details on his desk in Skorpios. Callas took the brunt of her lover's anger; it was several days before he had calmed down enough to think out his moves. The "Lausanne gambit" (the idea had been devised by a Lausanne law professor) had been carefully structured to avoid the unprincely suggestion of nationalization. "We calculated that the share-creation shift had plunged Rainier's treasury into the red, or damn close to it. It was a gamble of a very high order," said a French banker on Ari's team. "It made the prince extremely vulnerable. Ari told us to spread the rumor that Rainier was planning to expropriate the 450,000 original shares still held in private hands, and to incite stockholders to organize protest committees and pressure groups. It was monstrous, reprehensible and bloody effective."

Callas turned her thoughts to the film of *Tosca* that Franco Zeffirelli wanted her to make with him. It was exactly what she needed "to exorcise those private demons," Panaghis Vergottis told her when she flew to London in August to attend his brother's funeral. The German producers were keen, the money was there, Tito Gobbi would costar. Encouraged by Vergottis's enthusiasm for the project, and temporarily beyond the influence of Ari, she moved swiftly ahead with the deal. But at the final meeting with the producers, she said she wanted Ari to look over the terms. And just when it seemed that he wanted nothing more dearly than to cut her free from his life, Ari appeared determined to scuttle the deal. His demands, his unwillingness to compromise, his propensity for histrionics, made any serious attempt at negotiation hopeless. At one point he offered to buy out the Germans and produce the film himself with Callas and her agent Sander Gorlinsky. Tired of the whole affair, the producers agreed and a new set of talks began. And collapsed. In October, Maria announced that she was no longer interested in making the movie.

Vergottis's disappointment, both as a friend and a music lover, cut deep; the thought that Maria had distrusted his advice hurt him terribly. He begged her to change her mind; he believed that *Tosca* would be the biggest achievement of her career. He was seventy-five years old, and he "prayed every night to be spared to see its completion." Although on the surface nothing had changed between the three friends, Vergottis was puzzled by Ari's behavior; he could not understand why he had gone to such pains to subvert the *Tosca* project. (Later he would evolve a theory that since Maria had rejected the movie he had set up with Carl Foreman, he was determined to thwart *all* movies.) Exactly what Vergottis said to Maria next nobody has ever discovered; all that is certain is that he would never forgive her reply. (From "asides and innuendos only," one of her English lawyers later suggested her remark was "a heated accusation of a homosexual intimacy between Onassis and Vergottis in the thirties.") She immediately wrote Panaghis a long letter explaining the strain she was under and the grief she felt for the harm she had done to their friendship. ("If ever a letter were written which was an *amende honorable* for any wrong that Madame Callas might have done Mr. Vergottis, that *amende honorable* is to be found in that letter," a British judge would later observe.) Vergottis did not respond. He refused to take her telephone calls from Paris. He was inconsolable. Bitter with age and ill health and a sense of betrayal, he removed the pictures of Callas and Ari from his suite at the London Ritz.

On November 25, one year after the celebratory dinner at Maxim's, and six days after she had received a check for $5,460, the second installment of interest on her loan to the Overseas Bulk Carriers Corporation, Maria decided to convert her loan into 25 shares and accordingly cabled Vergottis Ltd in London: "This is to notify you that I have today decided to request you to convert my unsecured loan to you of 60,000 pounds [$168,000] into $25/100$ shares of the M/S Artemision in accordance with the option given to me verbally by your President, Mr. P. Vergottis, in consideration of granting you this loan. Please issue the corresponding certificate of these 25 shares and mail it to me 44, avenue Foch, Paris. Maria Callas."

Vergottis's reply was brief, "Reference your telegram refute your claim as totally unfounded."

Ari's reactions to most events were intuitive, swift and direct, yet when Callas told him what had happened he counseled patience. Legally he had no interest in the matter; he was anxious to keep his distance from Callas. His eventual intervention in the affair was not wholly the result of conscience, but of pride. For weeks he had been quietly pressuring Vergottis to take the issue to arbitration before any one of a number of well-known figures in the Greek shipping world, in the city of London or, failing that, an independent panel of lawyers. "I think we should avoid the publicity of a public trial, don't you?" He kept at Vergottis, knowing that publicity is the thing that old-money Greeks abhor more than anything else in the world. But any hopes that he had of avoiding a court case ended one evening at Claridge's when a chance encounter in the dining room culminated with Vergottis brandishing a bottle of brandy and shouting, "Get out of here or I'll throw it at you!" The stage was set for a play, which as a judge later perceived, had "many of the elements of a Sophoclean tragedy about it."

"Face was at the root of the case—not the ship, not money, not shares. None of those things mattered. It was a sort of catharsis, a sex case in the end. It was the good sporting stuff of which litigation ought to be about. And they could all afford it. There was no law in the case at all. The judge simply had to decide who was most believable," a senior lawyer said afterward. "Our old gentleman was convinced that they had done him dirt," said one of Vergottis's advocates. "But I would be as wary of anything a Greek shipowner told me as I would the wiliest inhabitant on the subcontinent of India. I advised him that if his story was accepted we would win, it was as simple as that. Unfortunately, Vergottis had no charm. Onassis was all charm. The shipping world didn't like Onassis one bit. They respected our old gentleman profoundly."

The case came before Mr. Justice Roskill in the Queen's Bench Division in London on April 17, 1967. It was bad timing, following hard on the heels of Ari's final defeat in Monaco. Claiming that the maneuver was unconstitutional, he had challenged Rainier's decision to create six hundred thousand SBM shares in the Monaco Supreme Court. In March the court found in favor of the prince. For Ari the game was over. He had been the most powerful man in the principality, the king of Monte Carlo, and now he was just another rich punter. He sold his holding back to Monaco for $9.5 million, claiming, "We were gypped," and sailed away. Claude de Kemoularia, Rainier's chief tactician and negotiator recruited for

the emergency from the French Treasury, didn't even try to hide
his jubilation. "If he'd taken our offer six months ago he'd have
been a richer fellow today and a damn sight happier. Even so, the
real pleasure is in beating him. He's never been thrashed before."
In his own private consciousness Ari took the loss of Monte Carlo
hard. But he had always resolved his disappointments with new
confrontations, new rules to manipulate, new people to charm and
conquer. All these things he found in an English court of justice.
The headline writers had a field day; in the dry language of English jurisprudence the case was listed simply as:

ONASSIS AND CALOGEROPOULOS V. VERGOTTIS

Contract—Option—Shares in ship—Whether party provided money by way of loan or for purchase of shares in
ship.

Dressed in a scarlet gown and white twenties-style turban, her
face heavily made up, Callas arrived on Ari's arm as if they were
attending a fashionable first night. In his opening statement for
the plaintiffs, Sir Milner Holland hinted at the drama to come. "I
am sorry to say that Mr. Vergottis said that if either Mr. Onassis
or Mme. Callas (claiming under her real name,* she was referred
to throughout as Mme. Callas) dared to appear in the witness box
they would be faced with a great deal of scandal, both in court
and in the press. It is perhaps natural that Mr. Onassis stigmatized
that as blackmail and unnatural that Mr. Vergottis laughed. The
breach between these two gentlemen and between Mme. Callas
and Mr. Vergottis has not been healed from that day."

Mr. Peter Bristow, counsel for Vergottis, had only recently
taken his silk,† and the case (which was filling the pages of the
press from *The Times* to the tabloids: "Onassis and Singer Sue
Over Million-Pound Ship Deal"; " 'Blackmail' Story in Action by
Callas") was a splendid opportunity for him to make a name for
himself. With allegations of fraud, treachery and criminality in
the air, and with heady intimations of sex and jealousy at the root
of the action, Bristow (later High Court Judge Mr. Justice Bristow)
addressed himself to the task of establishing the exact nature of
the relationship between Ari and Callas. There were many ex-
changes like this one:

"After you got to know Madame Callas did you part from
your wife and did Madame Callas part from her hus-

---

* Misspelled in all the trial documents.
† An English legal term denoting that a barrister is held in high esteem by his peers and
entitled to wear a silk gown, a step toward becoming a Queen's Counsel: Q.C.

band?" "Yes, sir. Nothing to do with our meeting. Just
coincidence." "Do you regard her as being in a position
equivalent to being your wife, if she was free?" "No. If
that were the case I have no problem marrying her, neither has she any problem marrying me." "Do you feel any
obligations towards her other than those of mere friendship?" "None whatsoever."

When it was put to him that he had turned Callas against
Vergottis (a man whom she admitted she had once considered
"more than my father") Ari answered without a pause: "Mme.
Callas is not a vehicle for me to drive. She has her own brakes and
her own brains." Although Maria recognized the necessary caution
and expediency of his answers, and no one could be more elusive
than Ari when he wanted to be, his unaffected offhandedness toward their relationship was yet another blow to her pride. His
denial of all obligations toward her went beyond legal discretion:
it eradicated the past, it was a public declaration of intent.
("It wasn't a trial," she later said, "it was a memorial service.")
When they were lovers, everything was possible; nothing would
ever be that good again. Yet still she could not draw away from
him. It was a weakness that the counsel for Vergottis pursued:
"You told us that you are still married to your husband, who
is in Italy?" Under Italian law, she answered, she was "very
much" still married to Meneghini. But she was rattled. "We
are here because of twenty-five shares for which I have paid, not
because of my relations with another man," she reminded the
judge.
    Her popularity diminished a little more every day as the
world saw her, in league with her rich and powerful lover, destroying a sick old man (his doctor always by his side) who had been
her friend and father-figure; yet she was a convincing witness;
Vergottis was not. His health visibly failing, bitterly convinced
that he was the victim of a conspiracy, he listened to the case
unfold with disordered emotions, and his uncontrollable outbursts
(spraying innuendo and venomous remarks before he could be
shut up by his own counsel, or the judge) did nothing to enhance
his case. "Is it pure coincidence that the 60,000 pounds which you
say was a loan happens to be just the sum appropriate to a 25
percent shareholding?" asked Sir Milner Holland, counsel for Callas and Ari. It was not coincidence at all, Vergottis answered. "I
am now convinced that he [Onassis] had it in mind in order to
trap me. I have heard so many things after this that it would make
your hair stand on end—the things he has done and how he

started. I have been to Greece and investigated lots of things. He is black in his heart."

After a ten-day hearing Ari was confident that he and Callas would "win by a mile," although the legal teams on both sides knew that it would be a photo finish: "The judge simply had to decide who would come in second," one of the lawyers later said. "There is no escape—one could wish there were—from the fact that perjury has been committed by one side or the other," Mr. Justice Roskill went straight to the heart of the matter in his summing-up. "If the defense is right there can be no doubt that Mr. Onassis and Mme. Callas have put their heads together, if I may be forgiven for using the term, to 'frame' Mr. Vergottis." If Onassis and Callas were telling the truth, he said, then clearly Vergottis had "lied and lied more than once."

The verdict went against Vergottis. He was ordered to transfer the disputed shares in the company to Callas and pay all their legal costs, amounting to some eighty-seven thousand dollars. Against his own legal advice, Vergottis appealed and won the appeal. Lord Denning, the master of the rolls, sitting with Lord Justice Salmon and Lord Justice Edmund Davies, found that Mr. Justice Roskill had "misdirected himself" in accepting that greed and avarice motivated Vergottis. A new trial was ordered. Callas and Ari immediately appealed against this decision to the highest court in England—the House of Lords. The day the news of their appeal was announced Ari telephoned Vergottis at the Ritz: "Not many guys your age, Pan, get two Judgment Days to worry about." "I'll handle the second one," Vergottis told him, still alert at seventy-eight. "The first one *you* worry about."

"No one wins in a law court. If you're lucky, you get less hurt than the other fellow," Ari said later. He would not know for eighteen months whether or not he had "come in second."

That summer Callas and Ari returned to Skorpios, although they were not on the best of terms with each other. Drawn together in a single will against Vergottis, their minds had shared a moment of unity; their hearts had never been more divided. At dinner the evening before they returned to Paris they talked as if they both knew they had spent their last summer together. "The only free people are those who love nobody," Ari said. She thought that was "too big a price to pay" for freedom. He asked her what she most wanted for herself, one of the half-dozen dinner guests later recalled the conversation that evening. "I just want to be on good terms with myself," she answered. During the following months they saw little of each other. She went for weeks at a stretch without leaving her new apartment on avenue Georges-Mandel.

CHAPTER 13

Love is very rich both in honey and in gall.

PLAUTUS

SECRECY WAS at the heart of all Ari's most serious ambitions ("He won more tricks hiding his own intentions than by trying to discover what the fuck the opposition was up to," said Meyer) and it was with the utmost secrecy and with more than ordinary persistence that he had continued to see Jackie Kennedy during her years of mourning. Still in the public eye as the Kennedy widow, she welcomed him to her duplex on Fifth Avenue. Although Jackie's travels with the widowed David Ormsby-Gore, Lord Harlech, a longtime family friend and the former British ambassador to the United States, and Roswell Gilpatric, former under secretary of defense in the Kennedy administration, her dates with men like Arthur Schlesinger, Jr., Mike Nichols, and chic homosexuals like Truman Capote, her lunches at the Côte Basque with various foreign aristocrats, bankers and politicians, created the speculation and filled the gossip columns, it was her secluded tête-à-têtes with Ari, unobserved, unsuspected, *unthinkable*, that were evolving into a serious relationship. ("She understood the art of pleasing men like Ari, and flirtation there certainly was," an Olympic aide in Paris later said. "I am sure they were not yet lovers.") He quarantined his servants to their quarters and served dinner himself the night she visited avenue Foch. "Ari loved all that, the clandestinity of the chase, driven on by the social clout Jackie would give him," says a former Olympic staffer in Paris. The secrecy also reflected his concern that the Kennedys, if warned of his growing closeness to Jackie, and the depth of the gratitude that his kindnesses inspired in her, might quickly move to end the relationship. He knew that it was not with affection that Bobby Kennedy referred to him as "the Greek," and described him as "a complete rogue on the grand scale." He knew that he could not win in an open confrontation with Bobby, who had assumed the leadership of the Kennedy clan after his brother's death and spent so much time advising and comforting Jackie and her children that tongues had started to wag. "He's spending an awful lot of time with the widder," Eunice Kennedy Shriver had pointedly put it to Bobby's wife, Ethel.

With the instinct of the politician, Bobby had seen the dangers that Jackie posed: it was unreasonable to expect her, aged thirty-seven, to continue to devote herself to a pure and virtuous widowhood, and that possibility made Bobby increasingly nervous as the 1968 Democratic primaries got under way and he dithered over whether to declare his candidacy. Although Jackie had tried to set herself apart from the rest of the family, to lead her own life and to raise her children beyond the spell of the Kennedy ethos, Bobby's influence over her was considerable. She was a Kennedy. She could not have private liaisons without public consequences.

The last thing in the world Ari wanted was premature disclosure of his deepening intimacy with Jackie. That Bobby had not discovered the growing importance of his sister-in-law's involvement with "the Greek" is remarkable. "I guess their very incongruity was an important element in their being able to hide what was going on for so long," says a former member of the Onassis hierarchy. "How could anyone be expected to tumble to what seemed in its nature incomprehensible?"

Jackie was in Mexico when she heard that Bobby was going to run for president. It reawakened her old foreboding; she was convinced that if he reached the White House he would die the same way her husband had died. ("Do you know what I think will happen to Bobby?" she said to Arthur Schlesinger, Jr. "The same thing that happened to Jack . . . I've told Bobby this, but he isn't fatalistic, like me.") Dutifully she prepared the required statement for the press: "I will always be with him with all my heart. I shall always back him." She knew that she could not much longer put off telling him how far her relationship with Ari had gone, and where it was heading. She had been reported dining with "the Greek," sometimes with Rudolf Nureyev and Margot Fonteyn; sometimes with Christina—at El Morocco and 21, at Dionysos and Mykonos in New York. ("Every fact in the world must have been printed about you now," Nureyev said. "To be this public is not good for soul." "Oh, but they're still on the fanciful embellishments. The essence is still untouched," she answered.)

In March, a few days after Bobby announced his candidacy and became embroiled in the internecine struggles between the conservatives who backed Lyndon Johnson's escalation of the Vietnam war and the divided antiwar liberals, Ari decided that "now the kid's got other fish to fry" it was time to edge toward a more open interest in Jackie. He had been searching all his life for the consummate woman and had always been disappointed, he remarked at a cocktail party at the George V Hotel in Paris. Garbo? Eva Perón? Callas? He answered with a smile, a shrug, another smile. Jacqueline Kennedy? "She is a totally misunderstood woman. Perhaps she even misunderstands herself. She's being held up as a model of propriety, constancy and so many of those boring American female virtues. She's now utterly devoid of mystery. She needs a small scandal to bring her alive. A peccadillo, an indiscretion. Something should happen to her to win our fresh compassion. The world loves to pity fallen grandeur." Riding back to his apartment afterward, he told Meyer, "That should set the cat among the pigeons on Hickory Hill." *

Bobby had heard about Ari's comment, recognized its implications, got mad, his right fist smashing into his left palm, and cooled down again by the time Jackie leveled with him in the voice that Callas had mischievously told Ari made her think of "Marilyn Monroe playing Ophelia." Although she did not suggest that marriage was imminent ("Jackie isn't a woman in whom passion is an absolute impulse," noted a woman friend who felt that "fallen grandeur" was beyond her imagination), it was a possibility in her mind; they both had something the other wanted. "I guess it's a family weakness," Bobby said, alluding to Ari's earlier liaison with Lee Radziwill. "I guess you know this could cost me five states," he added. Although the idea of the First Widow as the second Mrs. Onassis was infinitely alarming, a union fraught with awkward consequences and the cause of much moral anxiety, he knew that it would be a mistake to take a hard line and risk incurring Jackie's alienation at a crucial moment in his campaign. Her allegiance meant everything to him. And he was genuinely sensitive to her situation. She was more vulnerable and afraid than even those people who believed themselves closest to her were aware. She had a sense of melancholy she could not shake. Assassination was her shaping experience; she had dreams of being murdered and worried constantly that her children would be kidnapped or

* *Bobby Kennedy's mansion in McLean, Virginia, bought from JFK in 1957.*

harmed. Aristotle Socrates Onassis had much to offer besides love, bread and dreamless nights.

Before she married Jack Kennedy in 1953 and became a model Washington wife (albeit with a weakness for collecting couturier bills), Jackie was an established member of America's aristocracy. From infancy on she had breathed an atmosphere fragrant with money. Her father, John V. "Black Jack" Bouvier III, a Long Island stockbroker, a Yalie who never stopped enjoying the good life even when most of his money and most of his health had slipped away, spoiled her dreadfully. The Bouviers divorced in 1938, and four years later Janet Bouvier married Hugh Auchincloss, a name prominent in New York society for more than seven generations. Through the Auchincloss connections and her stepfather's generosity (the family stake in Standard Oil had paid for an estate in McLean, Virginia, and another in Newport) Jackie pursued a life of hunt balls, sailing, skiing and fast cars; with the rich girl's elegant antipathy to enthusiasm, she displayed no surprise when society columnist Cholly Knickerbocker named her Queen Deb of 1947. In the words of a friend who attended the same deb dances at Newport's Clambake Club on Easton's Point, "She was almost utterly unconscious of the possibility of any mode of living other than her own." After Dallas, although she never gave way to public despair, an aura of sadness clung about her that came from the consciousness of her history. Now in Ari's world it was as if she had rediscovered familiar ground beneath her feet: a return to safer and more splendid times.

Bobby intimated that it might be easier for him to adjust to the idea of Ari once the campaign pressures were off. And although the thought was politically pragmatic (Ari was too Levantine, too vulgar and moving much too close to the Greek military dictatorship of Col. George Papadopoulos ever to be condoned) it was a more encouraging response than Jackie had expected, and she gratefully offered to suspend her retirement from public life to campaign for him and promised to wait until after the election in November before making any public announcement about her future plans. Those insiders who knew what a close-run thing "the Greek crisis" had been breathed more easily, for even the Kennedy women who did not like her recognized the potency of her totemic presence. That Easter she flew to Palm Beach aboard Ari's private plane to spend the holiday with her children. Ari refused to appear for the waiting photographers when Jackie left the plane in Florida; he continued on to Nassau to spend Easter with his daughter.

In May Jackie had a rendezvous with the *Christina* in the Virgin Islands. None of Ari's guests was told the identity of the ex-

pected V.I.P.: "We were only warned that whoever was coming
had the clout to dismiss anyone deemed unsuitable." (Although it
was academic since all but one guest had already arranged to
leave the cruise at St. John to return to New York the day before
the mysterious new arrival was due.) He had been on edge for
days, "sweating more profusely than usual," according to a guest.
"I thought that a very big deal must have been in the works. In
the past, no matter how many important matters were on his
mind, he had been able to shut off and concentrate on the most
trifling thing when he was entertaining aboard the *Christina*."
Finally he had more vanity than discretion. Just before the time
came for his guests to go the speculation ended. Silver-framed
photographs of Jackie and JFK suddenly appeared in the saloon
and smoking room as well as on the Louis Quinze table in his teak-
paneled study. "It was always amusing to watch Ari operate. He
had such a wicked charm, a ruthless sense of pursuit. It was
bloody effective," recalls the remaining guest, Joan Stafford. Then
Joan Thring, she was Nureyev's personal assistant. An attractive
Australian, her dry, deadly humor and lack of affectation appealed
to Ari. "He thought she was a great, no-bullshit lady. He respected
the way she handled Rudi, who could be a handful," Meyer later
recalled. "She would always tell Ari what she thought, and he
didn't have too many people left around him who would do that."

Jackie arrived in the early morning, without her Secret Service agent. She wore a brown Valentino suit and dark glasses
pushed to the top of her head. In the words of one steward who
witnessed her arrival, "She looked like the kind of lady who would
keep a manicure appointment on the morning of Armageddon."
Ari told Joan, "For Christsake, stick close. Don't leave her side."
Ari and Jackie would never be free from the curiosity of the world.
"I don't want any sonsofbitches getting any of those Peeping Tom
pictures of just the two of us, making it look like we're horsing
around alone out here." Joan suspected that he was more concerned about the problems a snatched two-shot would create for
him with Callas than about what the world at large might make
of it.

If Jackie had marriage on her mind, "they were certainly not
yet lovers," Joan said later. Women acquire information in surprising ways, but it is in the little things that the strongest convic-
tions are often founded. When one evening Jackie ordered
bouillabaisse (a saffron-flavored fish soup invented by Venus as a
treat for the handsome Vulcan, as Ari liked to relate its legend) it
turned out to be not very good bouillabaisse, and she became
rather ill. Her embarrassment was extreme. "A woman who has

been sexually involved with a man simply does not get that flustered over an ordinary human frailty like an upset stomach," said Joan. "She was far too distraught for anything but the very mildest intimacies to have passed between them. It was rather sweet, actually. A touch of genuine innocence aboard the *Christina* was a rare thing."

Jackie and Ari pursued the question of marriage over tea together each afternoon, the only time during the cruise when they were alone. Putting aside the potentially troublesome disparity of age, personality and background, there were some tricky problems to be faced; not the least was the matter of religion: a Roman Catholic wanting to marry a non-Catholic and a man who was also a conspicuous adulterer and divorcé would create more than a spiritual struggle for Jackie. Ironically, the words of Jack Kennedy himself would demolish some of the most vehement opposition to the match: "When the chips are down," he had once said, "money counts more than religion." One close Kennedy acquaintance says, "That remark was enough to resolve Jackie's theological dilemma, if she ever had one. More than an excuse, it was a *reason*, a whole philosophy."

Ari was skeptical about Jackie's deal with Bobby ("He's making it too fucking easy," he fretted). He was convinced that she would never be mistress of her own fate as long as Bobby "has a political bone left in his body." The Kennedys were incapable of putting a moratorium on their feelings and prejudices. Cast in the villain's role by Jack, Ari knew that Bobby's opinion of him could only have deteriorated since the death of the president. "He just sees me as the rich prick moving in on his brother's widow woman. Sooner or later it'll come to a test of wills," he told Meyer. Nevertheless, Jackie's reluctance to give Ari a straight answer before she left the *Christina* that spring, Costa Gratsos would later suggest, was due not to her fear of the Kennedys but to her instinctive wiles: "Although she knew they had a deal, she'd promised Bobby that she wouldn't make any waves until after the election. I think she figured it would be interesting to see the glimmer of uncertainty in Ari's eyes. It was a nice touch. Keeping him waiting, turning the thumbscrews."

The day Jackie returned to New York Ari invited Joan Thring to share his bed; she declined. "He kept pumping me about Jackie, especially about her and David Harlech. Did I think they had been lovers? (It was the election year's number-one sideshow—"the greatest romantic cliff-hanger since Taylor and Burton, or maybe even since King Edward VIII abdicated back in 1936, and married Wally Simpson. . . . Will Jackie marry David?" a profile in *Esquire* magazine would begin that November.) Who else had she been seeing? What did I think of the men she'd been around with? Why was she attracted to gays? It was meant to be casual, gossipy, the sort of conversation he loved. He was fascinated by scandal." Only this time his curiosity had a more serious purpose. "I knew that whatever I said was important to him. Winning Jackie meant everything to him. It was the only time I ever sensed vulnerability in the man. It was an interesting new dimension," Joan later recalled.

Despite the secrecy, Jackie's trip had not gone unobserved in Washington. On May 17, Hoover personally replied to a White House "name check request concerning Aristotle Socrates Onassis." Although he had already announced his decision not to run in 1968, President Johnson kept close tabs on anything to do with Bobby, whom he "deeply despised, and vice versa." But the president's interest in Jackie's host in the Virgin Islands may have transcended the compulsions of a personal vendetta, and even the fact that he actually "enjoyed reading FBI files." Johnson was relaxing with old friends Drew Pearson and David Karr on the evening of April 3 when Karr disclosed that he had been asked by Ari to advise him on a massive, secret deal he was doing with the Greek colonels. Code-named Project Omega, the deal included the building of a refinery near Athens. Ari, claimed Karr, was toying with the idea of buying his crude oil from the Soviets. This intelligence undoubtedly sharpened Johnson's interest when he learned of Jackie's presence aboard the *Christina* in May. Karr, whose name originally was Katz and whose mother was born in Russia, had come up in the world since his days as a Fuller Brush man, *New York Daily Mirror* staffer, free-lance reporter for the Communist *Daily Worker*, and a star legman digging up dirt for Drew Pearson. In 1948, he branched out into public relations and show business (he produced a Broadway play and a couple of movies, including E. L. Doctorow's *Welcome to Hard Times*) before moving to Paris and establishing himself as a financial consultant with a special interest in the Soviet Union and Eastern Europe. "He had a tendency to be involved with two sides of every equation," Samuel Pisar, an American attorney in Paris and expert on East-West trade, later said. "Yet he was always able to supply the missing ingredient to make the deal." In his bargaining with the Russians, just as in his wheeling-dealing with everyone else, Roy Rowan wrote after Karr's death in Paris in 1979, it was always difficult to be sure whose side Karr was on. Stories of a KGB link were inevitable, and almost certainly true. He would continue to infect Ari's affairs, even after Ari was dead.

On June 5, 1968, at the Ambassador Hotel, in Los Angeles, Robert F. Kennedy was shot. In London, shortly after ten o'clock on the morning of the sixth, within minutes of Frank Mankiewicz's announcement in California that the senator was dead, Ari telephoned Gratsos. "She's free of the Kennedys, the last link just broke," he said. He showed no hint of regret, no trace of surprise, merely "a sort of satisfaction that his biggest headache had been eliminated," said a London aide. Gratsos was shocked by the killing; he was not surprised by Ari's reaction to it. "Ari had always taken what he wanted, and for the first time in his life he had come up against a younger man who was as tough, competitive and determined as he was. And now that man was dead." The night they buried Bobby by candlelight alongside his brother in Arlington Cemetery, Ari said to Meyer: "I guess the kid had everything but the luck." But the man who had been a guest at the White House for the funeral of John F. Kennedy found his name conspicuously absent from the list of those invited to Robert F. Kennedy's funeral services at St. Patrick's Cathedral on June 8. "In the circumstances his presence would have been in very poor taste," David Harlech, one of the ten pallbearers, said later.

Ari's first reaction that Bobby's murder had "removed the problem," quickly gave way to a suspicion that his death would obligate Jackie even more deeply to the Kennedy ethos and reinforce the unwritten tenet that she must never hurt the family prestige by a disapproved-of remarriage. Dead, Bobby could exert even stronger claims on her loyalties than when he was alive. Nevertheless, Ari's fears that the second assassination would "just double their [Kennedys'] right of veto over Jackie's life" were off the mark. More than ever Jackie wanted out. If she owed America a life after Jack's death, the debt was now canceled. "I hate this country. I despise America and I don't want my children to live here any more. If they're killing Kennedys, my kids are number-one targets . . . I want to get out of this country," she succumbed to the hostility, hurt and panic that had been welling up behind the glacial style she used like a shield when the pressure was on. At the hospital in Los Angeles, in the hours when Bobby fought to live, before the void that he would leave hit her, she had revealingly talked to Frank Mankiewicz, one of his Senate staffers, about her feelings at the funeral of Martin Luther King, Jr., in Atlanta back in April. Black people and Catholics, she told him, understand death: "As a matter of fact, if it weren't for the children, we'd welcome it."

More than anything now Jackie wanted seclusion, and there was no one better than Ari to see that she got it, whether it was aboard his yacht, on his private island, inside the guarded splendors of his homes in Paris and Athens, or in one of the permanent suites he maintained in hotels from London to Buenos Aires: addresses to conceal her whereabouts. She began a campaign to convince her family and friends that Ari was not a monster, but a man of sympathy and dimension. However, it was a mistake to introduce him to the Auchinclosses, with their refined sensibilities, so soon after Bobby's funeral. And if a trace of extra animus seemed to underlie Janet Auchincloss's cool manner toward him that June weekend at the family estate in Newport it was because their paths had crossed before. Staying at Claridge's some years earlier, she had been told that Lee was visiting Ari at the hotel. Wishing to see her, Janet had gone to his suite, to be greeted by Ari in his dressing gown. "She was shocked by his déshabillé at an hour when a proper gentleman would be savoring his preluncheon martini," one of her crowd would later tell the story. She demanded to see her daughter. "And who exactly *is* your daughter, may I ask?" Informed that she was Princess Radziwill, he said: "In that case, madame, you've just missed her." Seldom can a man have been presented to his future mother-in-law with more certain knowledge that he would be unpopular.

All that summer Jackie continued her mission to elevate Ari's credibility in her crowd, shuttling between Cape Cod and Newport, making him familiar with the people who mattered to her; getting Caroline and John used to having him around. He had a lot to learn: although he had lived close to her world for a long time, it would never be his world: he bestrode it like a maître d', sniped one of Jackie's gay companions. And while many of her friends accepted his presence, few genuinely welcomed him: he was "not one of us," said a member of their caste. His affair with Callas, his Levantine looks, the subterranean complexity of his deals, gave them a feeling that he was a shady customer. And although it was apparent to many that an affair was in the air, their disparate backgrounds would still have demanded a quantum leap of the imagination to contemplate anything more profound.

That the Kennedys continued to have interests of their own (there would always be another election, another candidate) that ran counter to hers as a woman no longer deterred Jackie. It was for the children's sake that she spent much of that summer at Hyannis Port. She took Ari to visit Rose and Joe Kennedy. She was deeply, genuinely fond of her father-in-law. The founding father of the dynasty had suffered a stroke in 1961, which paralyzed his right side from head to toe as well as that part of his brain that controlled his speech. Nobody knows what Joe Kennedy thought of Ari. Ari found it hard to accept, as he looked at the old man who was now barely able to utter anything remotely comprehensible, that they had long ago "had a little fun" with the same woman, Gloria Swanson. As Rose later described the visit, Ari sat "scrunched up in one of our tall fan-back white wicker chairs. Others of us were in other white wicker chairs, and still others were seated, reclining or sprawled out on cushions that were somewhat the worse from summer sun and wet and frogs and hard use from grandchildren. The white paint on the wicker was beginning to flake, as it always does. Everything was pleasant, attractive, practical, but far from elegant. And knowing of Onassis's fabulous wealth and style of life . . . I wondered if he might find it a bit strange to be in such an informal environment as ours. If so, he showed no sign of it. He was quietly companionable, easy to talk with, intelligent, with a sense of humor and a fund of good anecdotes to tell." She liked him, she said. That was before anybody told her what her daughter-in-law had in mind.

Jackie spent her thirty-ninth birthday on July 28 at Hyannis Port. The matriarchal Rose (*belle-mère*, Jackie called her affectionately) organized a family dinner, and afterward they watched *The Thomas Crown Affair* in which Steve McQueen played an insatiable millionaire who robbed banks. Later, Jackie told Teddy of her determination to marry Ari. As the oldest surviving brother and effectively the head of the family, the care of her future was now his responsibility. "He knew there was no point in trying to compel Jackie to be as steadfast to him as she had been to Bobby or more loyal to the family than she wanted to be. Yet some Kennedy intervention in the matter was necessary, and probably requested," says a family friend. At the beginning of August Teddy called Ari and suggested a meeting; Ari invited him to Skorpios.

"I hear he's exactly like Jack," Ari told Meyer, who was helping organize a party for Teddy. "Ari told me to see that there were some good-looking broads around. He didn't want the kid getting bored," Meyer recalled. One of the members of the *bouzouki* band brought from Athens was Nicos Mastorakis, a Greek journalist whose notes give some indication of the mood of the evening. ("Teddy holds a blonde goddess . . . Teddy drinks ouzo, permanently. Jackie prefers vodka at first . . . the *bouzouki* music reaches its peak and Teddy gets up and tries to dance . . . Teddy returns to his ouzo.") Jackie wore a long peasant-style skirt, a scarlet silk blouse. Teddy wore a pink shirt and matching scarf. Ari danced the *surtaki* and sang a brooding Greek ballad about lost love. He had a good repertoire of ballads, of which he was inordinately

proud. "Am I not a son of the people too?" he asked when his
guests applauded his laryngitic performance. "Yes, but a son with
money," the bandleader said. The evening ended badly for Mastorakis when somebody saw him taking pictures; the film was
removed from his camera. "Kennedy told him, 'If you print one
word out of place about this, if you hurt me, I'll have your ass,'"
Meyer later said. "I don't know what he thought he was going to
do, the senator from Massachusetts, to this Greek kid. But he was
right to be worried. He'd had a snootful, he hadn't exactly been a
boiled shirt all evening." Ari used his pull with the colonels, and
Mastorakis was picked up in Athens. "I guess they put the frigh-
teners on him because he did an okay piece, although later Ari
showed me a copy of his original story, which had been cut to
ribbons by the military censors," said Meyer. "If it hadn't been for
Jackie, Ari wouldn't have given a damn. He didn't have much time
for Teddy."

It was never easy to gate-crash Skorpios; on such an important and private occasion it was a formidable challenge, and the
infiltration of Mastorakis arouses the suspicion that Ari wanted to
provoke a situation that would compromise Teddy. It was only
later, after the marriage and Ari's intense dislike of the Kennedys
properly surfaced, that Meyer began to wonder whether Ari had
known about Mastorakis's identity from the start and deliberately
got Teddy drunk. ("Ari was too old a dog to learn new tricks,"
Gratsos conceded, recalling the time Ari had got Geraldine Spreckles's clean-cut all-American boyfriend paralytic.) The photographs and an eyewitness report of the festivities would certainly
have put Teddy in a nervous mood on the eve of the negotiations
with Ari—"It was the kind of stunt that amused Ari, it was in line
with his fix-the-bastards attitude," agreed an Onassis chieftain.
"Plenty of people thought they had him figured out. They never
did. He came on as the apotheosis of the regular guy, but he manipulated everybody as naturally as he breathed."

Ari went into the talks with Teddy with an easy mind. "I
wasn't looking for a dowry," he later told Willi Frischauer. "What
did I have to worry about?" Teddy had the toughest role. He had
to wipe out his personal feelings toward the task that destiny had
assigned to him. Playing a peculiar and delicate game (now the
standard-bearer of the Kennedy Legacy, he was concerned to protect the political interests of the family, yet was also a broker
required to get the best possible deal for Jackie), he opened on a
cosmic note. It was more than a family matter; to millions of
Americans Jackie was practically a religious symbol. Ari (who
later likened Teddy's role to "a priestly hustler peddling indul-

gences") said that he understood the sensitivity of the situation; however, he was sure that he and Jackie were capable of handling it. Although a man worth millions of dollars who started out with so little seems an American ideal, Americans had never warmed to Ari, and Teddy reminded him that it might cause especial indignation if he were to become the stepfather of the late president's children; at the very least it would put him under intense scrutiny. Ari smiled. The FBI, the CIA, the KYP (Greek CIA) and the DST (French security service: Direction de Surveillance de la Territoire) as well as Britain's MI5 had been watching him for twenty years. "I know about scrutiny," he said, removing his dark glasses, slowly polishing them with a large blue silk handkerchief, holding them up to the light, replacing them. It was a familiar all-purpose gesture: he used it to irritate, to play for time, to show his contempt, to express his boredom.

Teddy played out the game: religion, politics, family loyalties and fear were the bargaining chips he put on the table. He also had a keen awareness of his limits. After many hours of talk it was clear that Ari was not going to fold. "We love Jackie," Teddy said, ending a silence. "So do I, and I want her to have a secure life and a happy one," Ari answered, looking hard across the desk. Teddy said that if the marriage went ahead Jackie would automatically forfeit the $150,000 a year she got from the Kennedy trust, and even her widow's pension from the government would go out of the window. The essence of it now was not politics, it was financial, and the serious talking began.*

Ari, who could ensnarl a deal better than any man alive, was also a shrewd clarifier, a superb synthesizer. He set out his proposals precisely and without hesitation, for he had hatched the deal in his head, like any other business transaction, over many weeks and months; now these were his terms. Although he would be generous, his largess would not in any way diminish the prospects of his own children. The arrangements made on Skorpios, later incorporated into the fine print of a marriage contract concluded in New York, revealed his deep sense of paternal susceptibilities as well as his ambivalent attitude toward his bride-to-be: Jackie would receive three million dollars for herself plus a further

---

* "This is in accordance with the Zeitgeist," according to Thomas Wiseman in his book The Money Motive. "If money is the universal measure of excellence in our society, then to be unpaid is an insult. Top women want top pay for what they do. They want the tribute of money; not to be treasured, cherished, looked after and given dress allowances. Jackie O gets monetary proof of her worth as a wife. . . . If it means being valued in terms of cows, or yachts, this is not nearly so bad as being undervalued. The ghastliness of the market is not of being sold, but of being sold cheap."

one million dollars for each of her children. He would be responsible for her expenses so long as the marriage lasted; after his death she would receive $150,000 a year for life, exactly the amount she would have received from the Kennedy trust had she never remarried. In exchange, she would waive her rights under the Greek law known as *nomimos mira,* which compels a man to bequeath at least 12.5 percent of his wealth to his wife and 37.5 percent to his children.* While Teddy and Ari talked on Skorpios, Jackie had diplomatically flown to Athens and was never directly involved in the discussions. Ari welcomed her back to the island with a silver filigree bracelet engraved J.I.L.Y.

The following morning, he sent his handwritten draft of the agreement to Athens to be typed and forwarded to André Meyer, Jackie's financial adviser in New York. But the terms were less acceptable to the legendary head of the investment banking firm of Lazard Frères than they had been to Teddy. Meyer, who profoundly disapproved of the proposed marriage ("He did not feel that it was a good merger," gibed an associate), promptly made a counterproposal, which included a twenty-million-dollar cash settlement up front. Ari flew to New York and on the evening of September 25 confronted Meyer at the banker's sumptuous apartment in the Carlyle Hotel. Convinced that Jackie was "every bit as keen to marry me as I am to marry her," he furiously resented what he perceived to be Meyer's meddling, although it seems unlikely that even Meyer would have acted wholly unilaterally in such a matter.† It was a tough and rather distasteful session in which Meyer justified his reputation as a man who would fight tooth and claw for "the ultimate buck." He insisted on going through the agreement item by item, making a word change here, altering a phrase there, questioning every clause. Ari gave little away, although according to his private secretary, Lynn Alpha, the encounter left him "badly shaken" and in a foul temper. "Where's the bottle we keep around here?" he demanded when he returned to his office afterward. She produced the Johnnie Walker Black Label and poured a stiff drink. He told her to double it. Sipping the Scotch, he dictated the revised terms, which were returned to André Meyer that same night.

Even so, he still felt that he had made a good deal; in that part of his brain that did the sums, the deal was more important than

---

* He later claimed to have persuaded the Greek government to change the law to recognize such private arrangements; the claim, like so many of his stories, could never be substantiated.

† In her biography Men, Money and Magic, former New York Post publisher Dorothy Schiff, who had lunched with Jackie on several occasions in 1968, wrote: "Jackie wanted to marry Onassis more than Onassis wanted to marry Jackie."

the conquest. Later, when a former steward on the *Christina* claimed that a secret marriage contract existed (stipulating separate bedrooms, her right not to have a child, and 168 other intimate clauses), he was bothered only that people might believe it and think that he had been "suckered." When Johnny Meyer offered "to fix the mother" who had started the story (a Greek named Christian Cafarakis was the primary source of information on it, although he had quit the *Christina* some years before 1968— "thanks to an inheritance which I wasn't expecting, I suddenly found myself in possession of a fortune"), Ari thought about it for a minute, then told him to forget it: "Anyone who believes that garbage can go fuck themselves." Later he would often embarrass or amuse his friends by dwelling on the calligraphy of their marital passion. He was capricious in his bestowal of confidences and told stories about Jackie that concerned his manliness in a very literal sense: "Five times a night—she surpasses all the women I have ever known," he informed a friend in Athens shortly after they were wed. One man who found his frankness disconcerting was Pierre Salinger, Kennedy's former press secretary and now ABC-TV bureau chief in Paris. "He could get very vivid in his descriptions of his physical relationship with her," he would later recall.

The next weeks were filled with both activity and anxious moments. While Ari was entering the final stages of a five-hundred-million-dollar industrial deal with the new military régime in Greece, Jackie was conferring in Boston with Cardinal Cushing. A big homespun American-born son of Irish immigrants, His Eminence was a close friend of the Kennedys and the man whom Jackie had long regarded as her own spiritual adviser and confidant. He had married her; he had said a prayer at Kennedy's inauguration as president; he led the Mass of the Angels when her infant son Patrick died; he officiated at the funeral of the president himself. Suffering from emphysema and clearly a dying man, he still spoke his mind and had the courage to say unpopular things. Although he had never been afraid of controversy, his mettle must have been tested to the limit when Jackie told him that she planned to marry a divorced man, a member of the Greek Orthodox church whose first wife was still living. She did not know that the Kennedys were already pressuring him to "stop all this from taking place." He both loved and admired the Kennedys, but perhaps because there was a part of him that would always be a rebel, he resented their tone; it was as if they merely wanted something that was due to them. Most of all he didn't like the way they were ganging up on Jack's widow.

Jackie was strung tight the day they met in his residence on

Commonwealth Avenue. She did not expect his blessing; she needed his understanding. Her children, she said, would keep their faith, their name and their closeness to their father's family: all their emotional strength and sense of continuity came from those ties. But after five years of widowhood, she needed to be free of the past. Her humility and the simplicity of her words were in marked contrast to the heat he was getting from the Kennedys. A few days after her visit he told her that although he could not answer for the Vatican, he personally would not speak out against the marriage. It was no more than a damage limitation commitment. However, he was probably the best-known and best-loved dignitary of the Roman Catholic church in America, and what he *didn't* say would be more important than the condemnation of a flock of bishops.

Too many people now knew the situation for rumors not to be flying. Doris Lilly, a gossip columnist on the *New York Post*, was booed when she predicted on "The Merv Griffin Show" that Jackie and Ari would marry; Jackie buffs jostled her when she left the studio and demanded to know where she "collected that kind of garbage." The hostility toward even the suggestion of the marriage energized Ari. He told Earl Wilson that "Lilly was flat-ass wrong." (He felt, with some reason, that he could always handle gossip writers: "You just blow into their ears"; he didn't like reporters who poked around.) The next day Wilson wrote in his column, "We think we can tell you with comparative assurance that Aristotle Onassis is not likely to be marrying Jackie Kennedy or anybody else . . . his friends are a little offended that columnists keep harping on his friendship with Jackie, trying to make a romance out of it. Their family friendship goes back several years. Onassis furthermore says to his friends that he doesn't expect to marry again for the simple enough reason: he's already been married!"

In the dynamics of gossip, the Wilson denial increased the speculation. By Labor Day weekend the Kennedys were wracked with new tensions as they gathered at the compound in Hyannis Port. The question was how should they respond when the rumors were confirmed? And when would the rumors be confirmed? They didn't know, and Jackie wasn't telling them. But events were moving at a pace that would soon take the decision out of her hands. The *Boston Herald-Traveler* had got a tip from "a usually reliable source" that she was "serious about a rich Argentinian." Reporters began checking out eligible Argentinians. The story seemed to be dying when a feature writer preparing a separate profile of Ari noticed that he was an Argentine citizen. The journalists returned to their Kennedy sources, and the door began to give; somebody suggested that they should talk to Cushing: "The cardinal's got the key to all this stuff." He was discreet but refused to lie. On October 15, 1968, the *Herald-Traveler* elevated the gossip column scuttlebutt and talk show tittle-tattle to a front-page news story claiming that John F. Kennedy's widow and Aristotle Onassis were planning to marry soon.

The morning the *Herald-Traveler* story appeared on the streets of Boston, Pierre Salinger got a call in his Washington office from Steve Smith (grandson of William Cleary, an Irish immigrant who founded the New York transportation company, Smith had married Jean Kennedy in 1956 and was known as the "inside brother-in-law"), who said he had to see Salinger urgently; Salinger flew to New York that morning. "Guess what's happened?" the diminutive Smith greeted him the moment he walked through his door. "Jackie's going to marry Onassis." Jackie had asked Jean to break the news to Rose Kennedy before she called her mother-in-law herself later that evening, he said. "We have to figure out some kind of statement for the family to put out," Smith said. "Have you got any idea of what you want to say?" Salinger inquired, lighting up his familiar cigar. The marriage wasn't news to him; Stas Radziwill had told him about it two weeks before in London. "How about," said Smith, who had majored in philosophy at Georgetown, " 'Oh shit!' "

Now all the wheels were turning. In Athens Prof. Yanni Georgakis, chairman of Olympic Airways (a former director of the Panteios Graduate School of Political Studies, he also held the Chair of Criminal Law and Sociology at the University of Athens), was summoned to the Glyfada villa, where Ari explained the situation. The secret could not be contained much longer, and Jackie wanted to move quickly, he said. Since the Kennedys were adamant that the wedding should not take place in the United States, Georgakis was told to sound out the possibility of holding the ceremony at the American embassy in Athens. He told an embassy official as much as he could without giving names. ("Let us say that a very important Greek should wish to marry a very important American widow, could the ceremony, for reasons of discretion and a mark of respect to that very important lady, be performed in the embassy?") He was pressed to be more precise. The official paled when he heard the widow's name; in words not prevalent in diplomatic circles he said that it was out of the question, Georgakis recalled. He reported back to Ari and suggested they use the chapel on Skorpios. Ari agreed. Worried that the *bizarrerie* of a Greek Orthodox wedding service might upset the Kennedy chil-

dren, he told Georgakis to find a priest "who understands English
and doesn't look like Rasputin."

An aging millionaire in the throes of love is a natural source
of concern to his heirs. Alexander and Christina were shattered by
the news. The idea that their parents would remarry had seemed
to them (but to no one else) a growing possibility as their father's
interest in Callas faded. Christina wept. Alexander left the house
and drove his Ferrari at great speed through the night, wondering
whether or not to go to the wedding. It was a bad time for Alexander. He had never been at peace with his father ("I admire him.
I also admire Howard Hughes," he had once revealed his ambivalent feelings toward him) and now there was tension between
them that transcended the ordinary tension between a strong-
willed father confronted with the emerging independence of a sub-
missive son.

Alexander had fallen in love with Baroness Thyssen-Bornemisza, a complex and beautiful woman who had achieved international fame as a fashion model (Fiona Campbell-Walter, daughter of a rear admiral; pronounced by the Italian painter Annigoni
one of three most beautiful women in the world) before she married Baron Heinrich Thyssen in 1955. Divorced nine years later,
the mother of two children, and sixteen years older than Alexander, she had become his "mistress, mother and priest confessor." Unable to stop the affair, Ari had done his best to ignore it.

Meanwhile, in New York, Meyer was dispatched on a most
sensitive errand: to find Gloria Swanson, the lady whose favors
both Ari and Joseph Kennedy had once enjoyed, and ensure her
discretion. It took him some time to convince the former movie
queen that Ari really was about to marry Joe's daughter-in-law.
"And what makes Mr. Onassis think, Mr. Meyer," she said finally,
"that our very brief friendship a long time ago is a matter I would
wish to rake up now?" She instructed him to inform Ari that she
regarded his injunction to be "a compliment to my memory and
an insult to my integrity." He never got around to mentioning the
considerable sum of money he'd been authorized to offer her to
keep her quiet. "She was quite a dame," Meyer recalled. In her
memoirs, published long after both men were dead, she never
mentioned Ari at all.

Rose Kennedy was "stunned" when Jean gave her the news.
She thought of the difference in their ages, the difference in religion; she worried whether Caroline and John, Jr., would be able
to accept Ari in the role of stepfather. Her thoughts "awhirl," she
waited for the call from Jackie. By the time it came she had
reached the conclusion that her daughter-in-law "was not a person

who would jump rashly into anything as important as this, so she must have her own very good reasons." She told her to make her plans "as she chose to do."

On October 17, at 3:30 P.M., forty-eight hours after the *Herald-Traveler's* bull's-eye, Jackie's social secretary, Nancy Tuckerman, announced in New York that "Mrs. Hugh D. Auchincloss has asked me to tell you that her daughter, Mrs. John F. Kennedy, is planning to marry Aristotle Onassis sometime next week. No place or date has been set for the moment." At exactly the same moment, Donald McGregor, a senior Olympic pilot who was preparing to command the 8:00 P.M. flight to Athens, got an order to get his crew together "for something special." The scheduled 707 had been canceled (bouncing ninety-three passengers), and he was to be ready to take off at six o'clock for Andravida, a Greek military base. "Nobody knew what the hell was going on," recalls McGregor, who insisted on filing a flight plan for Athens anyway: "We'll amend it when airborne if necessary." (A former BOAC captain, McGregor was getting used to the relaxed ways of Olympic and its frequent management changes: "I used to go around saying, 'morning, sir' to everyone; I didn't know who the hell was going to be my boss next day.") At 5:30 that evening, accompanied by Caroline and John, a nanny and their Secret Service agents, Jackie left her fifteen-room apartment on Fifth Avenue and drove to JFK International, where they were joined by her mother and stepfather and her Kennedy sisters-in-law Jean Smith and Pat Lawford. "There were eleven of them altogether," says McGregor, who flew the 707 to the military base, where Ari's Piaggio was waiting to take them on to Skorpios. (The following morning Richard Burton called Rex Harrison from the Plaza-Athénée and asked him to invite Maria Callas to the party he was planning for the Paris opening of his latest film, *A Flea in Her Ear*. Burton and Elizabeth Taylor had often enjoyed her hospitality when she had been Ari's hostess. "I just heard the news from New York," he told Harrison. "She'll need a bit of cheering up, I fancy.")

It was raining on Skorpios on October 20, that fine rain that comes and goes in the autumn on the islands in the Ionian Sea. Artemis Garofalides said that rain was a good omen on a wedding day. Later she placed charms beneath the mattress of the nuptial bed. Jackie looked solemn and drawn in a long-sleeved ivory lace Valentino dress with a matching ribbon in her shoulder-length brown hair. The groom, three inches shorter than his bride, seemed slightly out of key in a blue suit, white shirt and red tie. Caroline and John, holding ceremonial candles, flanked the couple. Alexander and Christina sat together in a sullen mood. ("It's a perfect match," said Alexander, who had agreed to attend the wedding only because Fiona had insisted he go "as a mark of respect" to his father. "My father loves names and Jackie loves money.")

At 5:15 P.M., as the evening breezes began to rustle the bougainvillea and jasmine outside, the bearded Archimandrite Polykarpos Athanassiou, in robes of gold brocade, began the service in the tiny crowded chapel of Panayitsa (Little Virgin), translating the key passages of the ceremony into English for the bride's benefit ("The servant of God, Aristotle, is wedlocked to the servant of God, Jacqueline, in the name of the Father, the Son and the Holy Ghost"). As sponsor, Artemis placed wreaths of white ribbons and lemon blossoms on the couple's heads and crossed over them three times. In the stillest voice, Jackie repeated the prayers. It was exquisitely exotic, and half the guests had never seen a ceremony like it. Yet for many in that tiny church the sense of what Jackie had lost drained the joy from all that was happening. The couple exchanged rings (both rings first being slipped onto Ari's finger, then onto Jackie's, finally one on each) and drank from a golden goblet of red wine. Then came the final Dance of Esiah, the priest leading the bride and groom three times around the altar to the chant of the cantors. Christina's tears were not tears of happiness. She took things harder than Alexander, who sniffed the air as if scenting betrayal behind the incense. Jackie's Secret Service agent wore a Kennedy PT-109 tie clip and had no expression at all.

Ari went into the marriage with as high hopes as she for happiness, and there were early signs of domestic tenderness. Jackie gave him her own special name, Telis; he tried to stop her from smoking, snatching away her L & Ms the moment she reached for the pack. Within days of their wedding, Jackie summoned Billy Baldwin to Skorpios to redesign the house. An old friend who had decorated her Washington and New York homes, Baldwin had never seen Jackie so "free." She appeared relaxed and radiant, in almost hoydenish high spirits. There was no sign of any disappointment over the Kennedys' coolness toward the wedding. (Teddy's statement wishing them well was "chilling in its formality and brevity," noted *Time* magazine.) "Billy," she said the day he arrived, "you are about to have your first experience with a Greek lunch. I will kill you if you pretend to like it." Exhausted after the nine-hour flight from New York, followed by the helicopter ride to Skorpios, the small fragile-looking designer retired early on his first evening aboard the *Christina*, which he considered "the epitome of vulgarity and bad taste." Only Ari's study pleased him; its masculine charm and leather-bound books "almost made up for the horrors of the rest of the ship." He awoke early the following morning to find a tray of Greek delicacies outside his cabin door with a note from Jackie: "Billy, you missed your midnight sweets —and the houris have been kneading unguents all day long . . . after the zenith of the moon and our evening prayer, which is sweetened by Turkish delights, we have a dainty feast, and since, O cruel Allah, you could not share it, before we find la Belle aux Bois Dormant we drop these sweetmeats by your couch, to make voluptuous the dawn for you. Mme. Suleiman le Brillant. " Ari gave him a free hand: "This house I want to be a total surprise. I trust you and I trust Jackie and I don't want to know anything about it." He had only one request, a long sofa by the fire "so I can lie and read and nap and watch the flames."

It was a nice idea, and clearly part of the fantasy life he envisaged for himself now that he had acquired Jackie. But it was not his style. He needed to make deals. Deals had always been essential to him, in some psychic way he needed them; a deal meant an opponent, an opponent meant confrontation, and confrontation was the source of his strength. He could not live without adversaries, no more than a tree can live without soil; like mangrove trees, which make their own soil, he could create enemies from within himself. And now four days after the ceremony on Skorpios, he was sitting beside Col. George Papadopoulos in the back of an armor-plated Mercedes-Benz as, flanked by the colonel's personal bodyguards, supported by 350 armed police, it sped out of the Old Palace of Athens and headed for the dictator's villa in Neo Psychico. The colonel took no chances since a mine had exploded beneath a bridge seconds after he had crossed it. The two men were in jubilant mood as they prepared the joint communiqué to announce Project Omega. It was an unforgettable moment for Ari. Odysseus had become his alter ego: to return to his homeland proclaimed and celebrated had become a haunting dream. (Smyrna was thought to be Homer's birthplace, providing the inspiration for his *Odyssey*, Ari frequently reminded friends.) At the villa they toasted the deal in Greek cognac, served under the watchful eye of Papadopoulos's mistress, Despina Gaspari, from a "secure" thermos flask. What Ari was to call "the biggest deal in the history of Greece," Project Omega was impressive even by his standards: a four-hundred-million-dollar investment program, including the construction of Greece's third oil refinery, an alumina refinery, an aluminum smelter, a power station, shipyards and an air terminal.

Although First National City, Ari's bankers, posted a seven-million-dollar performance guarantee, it is unlikely that he ever considered investing any of his own money in Greece. The big attraction of the package was that it would keep his fleet fully operative at a time when more and more tankers were being laid up. Having won the concession for the building of the third refinery, he had in addition obtained the rights to handle the oil from beginning to end: he would buy the crude from the producers, transport it in his own tankers, refine it in his own refinery and sell it through his own distribution network. And by wrapping up his refinery in the same package as the alumina complex (and its concomitant power station run on oil that his fleet would carry and his refinery process) he was convinced that he could do a deal with one of the American aluminum giants (Reynolds Metals, Alcoa), which would provide the capital investment for the whole shebang.

Teddy Kennedy's worst fears must have been exceeded when Ari climbed into bed with the colonels four days after he married Jackie. "The boss is the only man in the world who can handle two honeymoons at the same time," was the favorite joke among Ari's Athens staff: "one with Jackie, the other with Papadopoulos." The dictator and his conspirators were all born into peasant or humble small-town families; all had entered the Greek Military Academy in the late 1930s when General Metaxas was attempting to re-create the heroic ideals of Hellenism on a Fascist model. Although they had promulgated a new constitution for the country and rigged a plebiscite to approve it, key provisions were suspended indefinitely, including those guaranteeing civil rights.

Ari emerged on the scene at an important moment for the colonels: he gave their coup a sense of credibility; Project Omega made them sound like shrewd businessmen as well as professional soldiers. And its announcement only days after his marriage to Jackie was a useful public relations bonus at a time when many European governments and public opinion were becoming seriously concerned about the régime's brutal treatment of its political opponents. Ari had no qualms about his partners. "Being with the colonels is preferable to being with the losers," he said, although later he would claim that he had merely repeated a private remark of United States Secretary of State Dean Rusk.

Not everybody in Greece was impressed with the Omega deal. The Athens newspaper publisher Helen Vlachos, under house arrest, was getting her thoughts and her anger down on paper. "With the coming of the colonels the worst traits of both the top star shipowners, and of all the discreetly following tribe, came out into the open. Their grabbing instincts were sharpened by the Great Junta Sale. Greece was being offered at cut prices, genuine bargains to be secured in exchange for a friendly pat on uniformed backs, the Greek flag devalued below the lowest-priced Panamanian or Liberian, taxes waived, laws forgotten."

Ari had been cultivating Papadopoulos for more than a year. One way or another, usually through a nexus of favors and kindnesses, he knew how to get people indebted to him; he made a permanent loan to Papadopoulos of his three-hundred-thousand-dollar villa at Lagonissi, an exclusive resort thirty miles outside Athens; when the colonel, abandoning his allegiance to the old simple virtues, ordered forty dresses at one thousand dollars apiece for his wife, Ari took care of the bill. And although they were using each other ("Colonel," he told him at the outset, "we're both people users, so let's do what we do best and see what happens"), the admiration was mutual. Born in a poor village in the northwest Peloponnesus in 1919, Papadopoulos was drawn to Ari's world. "He was terribly impressed by the glamor and style of the millionaire who had once been poor like him," said one of his officers. And Ari was aroused by his proximity to real power. Papadopoulos's arbitrary rule—a man answerable to no parliament, encumbered by no electorate, and who had a whole army at his command—caught his imagination.

During the Nazi occupation, Papadopoulos had been a company commander in one of the infamous German security battalions; after the war he went to the United States and studied at the NATO Psychological Warfare School. On his return to Greece he was said to have begun working for the CIA* and had successfully moderated the extremist tendencies of some of his colonels after the coup d'état. It was Papadopoulos who received the full force of Ari's charm and generosity; it was Col. Nicholaos Makarezos, the third man in the military triumvirate that had led the coup, who was left to work out the details of the euphoric but alarmingly vague Omega agreement. Although he had never studied economics (he deported an expert sent by the Organization of Economic Cooperation and Development who questioned the basis of his statistical data), Makarezos had been appointed Minister of

---

* No serious evidence was ever presented to support the allegation. C. M. Woodhouse in The Rise and Fall of the Greek Colonels (London: Granada, 1985) wrote: "At the second of the major trials of 1975, Papadopoulos said that he had never been trained or employed by the CIA, and that he knew the USA 'only from TV and the cinema.' His claim was not rebutted. It was even corroborated by the evidence of later investigations conducted by members of the U.S. Congress hostile to both the dictatorship and the CIA."

Economic Coordination. He had served as military attaché in the Greek embassy in Bonn before joining KYP (Greece's CIA); nothing had prepared him for dealing with a man like Ari.

"We'd spend a week getting agreement on a single point, then he would quickly concede several points with no trouble at all, and just when you were beginning to feel the momentum, he would return to the first point and want to insert a new proviso or add a clause that would negate everything," said one of Makare-zos's Omega team. Although he surrounded himself with experienced, high-priced advisers, Ari was his own principal architect of a deal; he kept his own record of a negotiation, making copious notes in his pocket notebook (dealing with the English or Americans, he wrote in Greek; in Athens he used French). After a particularly difficult Omega session, one of his own team pointed out that a specification Ari had quoted from his notes totally contradicted the facts his own experts had given him. Ari said, "My dear chap, two and two do not necessarily make four if your interests are affected by that answer."

The talks lurched from crisis to crisis. At the heart of the matter was Ari's failure to persuade the powerful United States aluminum corporations to stake the project on his terms. In spite of the colonial privileges of foreign capital offered by the junta (including freedom from taxes, duties or levies in any form for the company or its foreign staff, and no account books), his determination to keep a 51 percent partnership in the aluminum plant was totally unacceptable to the Americans. Said one senior Alcoa executive, "After his marriage he just lost all sense of proportion. His must-win mentality tipped over into pure megalomania. His terms were not terms, they were commandments. You couldn't reason with the guy. He seemed to think that we'd agree to just about anything for an invitation to dine with him and Jackie aboard the *Christina*. It was obvious that he saw that marriage as a good career move." A Reynolds director said, "We had discussions; the man was too greedy. He threatened to go to Pechiney [a French company that already had large aluminum installations in Greece], but we knew nobody was coming on that tab."

Since the beginning Papadopoulos had assumed that his prodigal Ulyssean hero was coming home with the goods; he thought that was the whole idea. Ari's sudden demands that Project Omega should now be financed by the government, and that the junta should lean on the Greek banks to provide loans on extremely favorable terms, were matters that Colonel Makarezos would have to handle. The military dictator refused to criticize his friend and benefactor; perhaps he could not see that the deal was conceptually flawed. And so the talks dragged on. Ari began making threats to pull out. He knew that the régime could not afford to let Omega fail. Twenty-four days after the putsch on April 21, 1967, it had signed a much-vaunted $250 million deal with Litton Industries, but the bargain collapsed. The colonels had staked their prestige on Omega. "It got so that every day, no matter how hard we worked, no matter how much we prepared, we seemed to end up in a deeper hole than the one we were in the day before," said one official at the Ministry of Economic Coordination. "He had some extremely able men on his team, men like Professor Georgakis, and Nicolas Cokkinis, experienced men, who came up with good feasible ideas. Onassis would disappear to Skorpios for a few days, and we'd reach an understanding with them; then he'd return, and in five minutes he'd destroy everything we'd achieved. It made Makarezos mad as hell."

Eleven days after the Skorpios nuptials, Ari got "the best wedding present I could ever hope for." He had at last beaten Panaghis Vergottis in his appeal to the House of Lords. But it was the narrowest of victories: the law lords upheld Mr. Justice Roskill's original judgment by a majority of three to two. Explaining the majority view, Lord Dilhorne said that the trial judge had been right in saying that the decision turned on the credibility of the witnesses and that he had approached his task with "great care and anxiety." Bearing in mind that "the greatest weight had to be attached to the findings of the judge who saw and heard the witnesses," the appeal would be allowed. Lord Pearce had argued valiantly for Vergottis: the advantage possessed by a trial judge in being able to absorb the atmosphere of the case was one that had its dangers, he said. The case was presented to him in an atmosphere of high drama. It was tried in the storm and tempest of emotion between old friends who had become bitter enemies. The class of case where love had turned to hate, where old friends wondered in amazement how they could ever have been friends, presented its own particular difficulties for the trial judge, said Lord Pearce, who had recognized, as perhaps Lord Dilhorne had not, the sheer professionalism of Callas and Ari in the witness box —their ability to smile, divert, put on a show. In view of this he felt that "where credibility was involved, contemporary documents were of the utmost importance." And in his opinion the documentary evidence supported Vergottis. Lord Wilberforce agreed with him. But it was small comfort for Vergottis. Ari had won.

•   •

Jackie was left a good deal to herself, to get acquainted with the villa and the island as best she could, and had plenty of time to think about herself and the changes in her life. Public reaction to the marriage made unpleasant reading as she waited on Skorpios for Ari to return from his frequent excursions to Athens and Paris, where less than a month after marrying Jackie he dined with Callas to celebrate their victory over Vergottis. Vatican sources said that "the case of the former Mrs. Jacqueline Kennedy is closed so far as the Roman Catholic church is concerned. She is barred from the sacraments so long as she remains married to Mr. Onassis." Hounded by hate mail attacking his refusal to condemn the marriage, Cardinal Cushing felt compelled to announce that he would retire at the end of the year, nine months earlier than he had planned. Publicly Jackie appeared to take it in her stride; privately she was dismayed and occasionally extremely distraught. When Ari was absent and as time passed, Billy Baldwin sensed her apprehension "about the course she had taken." She poured out her anguish in long letters to the friends who had stuck by her. "I had a letter from her that would be worth hundreds of thousands of dollars if I allowed any of the national secular magazines to publish it," said Cardinal Cushing. "I burned the letter. That letter was thanking me for understanding her."

To her former escort Roswell Gilpatric she wrote simply:

Dearest Ros—I would have told you before I left—but then everything happened so much more quickly than I'd planned. I saw somewhere what you had said and I was touched—dear Ros—I hope you know all you were and are and will ever be to me—With my love, Jackie.

Instead of fading, the publicity got worse. "Come on, be honest, would you sleep with Onassis? Do you believe she does?" Joan Rivers was asking audiences in Las Vegas. "Well, she has to do something. I mean, you can't stay in Bergdorf's shopping all day." When Ari heard that the story had upset Jackie, he told Meyer, "She's got to learn to reconcile herself to being Mrs. Aristotle Onassis because the only place she'll find sympathy from now on is in the dictionary between shit and syphilis." He underestimated the loyalty and understanding of her friends. Pierre Salinger sent a long hand-written letter telling her that it was her life and she should go ahead and do as she damn pleased . . . in the end it would be all right: she just had to remember that. She later told him the letter meant a lot to her. "She was getting a lot of heat," he said. "Not as much in the United States, incidentally, as in Europe. I was in Paris at the time, and whenever I went out at

night people would come up to me and say, 'How could Jackie do
such a thing? It's terrible. How can this wonderful woman betray
the memory of John Kennedy and marry this Greek merchant?'
Greeks are not well seen in France. In the United States there was
some resentment, but it was in no way equivalent to the heat
which she was getting over here," Salinger would reflect in Paris
fifteen years later.

Three days after the ceremony on Skorpios, Clyde Tolson,
Hoover's closest companion inside, and outside, the FBI, ordered
yet another review of Ari's files. And three days after that, Hoover
got the kind of memorandum he cherished:

> As you might have noticed, recent news stories concern-
> ing the marriage of Aristotle Onassis and Mrs. Jacqueline
> Kennedy have reported his age as 62. I thought you might
> be interested in knowing that information furnished to
> the Department of State by Onassis's daughter and son,
> Christina and Alexander, show he was born in 1900. Files
> of the Passport Office disclose that Christina Onassis, born
> on 11/12/50 at New York City, NY, was last issued pass-
> port Z-762056 at the Embassy in London on 10/27/67. In
> her application she listed her father as Aristotle S. Onas-
> sis, born at Smyrna, Turkey, on January 20, 1900. The
> passport files also reveal that Alexander Socrates Onassis,
> born on 4/30/48 at New York City, was last issued passport
> Z-578696 at the Consulate at Nice, France, on 10/18/66. In
> his application for this passport, he listed his father as
> Aristotle Socrates Onassis, born at Salonika, Greece, on
> January 21, 1900.

According to a member of Hoover's immediate staff, the bureau chief was "pleased as hell" by this routine report. "The fact
that Onassis's own kids didn't agree on when and where their
father was born convinced him more than ever that Onassis was a
total fraud, a liar, a man who couldn't trust even his own family
with the truth about himself."

On March 8, 1969, Stavros Niarchos offered the colonels an
investment package worth $500 million including a $150 million
long-term low-interest-rate loan in hard cash to help ease Greece's
perennial balance-of-payments difficulties—provided he, and not
Ari, got the concession for the third oil refinery. Colonel Makarezos, who now made no secret of his hatred for Ari, and barely
disguised his jealousy of his affinity with Papadopoulos, quickly
supported the Niarchos bid, which was in every way an improvement on Omega. "If Onassis is going to strip the meat of the refin-

ery he must deliver the rest of the animal," he warned
Papadopoulos. So far, he pointed out, all they had got from him
were broken promises and threats. The dictator had clearly had a
great deal more than that and sided with his benefactor. Two days
later it was announced that the Niarchos bid had arrived too late
to call off the Onassis deal: the contracts were already with the
printers. It was a blatant lie; the slow progress of the negotiations
was a matter of grave concern inside the junta. The conflict between Papadopoulos and Makarezos was suddenly dangerously
exposed. Makarezos wouldn't let the matter drop, and Papadopoulos was forced to commission the under secretary of economic
coordination to study the two bids and submit an independent
report.

Like Makarezos, Under Secretary Orlandos Rodinos was a
Niarchos man. He was also a pragmatist. Before he began writing
the report he asked Ari whether he would care to offer any suggestions that might give him "a new perspective" on the situation.
Ari suspected that it was a proposition and responded angrily. He
had Prime Minister Papadopoulos on his team, why should he
have to buy off an under secretary too? Whether because he had
been rejected or scurrilously misunderstood, Rodinos's report was
a model of political reckoning. He began with a summary of the
"lengthy and laborious" Omega negotiations, throughout which
the Ministry of Economic Coordination had had to contend with
"the well-known stubbornness of one of the leading Greek business
practitioners." The intervention of Niarchos created a new climate
of affairs. The difference between the two bids amounted to much
more than the apparent $100 million. Niarchos was offering to sell
to the government crude petroleum at $11.80 per ton against
Onassis's $14.32. Over ten years this would mean a loss of $150
million to the Treasury if they stood by the Omega deal. Add to
that the difference in shipping charges between the bids, and the
total spread would increase by a further $100 million. "Not only
do the economic, legal and ethical aspects of the matter compel
the examination and consideration of the new offer, but the political aspects argue in its favor," he opined.

It was Rodinos's conviction that this was much more than a
contest of pride between two powerful shipowners battling like
gods for supremacy on Mount Olympus: it was a battle for Greece
between British and American petroleum giants, with Onassis and
Niarchos bringing ships and a sizable grudge to their roles of
"men of straw." (Ari, he felt, was backed by British Petroleum;
Niarchos was probably working with Standard Oil of New Jersey.)
"It is especially useful for us to be conscious of the possible extent

of the conflict, and the eventual means by which it may be quelled. I feel, Mr. Prime Minister, that the key to the clearing of the whole matter is offered by Mr. Niarchos." His conclusion: Ari's offer should be rejected and a new round of tenders for the third refinery and other developments announced immediately.

"I guess I should have done business with this jerk after all," Ari told Papadopoulos after he'd read the report; he explained the conversation he had had with Rodinos. Papadopoulos sent for the under secretary at once and asked for an explanation. Rodinos insisted that he had suggested no such deal, although Ari had. Then why hadn't he informed the prime minister immediately? Rodinos said that he did not wish to expose Mr. Onassis . . . he was a friend of the prime minister's, he was an important man whose role was integral to the development of the Greek economy. Ignoring the essential discrepancy in their versions of the incident, Ari raised a question of moral principle. "Look here, you! I'm a businessman and am free to employ all means to succeed in my business. You are a minister of the government!" He became very excited. "Now you see, Prime Minister, why we are still arguing over Omega," Rodinos said. It was a delicate situation for Papadopoulos. Aware of the international scrutiny he was under as criticism of his régime mounted, uncertain of the strength of the faction behind Niarchos, he was not inclined to impose his dictatorial will. On May 20, he announced his decision to call for fresh tenders. He also ordered the chief prosecutor of the Supreme Court to launch an investigation into "the circumstances that led to the breakdown of the negotiations" with Ari. Orlandos Rodinos announced his resignation.

Arguments, accusations and counteraccusations flew between Ari and Niarchos (Ari had a simple unwavering attitude toward his former brother-in-law: "Stick it to him before he sticks it to me"); Papadopoulos and the pro-Niarchos forces inside the junta were now in conspicuous disarray and ordered the press not to print anything more about the crisis, or anything that would be "against the best interest of the country's economy." Finally the colonels produced the King Solomon solution: the rivals were each offered an oil refinery in exchange for guaranteed investment commitments. Niarchos got back the state-owned refinery at Aspropyrgos (his original concession to operate it had ended in August 1968) and announced an impressive two-hundred-million-dollar building program to increase its capacity; he would invest a further one hundred million dollars in other projects including the redevelopment of his shipyards at Skaramanga. On March 13, 1970, Ari pledged to invest six hundred million dollars in specified industrial projects in return for a fifteen-year concession for the operation of the new refinery scheduled to open in 1973, although the terms were less attractive to him than the terms of the original deal with Papadopoulos. It was all academic in the end. His attempts to revise contracts never let up. Complained a senior Greek civil servant, "His method was to smile and sign all the agreements we gave him—and then start to shuffle out of the pack the unprofitable ones." No matter how large and complex a deal became he still basically "applied the labyrinthine logic of the bazaar," says a former Omega coordinator in Athens. "The whole world had grown more sophisticated, and the market structures were getting more and more technical, yet in some curious way his wily rug-peddler approach to a deal continued to work for him in the shipping business. But there was simply no way that kind of behavior could be tolerated in the huge capital-intensive schemes he was discussing with the government. Watching him, doing his number, keeping track of it all in that little notebook of his, it was kind of sad. He was a dinosaur. It was all over for him. The conviction began to grow even on Papadopoulos that everything Ari now touched was going to be a mess, a disaster."

CHAPTER **14**

*The desire for happiness is the incentive
that moves us in all our undertakings.*
ARISTOTLE

WHEN HE WAS twelve years old, Alexander Onassis saw her climbing out of a sports car in St. Moritz in a snowstorm. She was dressed in a long leather coat with a fur hood, and he thought she was the most exciting female he had ever seen. When he was eighteen, and his mother wanted him to attend a dinner party she was giving in St. Moritz, he said: "I'll come if you ask Fiona Thyssen to come too." More amused than surprised by the suggestion that she invite one of her own friends for her son (she knew of his penchant for "older" women, and the Baroness Thyssen-Bornemisza, at thirty-three, was, in Alexander's own words, "tormentingly lovely"), Tina agreed.

There was no mystery about his fascination for women older than himself. At fourteen, one of his father's assistants charged with taking care of him during his parents' frequent absences, introduced him to many of his own women friends, most of whom were in their thirties and habitués of some of the more risqué nightclubs of Paris. "They were paid a lot to take care of Alexander because the secretary was paid a lot to take care of him," says Jacinto Rosa, Ari's chauffeur, who had known Alexander since he was twelve years old. He had taught him to drive and took a special pride in his enthusiasm for cars and knowledge of engines. Alexander's precocious interest in more corporeal skills disturbed the chauffeur. "Many times he asked me to drive him to the Bois de Boulogne, where he liked to spy on the prostitutes working with clients in their cars," says Rosa, who worried that Alexander's

239

voyeurism was unhealthy, as well as dangerous. Perhaps more than anything else it revealed the solitariness of his existence; he had no genuine friends, only employees. "Sometimes I tried to tell him what's better to do and what was better not to do, but I had to be diplomatic because he would not have accepted any kind of reprimand from one of his father's employees," Rosa recalled.

Despite being set up with his own tutor and a private apartment in the Hotel Baltimore, at sixteen he failed his exams at the lycée in Paris after returning several days late from a tryst in the south of France. Although Ari took pride in his son's sexual adventures ("what's bred in the bone comes out in the flesh") he was furious at his poor exam results. Refusing "to piddle away good money on a lazy kid," he put Alexander to work in his Monaco headquarters. Rosa watched his progress with a mixture of apprehension and amusement. "He considered the young ladies of his own age boring. He would rather be taking an engine to pieces than go out with 'kids without any interest.' His first serious love without any doubt was Odile Rodin—although nobody was supposed to know it," Rosa recalled. "He was around seventeen when he lived with her in Monte Carlo [shortly after the death of her playboy-husband Porfirio Rubirosa in 1965]. They stayed for a time in Tina's apartment in Paris when she was away. He gave very big tips to the staff to keep their mouths shut. Onassis knew. He knew everything. [He always looked as though he knew more about you than you wanted him to know, Costa Gratsos said later.] He seemed to be happy to see his son with such an expert."

In spite of his unobtrusive concern for Alexander's education as a man, Ari treated him in front of his staff as a glorified office boy (at twelve thousand dollars a year plus expenses). "He was just a nice shy kid learning the ropes," recalls one of his father's Monaco managers. "He didn't seem in any great hurry to prove himself an Onassis." Later Alexander said that he felt there had never been a day when he had "not been intimidated by the old man's wealth." And although he began to appreciate the miracle his father had performed in creating that extraordinary empire, his disaffection was slowly turning to hostility. Nightly and alone he pushed his Ferrari to the limit on the twisting corniche between Monte Carlo and Cannes to expiate the anger and inadequacy with which he was tormented. When an acquaintance accused him of having a death wish, he said that he didn't believe that there was any escape from his father's tyranny "except by living it out."

This was the young man Fiona Thyssen met on the night of Tina's dinner party in St. Moritz. Always at ease with men (she had been mixing with millionaires and with men of power and fame of one kind or another almost all her life), she was not aware that Alexander had been waiting six years for that evening, and that it was to be one of the crucial moments of both their lives. She was surprised by his understanding of so many things, for she had assumed that young men of his generation "were gauche, unable to make conversation." Most first words spoken between lovers have the habit of being both ordinary and unforgettable, and the first thing she remembers saying to Alexander was "My God, you can *talk!*"

Later that evening in the discotheque of the Palace Hotel the man with whom Fiona was dancing complained that she had spent far too much time with Alexander and suggested that she would "not have given him a second look if his father had not been a millionaire." She punched him so hard in the face that he fell down. "One thing that I have never been accused of, and, in fact, probably the only thing, is that I am obsessed with money." She fled the dance floor in tears, pursued by Alexander. "I discovered that he was quite amazingly warm and caring . . . it was just an immense surprise," she recalled. He was not especially good-looking. He wore his thick black hair short and neatly parted in a style that goes with expensive three-piece suits, which were what he liked best; heavy horn-rimmed glasses, often with dark lenses like his father's, gave his young faintly olive face strength as well as solemnity. He was slightly taller than his father. He had the Onassis nose, which Fiona would later persuade him to have fixed.

To her surprise and embarrassment—"being sixteen years older, I didn't know whether he saw me as a substitute mother figure or what"—they began an affair. Convinced that it would be a brief thing ("like maybe once") she was thrown to discover that he had other plans. From the beginning he wanted a relationship, a *commitment*. Having gone through most of his life almost friendless, living for so long without loving relationships, he was hungry for a promise of permanence. Although it was fun, their affair did not fit with the image she had of herself, and threatened her future. She had been divorced three years before from one of the richest men in the world; she was still young, extraordinarily beautiful; she had money and a social position. "I was boringly square," she says now. She wanted to be married again, but Alexander was out of the question. He was too young for her; and she knew enough about the politics of dynasties to know that his bride would have to be a wealthy Greek virgin from an approved shipping lineage. She did her best to break free. Alexander refused to give up. Soon it was very clear to both of them that there was an underlying strain of brinkmanship to the struggle and that they had embarked on a very serious affair. "It took me a long time to stop fighting and accept that we had become indispensable to each other and should just try to survive together on a daily basis, and whether it lasted a week or a month or a year we should enjoy it and be grateful," she said.

Her imperviousness to his wealth confused him. He had been brought up to believe that everybody has a price and that he could impress any woman with his fast cars and private planes, with his father's island in the sun and all the facilities of his life. At first it had amused her that he was unable to comprehend a world of values "so at odds with his own." Eventually it led to their first serious fight. "When you were still in your diapers, I had my own private plane and my forty servants and my two, five, ten cars, and the houses. The last person you are going to impress on that level is me," she told him. By Fiona's standards the Onassises were still "uneducated peasants." She told him truths he had never heard before: plastic flowers (a familiar sight in the Onassis homes) are infra dig (Wendy Reves had once suggested to Tina that she remove the plastic covers on the draperies in New York and was told, "Ari wouldn't like it"); a gentleman does not wear a white tie with a white shirt. It was the stuff of lovers' quarrels; at another level it epitomized the gulf between them. She had a gold medallion made and engraved with the date and the valediction: *To my beloved savage.* Meant to show her affection and express their unbridgeable worlds, it made him weep. "I thought, 'My God, what a bastard I am,' " she would recall. His tears scuttled her determination to break away.

As the affair continued and strengthened, Tina went to extraordinary lengths to end it. Fiona had been a high-class whore, she warned Alexander: she claimed she knew a man in London who had paid her fifty pounds to go to bed with him when she was only seventeen years old. Her tales became more incredible as they became more lubricious. Alexander and Fiona invented a game in which they tried to anticipate her next canard. "We were never even close to the stories she came up with," says Fiona. "She always surprised us."

Ari's effort to end the affair was subtler. There was no shift in his domination. Alexander possessed almost nothing that did not ultimately belong to, or was controlled by, his father; his apartment above the office in Monte Carlo, his cars, his credit cards and restaurant accounts, everything was down to one Onassis company or another. Early in 1970 he bought his son a two-million-dollar villa outside Athens. It was not a company house, it was Alexander's. Fiona understood his delight at finding himself suddenly a property owner, and at least partially free from the spell of Ari's power. And although he missed the note of ambivalence in her congratulations, her feelings became clear when she announced that she would look for a house to rent nearby so that they could spend the summer together. "Rent a house nearby? What do you mean? You will live with me," he told her. "My dear friend, I wouldn't put a foot inside that house. Your father is not buying that place just for you. He's also buying it for your mistress. He wants to prove that everybody can be bought," she told him. If she were to move into the villa, she had perceived with her native Scots canniness, she would become just another Onassis object—"to be manipulated, brutalized and treated on any level and on any terms he chooses."

Eventually convinced by Fiona's reasoning, he told his father that he did not want the villa. Ari, Fiona suspected, probably heaved a sigh of relief that she had seen through his game. "I suspect that very few people in his life had told him to go and stuff himself, although my intent was not just to tell him to stuff himself: I just wouldn't allow myself to be bought as his son's mistress." Fiona and Alexander never lived together. He worked in Monte Carlo, and she kept her home in Morges, near Lausanne. Later she rented an apartment in London. They spent almost every weekend together. She had her self-esteem to maintain and to her children, Francesca and Lorne, Alexander was simply a family friend. Few people suspected the truth. When he flew to St. Moritz, she would meet him at the airport in a Volkswagen that had seen better days and of which she was inordinately fond, and he, inordinately embarrassed. Its frequent breakdowns offended his mechanic's sensibilities. " 'I'm going to buy you a decent car,' he would say every time it packed in on one of the steep roads up to the house. I would say, 'Fine, if you're going to save up your pocket money five years from now we'll have a nice reliable car.' " She refused to accept anything from him that he hadn't paid for out of his savings. Whenever they traveled together they each paid their own way, except when they flew Olympic Airways and it cost them nothing at all. Slowly she convinced him that "not everybody could be bought and not every woman is on the make." Slowly she rid his head of the misanthropy of his father's inculcation. But there were some family traits she knew she would never change: although she had been close to the Niarchoses for a very long time, faced with Alexander's them-or-me ultimatum, which was in him as it were by nature innate, she wrote to Eugénie Niarchos—"one of my dearest and best friends ever, the only civilized human being in the whole bunch"—explaining that she was in love and that it had to be Alexander. They never met or spoke again.

"His affair with Fiona put more pressure on his relationship with his father, but he felt better about himself," said a friend who knew the score. Her confidence in him strengthened his resolve to

excel in his own right. In the office, people began to go to him for
advice, seek out his opinion. He had a sense of proportion that was
often lacking in his father. It made him a useful man to have
around when the unions had to be pacified. Eventually, he was
put in charge of Olympic Aviation. It was a small outfit, a subsid-
iary of Olympic Airways, providing services to the Greek islands,
charter flights, air taxis. (Although the thickness of his glasses
prevented him from getting an air transport pilot's license to fly
scheduled aircraft, he held a commercial pilot's license, permitting him to fly air taxis and non-scheduled carriers; he flew his
own plane and could handle a helicopter with great skill. "When
other pilots wouldn't even think of taking off because of the
weather, he wouldn't hesitate if it meant getting an emergency
case to hospital on the mainland. He was becoming a sort of folk
hero in the islands," Fiona recalled.) Alexander managed the company with flair, even if he had yet to display Onassian propensi-
ties for the big deal. Having less success with his national airline,
Ari reminded him: "The planes are the leaves of the tree. The roots
are the ships." ("Ari had a feeling of warmth toward his ships
which he often withheld from his human relationships; ships
probably reflected a nostalgia for his youth," a family friend observed.)

Now in his sixties, Ari was not prepared to yield an inch of
authority or give an ounce of credit to his son. Nor was he, in
Fiona's opinion, likely to do so in his lifetime. It was a question
that she and Alexander discussed constantly. "Ari didn't want to
have a son who was going to threaten him on any level. He was
jealous of his attractiveness and his charm. His reactions to Alexander's success were not the normal reactions of a father toward
his son. He did everything to humiliate him, to belittle him . . .
look how he impeded his education by removing him from school
on the flimsiest pretext. He simply didn't want Alexander to be
cleverer or wiser or better educated than he was."

On the evening of May 3, 1970, on the Niarchos private Aegean
island of Spetsopoula, Eugénie Niarchos undressed, slipped into a
nightgown and swallowed twenty-five Seconal tablets. "For the
first time in all our life together I have begged you to help me. I
have implored you. The error is mine. But sometimes one must
forgive and forget," she wrote Stavros in red pencil, in English. As
she waited, in the words of a favorite poem she had learned as
a schoolgirl, for "kinder skies and milder suns, and seas pacific
as the soul that seeks them," she picked up a ballpoint pen and
added a cryptic, almost indecipherable, postscript: "26 is an unlucky number. It is the double of 12.10b of whisky." At 12:25

A.M. on May 4 she was pronounced dead. She was forty-four years old.

Eugénie's fatal distress was caused by her discovery that Stavros planned to entertain his four-year-old daughter, Elena, and her mother on Spetsopoula that summer. Elena had been conceived in a bizarre interlude in 1965 when he married Charlotte Ford, daughter of Henry, in a Juarez motel suite two days after Eugénie had divorced him in the same Mexican town on the grounds of incompatibility. In 1967, after Charlotte returned to Juarez and ditched Stavros,* he found his way back to Eugénie and their four children. They never remarried since it was claimed that in the eyes of the Greek Orthodox church his marriage to Charlotte never happened.

Millionaires make few concessions to the rules and conceptions of ordinary society, their reactions in human crises are unforeseeable, and Niarchos's behavior during the hours between 10:25 P.M. on May 3, when he discovered Eugénie unconscious in her room, and the time she was pronounced dead, was to cause ugly rumors for a long while to come. Suspecting at once that she had taken too many sleeping tablets, which she had done before, he began shaking and slapping her in an attempt to revive her; when she slipped to the floor, he took her by the neck and hauled her upright. She fell several times as he struggled to get her back on the bed. He sent for black coffee, and with the help of his valet, Angelo Marchini, tried to force it down her throat. It was more than half an hour before he called his sister, Maria Dracopoulos, in Athens and told her to send the company physician. Dr. Panayotis Arnautis arrived by helicopter about ninety minutes later; it was too late. Since death was not from natural causes, Dr. Arnautis refused to issue a death certificate, and the body was flown to Athens for a postmortem examination.

The autopsy report listed multiple injuries to Eugénie's body. They included a two-inch bruise on the abdomen with internal bleeding and bleeding behind the diaphragm in the area of the fourth and fifth vertebrae; a bruise on the left eye and swelling on the left temple; an elliptic hemorrhage on the right side of her neck; a hemorrhage to the left of her larynx with small contusions above the collarbone on the left side of her neck; and there was also bruising to her left arm, ankle and shin. Dr. Georgios Agioutantis, professor of forensic medicine at Athens University, and Dr. Demetrios Kapsakis, director of the Department of Forensic Medicine in the Ministry of Justice, concluded that all these injuries

---

* *"He drove me nuts," she told Ford biographer Booton Herndon: "I found out that he was married to his telex machine."*

were consistent with strenuous attempts at resuscitation. Death, in their expert opinion, was caused by an overdose of barbiturates. "She had many injuries; more than you usually see in those kind of cases," said a mortuary technician who handled the body in Athens. "Right away I noticed that they weren't defense wounds, the kind of injuries you see when somebody's been warding off an attack. She was a fragile-looking woman, and somebody had used a lot of force on her. But a guy in a panic doesn't always know his own strength. And people trying to save a suicide, especially somebody close to them, can get damn angry. She looked as if she had been slapped around; I still think Agioutantis and Kapsakis called it right."

Not everybody was satisfied with the doctors' conclusions. Ari was far from convinced and went around saying so. "Why the hell did Stavros wait so long? Why did he have to send all the way to Athens for a doctor when there was a doctor minutes away on Spetsai? Couldn't he see that his wife was dying?" The incident on Spetsopoula was more than a private tragedy; potentially it was a political one as well. Ari knew that as long as there was a breath of scandal in the air, Colonel Papadopoulos, a conspirator by instinct, would be only too willing to delay the ratification of Niarchos's refinery deal, since Niarchos's patron was his rival, Colonel Makarezos. But with two thousand political prisoners locked away on barren Aegean islands and ugly rumors about the murder and torture of hundreds of political suspects circulating in Athens and throughout the world,* Papadopoulos's qualms about doing business with a man who was under a cloud because of a single death were less than convincing.

The "mystery" of the delay in summoning a doctor for Eugénie surfaced in the *London Times* on May 20. The following day a letter was published explaining that the physician on the nearby island was not summoned because it was known from "previous experience" that special equipment would be required that the Spetsai doctor did not have. "As a helicopter was already in Athens," wrote a Mr. Zervudachi at Niarchos's request, "a doctor with the necessary equipment was flown from there in about an hour and a half; in any event the Spetsai doctor could not have arrived much sooner, as he suffers from arthritis and has refused in the past for this reason to travel by speedboat and only been prepared to go to Spetsopoula by small caique." In a terse letter to *Elefheros Kosmos* (*Free World*, the dictatorship's own newspaper in Athens) the minister of social services rejected the Niarchos explanation

---

* *The junta gave credence to these reports by choosing to quit the Council of Europe rather than permit it to investigate the situation.*

as "unjustified." The physician appointed to Spetsai, he said, "served the needs of the inhabitants satisfactorily."

The strain was telling on Niarchos. Locked in a psychic battle with Ari, which transcended private anguish, he reminded people of his contributions to the Greek nation. "Now my antagonists pour accusations and gossip against me," he said. "They try to destroy what I have made for the good of Greece, I say again, 'for the good of Greece.' "

Nevertheless, the minister's brief declaration in the official mouthpiece of the junta was widely seen as a signal to Constantine Fafoutis, the Piraeus public prosecutor handling the case, that Niarchos should not be given any special privileges. A second autopsy was ordered. This time the examining doctors decided that the Seconal found in Eugénie's body (two milligrams of barbiturate in one hundred cubic centimeters of blood) was not a lethal dose and that her death resulted from physical injuries.

The divisions inside the junta, exacerbated by the death on Spetsopoula, were now in the open. Within days of the second verdict, Fafoutis felt compelled to order a third postmortem examination of the body by the four doctors whose verdicts were already in conflict, plus two Athens University professors of morbid anatomy and two experienced pathologists nominated by Niarchos. This time they produced a unanimous verdict: "The injuries found on the body were slight. The deceased was already in a comatose condition when they occurred and they did not contribute to the fatality which was partly due to the effects of Seconal and partly to the action intended to revive the deceased."

But Papadopoulos continued to use Eugénie's death to discomfit the Makarezos faction. "You can't operate as a straight arrow at this level," Ari told one close associate, acknowledging his own hand in the affair. On August 21, 110 days after Eugénie died, the public prosecutor recommended that Niarchos be charged with causing bodily injuries leading to his wife's death. He proposed that the sixty-year-old shipowner be tried under Article 311 of the Greek penal code: involuntary homicide, which carries on conviction a maximum penalty of eighteen years in prison. The proposed indictment was submitted to the High Court for approval. The judges ruled that the evidence merely confirmed that Eugénie Niarchos had taken her own life during the night of May 3 to 4, and the case was precipitately closed. The junta ratified the Niarchos deal. Colonel Makarezos was the guest of honor when a new dry dock, named after Eugénie, was opened at Skaramanga. "We are confident that the inspirator and creator of this shipyard will face the blows of fate with the same courage which enabled the ancient Greeks to triumph over the power of death," he told the workers.

There was as much dismay on Skorpios as there was relief on Spetsopoula when the judges dropped the case. "Ari wanted to keep Eugénie's death an issue," said Meyer, who perhaps more than most of those close to Ari had seen his hatred in action. "Except for Christina, he was the only one in the family who seriously blamed Stavros for what happened that night on Spetsopoula, although I guess Stavros himself felt some guilt, a sense of responsibility for the tragedy. Even Arietta stuck by him. Tina took the two youngest Niarchos kids to stay with her in England. It was Alexander who finally convinced his father to drop the whole business. It was the first time I'd ever seen him square up to his old man. He told him to drop it because he was hurting nobody but the kids: 'Their mother's dead, and all you can think about is getting even with their father,' he said. Ari eventually backed off."

Ari had plenty of other problems to think about. Not only were the colonels still unable to persuade the banks to deliver favorable long-term loans for Omega, but freight rates had more than doubled since he fixed the price at $3.30 a ton for the exclusive right to transport all the oil for the refinery for the life of the fifteen-year concession. It had been a gamble on his part, considering the volatile price of oil; but given the overcapacity developing in the tanker market, it seemed a gamble worth taking. But his botched attempts to involve Alcoa and Reynolds in Omega, failing to get the Americans to provide the basic capital investment, convinced even his most loyal aides that he was losing his touch, if not his piratical disposition. Talking with one of his Greek lawyers shortly after the collapse of his negotiations with the aluminum giants, he hinted at "a Moscow interest" in Omega. The Russians, he said, had "no compunction or twinge of conscience" about dealing with the junta and were willing to talk business immediately. An executive who visited the *Christina* on an unrelated matter heard the same story. Shortly afterward, Ari dispatched Yanni Georgakis to Moscow to prepare the ground.*

---

* David Karr claimed that he had also been deeply involved in the Soviet-Omega talks at Ari's request. "How do you deal with these people?" he recalled Ari asking about the Russians. "Just like you eat an elephant," Karr told him. "Bite by bite." Later Karr hinted to friends that his yacht, which caught fire, exploded and sank at her berth in Cannes in 1971, was a CIA reprisal for his part in Omega. But Fortune magazine, on December 3, 1979, four months after he was found dead in his avenue Foch apartment, in an article entitled The Death of Dave Karr, and Other Mysteries, suggested that his links with the Russians evolved out of his business association with Armand Hammer, chairman of Occidental Petroleum, in 1972.

The State Department viewed Ari's Soviet initiative with grave concern. Not only did the United States have vital stakes in Greece—strategic access to the Middle East oil fields, military and intelligence bases for the eastern Mediterranean—but the deal would have given the Russians a valuable toehold in a key NATO Pact country. Fortunately, Ari was treating the Russians in the same way he had treated the colonels, and the talks dragged on. In October 1971, Vice-President Spiro Agnew paid a state visit to his family homeland, the first top-ranking Western leader to set foot in Greece since the 1967 putsch. In three days of private talks he spelled out the facts of life to Premier Papadopoulos and his colonels, who, anxious about the possible collapse of Omega, desperate for the kudos of success, were disturbingly ambivalent about Ari's Russian initiative. Said Gratsos, one of the few around Ari to have spoken up against the Moscow alliance, "Ari asked for and got a lot of trouble. It isn't hard to imagine what Agnew told Papadopoulos. I should think he just reminded him of his dependence on U.S. military and economic generosity—and, 'Oh, by the way, George, if you don't want Nixon to cut off your aid, Onassis has to be dumped.' " Certainly some kind of deal was struck in Athens. In exchanging toasts at the vice-president's farewell dinner in the old Parliament building, both Agnew and Papadopoulos spoke scornfully of "sophists"—such men, said the premier, "jeopardize the effort made in defending our civilization." Later, Agnew told accompanying newsmen that continued military aid to Greece "is a matter of overriding importance to the United States." And he had barely shaken the Athens dust from his shoes in Washington when the colonels announced that Omega had been abandoned. Ari blamed Nixon. "He must be rubbing his hands tonight, getting a Greek to pull the cork on me," he said bitterly. "And after all I did for that son of a Greek bitch Agnew."*

Ari was not prepared to give up his Omega dream without a fight. When the refinery was again put out to tender in January 1972, he submitted a new bid. His persistence embarrassed the colonels, and especially Papadopoulos. Ari knew it too. "If he thinks he can shunt me to the sidelines now, he'd better think again," he told an Athens attorney who had helped him prepare the new tender. Two weeks later, on February 18, Ari's Learjet, SX-ASO, crashed into the sea off Cap d'Antibes, killing his per-

---

* When Agnew ran for governor of Maryland in 1966, Spyros Skouras invited Ari to contribute to his campaign fund, apparently with more success than he had had in persuading him to contribute to the Greek War Relief Fund in 1942. Washington columnist Jack Anderson included Ari's name in a list of prominent Greeks and Greek-Americans attending an Agnew-for-governor luncheon in 1966.

sonal pilots, the Kouris brothers. Ari was convinced that it was sabotage, but less certain who it was who had tried to kill him. He variously blamed the CIA, Papadopoulos, business rivals, and the KGB. His friend Willi Frischauer later said, "He could make out a convincing case against any single one of them, and frequently did, but it was mostly conjecture, innuendo, theory. He had no hard evidence, not a scrap."

The crash, during a night visual approach to Nice airport, was probably due to pilot error. "What happened I don't know," the dead fliers' successor, Don McGregor, said. "Whether the captain called for full flap and his brother put out air brakes or what . . . I'd heard bad reports about the younger brother's flying ability." Mike Jerram, an experienced pilot and aviation writer, said: "They may simply have lost visual reference while flying the downward portion of the approach, descended too low and hit the drink. Nice can be a tricky airport to get into, especially at night." Ari refused to consider any of the many possible explanations. He talked about hiring permanent bodyguards, in addition to the security men who protected his various homes and the *Christina.* "Ari, if somebody's prepared to knock off a plane to nail you, I don't think a whole army of gorillas is going to be much help," Meyer told him truthfully.

Alexander had been fond of the Kouris brothers, and their death troubled him. He spent several weeks searching the coastline, studying tide and wind charts, looking for traces of the wreckage. He found nothing. Nobody ever did. His concern about the Kourises' fate had no connection with his father's paranoia. "I guess it was one of those things," he finally told Fiona, who had walked the beaches with him. "It happens."

Little had gone right for Ari since his marriage to Jackie and his triumph over Panaghis Vergottis in the House of Lords. After Omega bit the dust he no longer had a serious goal. And yet he never stopped plotting. It was a psychological compulsion for him to manipulate and pressure people, even when those people were his own family. In the summer of 1970, when Omega first began to drift and disintegrate, he still found time to involve himself in Christina's affairs. He decided that she should marry Peter Goulandris. A Greek shipping heir, Goulandris was twenty-three years old, darkly handsome and keen on Christina. The Goulandris family ran four shipping lines, totalling over 135 vessels with a value in excess of $1.5 billion. His mother was a member of the distinguished, and even richer, Lemos family. Ari considered it to be the perfect match. "Some marriages are made in Heaven, the best ones are made on Skorpios," he said. Christina was wise enough to see the significance in his remark; wise enough not to accept it without question. "Loving is a quest, not a business deal," she told a friend on Skorpios that summer shortly before she fled the island and her chosen fiancé. Nervous dyspepsia, Ari explained her hasty decampment on the eve of the engagement. Jackie thought that she had "a case of the blahs."

But she simply felt entitled to the dignity of her own decision. The days of irrevocable trust in her father, whose devotion she felt sure she could rely on, were coming to a close. He had always been the center of her rich, unstable universe (for her seventeenth birthday, he had given her fifty thousand dollars' worth of trinkets wrapped in a Greek peasant shawl), but now between business and Jackie he was neglecting her more and more. "I don't think he realized what a melancholic, metaphysical age nineteen can be for a girl," said a Skorpios guest that summer. "She desperately needed his love, or at least the display of it." Yet she could not have been totally surprised by her father's behavior. Fixed on power, thriving on the thrills of wheeling and dealing, the games tycoons play for fortunes and revenge and dynastic grandeur, he had once told her: "To begin to think is to begin to make deals." It was flawless wisdom in an imperfect education. "I learned for myself that to begin to feel is to begin to hurt," she told a friend.

Alexander had little time for his little sister; there was a distance between them that was more than a measure of their need for separate lives. "He was frightfully jealous of her because she was a spoiled brat and everything she wanted she got," says Fiona Thyssen, who estimates that Christina was going through two hundred thousand dollars a year, spent on clothes, jewelry, apartments and travel at a time when Alexander was scraping along on the twelve grand he was earning with Olympic; he did, however, share her concern about Jackie (the Widow, as he privately called her) who was occupying so much of their father's attention, trespassing on their territory. Christina, he thought, was determined to concentrate Ari's mind on her "at any cost . . . we all take care of our own skins in the end."

By the indoor swimming pool of the Hotel de Paris in Monte Carlo Christina met Joseph Bolker. He was forty-eight years old; tennis, skiing, scuba diving and a daily workout in the gym had kept his body lean and taut; his silver hair was almost boyishly tousled. A teetotaler and a nonsmoker, he had a subdued likable manner, virtues that helped him in his civic and cultural life back home in Los Angeles. There was still a hint of his native Nebraska in the softer edges of his southern California accent. He was interested in people, a compulsive joiner (Republican Task Force; Americans for Change; Los Angeles Beautiful Committee; American Friends of the Israel Museum; Navy League of the United States); worldly (twice-divorced, four daughters); and, as Christina told a friend, judging his wealth on the Onassisian scale, "a dinky millionaire in real estate."

In Monte Carlo for the convention of the Young Presidents Organization, Bolker had struck up a poolside acquaintance with Christina, which did not go beyond first-name introductions. She talked little but was always pleasant and responsive, he recalled. When it was time for him to leave (he was returning to Los Angeles via Germany and London) she suggested that he look her up in London and wrote her number in Reeves Mews, her apartment near Grosvenor Square, and her name in a Filofax notebook. It was not until she tore out the page and gave it to him ("Don't lose it. I'm not listed") that he realized who she was. He called from Germany and arranged a date. "We had a good time," he remembers fondly. "She was a very bright, attractive, interesting person." He was surprised that she was still only nineteen years old.

He returned to Los Angeles; during the following months they met in Paris and London and in discreet hotels on the south coast of England, and the relationship deepened on Christina's part to a degree of dependency, demonstrated in letters and telephone calls, that gave him cause for concern. She told Bolker that her father was giving her "a particularly bad time and she was very, very unhappy." In bed for ten days with the flu, she had bought a television set for her sickroom; Ari flew into a rage when he got the bill and refused to pay it. "Yet a week before he had given her an emerald necklace and bracelet worth maybe three hundred thousand dollars, and she didn't understand. I said, 'Christina, it's obvious, the television set only the maid sees, or whoever you invite into your bedroom. When you wear those jewels the whole world sees them, they reflect on *his* wealth and on *his* image, and that's why he does those things.' "

Bolker did not like Ari ("He used his children, his family, he used everybody: he would publicly say 'I love my daughter, I love my son,' but there was no love, he had no feelings, no conscience, he was a user of everybody") and recognized the degree to which his marriage to Jackie had disturbed Christina. He had daughters of his own; his first wife, Janice Taper, had been an heiress with a tyrannical father; he understood the stresses and strains on young girls moving into a world more emotional and more complex than anything they had ever known. And in spite of his apprehensions about the direction his relationship with Christina was taking, he wanted to help her. She was not an easy person to reach; he lost count of the hours of failed communication they spent on the transatlantic telephone. Although her despair was authentic, she often complicated it to torment herself and provide an affecting touch of vulnerability. Her claims on his energy and patience, the violence of the shifts in her moods, escalated to a level of desperation. "Although she wanted people to think she was a smart apple, she was there to be loved by anyone who pressed her button," a friend recalls that period.

Joseph Bolker was far from happy to see Christina when she arrived unannounced in Los Angeles. His condominium apartment on the twenty-fourth floor of Century Towers West was a perfect bachelor setup (he made no secret of his fondness for beautiful women: "I enjoy women, and I have had experiences with some of the loveliest and most interesting women in the world; I don't see anything wrong with that") and after a couple of divorces he had no desire to cramp his style with an uninvited emotionally volatile live-in mistress, even if her name was Christina Onassis and her father was one of the richest men on earth and married to the widow of the thirty-fifth president of the United States.

"Does your mother know where you are?" he asked. When Christina admitted that she didn't, he insisted that she call Tina immediately. The marchioness, in the south of France, responded in an extraordinary way: "I do not want my daughter living with a man she isn't married to." Christina must return to Europe immediately, she said, "or make it legal." Bolker protested that in the first place Ari would never approve; and in the second place he didn't want to marry Christina. Tina told him that her daughter loved him very much, and if he cared so little about her feelings, then he should put her on the next plane back to Europe. The conversation upset Christina. She saw Bolker's reluctance to marry her (he was, he had politely pointed out to Tina, twenty-seven years Christina's senior, and not in love with her) even in the face of her mother's encouragement, as a slur on her desirability. Her paranoid outburst should have alerted him that Christina was not thinking rationally: "What's wrong with me? Why won't you marry me? Aren't I good enough for you?" she demanded to know.

Later she shut herself in the bedroom. Bolker stayed in the living room. After a while he grew restive. "I didn't hear any sounds, so I went back to the bedroom and she was lying there. She had taken some pills. I thought, 'Oh my God, what have you done?' There was a young doctor in the condominium across the hall, and I went and grabbed him. He started walking her around and pouring liquids down her and finally brought her round." She was unrepentant. "If you won't marry me, I will just keep doing this until you will," she told him. "I guess if you feel that strongly about it," Bolker said, aware that it wasn't much of a proposal

after the ritual proof of her love, "we'll get married." What her
father would think, what he would feel, what he would do when
he heard the news, she barely dared to think about.

Ari was celebrating Jackie's forty-second birthday on Skorpios
when the wire came from Las Vegas: *Chryso mou* had married Joe
Bolker. "Ari went ape," said Meyer. "I'd seen him fly off the handle
plenty of times but never like that. He was rampant, he was mad
enough to chew nails. That was a day I'd just as soon not have to
go through again." Ari knew all about Joseph Robert Bolker, of
course. Christina's London phone had been bugged for some time.
(One of his London aides who saw a transcript of a conversation
between Christina and Alexander—"total chitchat, domestic
trivia about the house Fiona was going to rent in Wilton Place,
Alexander's disenchantment with St. Moritz"—wondered about
"the psychopathy of a man who did not hesitate to bug even his
own family.") The idea that Christina could fall in love with this
stranger to her race and country had never crossed Ari's mind. It
was a measure of the distance that had come between them. "A
few years earlier, he would have anticipated the danger of expos-
ing a girl like Christina to such an unusual fascination," said
Gratsos.

"The Christina problem," as it became known among Onassis
insiders, restored Ari's flagging energies. He loved a fight. When
he didn't have a battle on his hands, his spirit was drained by
boredom and black moods. "He needed to test his edge on other
kinds of men once in a while just to know that he still had it," said
an aide. The problems with Jackie were not yet significant, although it was evident that her wanderlust had been aroused by
her permanent income, and he had already felt the necessity to
explain their frequent separations to reporters ("Jackie is like a
little bird that needs its freedom as well as its security. She gets
both from me. We trust each other implicitly"). The appearance
of a new enemy exhilarated him. It was always the same: the
closer the foe, the more deadly was his appetite for action. Bolker
replaced Niarchos as his private enemy number one.

Meanwhile, Christina began settling in as the third Mrs.
Bolker. She gave small dinner parties for his friends, played tennis, read a lot, surfed and went for walks by the Pacific. "The ocean
air is healing," she said, acknowledging the hurt inflicted by her
father's reaction to the marriage. "The ocean is life to a Greek."
She also knew that Ari would not, could not, leave them in peace
for long. "We enjoyed sleeping together and talking to each other
and everything was good. We satisfied each other's needs," Bolker
said about those early days as man and wife, although an early
incident with inescapably symbolic overtones was the loss of her

wedding ring in the surf at La Jolla. "It was washed off her finger, she became very distressed. She had me diving around for hours in those waves trying to find it. We both knew it was hopeless, but she didn't want to give up," Bolker recalled.

Although Ari secretly admired, even respected, his daughter's insurrection—"Obedience isn't worth shit," he growled after his initial rage, "if you don't have it in you to bust loose once in a while"—it did not follow that he would tolerate it for any longer than it took him to make the necessary arrangements to crack down on her. On her twenty-first birthday in December, she was due to collect some seventy-five million dollars (after taxes) from her trust fund; he rewrote the terms, delaying her access to the money. "She can't run her act on me. As long as she remains married to that man she doesn't get a penny," he told Meyer, who was dispatched to California to talk to Bolker. Bolker, Christina and Meyer met for lunch at the Beverly Hills Hotel. Prepared to listen to whatever Meyer had to say, Bolker remained wary. He knew that Ari's emissary was "capable of having people assassinated, having your legs broken or something. Christina said that he did a lot of things for her father, he took care of a lot of situations for him." She understood Meyer pretty well, and he liked her and was on his best behavior; he had the power to beguile, no less than the faculty to frighten.

In the Polo Lounge, Meyer went over the situation, conveying Ari's disapproval of his marriage, his "deep hurt" at being informed only after the ceremony had taken place. When the business of the frozen trust fund came up, Christina interrupted to express her own "deep hurt" that her father should have punished her by withholding "what is rightfully mine." She knew the solution, Meyer answered: the money was waiting for her the moment she divorced Bolker. Bolker stayed calm. He was perfectly capable of supporting his wife, he said with a display of loyalty that was admirable in a man who had hardly gone into the marriage in a fever of enthusiasm and was less than eager to sustain the burden of the passion that he had inadvertently incited.

Meyer turned to "the serious implications" the marriage might have on Ari's business arrangements. He looked at Bolker and said, "You see, Joe, Ari has a lot of dealings with the Saudis. Maybe they won't like the idea of a Jew in the family. If they pulled their contracts, the banks could get nervous. Nervous banks are bad news. It'd do more than scrape the paintwork if they called in their loans, Joe." Bolker said that he had many Saudi friends and understood the geopolitical problems of the Middle East: "I really don't think the Saudis have any animosity toward Jewish Americans," he said.

Bolker felt that the lunch had gone well and that they had got across their side of the story. "We felt that he understood the situation, that we had a friend; unfortunately, it didn't turn out that way. We heard later that he gave us a very bad report." Shortly after Meyer returned to Paris, Ari stepped up his efforts to end the marriage. "The moment I left for the office in the morning Christina started to get telephone calls from people trying to talk her into getting a divorce, telling her things about me, all kinds of incredible and dumb and untrue things, anything to discredit me." Stories that he was mixed up with organized crime began to circulate. "I would get home and she would be so distraught. Like somebody had called and said I was a member of the Mafia. After a while it just wore her down," Joseph Bolker recalled later.

In September, less than five weeks after the wedding in Las Vegas, she flew alone to talk to her mother in New York. They met in a suite at the Regency Hotel. "I'm just trying to work out a life I can live with. Doesn't Daddy want me to be happy?" Tina told her that he was testing her conviction. "You must prove to him that you're right and he's wrong. It's a game of nerves. Just stand up to him." To help make amends for the blocked trust fund, Tina secretly gave her daughter two hundred thousand dollars (an exceedingly generous gift from a woman notorious for her thrift: "To get Tina to break into a five-pound note was a goddam miracle," said Fiona Thyssen) with the suggestion that she look for a house on the beach in California.

Although it may have relieved Tina of some burden of guilt, the money, like the advice, was given not entirely without self-interest. Her marriage to the marquess, rocky for some time, was shortly to end, and she was already planning to marry Stavros Niarchos. To the cunning of a dissatisfied wife, Tina added an inherited disposition toward secrecy: so far she and her brother-in-law had covered their tracks, and while her pleasure was stimulated by the deception, she was nervous about Ari finding out and making trouble. "The Christina problem" was one sure way to divert his attention: "Joe Bolker has replaced Stavros as the man he loves to hate," Tina told a Paris friend. Unaware of her mother's plans, and of the real motive behind her counsel and her cash, Christina returned to Los Angeles with a new sense of resolve. It was short-lived.

On October 22, eighteen months after Eugénie's death on Spetsopoula, Tina and Stavros Niarchos were wed in Paris, with Arietta Livanos's blessing and, it was generally agreed, with her considerable abetment too—"Arietta was bent upon hatching an exclusive alliance, countenancing no marriage with outsiders," a Greek shipowner said. Alexander was informed in a courier-delivered letter one hour after the ceremony; Christina got the news via the message operator at Century Towers. "It was a very emotional time, a lot of yelling and screaming, a really bad scene," said Bolker, who believed that Tina "married Niarchos just to hurt Onassis—a revenge situation." Christina still harbored the gravest suspicions about her uncle: she feared that he would cause some terrible harm to come to her mother—"She was convinced that was part of his nature . . . she believed that Niarchos killed her aunt Eugénie and was going to kill her mother," said Bolker.

Tina was smart of course, and selfish, and on the evidence she was more hard-boiled than anyone had ever thought possible, including Ari. The marriage had shaken him every bit as profoundly as it had Christina. It was not, as he later said so often, "that the grave had hardly closed on her sister and Niarchos's wife," that upset him so much, but that he still regarded Tina, a decade and two marriages after their divorce, as his wife—she was and ever must be his wife, and wife absolutely, and wife eternally: she was the mother of his children. Her marriage to "Sunny" Blandford had never in truth distressed him; on the contrary. But Niarchos was something else entirely. "Ari behaved like an injured lover," said Gratsos, who felt infinitely sorry for him, yet amused. "His anger was intemperate. He could think only of the evil which he felt Niarchos had done him." Yet the hard part of his rage was that they had actually married. "If they had been having an affair behind Blandford's back, Ari could have lived with that," suggested one Paris aide. "Then he could have really turned on the fireworks . . . for him that marriage was every violation of the moral law. It was a strangely immature reaction from a man who was so far from young."

But while it was easy to dismiss Ari's rage as a ritual performance, it was not so easy to dismiss Christina's fears. Said a girlfriend in California, "There was such a goddam aura of Greek tragedy about the whole situation, anything was possible." The marriage seemed to Christina "an act of madness, the greatest disloyalty to the memory of her aunt and an outrage to her father's pride," said another West Coast friend, adding that "she couldn't shake the notion that something real bad was going to come out of it. It was just the worst time for her. The battle of wills with her father, her growing suspicion that she had made a big mistake marrying Joe, had taken a lot out of her. And now there was this shit. Tina couldn't have contrived a situation more likely to unglue her daughter's fragile state of mind." And so while Ari ranted and raved, Christina dealt with her hurt in her own fashion: it was reported that she had taken an overdose. However, in November she was well enough to fly to London, alone. Bolker issued a statement to the press: "Since our marriage, Christina and I have been subjected to extraordinary parental pressures, which are now seriously affecting her health. She is a young woman and should not be alienated from her father. At my suggestion, she has gone to London to see her doctor . . . and hopefully to resolve family problems."

It was Fiona Thyssen to whom she confided her deepest feelings. Fiona was probably the wisest friend she had; she admired the way her brother's mistress had handled her own difficult times and appreciated the influence she had had on Alexander's life (it was Fiona who had brought about her reconciliation with Alexander after years of mutual hostility). She was clearly on the edge when she arrived one evening in early December at Fiona's house in Belgravia. Joe, she said, was a genuinely nice guy, and they were sincerely fond of each other; however, the marriage had not worked out. Even without the pressures coming from her father, there was no way the marriage could survive. Fiona listened, thinking how grave and beautiful she was ("She was sensational-looking in those days, very bad table manners, like most Greeks, but a sensational face"); it was painful to see someone so young so distraught, so surprised by the things that were happening to her, and so fearful of the future.

A few nights before Christina turned up in London in such a bad state, Fiona had acquired a piece of information that she found especially disquieting. Unable to sleep and searching for a cigarette, she noticed several typewritten pages on the desk in her study in Wilton Place. Assuming they were from Alexander (it was a habit of his to leave overnight notes, reminding her of an arrangement, asking a favor, outlining some idea on which he wanted her opinion; sometimes it was no more than an affectionate or funny thought he'd had), she lit a cigarette and began to read. Slowly she realized that it was a transcript of a conversation between Meyer and another Onassis chieftain. "It was quite definitely threatening," she later remembered the tone in the pages inadvertently left on her desk by a houseguest, an Onassis executive and a friend of Alexander's. "Ari was determined to do a number on Bolker, he wanted to hurt the fellow, not do him in, but certainly do him harm in some way." It came as no surprise to Fiona; both she and Alexander had for some time accepted that Ari "was an extremely dangerous person who would stop at nothing to get his way." Although the depth of Alexander's concern for her safety became clear to her only after he told her that he'd deposited certain documents that would dissuade his father from allowing harm to come to her.

And now she knew that unless Christina acted quickly, Bolker would be in a lot of trouble. "And for what? The guy didn't want to marry her in the first place; Christina had made a mistake . . . and it was all incited by Tina for her own very dubious ends," Fiona later said. At the end of a long night in Wilton Place during which Christina had poured her heart out, Fiona advised her: "You don't want to be married to Joe. He doesn't want to be married to you. There is no question of anybody ripping anybody off. Go back to California on the first plane tomorrow, tell Joe that you want a divorce, and in a few weeks it will be all over and nobody need be involved except you and Joe." She said that if she didn't act at once her father would turn the business into a media circus, in which to parade his own anti-American prejudice: the Yanks ripping off the Onassises again. "Who needs it, Christina? Do something with dignity, which is a word your father doesn't even begin to understand," Fiona said with undisguised contempt.

Christina returned to California in time for the celebration Bolker had arranged at the Bistro in Beverly Hills for her twenty-first birthday. "I had to get away for a little time to deal with my feelings," she told a friend at the party. "I needed to come to terms with myself." In February, seven months after the Las Vegas ceremony, the Bolkers started divorce proceedings. "Although he may soon be my ex-husband, he will always be my best friend," she told reporters. What went wrong? "I'm too Greek and he's too Beverly Hills," she said. Meyer and two heavies were dispatched to escort Christina back to London. At Los Angeles International the Greek gorillas' .45's set the metal detectors "ringing like somebody had short-circuited Quasimodo," said Meyer. On the plane, they were ordered to deposit their guns with the captain; they didn't want to give them up. Meyer finally convinced them that the captain would not take off until they complied. "Then they were pacing around the cabin, watching everyone. They were acting a little weird, rattling the hell out of some of the passengers. I had to get Christina to tell them in Greek that one of them should just sit down in front of us, and the other should go up to the lounge and keep watch there. Those guys were the hardest part of the whole thing."

Ari still wasn't finished with Joe Bolker. He told Meyer to make him pay Christina's maid's airfare home to Athens. "I pointed out that the girl could fly home free on Olympic. Ari wouldn't hear of it. 'Make him pay,' he said." Inevitably, the story got around that Bolker had been handsomely paid off by Ari.* It was untrue. The marriage "in real terms" lasted less than ninety

* A marriage contract signed in October 1971 affirmed that they had no claims whatsoever on each other's properties and finances.

days; it cost Joseph Bolker "about fifty thousand dollars in attorney fees" to end it. "When a billion dollars leans on you, you feel it," he was reputed to have said afterward, and although he denies he ever expressed it in those precise words it is evident to him that Ari did set out to "destroy my credit, destroy my credibility."

In winning the battle Ari had lost the war with Christina. "The energy he put into destroying that marriage was extraordinary. If he had just been a little more patient, it would have collapsed under the weight of its own improbability," said an Onassis functionary in London. "It was doomed from day one, born in petulance and unhappiness—the result was chaos. I don't know what Christina told her father, but I do know that he genuinely believed that the divorce was all his doing. He felt good about that, but he also felt that he owed her one. If Christina had planned it that way, it would have been perfect, only I don't think she's that Machiavellian."

The months following the divorce were hectic; she was in great demand, a string of suitors came and went—barons and heirs and playboys, the movers and shakers of the Beautiful People. "It was the best time, the best time there ever was," she told a friend in Paris. In one month she was sighted with Baron Arnaud de Rosnay, Mercedes-Benz heir Mick Flick, and skier Patrick Gillis, a former lover of Brigitte Bardot's. It was reported, plausibly enough, that she often made the first move; at least one young man whom she wooed too vigorously felt compelled to flee her overtures. "It was her tragedy to be passionate without being lovable," said a former boyfriend. A hint that she had not lost her penchant for falling in love inconveniently came in a meeting between Flick and Meyer. Flick called Meyer at 7:00 A.M. in New York and asked if he could drop by and talk to him before he caught the morning flight to Germany. "I've been dating Christina," he said when he arrived an hour later. "I like her and I respect her, only I don't want to get married yet." He had decided a long time ago that he would not wed until he was forty-five; he had about eight years left. "Would you please tell Mr. Onassis that for me? Tell him I respect him and I respect his family, but I don't want to get married yet."

"The prodigal daughter," Alexander called her with his fondness for labels. "What happens next?" he asked her at dinner one evening. "I've no idea," she told him. "Isn't it exciting?"

CHAPTER 15

> *Coming events cast their shadows be-*
> *fore.*
>
> CICERO

DISSATISFIED WITH his own marriage and shrinking from analyzing himself in any way, Ari blamed the woman he had once lyrically compared to a diamond: "cool and sharp at the edges, fiery and hot beneath the surface." Jackie was now "coldhearted and shallow," and he no longer called her "my class A lady" (inspired by the slogan on her packs of L & Ms: "20 class A cigarettes"). Tina's marriage to Niarchos and Christina's crises had exposed in him an excessive desire for revenge, and a need to make a show of his griefs that must have been distasteful to Jackie, whose own emotions under stress were inviolable. "Jackie will never understand Ari. You can't know men like that unless you are born knowing them," Tina told a friend.

For over a year he had been turning back to Maria Callas for understanding, and much more; at first they met in the privacy of her avenue Georges-Mandel apartment in Paris. Following the publication in February 1970 (after it had fallen into the hands of an autograph dealer in New York) of the note Jackie had written to Roswell Gilpatric while still on her honeymoon on Skorpios, Ari made no secret of his rapprochement with his former mistress, nor of his pleasure in her company. The fifty-three words (quoted on page 234) were evidence of a close and valued friendship; and although it was barely more than the kind of note that is regarded in Jackie's milieu as good manners, Gilpatric's wife sued for divorce the day after it was published. Ari told Gratsos: "My God, what a fool I have made of myself." In May 1970, he was photo-

261

graphed dining with Callas at Maxim's; it looked a bit too much like the old days. Jackie flew to Paris immediately, and the following evening she was by Ari's side at the same restaurant. Told to get the photographers to record the tête-à-tête as if it were a formal banquet, Meyer said later: "For Jackie it wasn't so much a supper as a sock in the eye for Maria."

Four days after this remarkable episode Callas was admitted to the American Hospital at Neuilly suffering from an overdose of sleeping pills; her stay was brief and said to have been for treatment for a sinus problem. Although she had been in an extremely depressive state the evening before (she pleaded with two friends who were dining with her at her apartment not to leave her alone) she successfully sued a radio station and a Paris weekly for claiming she had attempted to kill herself in a fit of depression over her affair with Ari. Three months later she was riding high again when Ari dropped in by helicopter to Tragonisis, the Embiricos shipping family's private island, to give her a pair of century-old earrings, and a lingering kiss on the mouth that was captured by a paparazzo. Again Jackie displayed her speed. "Responding like a dalmation to the fire bell, Jackie flew to Greece, to Onassis, to the yacht *Christina*, and to squelch rumors," reported *Time* magazine.

Her sense of togetherness was not always so acute, and Ari had trouble hiding the fact that frequently on his visits to New York there was no room for him at 1040 Fifth Avenue: the decorators are in, Jackie would apologize ("She has a thing about decorating," he told Willi Frischauer with an air of resignation), or Caroline or John have friends staying. And while his permanent suite on the top floor of the Pierre was explained away as a business accommodation, it added weight to the stories of the many strings said to be attached to the marriage contract (according to Christian Cafarakis, still the primary source of information on the document, she had agreed to spend only Catholic holidays and summer vacations with Ari, "and for the rest of the year reserved the right to travel alone and to visit her friends and family without asking her husband's permission"). However, he did not want for companionship in his wife's absence. He would call one of the many beautiful women he knew and take her to a place where they were sure to be noticed. In Rome he guaranteed attention by throwing a glass of champagne over paparazzi who were trying to photograph him dining at the Osteria Dell 'Orso with Elizabeth Taylor (sans spouse Richard Burton, the actress slid under the table). It was becoming apparent not only to Onassis insiders that an implausible marriage was rapidly becoming an impossible one.

Jackie's extravagance was absolute, a fact neither capable of explanation nor, in her view, in need of it. No stranger to prodigal gestures himself, Ari had encouraged her expensive whims in the beginning; nevertheless, after getting a nine-thousand-dollar bill for gowns from the Rome couturier Valentino he slashed her thirty-thousand-dollar monthly allowance by a third and moved its control from New York to his Monte Carlo headquarters, where he could keep closer tabs on her spending. Another augury of his hardening attitude toward her extravagance was his refusal to make good the reputed three hundred thousand dollars she had dropped playing the stock market. "She should have left the money in tax-free bonds," he said with asperity. Obsessed as the very rich often are by stratagems of thrift, Jackie began unloading her outfits from Saint Laurent and Halston through some of New York's classier secondhand boutiques, taking sixty cents on the dollar. Yet often before the month was up she still felt the need to dispatch her secretary and ombudswoman Nancy Tuckerman (who was now on the Olympic Airways payroll) to ask Ari's New York money manager Creon Broun for funds.

"At first the kindly Broun advanced money until Ari put a stop to it," reported Jack Anderson, who had been invited to New York to lunch with Ari at 21. The lunch yielded little beyond a few elliptic asides about Jackie's inordinate interest in fashion ("What does she do with all these clothes? I never see her in anything but blue jeans!"), but afterward the syndicated Washington columnist was taken back to the office to meet several of Ari's top people while the man himself disappeared to attend to some suddenly urgent business. Well acquainted with the techniques of the unattributable source, the perfidies of plausible denial, a Washington art form practiced by politicians, lobbyists, bureaucrats and sometimes just spouses with a grudge, Anderson was not surprised when the aides began entertaining him with stories of Jackie's capers and the harmful effect her ungovernable spending was having on her relationship with Ari.

He wanted to be free of her; he ordered Meyer to tap her phone in New York. "I brought in a guy who was supposed to be a whiz at tapping phones," said Meyer, who had arranged the bug on Christina's phone in London; the plan was aborted when it was decided that "Jackie's Secret Service agents kept too close a watch on the apartment."

When she wanted to sue the photographer Ron Galella for invasion of privacy and mental anguish Ari advised against it. It would merely give Galella "millions of dollars' worth of free publicity at our expense," he told her and wanted nothing to do with it. Nevertheless, she had Galella arrested for harassment and sought a permanent injunction to keep him two hundred yards from her New York apartment and one hundred yards from her person anywhere else. Galella hit back with a claim seeking $1.3 million in punitive damages for false arrest, malicious prosecution and interference with his livelihood as a photographer. After listening to almost five thousand pages of testimony, the judge ruled in Jackie's favor; a year later the Court of Appeals overturned the ruling and reduced the *cordon sanitaire* to a token twenty-five feet.

The bill for Jackie's legal costs from her law firm, Paul, Weiss, Rifkind, Wharton and Garrison, eventually landed on Ari's desk. He consulted Roy Cohn, described by *Esquire* magazine as a legal executioner, "the toughest, meanest, vilest, and one of the most brilliant lawyers in America." It was also not far from his mind that Cohn was no friend of the Kennedys. He had had to be physically restrained by aides from swapping punches with his co-counsel Bobby Kennedy during the McCarthy-Army hearings in 1954. Ari told Cohn the story: how he had tried to dissuade Jackie from bringing the suit and told her that he would have nothing to do with it—"only now I am involved," he concluded, producing the bill. It was for over $300,000.

"Ari said, 'I think it's outrageous for a nine-cents case like this,'" recalls Cohn. "He said, 'No jury, no nothing and three hundred thousand dollars! It's absurd! I'm not going to pay this bill, and what I would like to know from you is will you go over the whole thing from top to bottom, and if you're satisfied would you testify as an expert witness for me as to the value of the services . . . as being considerably less than this?'" Even though Cohn "had a high regard for certain people in the law firm involved," he agreed to examine the costs and, if he concluded that they were out of order, testify on Ari's behalf.

Jackie's anger at her husband's maneuver turned to embarrassment when her law firm itself resorted to law to recover its costs. She complained to friends that Ari was a skinflint, although many felt that it was his "haggling tactics" that offended her more. "They finally made a settlement for over half the amount of the bill ($235,000), although he was very much annoyed at even paying that," says Cohn. During the course of their negotiations, Ari conveyed to the lawyer "a lot of displeasure with Mrs. Onassis's way of doing things and what he thought was a lack of judgment . . . all of these things were building up to a point of great grievance in him."

Nothing could have symbolized more explicitly the state of their marriage than the cruise on which they embarked that Easter with Andrew and Geraldine Spreckles Fuller. It was she who had stood up Ari at the altar in 1942. Jackie joined the yacht in Puerto Rico, expecting to be taken to Europe. She appeared exhilarated by the weather and by the prospect of the voyage. It soon became obvious that the *Christina* was going round in circles, never moving more than a few miles beyond Haiti. Geraldine finally expressed an interest in their cyclic progress. They were having engine trouble, Ari apologized; to Geraldine it seemed "a puzzling explanation" as they continued to move graciously around the Republic of Haiti.

Geraldine was pleased that she and Ari had remained good friends, and that Andy had grown fond of Ari. And although they appeared to be going nowhere, it was for Geraldine Fuller a voyage of discovery as they sat up long into the Caribbean night reminiscing about old times together in California and New York. But there was something about Ari that troubled her. "I began to feel very sorry for him," she later recalled. His relationship with his wife perplexed her: it was as if he was angry with Jackie and anxious to assuage her at the same time. Jackie often made fun of him, she remembered, and once alluded cryptically to the sexual proclivities of Greek men. Geraldine, who had grown up in Turkey and understood the nature of attachments between Levantine men, later wondered whether he had made the mistake of confessing his adolescent relationship with the Turkish lieutenant. Jackie's teasing sometimes turned to anger; the anger was capable of dissolving in self-mocking submission. One evening she retired to her stateroom with a bottle of champagne, leaving Ari and the Fullers talking over drinks in the saloon; sometime later she returned at a stage of gentle intoxication. "She said to Ari in this little-girl voice she puts on: 'I went upstairs, darling, and I put perfume wherever Mr. Lanvin'—or one of those big perfume people—'told me to put it, and you never came up. I put perfume *everywhere!*' And then she roared with laughter," Geraldine remembered.

Several days later she discovered the reason why they continued to hang around Haiti. Ari confessed that he had been trying to persuade Jackie to slip ashore for a quickie divorce in Port-au-Prince, on the understanding that they would remarry the following day. "I said, what do you mean, Ari, get married the following day? He said, 'Well, that's what I told her. It was an idea. I said that because of all this trouble between us, with people thinking that she didn't love me because she took the money, and there was always this money thing, I said to prove to me that she really loved me, we'd go ashore, get a divorce and immediately remarry to prove absolutely that she did love me.'" Geraldine thought it was one of the most unconvincing propositions she had ever heard in her life. "Of course, she wouldn't do it. You couldn't fool her."

Geraldine said, "You damn fool, Ari, she'll never buy that. *Never.*"
He finally laughed and said, "Yes, but I was hoping." He proposed
a settlement, Geraldine recalled. "He didn't tell me how much,
but he said that he had offered her a big payoff. I asked him why
he was doing all this, going to so much trouble. He said, 'Because
I don't want lawyers dancing on my grave.' I still think it was sort
of silly, thinking he could talk a smart lady like Jackie into such a
deal, falling for a ruse like that." Failing to deceive hurt his pride
almost as much as allowing himself to be deceived, he told a friend
shortly afterward.

Jackie never did get to Europe on that cruise. The *Christina*
returned to Puerto Rico, and she flew back to New York. She was
still, however tenuously, Mrs. Aristotle Onassis.

Alexander's success with Olympic Aviation was ignored by his
father. Said an Olympic executive close to what was happening in
Athens: "Ari had no scruples at frustrating Alexander's aspirations
in order to gratify the smallest whim of his own; there was no
kindness in his attitude toward his son. High on his own Der Tag,
he'd rather sacrifice love than give up the smallest piece of control
over his empire. Instead of preparing Alexander to take the helm,
he seemed out to destroy the boy's belief in himself." * Alexander
had come to dread his father's summonses and even his telephone
calls. "It got so that his whole day was spent trying to avoid the
old man," an aide said. Fiona Thyssen nevertheless believed that
it was up to Alexander "to make the effort to break out of the
ridiculous cycle of noncommunication" in which they were
caught; she believed that only he had the potential and the flexi-
bility to resolve "the horrendous deadlock," particularly since he
had broken entirely with his mother following her marriage to
Niarchos.

Unable to convey to Fiona the extent of his father's irrational
behavior, Alexander began taping their phone conversations.
Later she listened spellbound as, calling from New York, Ari began
a croaky rendition of "Singin' in the Rain." The words and music,
mixed up with a medley of complaints, orders, queries, inanities
and oaths, spilled out without interruption for ten minutes. "Listen to him. It's two o'clock in the afternoon over there, and he's

---

* *Ari's refusal to approve funds to replace two ageing Piaggios (which Alexander had
been telling him for months were "death traps") with helicopters, was a special bone
of contention. Only a lucky accident had saved Ari's own skin, as well as Jackie's, when
Donald McGregor, the former Olympic captain who had flown Jackie and her entourage
to her wedding, forgot to lower the wheels for a dry landing during a familiarization
flight in the* Christina's *Piaggio. "Best turn I ever did Onassis," McGregor recalled the
classic amphibian pilot's goof. "Checking out the damage, they discovered that the
whole interior was corroded beyond repair, and the plane had to be scrapped."*

completely pissed out of his mind." Alexander sounded like a man reconciling himself to a reign of unending oppression. "Yet in his own way Ari loved the kid," insisted Meyer. "He was jealous of his youth, he was jealous as hell of the baroness, but he still loved the kid. Only he wanted him to be a replica of himself, a made-over Ari. He couldn't bring himself to let the kid evolve his own ethos, work out his own life."

Beyond a few close friends, the nature and depth of Alexander's relationship with Fiona continued to be a well-kept secret. They rarely went out in public together, were never seen at smart restaurants or at the theatre: it was a discretion that put a severe strain on Fiona's social instincts. And although she accepted that one day he would probably leave her for someone younger ("I had all the anxieties of the older woman"), it was she who made the first move to end the affair after he had "freaked out" when he discovered that a smart christening party they were attending was swarming with paparazzi. "If I've been able to live with this difficult situation for four and a half years and you still can't face it, there really is no point in going on." And she left him.

Ari was delighted, arranging parties and cruises for him, giving dinners for him, spending nights on the town with him. There were always plenty of beautiful women around, including actress Elsa Martinelli, Princess Ira Furstenberg and Alexander's first love, Odile Rodin. "I was terribly sad," Fiona recalled their separation. "Still I was determined that it was finished between us and kept telling myself, 'I'll survive,' which, of course, one does." A month later Alexander called and confessed his own unhappiness. They spent a weekend together, and it was obvious to them both that they wanted only to be with each other, yet they could not go back nor could they endure a future so vulnerable to his father's tyranny. Alexander accepted that he had to become free of Ari and his empire. "It's the only way I'm going to survive. I can't take this grotesque man's domination for much longer." They had never been able to make plans about anything. Alexander had always been at the beck and call of his father, who disliked pinning himself down even to vacation dates for his top people. When Alexander insisted on a vacation and asked for the dates to be agreed in writing, Ari told him: "Don't be ridiculous. My word is good enough." Alexander said it was not. "Your word means absolutely nothing, especially to me: you have never kept your word to me in your life." Ari signed the agreement. Two days before Alexander and Fiona were due to leave for Africa he told him to cancel the trip because he needed him in Paris. Reminded that he had given his word, Ari said he was taking it back. "My piece of paper means nothing, whether I write it or say it. If I require you to do this or that you will do it." Alexander stuck to his guns.

"I thought, God, this man is just so *valuable*," says Fiona now. Although their future "did not necessarily include or exclude marriage," they recognized that they loved each other and were "prepared to make a statement about it" by living together. She bought a house in Switzerland, and he prepared to resume his studies to get the qualifications to give him a start in the outside world, beyond his father's Olympian reach. "The plan was that as soon as the house was ready he would say to his father, 'Right, I'm going to live with Fiona; I'm going back to university; I'm going to get a degree, and I'm going to get a job.' He actually had the guts to do that, to walk away and probably be totally disinherited."

Meanwhile, in New York, Ari was talking to Roy Cohn again, and again it concerned Jackie. "Mr. Onassis had definitely concluded that he wanted to break the marriage and had been consulting his Greek lawyers and so on, and there were a lot of complications over there, and he wanted to know whether I would be prepared to handle the American end, because he had assets over here, and participate in the overall strategy," Cohn recalled the situation. "He anticipated that the matter would be settled because he did not think that Jackie would want to make a big thing out of it, but he also viewed the possibility that her appetite for money would be such that it might not be amicably settled. He had a number of questions about American law and what the relative rights of the parties would be under that."

At a meeting in Cohn's townhouse office on East Sixty-eighth Street, Ari said that he felt he was being "taken for a sucker." "What annoyed him were two major topics. The first was her spending. His second complaint was that she was apparently everyplace except where he wanted her to be. If he wanted her to be someplace she just wasn't there; if he didn't want her to go someplace she was there." The marriage, he told Cohn, "had gotten down to a monthly presentation of bills."

Even with the formidable Cohn in his corner, Ari was determined to leave nothing to chance; he ordered Meyer to hire around-the-clock private investigators to seek evidence that could be used against his wife. Cohn had known Meyer since his days with Howard Hughes and recognized his ability to handle the situation. "Johnny Meyer was a truly enterprising man, one of a very small group of people in life who surround themselves with very rich and powerful people . . . whenever a problem came up or something had to be done, be it a reservation or a discreet arrangement at a hotel, or checking somebody out, or getting the dirt on somebody, Johnny was always there, ready to act with a wide circle of contacts upon whom he could call."

On January 3, 1973, Alexander had dinner with his father in Paris. He had learned to play his cards close to his vest and still did not mention his own plans; Ari revealed two facts that pleased his son immensely. He had decided to divorce Jackie and agreed to buy a helicopter to replace the Piaggio. He would take the amphibian on one last trip to Miami in February and sell it there. Alexander telephoned Fiona, who was vacationing in Mexico with her children, Francesca and Lorne. "The old man's seeing sense at last. He's divorcing the Widow and selling the albatross," he said.

Sunday, January 21, 1973, was not like any other day for either Fiona or Alexander. Even now, and she has thought about it a great deal, she is unable to say what made it so different from all the other Sundays they had spent together in Morges. There were no glances and innuendos, just an atmosphere of awareness that had permeated her apartment since early morning. They had never been as happy as they had that winter; so many things had been settled, and they were looking forward to moving into the house she had bought, which was being remodeled and decorated. She was leaving that afternoon for her brother's wedding in London; Alexander was going to Monte Carlo to fly a charter party to Athens. Although it was one of the rituals of Sunday that they lunched alone, that day he said: "I would like to see Chessie (Francesca) and Lorne; can we all have lunch together?" Afterward they played tabletop football, Francesca and her mother versus Lorne and Alexander. "He so strangely wanted to be with the family. I felt that he knew something or sensed something that made him sad, and I must have been picking up his vibes all day." How else could she account for her own disquiet and the unusual patterns of that Sunday? She asked if there was anything troubling him. He said, "It's as if I've never known the children before." Because of Fiona's own discretion, and Francesca's self-protective hostility toward any of her mother's men friends, it was true he had never become more than a shadowy guest. When he left that afternoon Francesca gave him a big hug and told him, "It's such a shame. We don't see you nearly enough. Next weekend, we'll play the return match and beat the socks off you."

It was raining when he left. A driver from Olympic Airways had come to take him to the airport, and although he was undemonstrative in public, and especially in front of an employee, he held Fiona very close when they said good-bye. She gave him a box of his special chocolates, Dairy Milk Tray, as she always did when he was going away; he ate only his favorite centers, picked from the little chart on the inside of the lid. He climbed into the car and on impulse got out and ran up the steps to hold her once more. "It was raining hard, and he hated the rain because it messed up his hair, he was quite vain, and for him to come back up those steps to give me this tremendous hug . . . it was all part of the strange mood of that Sunday," Fiona later said.

They talked the following morning when Alexander called her from Athens. They were to meet in London the next day. It was a long conversation, more than ninety minutes, and although he sounded in good spirits, he seemed unwilling to end the call. Later that day he had to check out the new pilot, Donald McCusker, who had just arrived from Westerville, Ohio, to replace Donald Mc-Gregor (grounded after an eye operation) as the regular pilot of the Piaggio. Although an experienced amphibian pilot, the American had never flown Piaggios, and Alexander had devised a plan to get him through the familiarization as quickly as possible. After only a couple of hours' sleep at the hotel, McCusker drove out to the airport to meet Alexander and McGregor.

"The idea was that McCusker would be treated as a charter customer," recalls McGregor. "To keep it legal, Alexander was to go with McCusker to check him out. McCusker would then 'hire' the aircraft, and I would go along as dogsbody to watch how things went, and we would fly furiously for a week to get Mc-Cusker's hours up before the Piaggio was ferried to Las Palmas to join the *Christina* before it sailed for Miami, where it was eventually to be sold."

Shortly before 3:15 on the afternoon of January 22, 1973, aircraft SX-BDC Piaggio 136 of Olympic Airways reached taxiway F of Athens International to hold for takeoff. Alexander sat in the right-hand seat; McCusker, the pilot under supervision, sat in the left-hand seat. McGregor took the middle passenger seat behind them. The plan was to carry out some water landings and takeoffs between the islands of Aegina and Poros. When they got to the plane Alexander discovered that he had forgotten the preflight checklist. He went through the safety checks from memory. The Piaggio flight manual lists seven ground checks; fifteen before-starting-engine checks; twelve before-takeoff checks; seven after-takeoff checks. From where he was sitting, McGregor was unable to see whether visual checks were made on the flaps and ailerons to be certain they responded correctly to the controls, but he had a high regard for Alexander's professionalism. "I know that when he checked *me* out he chewed me up for not making a visual check," remembered McGregor, who had come straight from 707s, in which it's impossible to observe the control surfaces from the cockpit. At 3:21 P.M. as an Air France Boeing 727 lifted off runway

thirty-three, the Piaggio was cleared for takeoff on the same runway with instructions to turn left when airborne.

The Piaggio lifted off. "Within three or four seconds the right
wing dropped sharply and stayed down," recalls McGregor. There
was no yaw or swing to indicate engine failure; there was no shud-
dering to suggest a stall. The plane simply seemed to lose its balance. He thought that the right float touched the runway; strapped
in the middle seat, it was impossible for him to see out. "By this
time we were in a right hand climbing turn which became quite
steep . . . I realized we were going to hit the ground." From becoming airborne to impact took little more than fifteen seconds, Mc-
Gregor estimates. He cannot recall a single word being spoken
inside the stricken plane in those fatal moments before they
ploughed into the runway.

Ari and Jackie were in New York when they heard the news.
Tina and Stavros Niarchos were in St. Moritz. Christina was in
Brazil and heard about it on the car radio. It was 6:30 in London,
and Fiona was preparing to go to her brother's wedding night
dinner when she heard. The news bulletins said that McCusker
and McGregor had been seriously injured and Alexander was in
surgery, undergoing an operation to remove blood clots and relieve pressure on his brain. The last scheduled flights had left for
Athens. "I spent the next three hours on the phone pulling every
string I knew, calling every person I knew who had a private
plane," Fiona remembers. "All I knew was that he was alive, and
I was going to look after him, he was going to be all right." At
eleven o'clock she got a call to say that a private executive jet
would be available at midnight. She arrived in Athens shortly
after six o'clock on Tuesday morning. Although he was on a life-
support system, he appeared to be remarkably undamaged. "It's
weird, the things you remember. He was always so proud of his
new nose, and I immediately thought: 'Thank God his nose is all
right,' " Fiona said later. Part of his hair above the right temple
had been shaved; otherwise there was little evidence of his injuries, and he was not bandaged.

While Fiona had been frantically telephoning all over Europe
trying to find a plane to get her to Greece, Ari had laid on a British
Airways Trident (passenger capacity 149) to fly one man to Athens:
the English neurosurgeon Alan Richardson. The family was still
gathering at the hospital from all over the world when Dr. Richardson confirmed the Greek surgeons' grim prognosis. Alexander
had suffered "irrecoverable brain damage." Yet it seemed inconceivable. Except for scratches on his hand ("as if he had fallen on
gravel," Fiona thought) he looked unmarked. Another neurosurgeon had been summoned from Boston, and while they waited for

his arrival somebody remembered that a sacred icon on one of the islands was reputed to possess miraculous powers. Ari ordered that it be found and brought to the hospital. An office next to Alexander's room was furnished with sofas and armchairs; Ari's sisters wept inexhaustibly, violently; their grief seemed very close to anger.

Outwardly calm, Fiona sat alone by the window with her thoughts. After a while Jackie came and sat by her side. She must have understood the loneliness of the woman who was probably closest of all to Alexander, yet, like herself, an outsider amid the almost tribal despair. She spoke in a quiet voice. She knew that Alexander told Fiona everything; she also knew that Ari had discussed their forthcoming divorce with his son. Could she tell her what figure Ari had in mind for her settlement? Expecting and dreading sympathy ("Sympathy, when you're that vulnerable, you don't need it"), Fiona was astonished by the question. Yet it was exactly the kind of distraction she needed at that moment, and as unreal as it seemed in retrospect she answered calmly. Although Alexander had mentioned a figure, she said she felt it was a question Jackie should address to her husband. Jackie agreed, and left Fiona to her thoughts.

By one o'clock in the afternoon of January 23, 1973, the Boston specialist had reached the same conclusion as the English and Greek surgeons. Alexander "was in the deepest possible coma, unable to breathe without the life-support system," Dr. Richardson said. Ari was told the situation: only the machine was keeping his son technically alive (he had suffered general contusion and edema of the brain matter; the right temporal lobe had been reduced to pulp and the right frontal fossa severely fractured), there was no possible hope of recovery. Ari told the doctors to wait until Christina arrived from Brazil to say good-bye to her brother— "then let us torture him no more." Dr. Richardson thought that he handled the situation "remarkably stoically, given the Greek temperament." It was the only thing he'd ever done in his life as a father that Fiona "respected on any level at all."

Ari left the hospital. Fiona was allowed to be alone with Alexander. "I just sat there thinking, I'll be able to get through, there must be a part of his brain left there. I held his hand and tried to let him know . . . even though I had to face the fact there was no way he was going to come back from wherever he'd gone to. After about forty minutes I got a bit weepy and thought, 'Oh, don't crack now, it's not going to help at all.' Then a doctor said he thought it was time for me to go." Christina arrived later that afternoon, and at 6:55 P.M. they switched off the machine.

When Fiona returned to the Hilton, the manager invited her

to go with him to open Alexander's room; it had not been touched since Alexander left on Monday, and he wanted her to see if there was anything there of hers, "letters, perhaps," that she might like to have. On the table by his bed were the chocolates she had given him when he left Morges. Three were missing: she knew which ones they would be. The brain defends itself to a degree, she said later; you drink a lot of wine, and take sleeping tablets, but it's the little things that break you in the end.

Ari walked the streets of Athens looking for the church in which he had prayed the night he learned of his grandmother's death. In the early hours of January 24, 1973, he found it and prayed for his son before the same altar at which he had prayed for Gethsemane. Time could not account for the distance he felt between now and then. Nothing could have summed up more poignantly the changes in his life than the note Ingeborg sent from Paris that morning: "Dear Ari," she wrote in French, and it was as if the language itself emphasized the passage of time:

> In thinking of everything that was good between us I cannot stop myself in order to say to you from my heart the shock and the grief that I felt when I learned this unbelievable news of the accident of your son Alexander. From a distance I sincerely share with you the bereavement and the profound grief that must overwhelm you. With my very best wishes, Inge.

He was buried on Skorpios, but only after Ari went through several changes of heart and mind before the final resting place was decided on. He had promised Fiona as well as several of Alexander's friends that he would be buried in Athens to make it simpler for them to visit the grave. Then he decided that he wanted the body deep-frozen and kept in a cryonic-care unit until medical science was able to rebuild Alexander's shattered brain; Meyer was ordered to contact the Life Extension Society in Washington, which specialized in cryonics. Ari drew back from that step after Yanni Georgakis, who had debated theology with him for ten years, protested that he had no right "to impede the journey of Alexander's soul."

The death of a son is a terrible blow to the psyche of a loving father; to a conscience-stricken father it is devastating. He could not accept that the crash had been an accident. He blamed the CIA and his old friend Col. George Papadopoulos, whose connections with the Central Intelligence Agency he believed went back a long way. "It's revenge for the Omega fuck-up," he said. It was true that the colonels' regime was looking increasingly shaky, and the failure of Omega was seen by the Greek public as the junta's failure and emphasized the serious economic difficulties the country was facing under the dictatorship.* Yet it seemed incredible that Alexander was killed to punish his father "for letting the side down," and most people who had to listen to Ari's emotional accusations put them down to grief and guilt; it was no secret that Alexander had been telling him for more than a year that the Piaggios were death traps.

"Ari was driving us all bananas, his paranoia didn't exempt anyone," said Meyer, who, within hours of the crash, had been told to find and destroy the tape recordings Alexander had made of the conversations with his father. "The strange thing is how he knew they even existed," says Fiona Thyssen, who still has no idea why Ari was so anxious to destroy them. "They were just tapes a young man recorded to prove to his girlfriend how impossible his father was." Meyer thought it was because "Ari didn't want to leave a shred of anything around that his enemies might one day use against him. He didn't trust anyone." At the Glyfada villa, the day after the funeral, Fiona overheard two of his most senior aides discussing the tragedy in terms that horrified her. "Do you know the German word *schadenfreude*? It means taking pleasure in another's misfortune. It was as if finally they felt he had been paid back for all the terrible things he had done to them over the years. That freaked me: the absolute hatred of this man by two people who couldn't have been closer to him. He didn't blow his nose without one of them being there with the Kleenex, and they *despised* him. I thought, 'God, this man's worse than even I thought he was.' "

The Greek air force took charge of the ill-fated Piaggio. With his own engineers denied access to the wreckage (Olympic was hardly impartial in the matter) until after the military experts had completed their investigations, combing through the debris on runway thirty-three, tagging and marking engine and other fragments, constructing a wreckage distribution map, interviewing eyewitnesses, getting statements from McGregor and McCusker, both of whom had survived the crash—McGregor with a compression fracture of the spine, concussion and leg injuries; McCusker, less physically injured, was suffering from amnesia—Ari's suspicions that the junta was attempting a cover-up grew and grew.

And the accident investigation report completed on April 20, 1973, could not have been more calculated to confirm his claim that the plane had been sabotaged. The crash had been caused

---

* On November 25, 1973, Papadopoulos was toppled in a bloodless coup led by Brig. Gen. Dimitrios Ioannides, an obscure commander of the Greek military police.

because the aileron connecting cables were reversed during the installation of a new control column: thus when the pilot, as instructed by the control tower, attempted to turn left on takeoff, the aircraft would have banked to the right; the harder he pulled the stick to the left the more sharply the plane swerved to the right.

The Olympic engineers disputed the official findings. In the first place they claimed that the vital color markings painted on connections before they are uncoupled (to establish what was joined to what at the time of the accident) were applied *after* the disconnection—including the markings on the reversed cables that the military investigators said had caused the crash. "They also claimed that the cables just weren't long enough to enable them to be crossed and connected up the wrong way round," said McGregor, who himself refused to buy the crossed-cables theory. The Piaggio had started its takeoff from almost halfway down runway thirty-three, one minute and fifty seconds behind the departing Air France Boeing 727. "I've read up an awful lot on wake turbulence since then, and in my opinion we were in the perfect spot to get hit with the full force of the 727's wake vortices [like the wake of a big ship, a jetliner's turbulence lasts for several minutes after the plane has taken off]. We did it the wrong way. We should have taken off from the runway threshold and made our turn before the 727's wake caught us, or waited for the prescribed time [three to five minutes] to let it subside. Ari blamed McCusker, but Alexander was the pilot in command regardless who was actually doing the flying," McGregor says bluntly.

The revenge motive festered in Ari's imagination; he offered a million dollars for information that would confirm that the plane had been sabotaged. "A cool million should be enough to bring something out of the woodwork," McCusker wrote Don McGregor. "If he doesn't come up with any leads, I think I will suggest he split that between you and I and we'll call it even, okay?" Although McGregor was visited once in the hospital by Olympic's operations director, who gave him a box of chocolates, neither pilot had heard a word from Ari since the accident; "not even a get-well card," recalls McGregor. "He must really be something," wrote McCusker, who had started fighting Ari through the courts for damages, having shaken off his attempts to charge him with Alexander's manslaughter.

Ari's thoughts were becoming morbid and dark: he repeatedly played a tape he acquired from Edwards Air Force Base in California of the last words of test pilots whose planes had got into uncontrollable dives ("Listen to these men, not giving up, fighting till the end, the way Alexander went out"); he had McCusker investigated for CIA links. He commissioned Alan Hunter, one of the most respected aircrash detectives in England, to make an independent investigation. By July 6, Hunter had reached the same conclusion as the air force investigators: the aileron cables *had* been reversed. And although Hunter explained how simple it was to make the mistake when installing new control mechanisms in that particular aircraft, Ari still insisted that Alexander had been murdered, and Hunter's report was locked away.

But the "murder" investigations continued to run up against blank walls. It was pure chance that Alexander was flying the Piaggio that Monday. Only a last-minute charter booking had prevented him from going to London with Fiona for her brother's wedding; only McGregor's failure to pass a medical exam had prevented him from captaining the familiarization flight with McCusker. In the time after it became certain that Alexander was going to be on the flight, it would not have been possible to switch the control cables.

In July 1974 Olympic gave Donald McGregor an *ex gratia* payment of fifteen thousand dollars (less 15 percent legal fees) for his injuries. Ari absolutely forbade the Olympic lawyers to settle the case with McCusker. "He couldn't bear to let it end; he wanted it to go on and on almost as if the case itself was the only thing keeping Alexander's memory alive. Even when McCusker's lawyers threatened to impound an Olympic 747 in the States he wouldn't give a goddam inch," Meyer recalled. "Right until the end he had this conviction that the CIA had killed his son, and as long as he could keep McCusker on the hook something was sure to come out."

Ari's head was "crawling with scapegoats, people he wanted dumped" because he had a feeling they were somehow involved in Alexander's death, said an executive anxious about the effect Ari's unconcealed suspicions were having on public confidence in Olympic Airways. Gratsos later recalled a story Ari told him about a Greek philosopher who didn't know whether gods existed or not, or even what they might look like, and decided that there were just too many things in the way of ever finding out. And Ari said, "Well, I don't know about gods either, Costa, but I do know about evil bastards, and I have a damn good idea what they look like, and no matter what's in the way, I'm going to nail one of them before my life is over."

In 1978, three years after Ari's life *was* over, Olympic settled with Donald McCusker for eight hundred thousand dollars.

16

Men have but a short time to live.
HOMER

H E HAD DECIDED to hold off on his plans for divorce. "He still intended to tell it to the judge," insisted Meyer. "Only now was not the time." Shortly after the funeral on Skorpios, Jackie called Pierre Salinger in Paris and told him that Ari was "so broken up" and wanted to take a cruise. Would the Salingers join them? The timing could not have been more inconvenient. That week he had started work for the French magazine *L'Express*; nevertheless, at eight o'clock the following morning he and his wife drove out to Orly, where Jackie and Ari were waiting for them. An Olympic Airlines 707 flew them to Dakar (they were the only passengers), where they joined the *Christina*. Salinger and Ari found a mutual interest in politics and journalism: "There were two things in the world that he hated more than anything else: one was politicians, and the second was press people," recalls Salinger, who has been both. It gave them plenty to argue about, and Ari still loved to argue, although some detected a hollowness in his passion now. Alexander was never mentioned. Long after his guests had gone to bed, the French writer Sabine de Labrosse saw Ari pacing the deck as the yacht headed toward the Antilles. He liked the feel of the sea beneath him. ("You know, Wendy, the ground doesn't really go with me," he once told Wendy Reves.) "Before Alexander died, he nearly always worked through the night on the boat," remembered Costa Konialidis. "Now you heard stories how he just walked up and down the deck until it got light, like he was afraid to sleep in the dark."

277

Hélène Gaillet met him for the first time shortly after this cruise. An attractive, intelligent, coolly ironic New York photographer, she is used to the company of successful men, and successful men are attracted to her. Her lover at that time was an investment banker whom Ari much admired. Hélène recalled: "There were about eight of us at dinner that night at a restaurant on Eighth Street, east of Washington Square. Men like Ari and my friend carry people with them because it projects their social image; if you had asked either of those men the next morning who was at the dinner, they would not have been able to tell you. They talked business together almost the entire evening." She saw that they were two of a kind, "men in whom everything is at risk." Yet by the end of the evening she had reached the conclusion that "Ari was a man who had decided that nothing was that important anymore. It was as if some essential part that held things together had gone out of his life."

The summer of 1973 was an exhilarating time for the tanker business; spot market rates climbed steadily, VLCCs and ULCCs —very large and ultralarge crude carriers, of over four hundred thousand tons—were making four million dollars' profit on a single run from Kuwait to Europe. With profits of some twelve million dollars a month coming in from his fleet of more than a hundred ships, and with the world's consumption of oil increasing by 8 percent a year, and United States consumption almost 40 percent of the total, going up by 8.7 percent, Ari ordered four more two-hundred-thousand-ton tankers from Japan, and two ULCCs from France. It was simply a response to market conditions, and the sense of triumph and celebrations that would once have accompanied the expansion of his fleet were missing. When Konialidis congratulated him, he said: "I can't get excited about it, Costa, perhaps I've used up all the excitement, perhaps I don't need it as much as I thought I did." His cousin was stunned. He had lived his life in awe of Ari's energy and drive, he had accepted him without question as head of the family, he had never heard him talk this way before. In that single sentence, in less than a couple of seconds, so it seemed, as he remembered it afterward, Costa Konialidis "recognized the end of an era." Ari had always measured the success of his life in simple arithmetic: three times three tankers make nine tankers; nine tankers make millions. And now he had found the flaw in the arithmetical progression: "Millions do not always add up to what a man needs out of his life," he said.

Although he was still capable of moods of great irascibility and fits of frightening anger ("Once a tough-minded sonofabitch, always a tough-minded sonofabitch," said Meyer), he sought more

and more the camaraderie of old friends like Gratsos and Konialidis, a few trusted individuals, men who went back a long way and
were rooted in a past that outsiders would never understand. He
loved to remember the early days. Sometimes he talked about
himself almost as some other person. Gratsos suspected that recalling the distant days disarmed memories of the recent past. He
revisited his childhood, like a man going through an empty house
he had lived in a long time ago, going from room to room, remembering scenes and names, trying to describe the sounds and the
smells of things half-forgotten: the sound of the *imbat*, the wind
that blew until sunset in Smyrna; the smell of the charcoal fire
Grandmother Gethsemane fanned with the feathered wing of a
turkey; the names of the United States destroyers that were anchored in the harbor while Smyrna burned; the first time his father offered him a cigar; the libidinous landlady in Naples and the
girls in the big brass beds at Fahrie's; the bitter taste of defeat
when he failed to be the *Victor Ludorum* at the Pelos club in '22;
the size of the sultan's *Fuad*, the most beautiful yacht he had ever
seen; the weeping of the emigrants on the *Tomaso di Savoya* as
they waved good-bye to the old country.

In the summer he went back to Skorpios for the first time
since the funeral. As if it were a symbolic gesture that the past had
been buried with his son, he invited Tina and Stavros Niarchos to
visit the grave with him. Their yachts rendezvoused between their
private islands. "It was a very strange meeting in the middle of
the ocean, those two enormous yachts . . . as if two warlords were
meeting to sign a peace treaty in neutral waters or something,"
recalls Geraldine Fuller. "But for some reason, Jackie was furious
with the whole idea. She wished Stavros hadn't come, and when
we were invited over to his new yacht [*Atlantis*] for lunch she
refused to go." The Niarchos crew, immaculate in white uniforms
and caps, was drawn up in a guard of honor to greet Ari and his
guests. "They weren't at all like Ari's crew, who were much more
informal—little T-shirts with *Christina* written across the fronts."
That evening they all went to a local island for dinner, and afterward Ari invited everyone back to the *Christina* for a nightcap. "It
was astonishing," recalls Geraldine. "We were met by Ari's captain and crew absolutely impeccably turned out in tropical uniforms and peaked caps; the captain wore more braid than any
admiral I've ever seen in my life. Where Ari got those outfits from
in the middle of the Aegean I don't know. That's the kind of thing
he would do." She also suspected that it was something deeper
than playful one-upmanship that drove him to such lengths. "He
was very rich and glamorous, but deep down he always felt that

he was the little Greek man from Smyrna. He had married the widow of the president of the United States, and Niarchos had certainly never matched that. Yet when Stavros's sailors looked smarter than his, he simply couldn't bear it."

On Skorpios life went on much as it always had, although the British diplomat Sir John Russell was not alone in noticing how isolated Jackie had become. "She always seemed to be off reading somewhere, or swimming, she did have an increasing air of aloneness about her," he said. "She occupied the island with an air of tacit disapproval of her husband's style and her husband's friends," said another frequent guest, who also suspected that she had decided that the only way to "survive with Ari was to maintain her own center of gravity." Ari continued to drink his favorite Black Label Scotch and sing the Greek ballads he loved to hear at night. Yet friends noticed that his sense of energy had gone. "He looked out of sorts and complained of headaches," remembered one. When his guests had gone to bed he would walk for hours alone in the darkness of the island, always ending the evening sitting on his haunches like a peasant beside the tomb of his son. Late one night, an American woman unable to sleep and out for a walk came within a few feet of him without being noticed. "For a man to be that enclosed, it seemed to be a kind of happiness," she later said. "I had the feeling that if Alexander were alive and at his side, Ari would have been no nearer to the boy than he was at that moment."

October 1973 saw the bottom fall out of the world tanker market as the Arabs applied the greatest oil squeeze in history to discourage the West from aiding Israel in the fourth Arab-Israeli war. Ari recognized that the implications of the oil warfare reached far beyond the Middle East battleground. Not since World War II had any event presaged greater global change. As nations finally faced up to the need to conserve fuel and began massive programs to develop domestic resources and new energy technology, the tanker depression would be no passing thing. More than a third of his tonnage was already laid up, none of the oil giants was interested in long-term charters, and he was forced to cancel the two French ULCCs, at a loss of $12.5 million.

Ever since the failure of Omega, he had been talking about building an oil refinery in the United States. And almost at the moment on Yom Kippur when Egyptian troops were pouring across the Suez Canal and Syrian soldiers were striking in the north on the Golan Heights, Costa Gratsos called to say that he had found the perfect site for an American refinery: Durham Point, a wooded headland above Great Bay on the Atlantic coastline in

New Hampshire. Tankers would discharge their cargoes at a deep-water terminal on the Isles of Shoals some seven miles offshore; a pipeline would take the crude from there to the Durham Point refinery. But Gratsos had done more than find the perfect location. He had hit on the one governor in the whole of New England who would welcome an oil refinery in his state. With New Hampshire's traditional cotton mills and timber industries in decline, its shoe factories closed, Governor Meldrim Thomson, Jr., had eagerly welcomed Gratsos's interest. There would be "no problems, no red tape." Ari gave the go-ahead.

Aware that not only beauty but university environmentalists are especially touchy about developing oil refineries in unspoiled towns like Durham, site of the University of New Hampshire, it was vital to move quickly. Executives of Olympic Oil Refineries (posing as ordinary house buyers, claiming to be "tired of the crowding of urban life and craving isolation," or trustees wishing to purchase land for such worthy purposes as a bird sanctuary or an old people's residence, or sometimes an exclusive beach club) began buying up property and estates in target areas in Portsmouth and Rye as well as Durham itself. More than thirty-two hundred acres, in a long narrow tract running down to the sea, were optioned (for around $4.5 million) before Ron Lewis, a blacksmith-turned-investigative reporter on a local weekly newspaper called *Publick Occurrences*, caught on to what was happening and spilled the beans. At a hastily summoned televised press conference in Concord on November 27, Governor Thomson unveiled plans for a six-hundred-million-dollar project that would mean, directly and indirectly, thousands of new jobs, and millions in tax revenues for the state (the refinery and its satellite industries would cut property-tax bills by 75 percent). Not everybody was impressed. Many objected to the secrecy with which the deal had been handled. Within days four thousand people had signed a petition against the refinery. "These ecology nuts piss me off," Ari told Gratsos when he heard. "A modern refinery's no worse than a modern apartment block. We're living in an age when people have to make up their minds what they want—survival or pretty picnic scenery."

Although he did not personally want to involve himself, by the middle of December opposition to the refinery had grown so vociferous that Gratsos pressured him into holding a press reception ("Let's show these people you're not an ogre, Ari") in New Hampshire's chief city, Manchester, which had a large Greek community, solidly Republican. Ari was confident the deal was sewn up. Not only did he have Governor Thomson on his team, but now

William Loeb had thrown his considerable weight behind the scheme. As publisher of the *Manchester Union Leader*, with a circulation of sixty-five thousand, the biggest paper in the state, and according to the *New York Times* most conspicuous for its front-page editorials "denouncing Negroes, homosexuals, Jews, Kennedys and others it views as menaces to civilization," Loeb's support was axiomatic; "Kissinger the Kike?" ran one *Union Leader* editorial during the Arab-Israeli war. "Welcome to the two Big O's: Oil and Onassis," read the paper's headline the day Ari helicoptered into Manchester. Hundreds of people carved a colder message in the snow covering the fields: Ari Go Home, and Ari O No in letters large enough to be read even at three thousand feet.

Ari was not at his best. He was not feeling well. He was cold. He was tired. His heart was not in it. He'd have liked Jackie at his side ("Shit, she's just got to stand there, she learned how to do that with Jack all those years"; Gratsos had advised against it, saying, "Loeb *hates* the Kennedys"). "I am not a Greek bearing presents," he began the press conference with a weak joke. The last thing he wanted to do, he went on, chewing nervously on a Montecristo cigar, was to impose an unwanted investment on the people of New Hampshire, "particularly if we bear in mind that the people of New Hampshire are part of the American aristocracy." However, even the aristocracy needs a kitchen, he said: "All this time, for years now, your supplies were coming from very far-away expensive restaurants. If we can manage to produce a refinery, clean as a clinic, and without any smell and without any smoke, and if we can persuade and convince the officials of the environment and ecology, I hope we are doing something good for everybody." He was asked, When you say you don't want to impose anything on New Hampshire, do you mean the state or the people? "The state is the pipple," one journalist accented his answer. "The pipple is the state." It was a lackluster performance. The wire-pullers and local pols lined up behind the refinery were dismayed. His fabled charm and relaxed confidence when dealing with the press had gone sour on him. Attempts to stage-manage the conference failed utterly when the governor himself got drawn into an argument with reporters. "It was a screw-up from beginning to end," Meyer said later. "Ari wasn't properly briefed, except for one ass-brained joke about the Governor's home-made maple syrup,* which was meant to defuse the question of why we'd been buying up land secretly. Nobody had bothered to talk strategy for

---

* *Ari had held up a bottle of syrup when the question came up and said, "Well, we certainly didn't come to say that we are going to build a distillery of maple syrup."*

the question-and-answer session with him, and even if they had, his consultant team was so unprepared it was unbelievable." (Gratsos gave little importance to the fact that Ari had been badly briefed: "He was never good at briefing-book answers. He was at his best playing it by ear.") As aides hustled him out of the room, reporter Anne Gouvalaris again tackled him about the tactics Olympic had used to get the land: did he think he had behaved honorably? "You don't force with money, my dear," he told her with a remnant of his old charm. "You seduce."

Jackie talked him into a trip to Acapulco to celebrate the New Year. The night before he left for the Mexican resort, three months into the Arab oil embargo, he got the latest figures from the American Petroleum Institute: oil imports were just over half the October volume and still falling. Each week more of his ships were becoming idle, and he knew that even if there was a Middle East settlement immediately, the Arabs would not open the taps as freely as before the war; they had discovered that the longer they kept the oil in the ground the more valuable it became. And the manic inflation would continue to depress the tanker market even when the fighting stopped, since industrial nations unable to afford the increases would simply be forced to cut their demand. When Ari boarded his private Learjet at the end of December 1973 he was hollow-eyed and disheveled, no longer thriving on crises and sleepless nights. According to an Olympic executive who accompanied him to the airport, "He looked sick as a dog."

The tanker crisis wasn't all he had on his mind. Olympic Airways had always been a problem and now, with its sad associations, it was a painful one, which he tried to avoid as much as possible; his attitude merely made matters worse for executives grappling with tribulations that ultimately only he could settle. He was also a lot less sanguine about the local opposition to the New Hampshire refinery and, complaining that he felt "so tired all the goddam time," a complaint that had become more frequent since he returned from Skorpios that summer, he was constantly on the telephone to Gratsos, to Loeb, to Governor Thomson, "kickin' ass."

It was a mistake for Jackie to permit her expensive whims to resurface at that particular time with the declaration that she wanted to build a house in Acapulco. He saw her desire to make a home in the town in which she had spent her honeymoon with Jack as "the final symptom of their misalliance," according to an Onassis insider. "She's a beautiful woman," he said to Gratsos in one of their several telephone conversations during the Mexican trip, "but millions beautiful she's not." The tension in their marriage, as he prepared for a survivable divorce, was felt by all around them. They were still arguing when they flew back to New York on January 3, 1974. Jackie was in a feisty mood and gave as good as she got, reminding him of every lapse of taste and style he was ever guilty of in their five years together; she could be cutting about the faults of others, and like all women "brought up to be adventuresses" (Gore Vidal's view of Jackie and Lee) and "Western geisha girls" (Truman Capote's summing up of the sisters) she obviously knew how to wound a man as well as how to flatter him. He eventually retreated to a quiet corner of the aircraft, and the flight became a spiritual journey as well as a geographical one as he filled page after page of a notepad. Overcoming his superstition and starting with the words, "To my dear daughter," Aristotle Socrates Onassis was drafting his last will and testament. Since Alexander's death he had been living with thoughts of his own mortality, and now he was embracing its reality. For many weeks he had been in pain, his whole body ached, and the physical and mental act of composing his will took a superhuman effort. For a man who had seldom troubled himself with the subtleties and paradoxes of legality and morality it was a carefully crafted document.

The woman who had come to him with such a dowry of history was dismissed with a kind of Catch-22: having already taken care of her, and having extracted a written agreement by which she had relinquished her hereditary rights, Jackie was bequeathed a lifetime income of $200,000 a year. (Caroline and John would each receive $25,000 a year until they were twenty-one.) If, however, she challenged the will or resorted to the courts she would immediately forfeit her annuity, and his executors and the rest of his heirs were instructed to fight her "through all possible legal means." If his death occurred before he had established a foundation in the name of his dead son, he wrote, his executors were to create such a foundation, to promote welfare, religious, artistic and educational activities, for the most part in Greece, and to make annual awards based on the Swedish Nobel Prize system. The Alexander Onassis Foundation, to be set up in Vaduz, Liechtenstein, was also to have another more businesslike purpose. The intricate network of corporations that he had manipulated and controlled all his life would die with him. His empire would live on through a structure comprising two new holding companies, Alpha and Beta: Alpha consolidating all his assets (painstakingly catalogued on the flight to New York); Beta containing only the shares in Alpha. His principal heir, Christina, was to get all the assets in Alpha (in addition to an annual allowance of $250,000 and, if she remarried, $50,000 a year for her husband). The controlling interest (52.5 percent) in Beta would go to the foundation. Its board of directors would be drawn from his inner cabinet, headed by Costa Konialidis, and would, in effect, run the empire for Christina.

Hour after hour, as the Learjet sped across the skies above the Gulf of Mexico, Ari scribbled away, dividing up his kingdom: sixty thousand dollars a year for life for his sisters Artemis, Merope and Calirrhoë, thoughtfully indexed against inflation; sixty thousand dollars a year for his cousin and loyal aide Costa Konialidis; to Costa Gratsos and to Nicolas Cokkinis, his managing director in New York, thirty thousand dollars annually; twenty thousand dollars a year for Costa Vlassapoulos, his man in Monte Carlo; chauffeurs, chambermaids, housekeepers were remembered with varying amounts of gratitude. The only interruption in his writing came when the plane put down in Palm Beach to refuel and the airport manager pointed out that his Shell Oil credit card had expired. He and Jackie were reported eating bacon, lettuce and tomato sandwiches in the coffee shop while the matter was straightened out. Jackie must have suspected what Ari was doing and observed the mood in which he was doing it. If she regretted her exigency in Acapulco, she succeeded in the coffee shop in giving the impression that their "period of togetherness heretofore unseen" was still in one piece. Between Palm Beach and New York, he put the finishing touches to probably the longest epistle he had written since he was a young man in love with Ingeborg Dedichen. "My yacht, the *Christina,* if my daughter and wife so wish, they can keep for their personal use," he wrote. If they decided that it was too expensive to keep (its running costs were estimated at six hundred thousand dollars a year), they were to present it to the Greek state. A similar clause covered the future of Skorpios. (Jackie was given a 25 percent share in both the island and the yacht.) As chief executor of the will he named "Athina née Livanos-Onassis-Blandford-Niarchos, the mother of my son, Alexander."

He did not return to New York refreshed. His people were appalled by his appearance. He seemed to have difficulty holding his head erect, and staffers who had grown used to his thick accent, especially when he was tired or angry, noticed that his speech was often slurred, even when they were sure he had not been drinking. ("I can't count on getting drunk anymore, even when I want to very much," he told a close friend in London.) "There was a pallor to his skin you wouldn't believe was possible after even an *afternoon* in Acapulco," said one of the public relations people brought in to work on the Durham Point campaign. "I sure as hell wish I could have given him some better news. He looked like a guy who had been short of good news for a long time." The Olympic team running the refinery project had discovered one thing about the people of New Hampshire: they were as prickly and unpredictable as everybody said they were. A pressure group calling itself SOS (Save Our Shores) was pumping out a stream of stories about the threat of oil spills and fractured pipelines that dismayed the public relations men and management consultants retained by Olympic Oil Refineries.

One of the most telling blows to Olympic's plans came during what was expected to be a routine public relations exercise at Rye Junior High School. ("They were traveling round with this dumb-ass Technicolored picture show, proving how you could eat off the decks of Ari's tankers . . . the only oil slick in sight was in Peter Booras's hair," said Meyer.*) Olympic's supertanker moorings would be sited off the Rye shoreline, and the pipeline to Durham Point would cross the town's beaches. And while Ari's experts and PR people were delayed in a TV studio, Frederick Hochgraf, a University of New Hampshire engineering professor, was disclosing to the six hundred people packed into the school gymnasium (many of whom were fishermen and lobstermen, or engaged in the summer resort industry) facts that even the strongest opponents of the refinery had not even guessed at. If the supertankers delivered 270,000 barrels a day to the refinery, 3,660 barrels a year would be spilled in the sea. And if the refinery handled even half of its 400,000-gallons-a-day capacity, a further 3,980 barrels were guaranteed to leak into the New Hampshire waters. And it took only one part per million of oil in seawater to kill lobster larvae, and possibly destroy the beds forever, a marine biologist said after they'd heard Hochgraf's chilling statistics. ("When I completed my initial study, I was appalled by the numbers, so appalled I just sat on the figures for a week until I could find confirmation from another study calculated by an entirely different method," Hochgraf said later.) When the Olympic team, headed by Booras, finally arrived, they were unaware of Hochgraf's presentation and again and again attempted to fob off questions with answers like, "There are no studies on that . . . when our studies are completed, everyone will know what's involved and what benefits it will bring. . . ."

---

* It was Booras who had first suggested the Durham Point site to Gratsos. A fellow Greek immigrant, an old family friend and owner of the Yankee Artists greeting card company, he was especially proud of his EBS invention, or the Endless Breadloaf System, which bakes bread without end crusts for restaurants, saving "the 15 percent of the loaf that nobody wants."

(The PR people had an office at the Ramada Inn and another opposite the capitol building in Concord; when people called with difficult questions, they were invited to dinner.) When for the umpteenth time he was asked what the chances of oil spills were and Booras answered for the umpteenth time that there were no figures presently available, Hochgraf walked slowly across the high school stage and threw his fat notebook of facts and figures at the feet of the Olympic experts.

Yet the real problem about New Hampshire, Ari had now discovered, was the principle of Home Rule, the right of every town to reject any state government policy it didn't like. And at the Durham town meeting in March the people voted against the refinery, 1,254 to 144. In spite of this "little local difficulty," Gratsos remained bullish. He was convinced that the legislature, with twenty-four senators and four hundred representatives, the third-largest parliament in the world, was too big to be susceptible to local pressure groups. "They've got to vote down this Home Rule nonsense. You can't run a state with every two-horse town able to tell its government to get lost." Ari wasn't convinced. A few days later supplements plugging the virtues and advantages of the refinery ("Don't Let a Noisy Minority Stop Our State") appeared in newspapers throughout New Hampshire. The home telephone number of every legislator was listed with an appeal to readers to call and urge them to vote for the development. The stunt merely brought out the Puritan ethic in the New Englanders. They telephoned in the thousands—telling their legislators to send the refinery to blazes and Mr. Aristotle Onassis with it.

The day the New Hampshire state legislature turned down the refinery project, Ari decided to get a checkup. For months he had been feeling weak, and once or twice had been almost unable to rise from his chair. The stamina that had driven him through the vicissitudes of his incredibly productive years was fading; the grit that had enabled him to overcome catastrophes and disappointments was nearly exhausted. He was also having difficulty opening and closing his eyelids; although it came and went, fluctuating in its severity, it worried him far more than his constant tiredness. Suspecting that he had muscular dystrophy, he was almost relieved when the doctors told him that he was suffering from a disease called myasthenia gravis, a disorder of the body's autoimmune system, which could be controlled by drugs. He had insisted on being told the score exactly and talked learnedly yet curiously lightly about his condition. "It usually hits men around their forties, so I take it as a tribute to my physical shape," he told friends. Although it was incurable, and had a tendency to remit and to relapse, "it's unlikely that it'll do me in," he said. Patients dying of the disease usually had some additional pulmonary condition, and apart from the myasthenia he was A-one. He would know soon enough if the drugs were any damn good: most remissions occur within the first five years of the disease process, and most deaths also occur within the same time span.

Although he suspected that the oil majors and Niarchos had conspired against him (Gratsos believed that "revenge was all that stood between him and complete collapse"), he took the New Hampshire defeat stoically and for a while seemed almost like his old self, although he was drinking more and holding it less well. At the Crazy Horse Saloon in Paris, much the worse for wear, he invited paparazzo Roger Picard "to photograph the secret of my success." In the men's room, he put his penis on the saucer in which customers left their tips. "There it is," he roared triumphantly. "That says it all. Sex and money—that is my secret." As his spirits seemed to improve, Jackie appeared to have fallen into an expression of habitual despair. "She had acquired that austerely religious look you see on the faces of peasant girls in Europe —ardent and unhappy and full of carnal sacrifice," one of her friends said. And certainly her mood could not have been improved when Maria Callas turned up in New York discussing her relationship with Ari, "the great love of my life," with Barbara Walters on the "Today" show, and declaring mischievously that love is "so much better when you are not married." Did she have any hard feelings about Jackie? "Why should I? Of course, if she treats Mr. Onassis very badly, I might be very angry."

In the spring he returned to Monte Carlo for the first time since his bust-up with Rainier. The two men dined together aboard the *Christina*, and a rapprochement of sorts was achieved. But the visit depressed him, and during dinner one evening at the Hotel de Paris, his jaw muscles became so weak that he had difficulty eating. Although the problem went away the following day, he had read up enough to know that it was a further symptom of his disease. The realization that in spite of the drugs and painful injections he was still vulnerable to sudden bad spells upset him immeasurably. "This place has too many memories, too many damned ghosts," he repeated, as if trying to shift the blame for his depression on to the locale. He decided to cut short his visit; on his last night there he went to Regine's. In a dark part of the club, away from the dancing, he was astonished to see one of his "ghosts." He said, "What are you doing here? You hate nightclubs!" Wendy Russell, now Mrs. Emery Reves, the woman who had arranged his first meeting with Churchill in the fifties, said she was with her husband and some friends; she still hated night-clubs. "He sat down beside me and said that he also hated night-clubs now. 'I have changed a good deal. I have had time to reflect . . . I am sad about many things. I am sad about you and Emery,' he said." Repeating it once more he kissed her cheek. She was moved by his appearance, his physical deterioration, his elegiac tone. She knew he was trying to apologize for having used them as he had used so many people in the past, for having betrayed their confidence, tipping off the press to Churchill's first visit to the *Christina*, all those years ago. "I took his hand. 'You need not ever be sad about Wendy and Emery Reves,' I told him." It was a kind of forgiveness, their last farewell.

CHAPTER 17

*Thou must leave thy lands, house, and
the wife of thy bosom; nor shall any of
those trees follow thee, their short-lived
master, except the hated cypresses.*

HORACE

PERHAPS ARI recognized the finality of the occasion
as the *Christina* sailed out of Monte Carlo in the spring of 1974.
Certainly a profound sense of urgency now entered his interest in
his daughter's destiny. "I think he suddenly became aware of her
in his conscience, and his conscience was the evocation of Alexander," said one of his Olympic aides. By dying, Alexander had
changed Christina's life forever. While she remained calm on the
surface ("perhaps she was simply numb, perhaps it was the repose
of inheritance," suggested a Paris friend), there was a hint of the
crises ahead in something she was heard to say the day they buried
her brother on Skorpios. "Things never happen the way you expect. It would be very comforting to say, with Medea, 'I, myself,
am enough.' Isn't that what we all really want?"

It had been decided that she should go to New York "to learn
the ropes" under Costa Gratsos's supervision. He treated her
rather as an intelligent woman than as a child or pupil. And it
seemed to work. "She's going to be fine," he assured Ari. "Already
I trust her intuition more than my intelligence, probably even
more than your sorcery!" Ari disclosed by the faintest catch in his
voice how much he was affected by Costa's words. And now he
took her along to conferences and business lunches, meeting people at all levels, although she seldom spoke. At one boardroom
lunch at the British Petroleum headquarters in London she did
not utter a single word, nor ask one question. Her withdrawn
behavior puzzled BP chairman Sir Eric Drake. Is she always that

aloof? he later asked Nigel Neilson. Ari's man in London could not explain her apparent apathy; it went against everything he knew she had been taught. Later he recalled a scene on the *Christina* when she was about ten years old and had returned from having her hair done. Ari said how pretty it looked and asked the name of the man who did it. She did not know. He asked whether the man had a family? She did not know. "You must always talk to people, always ask questions, find out things, always be interested," her father had lectured her. At a cocktail party at the Savoy, Sir Eric, surprised by her animation, inquired why she had been so silent at the working lunch. "My father told me I had to listen to every word, to observe, and to keep my mouth closed until I knew what I was talking about," she told him.

Ari took pride in her progress. She began to change her life, or tried to. She worked with seriousness and application, and although she did not entirely neglect her nightlife she was seen much less often on the circuit. Ari seemed satisfied. He said, "It seems just possible she might some day prove herself capable of running the family." It was the highest compliment a Greek could pay to a woman. Yet in spite of his growing confidence in her, and in spite of Gratsos's reassuring reports, friends began to notice disquieting signs in her behavior. "One minute she'd be fine, smiling, relaxed—then wham! Her fuses were getting shorter all the time," recalled a junior executive in the maritime insurance department of Frank B. Hall & Co., where she spent a month of her apprenticeship. "She could cold-eye you like nobody I know," a secretary remembered. "You never knew what you were supposed to have done that was so terrible."

At the beginning of August, the month she usually spent on Skorpios, she disappeared. None of her friends in New York, Paris, or the south of France knew where she was. Phone calls were not returned, letters went unanswered. "I thought, 'Oh, Christina, she's found a lover she wants to keep to herself.' She's very protective about that part of her life," one of her oldest friends in Paris said. "I was hoping to spend August on the island, and although I was disappointed I thought, 'Good luck to her.' I hoped she was happy some place." She was far from happy. On August 16, under the name of C. Danai, she was admitted to the public wards of Middlesex Hospital in London, suffering from a massive overdose of sleeping pills. Tina flew up from the south of France in a private jet and for forty-eight hours did not leave her daughter's side except to catnap in an armchair in a waiting room at the end of the ward. Amazingly, the drama was kept from the press. Not until

Christina was out of danger and moved to a private room was even her father told.

Tina possessed few emotional reserves, and the stress of comforting Christina at that particular moment was especially trying. Her marriage to Niarchos had not brought her the satisfactions she expected, and friends suspected that divorce was in her mind.* She had discovered that the Greek civil code forbids marriage between a brother-in-law and a sister-in-law. "It was one way out of an unhappy situation, yet it also seemed to upset her, as if she had trespassed," said a family friend. Christina's crisis, after the death of Alexander, after the death of Eugénie, renewed Tina's fears that a kind of retribution was at work. "I suppose we are all apt to expect too much," she said when she returned to Paris in September. Her beauty was fading, partly because of her habitual reliance on barbiturates. Once absorbed only with such anxieties as which party she should attend, which lover she would take next, she now faced all the shock and betrayal of an unprepared-for middle age. "I'm *suddenly* forty-five years old."

On the morning of Thursday, October 10, a maid found her dead in her room in the Hotel de Chanaleilles, the Niarchos Paris mansion. Her husband was asleep in another room. There were conflicting reports about the cause of her death. At the headquarters of Niarchos's company in London, a spokesman announced that Tina had "a blood clot in one leg and that death resulted when the clot moved to the heart, obstructing blood circulation." In Paris, her secretary said that the cause of death was "a heart attack, or a lung edema"—excessive accumulation of fluid in the tissues. Christina was in New York when she heard the news and flew to Paris immediately, arriving in the early hours of Friday morning. Newspapers were already comparing Tina's death with the death of her sister on Spetsopoula four years before. The news agency *Agence France Presse* and the mass-circulation afternoon paper *France-Soir* promptly raised the possibility that death could have resulted from an overdose of sleeping pills. "Sources close to Niarchos said that her death was caused by an overdose of barbiturates and tranquilizers," reported the *New York Daily News*'s Bernard Valéry, a journalist who had known the family since the early days in Monaco.

Christina moved fast. By eleven o'clock that morning she had

* *"Helene Rochas was chucking Stavros under the chin while his recently dead wife Tina was still alive,"* reported gossip writer Suzy in her New York Daily News *column on February 6, 1975. "Tina was not even slightly amused by all the flirting. It embarrassed her terribly to be so put down but there wasn't a bloody thing she could do about it."*

got a magistrate's warrant ordering a postmortem examination. "Ari went along with it. I don't think it had anything to do with trying to hurt Niarchos. He just wanted to put the zipper on the rumors for Christina's sake. She seemed so shaken that he actually feared she would try to kill Stavros . . . there was a lot of speculation, a lot of ugly gossip," said Meyer. Onassis and Niarchos issued a joint statement claiming that although Christina had demanded the autopsy, the two families "not only are not opposed to it, but on the contrary welcome the decision."

Tina died from an acute edema of the lung, the two pathologists appointed by the public prosecutor's office confirmed without amplification on October 13. There were no traces of violence on the body, reported the London *Times*, and the public prosecutor issued a burial permit. She was buried at the Bois-de-Vaux cemetery in Lausanne, beside her sister. Ari was notably absent. Niarchos wept throughout the service; opposite him stood the duke of Marlborough, Tina's second husband, also in tears. It was to the Englishman that Christina turned for comfort when she broke down at the graveside. ("My aunt, my brother, now my mother— what is happening to us?") One close friend said he was sure that "death was of her own choosing." Said Peter Stephens, who covered the story for the London *Daily Mirror* and had known Tina well: "I've never been able to decide in my own mind whether Tina killed herself deliberately or not. But she must have expressed a wish to be buried next to her sister and not with her son on Skorpios, which I think implies that she suspected she would arrive there through the same channels."

Still seething at Christina's intervention, Niarchos put out a statement disclosing for the first time her suicide bid—"at a time when her mother still mourned the death of her son. Tina never recovered from the depression into which these blows plunged her." The implication of the public rebuke was cruel and clear: Christina herself had calamitously worsened her mother's already failing health.

The continuing decline in Ari's own health after Tina's death was at first explained away as exhaustion, but "the psychic wounds inflicted by the tragedy in Paris and the renewed bitterness between the families exacted a dreadful price," an Olympic executive in Monaco said later. Only weeks before Tina's death he appeared to a friend who spent a week alone with him on Skorpios to be "not a hundred percent fit, although in better shape and better spirits than I'd seen him in a long while." The visitor was Hélène Gaillet. She had been waiting in Paris for the postponed

Muhammad Ali–George Foreman fight to be rescheduled in Zaire, which she had been commissioned to photograph. "I called him on Skorpios and said, 'Ari, I'm really in a dilemma, I don't know what to do, can you advise me?' He said in that hoarse voice, 'What is it, Hélène, what is it you want?' He was always very direct, he didn't have those old social graces that we are supposed to abide by. He said, 'Do you want to come here?' I said, 'Yeah, I was hoping.' " She said she had talked to her lover, Ari's friend, and he had said it was fine for her to call Ari. Ari asked the name of her hotel, and within an hour one of his people in Paris called to say she would be picked up at nine o'clock the next morning. His Learjet flew her to Athens; she stayed overnight at Glyfada, had dinner with Artemis and Christina. "Christina was very dark, very thin, a very stormy woman, a strong personality," she recalled. "I found her fascinating. She had this underlying aura of . . . I don't want to say doom, but doom's close. There was something about her that you sensed was getting out of control, something in her eyes."

Helicoptered to Skorpios, Hélène was surprised to discover that Ari was alone on the island. "He never made a pass. I slept on the *Christina*, he stayed in the house." Once, at dawn, she saw him walking alone on the beach, like an early morning animal. "I don't think he ever wanted me physically, it was not something that was necessary to our friendship. The day after I arrived he called and asked what was I doing? What am I doing? I'm doing nothing, reading books, having a wonderful time. He said, 'Come on, let's go for a ride.' He drove me all over the island, showed me the orchards, the farm animals, the flowers. The island was like a medieval domain, a self-sufficient economic unit, producing its own milk, bread, meat, figs; only fresh water had to be shipped in and stored in reservoirs. He showed me where Alexander was buried. It wasn't a sad visit; he talked as if he expected him to join us any minute. 'Alexander is just as living to me as you are. He comes to me often. Unfortunately, till I die I cannot go to him,' he said." He had, for a brief moment, "a haunted face, a look of terrible longing." Afterward, they drove to a beach. "We stripped and went into the sea. And again the beauty and simplicity of this man, there was never any kind of sexual innuendo. Perhaps I can think of moments inside my head when I thought, 'I could really get involved with this person. . . .' He was like an animal to look at naked, and under other circumstances, a man and a woman on a deserted beach would be attracted to the idea of making love. Somehow I think he rather liked the idea that there was a woman who was off-limits." In the evenings, they dined, just the two of them, aboard the yacht. "This is the only place on earth in which I don't feel myself alien," he told her.

At the beginning of November he checked into a New York hospital under the name of Mr. Phillips. Christina returned to be with him, and the identity of Mr. Phillips was quickly discovered by the press. "He was visibly going downhill, yet the people at Olympic, even Johnny Meyer, were insisting that it was something that was going to be fixed," said a *Paris Match* journalist who had become especially close to Christina. "I honestly don't know what she believed at that time, although she seemed to have reached a closeness with Ari she hadn't had before, her old feelings of not giving him all he expected of her seemed to have gone."

They spent hours together. When his eyelids became too weak to stay open, she cut strips of Band-Aid to tape them up and, aware of his vanity, ordered darker lenses for his glasses to hide the plaster. "This is God punishing you for all your sins," she teased him. "I never think about sin," he told her, his voice gruff with age and nicotine. "It's my nature." It was a cruel time, Christina felt the darkness closing in. "My most fervent wishes are that my father may get better and that I shall meet a man who loves me for myself and not for my money. Happiness does not depend on money. Our family is the best proof of that," she said, affectingly reminiscent of her mother's divorce statement the day she left Ari. "Since the death of my mother and of my brother we have both learned how short life can be and with what terrible suddenness death strikes."

Although he felt strong enough to discharge himself from the hospital in November, his face was swollen from cortisone injections prescribed to counter decreased adrenal function, his temper more unpredictable than ever, but behind his bluster, he was a frightened man, frightened for himself, for his daughter and for his empire. His airline was in deep trouble. The increase in oil prices had hit Olympic harder than most other carriers, since the threat of war with Turkey over Cyprus that summer had all but wiped out the vital Greek tourist trade. He was almost the last person to know how bad things had got. Old hands around the company could scarcely believe how out of touch he had become since Alexander's death. On the day on which Ari discharged himself from the hospital, the cashflow fell to a level where the company could no longer maintain its regular schedules. Costa Konialidis, who had been in charge of the troubled airline almost from the start, was finally forced to summon up the nerve to confront him with the situation.

The Olympic staff in New York had never seen him in such a

rage as the day Konialidis broke the news to him. And his rages were notorious at the Olympic offices; his habit of pressing the ground-floor button and ending up in the basement and not at street level, as in Europe, caused such tantrums that the Olympic elevators had to be rewired European-style. The bad news came right on top of the formal opening of the Olympic Tower, a fifty-two-story Fifth Avenue condominium, which he had built in association with the Arlen Realty Corporation. Designed for the very rich, the midtown skyscraper was considered a great gamble at a time of inflation and fears of deepening recession. Only 35 of the 230 apartments had been sold, and although occupancy was still some months away, it had already been considered necessary to push "Olympic Tower with a promotion campaign rarely equalled even in the real estate industry," reported the *Wall Street Journal*. The last thing Ari wanted at that moment was a lot of publicity about another Onassis failure.

Meanwhile, in the first free elections since 1964, Constantine Karamanlis's New Democracy party had just swept to victory in Athens. It was Karamanlis who had urged Ari to take over the airline, and having wrangled concession after concession out of the prime minister in the early days, Ari was sure he could still "take care of the situation." However, his demand for a massive injection of government money into Olympic Airways was dismissed out of hand. "He was so out of touch," recalls a former Olympic executive. "There was no way Karamanlis was going to bail him out. Ari was poison, *poison*. With Greeks it's love or hate all the time." Papadopoulos and the rest of the dictatorship's inner circle were in Korydallos Prison, awaiting trial on charges of insurrection and high treason. Karamanlis was under pressure to deal severely with former junta members and their collaborators. So intense was the antijunta sentiment that demonstrations calling for execution of the leaders occurred almost daily. "Karamanlis wasn't going to lift a finger to help a man whose relations with Papadopoulos were generally thought to have far exceeded the ordinary requirements of business tact," said an Athens attorney who had been on the Omega team.

Still Ari didn't get the message. "It simply never occurred to him that he was looking defeat in the face. He reacted as he had always reacted in the old days when he didn't get his way, threatening to wash his hands of the whole business, grounding the entire Olympic fleet, freezing salaries. He really pulled out all the stops," Meyer recalled. Instead of caving in and pleading with him to stay on, as he had done so many times in the past, Karamanlis appointed an emergency management board and announced that the government would open immediate negotiations to repossess the national carrier.

He, Aristotle Onassis, to whom bluff and brinkmanship had been the breath of life, still believed that the prime minister was simply establishing a negotiating position. He was nevertheless shaken by Karamanlis's tough response, for he did not want to let go of the airline and the planes that he had so often told Alexander were merely "the leaves on a tree whose roots were ships." The loss of Olympic was a failure appalling to contemplate and impossible to ignore. In December, against his doctors' advice, he flew to Athens. Determined to keep control of the airline while appearing willing to conclude the transfer, for several days he discussed various clauses of the transitional documents, waiting for the counterproposals to be put forward. When he realized that the government was seriously intent on taking back Olympic he switched tactics. "Each morning he'd confront us with a fresh list of demands and queries, denying points we'd all agreed on twenty-four hours before," said a Karamanlis aide stunned by "the sudden change in this man and the whole mood of the talks." Ari was scarcely in a condition to conduct exacting and complex negotiations. He had ventured beyond his threshold of fatigue. "His manner was peremptory, his language was sometimes almost incomprehensible, a lot of his answers were frankly unfathomable," said another federal negotiator, whose earlier sympathy for Ari was replaced by irritation as his prevarications grew, and the talks dragged on in flurries of Onassissian rhetoric and bewildering revisions that raised boardroom sophistry to new levels of exasperation. Although most of Olympic's planes and plant were leased from and controlled by a baffling structure of interlocking Panamanian corporations, a senior government lawyer urged Karamanlis simply to suspend the talks and take back the airline, announcing the *fait accompli* in a brief statement, emphasizing "the government's sufferance and the shiftiness of Onassis." Said an Onassis advisor: "We were all bystanders. Ari was the quintessential nonteam man, he was the only one who really knew the numbers. He saw this as a contest between himself and everyone else."

Jackie was with some of the old JFK team at Ted Sorensen's apartment in New York watching *The Missiles of October,* an ABC-TV special about the Cuban crisis of 1962, while Ari confronted his crisis in Athens. Afterward, she took off for some skiing with her son on the Swiss slopes of Crans-sur-Sierre. Said an aide who watched Ari's performance with growing dismay and sadness: "Jackie seemed determined to stand aside from Ari's problems.

There was not a lot she could have done in Athens except *be there*. They were some of the worst weeks of his life. He could have used some wifely comforting, not to mention her public relations pull . . . he was putting up the backs of the very people he needed to beguile. His language even to those whose help he needed most was either sullen or griping. He'd lost his touch completely, he was played out. His name had once acted like a spell in Athens, now his world had turned upside down. He had become . . . assail-able. Maybe it was the cortisone [the most frequent explanation for his behavior], maybe his age had suddenly caught up with him. He was extremely pale, and I've never seen a man sweat so much outside a sauna bath." Meyer, in retrospect, had no substantial recollection of the talks: "I just remember that in some way he seemed resigned to the fact that he was beaten, yet appalled that he had let his guard down and determined to make those bastards fight every inch." There was something about this battle that touched everybody who watched its progress. Perhaps the man most affected was Gratsos: his association with Ari was so per-sonal and so deep that to see Ari's last big prize being wrenched from his grasp was almost unbearable.

Karamanlis's chief negotiator and the man who was to run the airline after Ari, George Theofanos, was wary of Ari's favorite strategy of prolonging talks late into the night before reaching agreement on a particular point only to reinterpret their under-standing when they met the following morning. At one crucial meeting when Ari eventually conceded a vital point, Theofanis suggested that they put it in writing immediately so that there could be "no wrong impressions, no misconceptions" the next day. Ari said that it was after midnight and all the secretaries had gone home. Theofanis went in search of a typewriter to type out a draft of the clause himself and get Ari's signature there and then. When he returned, Ari had left.

It was a losing battle for Ari. On January 15, 1975, in spite of all his efforts, and after almost twenty years, he handed back Olympic Airways to the Greek government.* The strain of those

---

* It was later revealed that an agreement was reached that gave Ari sixty-nine million dollars for Olympic's assets. "To casual observers, it looked like a favorable settlement," reported Lewis Beman in Fortune magazine. "Actually, all of the money that Onassis was to get from the government was earmarked to pay Olympic's outstanding debts. The agreement left him with Olympic's accounts receivable and working capital—all together a little more than fifteen million dollars—as well as its real estate, worth roughly ten million dollars. He was also allowed to sell two 707's to Jordan for nine million dollars, and to keep for his own use a Learjet and two helicopters, valued at five hundred thousand dollars." Adding it all up, wrote Beman, even thirty-five million dollars was not much of a return for the money and effort he had put into the business.

weeks in which he struggled to keep control of the airline he professed to disdain and had once dismissed as "a hobby enterprise," hastened the pace of his illness, and he knew that he was a dying man. He also knew the capricious turns by which vast fortunes and great families can be ruined and forgotten. "It's not so difficult for one man to make a fortune," he had said. "But if the fortune is to endure and grow, a man must not only have heirs, he must make plans." During the following weeks he acted ruthlessly to secure his empire.

With the lapse of time it seemed that the question of divorce had become unimportant to him but now, on the strict understanding that he would end his marriage to Jackie, he extracted a promise from Christina that she would marry Peter Goulandris, to whom she had been almost engaged on several occasions. Harvard graduate Goulandris was heir to the world's third-largest shipping dynasty. The alliance would be formidable ("Think about it, Johnny, the greatest tanker fleet the world has seen," he had said to Meyer). "Thirty years earlier, he consolidated his own fortune by marrying a Livanos; now here he was trying to secure their daughter's fortune with a similar stroke," said an Athens associate.

On February 3, Jackie received a call from Athens to say that he had collapsed with severe abdominal pains. His doctors diagnosed an attack of gallstones and stressed that because of his impaired nutrition, caused in part by his increasing difficulty in chewing food, in part by his failure even to try to eat regularly during the Olympic struggle, and a bout of flu, he was in an "extremely vulnerable" state. Jackie left for Greece immediately. Christina, also informed of her father's condition, flew back from Gstaad, the Swiss ski resort, where she had been holidaying with Goulandris. Ingeborg Dedichen, who had been having bad dreams and nightmares about Ari for some months, recorded in her diary ("September 9: Nightmares AO! September 10: Bad night. AO dying!!?"), noted with presentiment on February 4: "Ari ill!" And on the fifth she wrote simply, "Ari?"

The situation at the villa had become tense. Specialists summoned from Paris and New York were disagreeing among themselves about the best course of action. The French liver specialist, Prof. Jean Caroli, advised an immediate operation to remove Ari's gall bladder; the heart specialist, Dr. Isidore Rosenfeld, felt that he was too weak to undergo major surgery. Shaken by the deterioration in her father's appearance, Christina became distraught. And Jackie, as she always did to ease her nerves, affected insouciance (although it seemed to Meyer that she "paled visibly" at the sight of Ari), and not for the first time was misunderstood by Christina and her aunts. "Jacqueline kept her feelings to herself, it's an implicit part of her nature to avoid any kind of public display; unfortunately, her ruminating propriety jarred terribly on their expressive Levantine sensibilities," said a family friend.

Ari himself made the critical decision to return to Paris and have the operation to remove his gall bladder at the American Hospital in Neuilly. On the afternoon of February 6 as he left his Glyfada villa for the airport, he sent a servant hurrying back to collect a book he had been reading. It was called *Supership*, in which Noel Mostert reported that the first million-tonner was on the horizon, a tanker so big that cathedrals could be lost within its bowels. Ari sat with the book unopened on his lap for most of the journey; memories of the *Ariston*, the fifteen-thousand-ton "monster" they said was impossible when he built her in the thirties, must have crossed his mind.

His exhaustion gave him an air of serenity as he sat between Christina and Jackie in the limousine moving through the darkening suburbs of Paris. But the women found no comfort in the look of tranquillity. His body weight had dropped forty pounds in eight weeks. He covered the gaping collar of his custom-made silk shirt with a dark blue cashmere scarf. "I want," he had trouble articulating, his voice a faint rasp and thickly accented. "I want to walk from this car under my own steam. I don't want those sons of bitches to see me being held up by a couple of women." Overwhelmed by the vehemence of his pride, Christina's natural melancholy deepened into despair, her eyes filled with tears. Jackie reached out and touched her sleeve, aware of the familiar dilemma —what to say, what to leave unsaid. In spite of her distress, the conciliatory gesture merely rekindled Christina's antagonism toward the woman she had dismissed as "my father's unhappy compulsion."

Not only were the usual paparazzi waiting outside 88, avenue Foch: agency reporters, five television crews, photographers from *Paris Match*, *Stern*, *Oggi* and many other international magazines and newspapers, as well as the simply curious, received them with the kind of hullabaloo usually reserved for eloping movie stars and disgraced politicians. The press watch was an affirmation of what the women already knew in their bones: he had returned to Paris for the last time. It was a dry, almost balmy evening; a mild east wind barely moved the crisp tangle of ivy and creeper that covered the tall wrought-iron railings. The night lit up with flash and klieg as he climbed slowly from the car. His legs were weak, and he could walk only with great pain, but Ari climbed the steps and, unaided, went inside.

• •

At the George V Hotel, Johnny Meyer was having a drink with a French journalist when he was called to the telephone. He rose slowly from the chair at his regular table in his favorite bar in Paris. "M'lord is back," he said when he returned a few minutes later. A paunch was creeping out under the crocodile-leather belt of his dark blue suit. He looked rich, a man with all the moves, the journalist thought, which is what he wanted her to think. "How is he, Johnny?" she asked the man who was so often described as "a reliable source" or "an Onassis insider."

"I think we're on the mend," answered Meyer. Little more than a bit player in the Onassis story, he had a shameless yet faintly touching sense of self-importance; in the notes for his never-finished autobiography, he would describe himself as Ari's Falstaff. "We're spending the night at avenue Foch before checking into the American Hospital for tests to determine whether or not they should remove our gall bladder," he said. The reporter expressed astonishment at the suggestion that Ari was getting better. "Whoever heard of anyone dying of droopy eyelids?" Meyer replied. Perhaps it was a genuine lack of understanding, or sheer optimism, but he was convinced that Ari would pull through. That morning he had talked to Gratsos, who had assured him that everything was going to be fine. He trusted Gratsos. It never occurred to him that Gratsos would keep him in the dark.

Ari slept for several hours after arriving at avenue Foch; shortly after waking he took a pyridostigmine slow-release capsule to get him through the night: the capsule released one-third, or sixty milligrams, of its dosage immediately and gave him a surge of energy into which he crammed as much business as he could manage. He sent for the people he wanted to see.

Meyer was shocked when he saw him propped up in the large antique bed, which dominated the master bedroom on the fifth floor. It was too warm, a greenhouse heat, in the room; the sound of Paris was muted by the thick old walls and the armor-glazed windows hung with heavy drapes. Ari was staring distractedly down the length of his legs: distinct bones extended beneath the covers. Freshly shaved and cologned, his face had a shellacked sort of pallor, and his head seemed too large and heavy for his stringy neck to support. *Jesus*, Meyer thought, feeling what later he could only describe as pity for the exhausted-looking man; it was the first time he had ever thought of Ari as old. He was sure he had not betrayed his feelings by as much as a blink and was startled when Ari said, "You didn't expect to see me looking like this, old friend? A bag of skin and bones. I apologize that my appearance distresses you so much." He simply needed feeding up, answered Meyer, who didn't trust himself to lie well enough at that moment to say more.

"I have a problem chewing. I find it hard to chew. I don't eat so much," Ari said. His speech was slurred. He held his chin as if attempting to support the weight of his head, but Meyer suspected it actually was to help him talk. "It's God punishing me for always biting off more than I could chew," he said. Meyer laughed dutifully, but beneath the cynical humor he could sense Ari's anxiety. He knew it was a natural fear of men who have lived their lives in conflict that their courage will give out, that their nerve will let them down in the end. "I don't think God would have the guts to punish you," he said and was pleased to see his remark light up the face of a man whose life, he realized now, was running out fast.

They began to talk about the past; blaming the present and admiring old times had become a habit between them. *Supership* had brought back memories of the *Ariston* for Ari. "It was the best time. I had so many plans then," he said. Meyer said he wished he had known him back then. "I said, 'Remember the stunt you pulled in Rotterdam, when the Greek consul was screwing you over a clearance?' It was one of his favorite tales, it always cheered him up. But he just stared at me. 'What story's that, Johnny,' he said. 'Remind me.' It was his favorite story! I'd heard him tell it two thousand times. 'That chickenshit official who was insisting on playing it by the book?' I said. 'Tell me about it, Johnny,' he said. So I told him his own story, word for word, like a ritual, right down to the same punch line: 'My friend, you are now aboard a Panamanian ship.' " Ari looked pleased, as if he had heard the story for the first time. "Jesus, Ari, you *invented* the flag of convenience," Meyer said, although he had heard other Greeks make the same claim, tell almost identical anecdotes. They talked about Hollywood for a while, the girls they had known, the good times; how old they had grown since then, Meyer thought. Ari asked how many pairs of shoes he now owned. Shoes were Meyer's passion; the best shoemakers in Europe had his lasts in their workrooms. "He said I'd have to sacrifice a pair for his funeral. 'My roads on Skorpios aren't kind to nice shoes,' he said. I told him, 'Ari, I'll give you dollars to doughnuts you'll be there to dance at my wake.' He said he wasn't a gambler, no bets. I told him he was the greatest long shot player I ever met. He said, 'No, Johnny, I was just a Greek kid who knew how to do his sums.' "

There was a long silence; Meyer thought Ari had slipped into sleep. Then Ari said, "Soon I shall be in Skorpios with Alexander.

You know I am dying, Johnny." The essence of death, Meyer remembered reading somewhere, was loneliness. He had never seen Ari look so lonely as he looked now. "You're crazy, Ari. Who ever heard of anybody dying of droopy eyelids," he repeated the joke he had made earlier that evening. Ari must have seen through the compassionate lie and patted Meyer's face. His fingers were almost fleshless bones. Meyer took his hand and held it tightly, surprised how cold it felt. "You want to die? You want to lose the decision?" he asked. Ari told him that he did not want to go on living with ghosts. "I don't want that, Johnny. I couldn't stand that."

Again Meyer became aware of the silence that filled the house. It was the sort of silence that he associated with dustsheets. But he knew that the apartment was full of people. He had not seen Jackie, although he knew she was about. Christina had greeted him in the hall with a family reunion sort of voice and asked him to arrange a suite for her at the Plaza-Athénée; she did not want to share the apartment with Jackie after her father had checked into the American Hospital, she told him.

There was no clock on the bedside table, just photographs of Alexander and Christina (but none of Jackie), the book called *Supership*, a small crucifix and a pocket calculator. A crucifix and a calculator! The juxtaposition lingered in Meyer's memory forever. He told the story over and over again and always ended it the same way: "His whole life was there on that tiny table, from the cradle to the goddam grave—a goddam calculator and a crucifix."

At 11:50 the following morning Ari left in a blue Peugeot from the underground garage and headed for the American Hospital on boulevard Victor Hugo. It was a mild bright sunny day. The car moved quickly onto the inner boulevard Périphérique at the place de Maréchal de-Lattre-de-Tassigny and turned right along the boulevard de l'Amiral Bruix to the Porte Maillot. At noon, as the crowd of photographers and reporters at the main entrance was distracted by the arrival of Jackie and Christina, he entered the hospital unobserved through the adjacent chapel, known to interns as the "artists' exit," since it is also the route to the morgue.

A spokesman said that he had been admitted to the hospital "shaken by very heavy influenza." On Sunday, February 9, his gall bladder was removed. Christina, who had moved into the Hotel Plaza-Athénée, also took a room adjoining her father's first-floor suite in the hospital's Eisenhower wing and spent most of her time by his bedside together with her favorite aunt, Ari's closest sister, Artemis. Clannish and exacting, these two women made Jackie feel like a stranger in the presence of her husband. The hurt of exclusion did not reveal itself in any outward way, as each day she visited Ari as determinedly as she spent the evenings dining with friends.

On February 22, *Paris Match* talked to one of the doctors who had operated on Ari: "Our last ally for saving him is his pride. And that is the final unknown quantity," he said. By the end of the month it seemed as if he was fighting back. Although he was still on a respirator and remained connected to a kidney machine, a hospital statement talked about "a slow but progressive improvement" in his condition. Jackie felt sufficiently encouraged to fly back to New York to see her daughter. She telephoned every day to check his progress and heard nothing to alarm her; his condition appeared to remain serious but stable.

Christina and Peter Goulandris went through the traditional Greek "giving the word of marriage" ceremony and afterward visited Ari's bedside to tell him the news and receive his blessing.

On Saturday, March 15, it rained for twelve hours and nine minutes in Paris; it was the longest rainfall of the winter, and when it stopped Aristotle Socrates Onassis was dead.

Jackie was in New York when she heard that she was a widow again. Before she left for France with her mother that evening, she called Teddy Kennedy and pleaded with him to accompany her to the funeral, and to bring her children. She knew she was going to need all the support she could get. Only Jacinto Rosa, the family chauffeur, was at the airport to meet her in Paris. And the press. "She simply smiled to herself behind those huge dark glasses and pulled her black leather coat close around her when she saw the reporters," remembered Peter Stephens, surprised by the smile. He suspected that she was compelled by principles and practice rather than by passion when she issued a short precisely worded statement at Orly: "Aristotle Onassis rescued me at a moment when my life was engulfed with shadows. He meant a lot to me. He brought me into a world where one could find both happiness and love. We lived through many beautiful experiences together which cannot be forgotten, and for which I will be eternally grateful." Later, accompanied by Miltos Argyropoulos, who had been Olympic's man in Paris, she drove to the hospital chapel to say her last good-bye to Ari. He was lying on a bier in the candlelit room with a Greek Orthodox icon on his chest. She made the sign of the cross and said a prayer. Seven minutes after her arrival, Jacqueline Bouvier Kennedy Onassis returned dry-eyed through the rain and the flashlights to avenue Foch. But the poise and the aura of courage admired so much in the traumatic days after JFK's assassination were now seen as too regally chilling, too cold-blooded.

Although few women could have been better able to understand the crushing effect of multiple tragedies, Jackie's efforts to comfort Christina were met with disdain. She had made a bad mistake in not returning to Paris forty-eight hours earlier; the family would never forgive her for being three thousand miles away when Ari died. For once her perfect instinct for self-preservation had malfunctioned. She was out in the cold. Conversations were conducted in Greek, and once-friendly aides avoided her; Christina was under sedation and could not see her at all. She had taken her father's death badly. Her left wrist was heavily bandaged when she left the hospital the day he died, and it was rumored that in an agony of grief she had again tried to kill herself. "It was an accident, a bathroom slip," a friend insisted. Whether or not the bandage did have a more ominous significance, she had composed herself sufficiently to fly home to Skorpios with her father's body three days later.

Thirty-four relatives and friends were on board the Boeing 727 that took his body home to Greece. It seemed as if there had been a rapprochement between Christina and her father's widow, the promise of a deeper understanding, as they left the plane together. When Christina saw the photographers and her anxieties came back, Jackie gripped her arm. "Take it easy, it'll soon be over." The two women and Teddy Kennedy shared the first limousine. Another plane carrying more relatives and friends from Athens had landed earlier, and now that the funeral party was complete, the cortege of cars and buses began its slow journey from Actium to the small fishing village of Nidri, where Ari's body was to be placed on a launch for the last ride to Skorpios. It was a cold overcast day. Village women in black shawls lined the route, holding small bouquets of purple flowers, and bells tolled in the churches. Then the motorcade stopped. Christina left the limousine she was sharing with her stepmother and got into the car behind. For a moment everything seemed to have frozen in the bare landscape ("It was very Daliesque, drained of reality," recalled a family friend). Teddy Kennedy closed the door, and after a small hesitation the motorcade continued on its way. "I don't know what was said, but something happened in that car between those two women. And Christina's pride means more to her than tact and propriety. She obviously felt the need to make a gesture, even on that harrowing journey, and she made it," a mourner remembered the episode. What happened on the road from Actium remained a mystery for a decade, but not long ago one of Christina's closest companions revealed the truth: Teddy Kennedy had attempted to talk about "financial matters" to Christina in the limousine. She was appalled by his insensitivity. "She knew that Teddy wasn't there to share her grief, or simply to hold Jackie's hand. He was there for a specific purpose; he was going to want to discuss business sooner or later. Ari always had money in his head, Christina understood that . . . the Kennedys had it in their hearts, she understood that, too. But Teddy's timing blew her mind. And that's why she hightailed it out of the limo that day."

On Skorpios the walnut coffin, made from one of the island's trees and bearing a brass plate inscribed simply: "Aristotle Onassis: 1900–1975," * was carried up the hill to the tiny chapel, past lines of employees in their work clothes—chefs and waiters, gardeners and sailors and maids—holding lighted candles. Below them the *Christina* waited with her Liberian flag at half-mast. A village priest read St. Paul's Epistle to the Thessalonians, and a small choir sang several verses, including: "I went to the grave and I saw the naked bones, and I said to myself, who are you? King or soldier? Rich or poor? Sinner or just?" The service was quickly over. Each mourner kissed the ikon placed on the coffin. As the sky darkened, a few drops of rain fell, and the fragrance of the almond and olive trees that he had planted himself drifted in the air, the body of Aristotle Socrates Onassis was lowered into a concrete vault alongside his son Alexander's.

Standing on the deck of the *Christina*, as the breeze that comes with sunset began blowing off the Aegean, the heiress who gave the yacht its name spread her arms and, driven by something deeper than the impulse of her grief, told the crew and her father's employees gathered around her: "This boat and this island are mine. You are all my people now." She spoke in Greek, and the words seemed to come from the depths of her being.

* *Evasive to the end, the dates on his tombstone read: 1906–1975.*

EPILOGUE

My father will leave me nothing to do.
ALEXANDER THE GREAT

THE DAY AFTER her father was buried on Skorpios, Christina flew to Lausanne "for a few days' rest." But the following weeks were anything but restful as she began the task of unraveling the legacy. On April 29, at the American embassy in Paris, she renounced her United States citizenship, which had exposed her global income to American taxes. But in abandoning her American birthright, and the specter of the IRS, she inadvertently created another problem. She was the sole beneficiary of the trust that controlled Victory Carriers, the American company set up as part of the settlement of the 1950s criminal litigation instituted against Ari by the Justice Department; and the agreement excluded foreign participation in profits from the company's four United States–flag tankers. Her answer was swift, creative and effective. Although the ships—now twelve to fourteen years old and operating in the volatile spot market—would continue to be controlled by Costa Gratsos in New York, she established another trust to hold Victory Carriers, and the beneficiary of that trust was to be the American Hospital in Paris. It was a neat move, and one that Ari himself would have admired. Admitted hospital director Perry Cully: "It looks to us like a tax dodge for Christina." *

* It was impossible to put a value on the bequest; shipping experts reckoned that the American Hospital stood to receive an annual income ranging from "very little to seven figures." To date, according to spokesman Bruce Redor, the Hospital "doesn't appear to have received a penny from the trust."

Although under the terms of Ari's will the majority interest in the business was held by the Liechtenstein foundation, ruled by the aging cadre of cousins and old cronies, at a hastily convened board meeting in Switzerland Christina intimated a determination to assert her authority over the empire. The will said the foundation would award prizes in various fields, including art, religion and education, based on the Nobel Prize system; she announced it would be devoted essentially to social welfare projects in Greece. It seemed to be a small modification, yet it signaled a profound change. For not only did it philanthropize Ari's image in Greece, where officials, still highly critical of his intimacy with the colonels, were looking hard at the question of an inheritance tax, but it also gave notice to Ari's executors that she meant to take control, whatever her father's last will and testament said. "Christina's reinterpretation of Ari's plans for the foundation was subtle. Konialidis and the other executors failed totally to recognize its significance," a Swiss lawyer who was present at the Lausanne meeting said later. Although none of the "uncles" objected to her forceful attitude, Gratsos certainly was aware of, and perhaps connived in, what she was up to. He was pleased to see how confidently she moved into her new role. "She is going to be one of the most expert shipping people in the world in a very few years, capable of running all of these things without the advice of old, dilapidated men," he was quoted in *The New York Times* on June 15.

High on the list of problems confronting Christina was the state of the company's tanker fleet. The oil crisis and economic depression were squeezing the shipping business to an unprecedented degree. All fifteen of Olympic's supertankers carried long-term charters with major oil companies, and were making good profits despite the tanker glut, but half those charters were due to expire within the following two years. "It was a lousy time to get thrown in at the deep end," said a London oil executive. "Yet it was precisely the kind of crisis situation that Ari thrived on. And now we were going to get a chance to see if his daughter was made of the same stuff."

In New York, she set up a special "task force" (presided over by Eliot Bailen, who had been Ari's counselor since the 1950s and was now with the law firm of Holtzmann, Wise and Shepherd) to review the situation and prepare a strategy for the difficult times ahead. Next she turned her mind to the manner in which the empire was run. It was a formidable challenge. Ari's autocratic style, the way he had parceled out authority to assorted satraps, his insistence on making every important decision himself, his failure to bring in young executives and modern business methods, had inexorably sapped management mettle. Olympic Maritime, which supervised the shipping side of the empire out of a *belle époque* building in Monte Carlo, with a staff of 130, was not even a conventional company, but a branch of a dummy corporation registered in Panama. Another sixty-five people, responsible for hiring crews and provisioning the fleet, worked out of the Springfield Shipping Company, headquartered in a shabby-looking building in the port of Piraeus. Each of the ships was run as a separate corporation, usually registered in Panama to avoid taxes. There was no central accounting system; the ledgers for one corporation were usually kept in the offices of another a continent away; profits were channeled through a labyrinth of tax-haven shells.

Ari had written at the start of an early notebook, "Never begin a deal, a battle or a love affair if the fear of losing overshadows the prospect of winning." And although that was written in a simpler time, when he was able to keep his business secrets all straight in his head, the sentiment made a strong appeal to Christina. She might have been perceived as a young girl of extraordinary naïveté in many ways, but she was still her father's daughter who was determined to perform in his image. Caution, which in another chief executive of a multinational corporation would be accepted as wisdom, in her seemed a kind of disloyalty, a violation of her legacy. It surprised none of her friends when amid the turmoil of those early days at the helm of Olympic she launched a lawsuit to have her dead mother's third marriage annulled on the grounds that it was unlawful for Tina to have wed her brother-in-law. A great deal of money was at stake, of course; one inside estimate put Tina's personal fortune at $270 million. But money was not entirely the reason for Christina's offensive. "You could say she was also settling a few private scores," said one of her lawyers in Athens, acknowledging Christina's deep distaste for the way her stepfather had revealed her suicide bid to the world. Moving swiftly between countries and crises, dealing with personal pressures and the constant stress of business, she seemed to be handling herself with a style and a strength that impressed even her severest critics. Through the death of her family she was realizing resources within herself that were changing not only her status but also her whole personality and outlook on life. Meyer recalled the exact moment he recognized the profundity and nature of her transformation. He said, "She called me from Monte Carlo at three o'clock in the morning to ask me to do something for her in Miami that day. Only Ari would have had the crust to do that. I told myself, 'This kid's really got what it takes.' She was making up for lost time, and loving every minute."

On April 18, *The New York Times* broke the news that Ari had been planning to divorce Jackie and shortly before he died had asked Roy Cohn to begin proceedings. "Several friends of the Onassis family have said that Mrs. Onassis wants more money," reported John Corry in a front-page story. Christina, he wrote, "is said to be bitterly hostile to Mrs. Onassis." Jackie "went through the ceiling" when she read the story, Cohn would later recall. "According to what I was told by very reliable sources on the Christina side, Jackie was calling up Christina in Monte Carlo after the story had been printed, threatening that unless Christina put out a statement saying that everything had been all lovey-dovey and wonderful between her father and Jackie, she was going to make no end of trouble over the estate, and everything else," claimed Cohn.

Jackie would have had to be a saint not to feel resentment at the stories of Ari's plans to divorce her, and the amount of his bequest, claimed to be the minimum sum he could get away with under Greek law, that were appearing in the press. Four days later, the *Times* carried an inside-page agency story from Paris headlined, "Miss Onassis Denies Her Father Planned Divorce." These stories are totally untrue," she said through her French attorney, adding that her own relations with her stepmother were based on friendship and respect and there were "no financial or other disputes separating" them. One of the few Onassis aides who remained sympathetic to Jackie, Johnny Meyer was not alone in believing that she should not have put so much pressure on Christina for a formal denial. According to Cohn afterward, "It was the kind of statement they would have been better off if it had never been issued. It really confirmed that things were not all right. It was like a confession of someone being tortured . . . it read like such a weak affirmation that it was clear to everybody that Christina was doing it just to get Jackie off her neck and that she was actually, in effect, confirming the fact that things had not been good at all."

Then Christina flew to New York and confronted her stepmother. Insisting that she speak to her alone, she asked how much Jackie wanted to renounce all further claims to the Onassis estate. Jackie was more than willing to talk business. The visit lasted for only fifteen minutes, but the parameters of a deal were agreed on, including a promise that Jackie would sell Christina her share in the island and the yacht. Jackie returned to Skorpios to collect her personal belongings, as well as mementos of Ari. It would take eighteen months of intense legal wrangling to settle the final figure of twenty-six million dollars. "It was a steep price to pay, but Christina didn't complain. She wanted to expunge the very thought of Jackie," said Meyer. Yet Christina would always be profoundly ambivalent about her stepmother. A few days after their summit meeting in New York, she volunteered a further statement to the press pleading that they both be left in peace "and all detrimental and harmful speculation cease." On April 24 they flew separately to Skorpios for the Greek Orthodox service marking the fortieth day after her father's death. Afterward, the worshippers completed the ceremonial rite of passage by eating of a loaf of sacramental bread, a symbolic act to send the soul of Ari to heaven. "Forty days," Christina said to Artemis that evening. "It seems like forty years."

If there was a certain inevitability about the entente between Jackie and Christina, however fragile it may have been—"they were two sharp ladies who recognized that a settlement was not only possible but palpably pragmatic," said a veteran Onassis banker in New York—nobody expected the schism between Christina and Niarchos to ever heal. However, a few days after she returned from the Aegean memorial service for her father—"after a little horse trading and a lot of soul-searching," according to a Niarchos source—Christina declared that there was now "complete harmony" between them. Once again pragmatism was at the heart of her *volte-face*. Her lawyers, playing the role of firemen, had managed to damp down her anger. "They convinced her that a courtroom was no place in which to turn loose the family skeletons," said a Niarchos insider who helped to arrange the *en famille* talks to settle Tina's estate.

But the most revealing testimony to the reality of her growing confidence was her decision to drop Peter Goulandris. "I am tired of everyone trying to marry me off. It isn't because it's too soon after my father's death but because I don't have plans to marry him or anyone else," she announced. Although it was also hinted that the archconservative Goulandris family had conspired to stop Peter marrying the divorced, headstrong daughter of a man they still regarded with considerable distaste. It was also a fact that Goulandris executives now viewed the business side of the alliance far less favorably than they had six months earlier, before it became clear that the tanker recession was not going to go away for a very long time. According to an Athens shipping broker, an Onassis-Goulandris marriage would have been "the biggest merger of white elephants in the world." However, a Goulandris cousin later said: "Of course there were business influences at work, but they were not finally responsible for what happened. Christina has a Greek soul but a very American mind, while Peter was brought up to believe in the ideal of female subservience to the male. No way was she going to buy that. Besides, she had smelled the blood of the boardroom. That's just about the most intoxicating smell in the world. Rejecting Peter, she took her first step toward adulthood and self-realization. It was her way of settling her debts with the past—when she was merely the daughter of the family." At a meeting with chairman Sir Eric Drake and the board of British Petroleum in London she announced, "From now on, gentlemen, if there is anything to discuss or to be decided you will be dealing with me." She put on a similar performance for Sir Frank McFadzean and his board at Shell Oil. "The sheer theatricality of big business seemed to appeal to her immensely," said one director. "She was like a queen determined that honor be paid to her throne. One instinctively sensed that she had caprices which had to be humored carefully, or else." Her show of strength made good business sense. "It's been three months since there was a boss at the helm, and many people have been wondering what was going to happen," Nigel Neilson said. "She is now reassuring our business associates there will be no change." But still the big question was how could a woman with so little business experience run an empire so raveled as Olympic Maritime? "She can draw on the advice of people with vast experience," Neilson repeated the familiar line, although privately he was concerned that all of those men were over sixty years old, and most of them were well into their seventies and better known for their subservience to Ari than for their brilliant careers. She had also inherited her father's notebooks, of course. And whoever possessed those books possessed the innermost secrets of Ari's mind. When the time comes, Ari had said before Alexander's death, his son would inherit his notebooks: "Then he will know as much as his father. But he will never be quite as clever—because I wrote the book!" But had she inherited something else? Something almost as important as those books? Once when a friend referred to Ari's instinct about people, Alexander asked where he sat when he visited avenue Foch. The friend replied that usually he sat on the chair placed in front of Ari's Louis Quinze desk. Alexander said, "You *always* sit in that chair. His instinct is a machine. It measures your breathing patterns. Technology tells him if you lie, not instinct." *

* Ari's favorite piece of technology, acquired a few months before his death, was a voice-stress analyzer, the size of a microcassette recorder, which, when attached to the telephone, indicated with a combination of colored pinlights whether the person on the end of the line was anxious, and probably lying, or at ease, and likely to be speaking the truth. He called these gadgets his toys, and occasionally "the tools of my wicked

Had Christina inherited the polygraphic gadgetry, too? "She has everything that's necessary to aid her judgment and to guide her decisions. But it's still Christina Onassis who makes the final synthesis of the information coming in," said an Olympic lieutenant in Monte Carlo. And Costa Gratsos was equally adamant, "She is making all the decisions, regarding even the smallest matters." The *Wall Street Journal*'s Eric Morgenthaler thought "that was laying it on a bit thick," but it was clear to him that Christina intended to run her own show. She also had more than her share of luck in those early months at the helm. Although Olympic paid out seventeen million dollars in penalties to cancel six supertankers Ari had ordered at the height of the 1973 boom, one of the three ships that were too far along in construction to be canceled, the 277,000-ton *Olympic Bravery*, ran aground during her maiden voyage, and the company collected fifty million dollars in insurance for a ship that was capable of running losses of up to ten million dollars a year in the daunting state of the tanker market.

Christina's stamina seemed astonishing. It appeared that she could cope with the technical complexities of her business and the involved problems in her private affairs with an ease that seemed hardly possible to those friends who were close enough to know that her emotional equilibrium had for a long time been precarious. But there was an augury of problems ahead in her increasing use of medication. In the first weeks after Ari's death, her uncle, Dr. Garofalides, had prescribed the antidepressant drug imipramine. But the side effects made her tired and weak; and to overcome her fatigue she turned to amphetamines, and very soon she needed barbiturates to sleep. After a while she found that the pills were not having any effect, and in an effort to break the "vicious circle" of uppers and downers, she switched to taking shots. A private nurse traveled with her everywhere to take care of the injections. "She was always trying to wake up or go to sleep," said a close friend in Paris. Olympic staffers noticed the way her moods switched, often in the course of a single day ("edgy, vivacious, peremptory, relaxed, you name it") and began to speculate about her ability to continue to function as company chief. Christina later admitted, "I was near the end of my rope." But although interest in the Onassis fortunes had increased rather than dimin-

---

trade." He had been using them for a very long time and was an expert. In a bar in the south of France in 1956 he demonstrated a wristwatch recorder to Alan Brien. "Let us suppose I want to know what the man next to us is saying. If we fall silent he will get suspicious. This is what I do." He spread his arms wide on the bar so that the "watch" was close to the man, who was in deep conversation with a pretty young woman. "And now I talk very loud and show no interest in his business at all." After the couple left, Ari played back the man's soft impeachments.

ished since her father's death, she managed to keep her unstable state hidden from the press.

In June, she found herself in love again. Her new beau looked a better bet than Bolker. He was young (thirty), rich and Greek: Alexander Andreadis, second son of Stratis Andreadis, one of the most prominent bankers in Athens and the owner of the largest shipyard in Greece. Indeed, the lovers had a great deal in common, not least that their fathers both maintained exceptionally close relations with the military junta. It was Stratis Andreadis who got the refinery contract after Ari had been ousted, only to lose it again when Papadopoulos was deposed as president in 1973. The colonels' successors also canceled Alexander's medical deferment from military service, and he still had nearly a year to serve in the ranks when he met Christina. The courtship was secretive, impassioned and swift. "I think I asked Alexander to marry me when I told him I couldn't live without him. He said, 'Then why don't we get married?' I was thunderstruck . . . I know it sounds ridiculous, but my heart skipped a beat," she later told friends.

In spite of Christina's indignation and her unconcealed antipathies, Artemis, who had become the family matriarch and Christina's closest confidante, persuaded her to invite Jackie to the wedding. The Onassis aunts and the Olympic uncles disagreed rather more among themselves about the wisdom of the marriage than they admitted to the outside world; Jackie's presence, with her son, John, indicated a need to convey unity instead of division within the family. Costa Konialidis said that Alexander was an untimely choice, which might have meant much or little, although the fact that her uncles disapproved of the marriage gave it an added interest in Christina's eyes.

It was assumed, especially by the media, that there was business logic as well as romance in the marriage. Although regarded as a playboy figure in Athens, an avid collector of antique Rolls-Royces, Andreadis had graduated from Zurich University with an honors degree in mechanical engineering. In London, the well-informed *Financial Times* reflected:

> Could Christina Onassis have managed her father's business empire? The question may now be academic since her new husband, though not as was predicted from one of the great Greek tanker owning families, is a businessman of formidable power. Granted the marriage lasts—she has already made one brief and sorry match—it is hard to see Alexander Andreadis not playing some management role in the Onassis line. The Andreadis interests cover banking, including the Commercial Bank of Greece,

the country's largest private bank . . . so although this is not one of those carefully arranged Greek dynastic marriages, and the pair only met apparently a month ago, it looks as if there is new management and financial muscle behind the Onassis interests.

On July 22, four weeks after meeting over coffee at the Athens Hilton, a hotel owned by the Andreadis family, the lovers were married at sunset in the private chapel of the summer residence of Prince Peter of Greece at Glyfada. The rush to the altar appalled most of the family (but not Jackie, who, with a remarkable turn of congratulation declared that she "so loved that child . . . at last I can see happy days ahead for her"). Ari had been dead three months, the family was still in mourning, and even in the beautiful Byzantine monastery above the Aegean Sea, as Christina and Alexander repeated the vows of the Greek Orthodox church, made the traditional three trips around the altar and were pronounced man and wife, it was the desolation of a death that most touched the tiny congregation. "You can't excuse Christina, but it's hard not to pity her," was the kindest word from an Olympic insider.

But it was not merely a matter of bad timing that aroused so much avuncular concern. Konialidis and other stalwarts of Ari's old guard knew something the *Financial Times* did not, and before the honeymoon was over Christina had been persuaded to take their advice. Working from a precise brief, she gave a press conference: she would, she made it clear, continue personally to direct the Onassis empire. Her fortune would not be merged with the Andreadis assets or interests in any way.

Precipitant passion is not the best harbinger of domestic bliss, and from the word go the marriage was not without incident. Private dissatisfactions erupted into public squabbles. When Christina insisted on playing backgammon with friends in the lobby of a Monte Carlo hotel into the small hours, Alexander, in a spectacular display of Greek virility, hurled the board across the lobby and dragged his erring bride into the elevator. But more often, unequal to the task of dealing with her vagaries, he simply withdrew. During one of their frequent fights, Christina flew to Moscow to negotiate with the Soviet shipping agency Sovfracht, a department of the Soviet Ministry of the Maritime Fleet, a deal to lease the Russians five bulk carriers on five-year charters. The man she was principally dealing with was Sergei Kauzov, head of Sovfracht's tanker division. (They had already met, briefly, in Monte Carlo. "Sergei says I wasn't very nice to him," Christina later recalled the occasion, and the fact that she had asked him how a Communist party official justified his presence in a town like Monte Carlo—"and with whose money?") Deeply disenchanted with Andreadis—perhaps intrigued and titillated by a sense of risk—she began an affair with the forty-year-old married Russian. Although he seemed an unlikely ladykiller—barely taller than Christina, with thinning brown hair, a pale face and only one eye, the result of a childhood accident—Kauzov had the quirky charm that some women have a taste for.

In the beginning, the relationship, in the words of a Paris girlfriend, was "physical and capricious"—a distraction from the despair of a new and already ailing marriage. The path to Kauzov's door had been prepared for Christina by Ari's old friend David Karr, whose exceptional closeness to important Soviet officials, including Premier Alexei Kosygin's son-in-law Dzherman Gvishiani, deputy chairman of the State Committee for Science and Technology, had aroused the interest of the CIA—and also the Direction Générale de la Sécurité Extérieure (DGSE, France's CIA) in Paris, where Karr now lived, and would soon mysteriously die, less than a hundred yards from the Onassis apartment on avenue Foch.

In the middle of her marital vicissitudes, her uncles' gravest suspicions about the Andreadis empire were confirmed. Following a routine check by inspectors from the Bank of Greece, three of the five Andreadis banks were placed under government control. Stratis Andreadis faced charges of fraud to the tune of thirty-eight million dollars. He was further charged with selling shares belonging to the banks he controlled to holding companies personally owned by him at prices far below their real value. This new crisis —at Olympic Maritime it was balefully referred to as the Andreadis Fault—ironically kept the marriage afloat. "She could hardly give Alexander the heave-ho in the middle of that mess," says a friend. "And on top of everything else, the poor fellow had fallen off his motorbike on Skorpios and broken his ankle." Christina's reaction was to ban motorcycle riding on the island and ship Alexander's bikes back to the mainland. "Biking was about the only pleasure Alex had on Skorpios. It just wasn't his year," said a former Andreadis mistress.

Alexander grew fat and waited miserably in Athens, brooding over the scandal that threatened the Andreadis fortune, and protesting over and over that although he loved Christina very much she had become impossible. "I don't know what I can do. She's so many women rolled into one. I never know which woman I'm dealing with," he told friends. It was clear to him and everyone else that the marriage was finished. In Paris she was reported hosting a dinner party for sixty guests (including uncle Stavros Niarchos) at Maxim's. What he did not know was that his wife was also hotly pursuing an affair with Kauzov in Paris, where the Russian had conveniently become head of Sovfracht's French bureau. It was no longer a capricious fling. Unable to be seen together, they conducted the extraordinary liaison in out-of-town hotels and restaurants, and once they even slipped away for ten days to Brazil. (After she returned from Rio de Janeiro a former boyfriend recalled her asking, "Who is Dostoyevsky?") Occasionally she made an excuse to visit Kauzov at his office, between a butcher's shop and a bar, on rue des Huissiers in the suburbs of Neuilly-sur-Seine. When he returned to Russia for business briefings, and to see his wife and nine-year-old daughter, Katya, she flew to England to telephone him on the London-Moscow direct dialing system rather than risk exposure by going through the Paris operator. Even her closest friends had no inkling that she was having anything more than a business relationship with Kauzov.

In October 1976, fifteen months after the short-order nuptials, Christina and Alexander applied to the Athens Archbishopric to help them in a reconciliation—a cynical formality of the Greek Orthodox church before starting divorce proceedings. The following March, they each filed, each citing "differences of character." In prepared statements read in court by their lawyers, Christina claimed that Andreadis was "despotic, foul-mouthed, blindly jealous and yet a womanizer, fanatically self-centered." He countered that she had "a peculiar and dictatorial character and didn't really care about me."

The marriage was dissolved in July 1977. She said, "I'm through with marriage and romance. I won't let anything stand in the way of running my business now. That is the one major goal in my life." She was not entirely telling the truth, but she was not neglecting her empire either. Part of the fifty million dollars' insurance she collected on *Olympic Bravery* she used to buy a 270,000-ton tanker from D. K. Ludwig. It seemed a risky purchase, even though she got the ship (renamed *Aristotle Onassis*) for some ten million dollars less than its current value, and fifty-three million dollars less than it would have cost at the height of the boom years. Conscious of her father's maxim that "in shipping the advantage is always to the one with the most patience," she calculated that even if she had to lay up the new tanker for five years, she'd still make a killing with it in a very short time if the market rebounded. "Christina's not a gambler. But, like her father, she's not afraid to take calculated risks," her lawyer, Stelios Papadimitriou, said.

When Maria Callas died of a heart attack in her Georges-

Mandel apartment in September, Christina sent flowers "from the
Onassis family." To friends she said, "Maria never did get what
she wanted most—she didn't fight hard enough for the important
things." Significantly, her own affair with a married man had
reached a critical stage. Kauzov had told his wife, Natalya, about
his mistress in Paris and said that he wanted a divorce. (The
columnist Jack Anderson reported that the Russian boasted to
friends afterward that he had tricked Natalya, claiming he had
been ordered by his bosses to seduce Christina. Unfortunately, he
had accepted gifts from the capitalist heiress, which he had not
declared, and the authorities were about to arrest him and confis-
cate the family car and apartment. A quick divorce, with all his
property signed over to Natalya, would ease the situation. When
he was released from prison, Kauzov promised, they would be
remarried.) A close friend says it was Christina who insisted that
Natalya had to go. "I don't think she felt particularly guilty. She
isn't the sort of lady to torment herself with sexual self-reproach.
She was simply tired of eating in suburban cafés and hiding
away."

The affair was first uncovered by the Service de Renseigne-
ments, the French secret service, when a routine surveillance operation turned up Christina's license plate number among the cars
visiting the Sovfracht offices. (A graduate of the Moscow Institute
of Foreign Languages, a designated KGB training school, Kauzov
was listed as a "target alien" by the French security services.) It
was something more than a juicy item for the gossip columns. For
although the meetings had the aura of lovers' trysts, they also
contained elements of intelligence activity. "Christina had access
to the kind of information which could reveal a great deal about
Western energy needs and fluctuations in the hands of Soviet intelligence analysts," said an MI5 officer in London. "The Soviets
must have been wetting their lips when they heard Kauzov's story.
It was a gift." Said a veteran company man in Washington: "I
don't subscribe to the view that it was a setup from start to finish.
Kauzov was a middle-rank KGB administrator. Nobody could
have reckoned on Christina falling for him the way she did. But
once it happened, Moscow squeezed it for all it was worth."

And so when Kauzov was suddenly recalled home—Christina
wasn't far behind. Tracked down at the Intourist Hotel on Gorky
Street, she was indignant when Western newsmen asked about the
rumors now openly circulating (leaked by the CIA, anxious to "cut
her off at the pass" with embarrassing publicity) that she planned
to marry Kauzov. The idea was *preposterous . . . untrue . . . stupid
. . . a lie.* "I don't know what the fuss is about. I am here as a

tourist," she said with the irascibility that had often made Ari so hard for the press to deal with in his later years. "I'll be returning to Paris in a few days," she insisted.

Western reporters were inclined to treat the story as a sort of mirror image of *Ninotchka,* the 1939 Hollywood romantic comedy about devout Russian Communist Greta Garbo falling in love in Paris with Western capitalist Melvyn Douglas. In Whitehall and Washington it was felt that the implications were closer to Le Carré than to Lubitsch. The source of the CIA anxiety was a French intelligence tip that Christina was planning to open an office in Moscow—with her lover at the helm. "If the Onassis tanker fleet were to fall under Soviet influence, the men in the Kremlin would have much more than a propaganda coup," said a Western shipping analyst. The expansion of the Soviet merchant marine was causing particular concern in the West at that time. The day after the political consequences were spelled out by State Department officials to Onassis executives in New York, Costa Gratsos took off for the Soviet capital. Christina saw him, listened to what he had to say, told him she would think it over. After the grave allegations about her lover's connections, it was hoped that she would back off from actual marriage. But they reckoned without what one aide wryly called "her Olympian disregard for prudence."

On August 1, 1978, ignoring the Cassandra-like forebodings of her aunts (one of whom, according to a Greek newspaper report, had threatened to have her forcibly examined by psychiatrists in order to prove that she was legally unstable), Christina married Sergei Danyelovich Kauzov in a $2.15 ceremony in a Moscow "wedding palace" on Griboyedova Street. A string quartet (optional extra) played Mendelssohn's Wedding March. The bride and groom solemnly promised registrar Klara Lemehkova that they would preserve their love for all their lives, be faithful and loyal and stand together in love and sorrow. Mme. Lemehkova wished them happiness and cautioned Sergei, "Wherever you go, don't forget your Soviet motherland." The ceremony was attended by eleven guests, none of whom was from the bride's family. (Artemis had made her disapproval clear the day Christina first told her about Sergei: "How could you love a godless man?" she asked.) The bride was accompanied by John Fotopoulos, the first secretary of the Greek embassy. Before driving off in Sergei's brown Volga sedan, the happy couple announced that after a Siberian honeymoon on the shores of Lake Baikal they would share a two-and-a-half-room apartment with Sergei's mother until they found a flat of their own. "We are just ordinary people," said Kauzov, who disclosed that he had parted company with Sovfracht two months before and was now earning $150 a week teaching English to Russian students; he omitted to mention that he was also lecturing on the ideological role of the Soviet merchant marine to Western and Third World union activists attending Moscow's Higher Trade Union School, run by the Second Chief Directorate (Department for Foreign Students) of the KGB. Said a French intelligence man who had followed Sergei's progress since he first showed up in Paris in 1976, "The ideological role of the fifty thousand dollars a year he collected as Christina's husband (under the terms of Ari's will) would have made the basis for a more interesting lecture."

The honeymoon never happened. Four days after they exchanged rings—before even the bouquet of red and white roses had died in the vase on the dresser in her mother-in-law's apartment—Christina took off for Greece. Just as Bolker and Andreadis had had to do before him, the abandoned groom put on a brave face. "She had urgent business," he told curious newsmen in Moscow. Tarrying long enough to be photographed in the pool of Aunt Artemis's seaside villa outside Athens, she rounded up a dozen friends to join her for the weekend on Skorpios. "Don't you miss Moscow?" a guest asked facetiously. She answered that she missed her friends—and her Learjet—far, far more. "Moscow was more meddlesome than she was disposed to tolerate," said one of the Skorpios dozen. "The bureaucrats refused to allocate airspace for what they called her 'capitalist self-indulgence' when she wanted to use her own plane for the honeymoon. She has a hysterical base to her nature, and to say the least she got pretty snitty." Her anger was directed not so much at the Russians as at David Karr, who was never far away whenever the Soviets were involved. "She felt that he hadn't tried hard enough to persuade the comrades to accommodate her Lear, although he was always boasting about how a few years earlier he had arranged landing rights in Moscow for Armand Hammer's Gulfstream. I think she saw it as a deliberate snub."

Her flight to Skorpios surprised nobody in her crowd. "It's where she always runs to when things get too hairy for her in the real world," said one chum. "On Skorpios she is Queen Christina —I've seen peasants literally fall on their knees to kiss her hand. Only on the island does she feel free to dance on tables if that's the mood she's in—it's where she's most like Ari, where you see the real Christina, and hear what she really thinks." Sitting around one evening, they began to play the what-if game. Christina said, "What if Alexander had not been killed?" Her friends were stunned. "How do you answer a question like that?" said one. It was Christina herself who came up with the answer. "I suppose I wouldn't have felt the burden of being an Onassis so heavily," she mused. "I would have been freer—but I wouldn't have been completely born."

On August 10, she flew to London for talks with the directors of British Petroleum, one of Olympic's most important customers. At lunch in the boardroom at Britannic House, BP's headquarters in the city of London, they were joined by a Foreign Office minister, whose presence according to one oil executive "had been ordained at a high political level." Convinced that a KGB man was now "profoundly influencing" Olympic Maritime affairs, the anti-Communist Saudis were unlikely to renew their charters and would have no difficulty in finding cheaper replacements for the Onassis ships, the minister informed her. She did not need to be reminded that more than 85 percent of Olympic's tanker trade involved the transportation of Saudi Arabian oil. As she left that evening, clearly badly shaken, to take her Learjet back to Athens, a senior BP man told a colleague: "Not for all the tea in China would I want a daughter of mine to be in that young woman's shoes right now." Her anxious state of mind after the day of talks with the British oil chiefs was not helped by an intelligence-inspired tip-off that in her absence Sergei was spending his nights with Natalya. Christina called him in Moscow and demanded, "Are you still in love with your wife?" "Of course I am. And I want you to come back soon," he answered nimbly.

She returned to Moscow on August 13. She refused to accept that Sergei might be a spy. Said a former lover in Paris, "She could not bear the thought that she might have been used. But she is also a realist. If it wasn't proved that Sergei was working for Russian intelligence, she knew that the scenario was perfectly plausible. The idea of a Moscow office was never mentioned again, although she did her best to make a go of Russia." Her stay with Sergei's mother was predictably brief; she flew in her favorite interior decorator, Atalanta Politis, to work on her new seven-room mansion apartment. She used her hard currency to buy the special certificate roubles to shop in the Beryozka stores, which provide luxury Western goods for foreigners and privileged Soviets. But the sense of isolation got her down. She spent thousands of dollars on telephone calls to friends in the West. Her attempts to learn Russian—and she is an excellent linguist—never got farther than the expletive stage. She put on over fourteen pounds (she blamed Russian Pepsi-Cola and caviar) and was listed among the world's ten worst-dressed women. "Moscow," said a friend who visited her there, "oppressed her. I never once saw any color in her face during the whole of that time."

But of all the doubts that assailed Christina, the most telling was the death of David Karr. Not only was he her most reliable link with the West—it was through his Kremlin contacts, he liked to claim, that the way was paved for her to marry Kauzov and set up house in Moscow—but also a friend she had come to rely upon. He had spent the Fourth of July in Moscow celebrating the opening of a luxury hotel he had developed, and Christina dined with him there only a few days before he was found dead in his avenue Foch apartment. Two doctors, Karr's own physician and a police surgeon, summoned to the apartment, agreed that the sixty-year-old entrepreneur had died instantly of a massive coronary attack. But their expert opinion was questioned by Karr's young widow, Evia, who flew from New York in time to get an injunction stopping the funeral and cremation service literally in mid-prayer at the Père Lachaise cemetery in Paris. She demanded an autopsy. According to a friend of the family, himself a Russian-born American living in Paris and, like Karr, deeply involved in emigré politics (according to Karr's own claims, he was acting as a private liaison between the United States and Russia on the issue of the emigration of Soviet Jews), "Evia was convinced that Dave had been murdered the way Markov had been tapped in London, and the way Kostov almost got his here in Paris." * According to confidential telex reports sent to the secretary of state by the United States embassy in Paris, Evia Karr claimed that her husband had either been poisoned by the Russians (he became ill after each visit to the Soviet Union, she told United States intelligence officers who questioned her in Paris) or had been murdered by the KGB in their apartment. But the autopsy found no trace of toxic substances; a small fracture of the larynx, attributed to Karr's dying fall, was not considered to be inconsistent with the original opinion that a massive coronary had been the cause of death. Evia was not convinced and insisted on filing an action that left the case open, recorded under French law as "Homicide charged against person or persons unknown." In a later message to Washington the embassy advised that the ". . . sensational aspects of

---

* A Bulgarian defector who broadcast anti-Communist propaganda back to Eastern Bloc countries, Georgi Markov was jabbed in his thigh while standing at a bus stop in London. When he turned, a man stooped to pick up an umbrella and said, "I'm sorry" before hurrying into a taxi. Markov died four days later, apparently from heart failure. Later intensive forensic tests on tissues, which included a section of the flesh surrounding the puncture mark on Markov's leg, were carried out at the Chemical Defense Establishment at Porton Down. What appeared to be a pinhead on one of the specimens was a metal bead .068 inch in diameter, with two .34mm-diameter cavities, which had contained the deadly chemical poison ricin. Vladimir Kostov, who had also defected from Bulgaria, survived an identical attack while traveling on the Paris Métro.

Karr's death . . . may not be fully put to rest by the autopsy report." It is still not known who killed Karr, if his death was murder, but it must have crossed Christina's mind, as it did so many others who had done business with him, and as *Fortune* magazine mused four months after his demise, that his powerful friends in Russia were potential enemies as well. And Karr had an unhealthy habit of bragging that more than a few of those Soviet bigwigs were in his pocket.

Christina had been brought up to believe that death, like poverty, was for other people, not for the Onassises; Karr's passing not only heightened her sense of vulnerability and isolation in Moscow but also reopened the emotional wounds caused by the deaths of Alexander and her parents. "She wanted out—out of Moscow and out of that marriage," said a friend who had been close to her during Ari's terminal illness and believed that her irrational behavior—"first the Andreadis affair, then the Kauzov business"—was not only an impulsive show of selfhood but also a symptom of pathologic mourning. Less than five months later she formally separated from Kauzov; the following May in a Swiss court the divorce was made official. The Russian collected a seventy-eight-thousand-ton tanker as part of his settlement ("Commie or not, little Sergei wasn't going to be screwed out of his plutocratic perks," said a former New York associate—or, as another put it, "Christina is magnanimous in divorce") and was promptly given a Soviet exit visa to develop his business interests in the West.

Back in Paris, as the 1980s began and she put behind her a decade in which she lost her whole family, became the most famous heiress in the world, and saw her three marriages fail (none of them surviving longer than two years), Christina was faced with "the challenge of remaking my life." Her early grief-avoiding days of activity and change at Olympic were replaced with an unusual calm, which some suspected was the calm of uncertainty, or perhaps the poignant satiety of the very rich. Although she was now the sole standard-bearer of the family, and much was expected of her, she confessed to friends that when she looked into herself she had difficulty defining or even determining what she wanted to find there. She reflected on the era that had ended as a downhill racer does on his last season, analyzing each run, replaying every heel push and hip flexion, blaming skis, wax and the weather when practice times were not converted into triumphs.

Occasionally, Kauzov continued to share apartments with her —in St. Moritz, in Paris, at La Jolla in southern California ("It's an open divorce," she told a friend who had the temerity to inquire into the nature of their continuing relationship). Mostly she played the field. Perfume heir Yvon Coty and Monaco's Princess Caroline's first ex-husband, Philippe Junot, were among the attentive escorts. "But she must be impossible to live with," said a close friend. "When she came into the bathroom that bathroom was like a stable five minutes later . . . although I must say her faults were always redeemed by the generous impulses which followed her unruly outbursts." Says Paris friend Jean-Pierre de Lucovich, "You dare not admire something in a store if you are with her because she buys it for you; if you don't want to act like a pimp, which, sadly, many of the men who get close to her do, you must keep your mouth shut."

As Christina passed her thirtieth birthday the threat of loneliness tightened around her. Increasingly she expressed the need to surround herself with people, and like Ari hated it when a party had to end. "She simply couldn't understand that loneliness isn't assuaged by numbers, and that one true friend is sometimes all the company a person ever needs," said one of the dozens of guests she invited to Skorpios the summer she shed Kauzov. She kept her Learjet fueled and permanently available at Le Bourget to fly friends to wherever she needed them. "Private jetliners are nothing special now, but Christina is the only person in the world I know who keeps hers completely exclusive. She could help cover its costs if she rented it out occasionally, but she refuses: the plane, the pilots, the mechanics—they wait," says Patrice Habans, a French photographer who has known her since she was a child. Such was her anxiety not to be alone that she engaged a socialite as her social secretary. Two of the Skorpios summer regulars later complained to Christina about this man and his girlfriend. "They were not amusing, they never said anything clever or interesting. They were simply boring. That was a mystery to us, because people in that position—it is their *job* to be entertaining, you understand? So we said to Christina, 'You know, if you want to buy people, and must have a couple around you all the time, we are sure that you can find for the same amount of money some people who are a little more charming.' She said, 'Oh it is so difficult, you know, finding staff.' It made us laugh." Christina began to laugh too, although, they suspected, with bewilderment and uncertainty.

Society shows us what we are, Tina had lectured Ari—"but Christina knew that it was solitude that would show her what she should be," said Costa Gratsos, who felt that she socialized too much, and was betraying her early promise in a business he had loved and shared for a lifetime with Ari. It was part of a dour warning against what he saw as a potentially wasted life. Nevertheless, Christina took it hard when Gratsos died at the beginning of December 1981. "I shall never have a friend like him again," she said. She would miss his calm, his wisdom, his strength. She knew he always told her the truth, and not many people did that anymore. An executive at the Paris fashion house Jean Louis Scherrer later talked about the lies they told her when she showed up ten pounds heavier for a second fitting: "Unable to get into the dress, she'd storm around in her underwear, blaming the designer, the fitter, the seamstress—totally ignoring the fact that she'd simply ballooned between fittings. I'd be agreeing with her—yes, yes, yes, it's intolerable! And you look so wonderful, Christina! How could she believe that? A fitting room—all those mirrors—is the cruelest place in the world for a fat lady. She knew she didn't look wonderful. She simply didn't care. She did nothing with her face, her hair was a mess . . . it was as if she wanted to punish the world for making her so rich and so bloody unhappy."

Her weight was an increasingly disturbing problem. She didn't drink alcohol, didn't use dope, but her consumption of Coca-Cola and junk food seemed to many friends to be blatantly self-destructive. She would confess with a kind of dégagé candor that her body felt clumsy and unlovable. "Thunderthighs," Greek writer and socialite Taki Theodoracopulos dubbed her after revealing pictures of her riding pillion on a motorbike in the Bois de Boulogne appeared in newspapers. It hurt, but she did not let people see that it did; in fact she enjoyed being recognized and reading about herself in the gossip columns; and being followed by the paparazzi, and the games of hide-and-seek they played together (although she did not always appreciate the pictures they got when she was off her guard).

Yet still she was often depressed and uncertain about her life. Some of her most trusted advisers and friends were no longer around: Uncle Theodore, David Karr, Gratsos and her favorite aunt, Ari's older sister, Artemis, had passed away one after the other; and Johnny Meyer, the last survivor of her father's entourage, was dying—although in a bizarre accident in Florida he would cheat the cancer for which he was being treated at the Mayo Clinic. Returning home alone from dinner one evening he stopped his Lincoln to relieve himself by the roadside when a defect in the transmission caused the parked car to jump into reverse, killing him on the spot. ("His death had all the ingredients of a perfect Johnny Meyer story, except for the fact that he didn't have a beautiful girl in the car—but it was still a better finish than the one he was expecting and dreading," said Brian Wells, a writer who knew him during his last rousing years in Florida.)

Christina's besetting sense of bereavement aroused in her a

keen interest in the health of her friends. "If you happened to
mention that you had a slight temperature," said one, talking from
personal experience, "she'd have you booked into a private room
at the American Hospital and be arranging specialists in nothing
flat." When she heard that the journalist Jean-Pierre de Lucovich's
sister-in-law was seriously ill, she insisted that she spend the summer on Skorpios. "Françoise was treated like a queen; Christina
was like a nurse to her," recalled a family friend. Tragically, the
illness worsened, and in September Christina summoned to Paris
a leading Houston cancer specialist. An operation was performed,
but ten days later Françoise died. One of her relatives later recalled an evening about a week after the funeral when the family
was having dinner together: "Christina's housekeeper, Hélène,
called and said that Christina was on her way over. She told us to
be ready to pick her up downstairs because she was alone and very
disturbed. It was when we were beginning to wear pretty good
masks, not talking about the bad times. Then Christina arrived . . .
this Greek widow figure, all in black, sobbing, weeping. It was
quite a production—'It was all my fault, I should never have asked
the surgeon from Houston to come,' etcetera, etcetera. We assured
her she was not to blame. Everybody knew that the operation had
been Françoise's only chance. Yet it was very strange, seeing Françoise's mother and sisters trying to comfort this distraught woman
who had suddenly descended upon them."

Her immoderate sense of compassion was a source of irritation to her former stepbrother, Jamie, marquess of Blandford. In
1983, when he was twenty-seven years old, the weak, handsome
heir to Blenheim Palace and the historic dukedom of Marlborough
developed a heavy heroin habit. He had discharged himself from
a Minnesota drug rehabilitation clinic after only a few days, and
his future seemed bleak. His father naturally was distressed. The
sense of romanticism Christina associated with the Marlborough
name had long ago caused her to forgive Sunny for marrying her
mother in 1961, when she still harbored hopes of Tina's reconciliation with Ari. Moreover, she had become genuinely fond of her
former stepfather, who had shown her much kindness at Tina's
funeral. Always more at home in matters of deed than of tact, she
invited Jamie to a party in Paris and dispatched the Lear to collect
him. "When I got there I was grabbed by four hefty blighters in
white coats, ambulances, the lot . . . Christina had cooked up the
whole bloody plot with my father to get me into a private looney
bin in some château in Paris," Jamie recalled the incident later,
feeling that the nature of his abduction was not of a kind that
helped drug addicts toward recovery.

•   •

Late one afternoon in the spring of 1983, Finn Bryde let himself into his aunt's apartment in Oslo. She was sleeping in a chair. It was still plain to see that she had once been extraordinarily beautiful. Bryde sat quietly for a few moments. After a while, she began to murmur in her dreams. "Ari, oh, Ari, wake up, my darling Mamico, please wake up . . ." A few days later Ingeborg Dedichen was dead—"I'm as old as the century," she told friends to the end.

In London, Christina had found a new lover, Nicky Malroleon, the old Etonian son of an Anglicized Greek shipping millionaire— and fashionably some ten years her junior. He was a charming young man but very unsatisfactory as a flatterer. When it was reported that she was pregnant, Nicky, in what was simply not naïveté, told London gossip columnist Nigel Dempster, "I'm pretty certain she isn't having a baby. But if she is, there is a possibility of me being the father." There was no baby, and not long afterward there was no Nicky in her life either. It was a bad time for Christina. Her weight rose to over two hundred pounds. Another affair began, and ended. Asked by a girlfriend whether there was a new man in her life, she answered that she had given up expecting "new raptures, new thrills." The only man with whom she said she had ever felt "a psychic bond," and who had never been far away, Sergei Kauzov, resurfaced on the scene. Concerned about the number of pills she was taking to help control her weight, and her faddy crash diets, he was seen by some of her friends as an emotionally stabilizing influence. Although still anathema to the "uncles," he had become a successful shipowner in his own right (although his fleet was estimated to be worth twenty million dollars, his new capitalist image did not disarm Western intelligence agencies, which continued to accord him KGB status) and was known to be giving Christina abundant professional guidance. A Paris friend said later on, "There was Sergei whispering who-knows-what in one ear, Aunt Calirrhoë* telling her something else in the other, the people in Monaco and Athens urging her to listen to neither of them; it was a regular axe-grinders' League of Nations."

On Sunday, August 28, 1983, Christina was held for three hours for questioning by customs officials at the Actium military airstrip before being allowed to leave the country in her Learjet. The problem was a matter of the $32.5 million it was claimed she owed in death duties, and fines for failing to submit tax declara-

---

* Ari's youngest half-sister and the widow of Olympic Airways executive Constantine Patronicola, Calirrhoë, together with a companion, George Tsaussis, some twenty-five years her junior, moved into the avenue Foch apartment in the summer of 1983; three months later she returned to Greece, alone.

tions.* Her stab at Onassisian guile in the way she had altered the foundation's aims to elevate in Socialist Greece Ari's tarnished memory and the family name had not come off. The affront at Actium, where Ari had enjoyed unique landing privileges and virtual immunity for twenty years, was meant to remind her that the Onassis name had lost its magic in Athens.

In December 1983, friends began observing a distinct improvement in Christina's mood. She spent several weeks in the Buschinger Clinic in Marbella, shedding twenty-four pounds—and a great deal of the gloom that had made the year such an ordeal for her and for those around her. The cynical ones attributed the transformation to the unexpected leniency and speed of the Greek tax settlement; few knew the truth. She had fallen in love with Thierry Roussel, heir to a pharmaceutical fortune, and, at thirty-four, considered to be one of the most eligible bachelors in France. In March they were married in a civil ceremony at the Paris sixteenth *arrondissement* town hall. After a blessing at a Greek Orthodox church, they held a dinner for 125 guests at Maxim's. A few friends loyally prophesied that this was the marriage Christina had been waiting for ("We plan to grow old together," said the groom); others read the signs less optimistically, and seemed to be justified when a week after the ceremony Christina told Roussel that she wanted out. "Par for the course," said an Onassis insider. "Call it Christina's seven-day itch." The quip covered the mounting concern felt about her largess in Monte Carlo. "Roussel is supposed to be a very rich man. Yet she still agrees to pay *him* a fortune in the event of a divorce. One Kauzov in a lifetime should be enough even for Christina." Nevertheless, the couple survived the rocky start, and the first months were filled with the familiar pattern of socializing, traveling, house buying; a one-million-dollar seven-bedroomed apartment in Grosvenor Square was added to the string of homes, but sold again four months later at a ninety-five-thousand-dollar profit. They built a storybook villa on the slopes of Lake Leman, near Geneva.

Christina's familiar weight problems made her condition not, for some time, evident. In the autumn, she announced the news, which was immediately followed by press stories that a scan had disclosed she was going to have a son, to be born on Skorpios, and named after his grandfather. On January 29, 1985, at the American Hospital in Paris where Aristotle Socrates Onassis had died ten years before, Christina gave Cesarean birth to a six-pound, two-

Christina appealed on the grounds that her father was a citizen of Argentina and never resided or owned property in Greece. In November 1983 the case was settled for $3.7 million.

ounce girl. The baby was named Athina, after her late grandmother. "It would be nice to end the story right there and say that
Christina lived happily ever after. But you know that for her, dis-
illusion will never be very far away," a London friend said after a
weekend at Lake Leman.

On July 15, 1985, beneath the headline "On Again or Off
Again? It's Stormy Seas for Christina O and Her Hapless Hubby,"
People magazine reported: "Since Athina's birth the home has become more like a maximum security prison." Christina lived in a
different dimension from the rest of us, a friend from her days at
Miss Hewitt's Classes in New York once said of the girl who grew
up in a miasma of money, and more money. And *People*—"24-hour
cameras are in every room, hired guards patrol their land. . . ."
The older she becomes the more her wealth encloses her. Now she
is seen only briefly, a remote, unhappy figure, reported by gossip
writers, freeze-framed, child-eyed, in flashlight. Sometimes she
seems to have no sense of future at all—only an aura of aftermath.

NOTES

CHAPTER ONE

I drew on dispatches in contemporary newspapers and periodicals published in the United States and Britain in describing the political climate and the background of the events of the period; I also relied substantially on British diplomatic and consular reports, including the Trade of Consular District of Smyrna, compiled by the Admiralty War Staff, Intelligence Division, and published in a confidential handbook prepared under the direction of the Historical Section of the British Foreign Office (January 1919); the summary of the official reports regarding the events that followed the landing of the Greek troops in Smyrna by the officer commanding the army of occupation and the High Commissioner of Greece in Smyrna from E. K. Venizelos, head of the Royal Greek Legation in Paris, to Georges Clemenceau, premier of France and president of the Paris Peace Conference (May 29, 1919); *An Atlas of Middle Eastern Affairs* by Robert C. Kingsbury and N. J. G. Pounds (London: Methuen, 1964).

For personal details I have drawn wherever possible upon primary source material, deriving from the talks I had with Ari and Artemis Garofalides over a period of seven years. Although Ari's Argentine passport issued in 1924 stated that he was born on September 21, 1900, his biographer Willi Frischauer accepted and printed Ari's claim that he was born on January 20, 1906, the date repeated in the book by *London Sunday Times* journalists Nicholas Fraser, Philip Jacobson, Mark Ottaway and Lewis Chester, *Aristotle Onassis* (London: Weidenfeld and Nicolson, 1977); and in Frank Brady's *Onassis, An Extravagant Life* (New York: Prentice-Hall, 1977; London: Futura, 1978). "Rethinking the evidence, and understanding Ari a lot better than I did when I began my research in 1966, I now believe that 1900 is the more credible year of his birth," Frischauer concluded shortly before his death in 1978, although he remained convinced that Ari was telling the truth about the month he was born: "Men as well as women often shave a few years from their age, but their star signs are sacrosanct," he told me. Never in his conversations with me, nor in Frischauer's notes, did Ari mention his father's first employer in Smyrna, the Jewish merchant Bohar Benadava. Benadava was identified in a letter from the Office of the Turkish press attaché in Washington, D.C., to Joachim Joesten, October 14, 1954. The full text of this letter was published on pages 22–23 of Joesten's *Onassis* (New York: Abelard-Schuman, 1963). This first Onassis biography had its genesis in a three-part profile that Joesten wrote for the *New York Herald Tribune*, June 1954.

31
But he would never forget his first time at Fahrie's: Throughout his life, Ari found himself irresistibly drawn to brothels, and prostitutes; when his own son, Alexander, was fifteen, he introduced him to Manuela, reputedly the most beautiful and sexually gifted girl at Madame Claude's in Paris. "She taught Alexander to be a loving lover," Fiona Thyssen-Bornemisza told me in London in November 1985.

CHAPTER TWO

The historical sources that most contributed to my understanding of the events and conditions described in this chapter, in addition to the newspaper reports of the period, especially those in the *Christian Science Monitor*, the *London Daily Telegraph*, *London Times*, *Chicago Tribune*, *New York Times*, and the *Manchester Guardian*, were the volumes entitled *Greek Atrocities in Turkey* (Ministry of the Interior, Department of Refugees; Ahmed Ihasan & Co., 1921); *Report of the International Commission of Inquiry to Investigate the Treatment of Greek Prisoners in Turkey* (London: Anglo-Hellenic League, 1923); *Papers Relating to the Foreign Relations of the United States, 1915 Supplement*, 1922, vol. 2; 1923, vol. 2 (U. S. Department of State, Washington, D.C.); Edward Hale Bierstadt's *The Great Betrayal* (London: Hutchinson, 1924); Marjorie Housepian's *Smyrna, 1922: The Destruction of a City* (London: Faber and Faber, 1972); and the sworn testimony of the Rev. Charles Dobson, the British chaplain of Smyrna.

34
"To me it is a calamity": Bristol letter to Adm. W. S. Sims, May 18, 1919, Papers of Mark L. Bristol, Library of Congress.

42
"Just then the phone rang": Holiday, December 1958.
According to journalist Michael Sheldon, writing in the English magazine *Everybody's* on September 4, 1954, Ari was "a ragged urchin who had been born in a broken-down old shack ... [his] father had hawked home-made trinkets around Smyrna, and his mother had swept offices and taken in washing to eke out their tiny income." After the Turks rose

against the Greeks, reported Sheldon, Ari escaped to Constantinople,
"leaving a murdered mother and father behind." According to an earlier
profile in *Time*, January 19, 1953, "his father and other members of his
family" were killed in the massacre of 1922. In the *Saturday Evening Post*,
July 25, 1953, in an article called "Monte Carlo's Mysterious Millionaire,"
Ernest Leiser reported, "The tycoon-to-be was born in Greece in 1906 and
raised in Smyrna. . . ." Ari did nothing to correct any of these stories until
May 1957 when his London public relations consultant Nigel Neilson
arranged a series of interviews with Graham Stanford for an "authorized"
life story that appeared in *The News of the World*, a British mass-circulation Sunday newspaper. This is the first known interview in which Ari
admits that his father survived the massacre. Two of his uncles were
killed by the Turks—"I saw them hang," he told Stanford. This is one
fewer than he claimed in the Joachim Joesten *New York Herald-Tribune*
profile, June 1954. The Turkish embassy in Washington in its letter to
Joesten of October 14, 1954, insisted: "No one belonging to the Onassis
family has been hanged, nor are there are any records of his or his son's
imprisonment." Joesten weighed the partisan bias, clash of interests and
motives for keeping the facts secret or misrepresenting them, and concluded that the denial "need not necessarily be taken at face value." According to Artemis Garofalides, three uncles were executed, although in a
conversation with me in Paris in 1974, she discounted Ari's claims that he
had seen any of their bodies on the scaffold. "He possibly believes he did.
It was a very confusing time. He had nightmares for years," she said.

The description of the Karatass sitting room, Gethsemane reading
the passage from Ecclesiastes and fanning the fire with the feathered
turkey wing, and the arrival of the Armenian fugitive and his story of the
death of Chrysostomos also come from talks with Artemis, without whom
Ari's early years would be incompletely perceived. According to Ari's enemies (and to a few of his friends; see Randolph Churchill footnote, p. 157),
to the wealthy Greek socialite and gossip writer, Peter "Taki" Theodorecopulus, who calls him "the old Turk" (*The Spectator*, August 13, 1983),
and to at least three old men who claimed to have known the family more
than sixty years ago (author's interview, Izmir, 1983), the Onassises were
not Anatolian Greeks, but Turks. Only in Socrates' lifetime for reason of
social status had they become Hellenized, and the classical Greek first
names adopted. (Appropriately, perhaps, since, as Miss Housepian re-
minds us in her excellent book, "Smyrna was the cradle of Greek legends,
the ancestral home of demigods and the mortal kings of Mycenae and
Lydia.") The family's ethnographic origins may never find a definitive
solution, and in the absence of historical records, the truth must largely
depend on the interpretation of what the Onassises themselves had to say
about their past.

CHAPTER THREE

Recounting his flight from Smyrna, Ari said that James Loder Park had persuaded "Lieutenant Tyrrell, who had the same initials as me" to arrange his passage aboard the *Edsall*. Ari never knew how finely balanced his deliverance must have been, for "Tyrrell" was almost certainly Lt. A. S. Merrill, Admiral Bristol's intelligence officer, who had sailed with the *Edsall*. "Merrill, like his chief, was contemptuous of the luckless Greeks and prepared to believe the worst of them": Marjorie Housepian, *Smyrna, 1922*, p. 113. "Merrill was feeling some disgust toward the refugees; whenever he caught the eye of a female she would break into tears. 'This steady weep business makes me ill,' he said. 'It looks so practised.' ": Ibid, p. 178.

Although Ari claimed that he was seventeen when he left for Buenos Aires in 1923, he also often added that he was "on the edge of manhood," which is usually regarded to be twenty-three in Asia Minor, especially among families from the interior, where the Onassises had their roots. In his study of moral values in a Greek mountain community *(Honour, Family and Patronage*, Clarendon Press, Oxford, 1964), J. K. Campbell writes, "As a son reaches the threshold of full manhood, 23 years of age, the importance of his prestige ranking within [his peer group] becomes incompatible with undue deference to any senior person, even his father."

The U.S. Office of Naval Intelligence report detailing Ari's insurance scam was obtained through the Freedom of Information Act. According to this same ONI report the *Maria Protopapas* ("renamed *Onassis Maria*") did not sink in Montevideo harbor during a storm, as Ari claimed, but "was lost almost immediately off Genoa." Wherever this freighter sank, ONI's implication that its speedy demise was another insurance fraud cannot be avoided.

Although Claudia Muzio was regarded as outstanding among the singers of her time, "with a voice of great beauty capable of intense drama and pathos," according to *London Times* music critic Noël Goodwin, her great fame, which rivaled Caruso's, a frequent partner, is now almost forgotten; her triumphs at Covent Garden, New York Metropolitan Opera, Chicago Lyric Opera and La Scala have received relatively scant critical study; she made many gramophone records, albeit pre-electric and generally of poor quality. While it is difficult to determine how important a role she played in Ari's life, Costa Gratsos, who said that it was "sexually minimal, emotionally nothing," conceded that her advice ("sing to just one person") started his "winning streak" in Buenos Aires. She died in Rome in 1936, aged forty-seven; a newspaper obituary notice concluded, "Her lonely and unhappy life probably contributed to her early death."

56
Alberto Dodero entertained like a Croesus: Time, May 16, 1949.

CHAPTER FOUR

The most reliable and important single source for the story of Ari and Ingeborg Dedichen is the collection of letters, telegrams, diaries, documents and photograph albums kept by Ingeborg from 1935 to her death in Oslo in 1983. And for access to this wealth of material, together with the loan of her revealingly annotated copy of Joesten's *Onassis*, I am deeply indebted to her nephew and executor, Finn Bryde. As well as explaining his family's history, Mr. Bryde contributed invaluable personal memories, from which I gained many insights into the character of his aunt, as well as the subtle complexities of her extraordinary love affair with Ari. And I am especially grateful for the unfailingly kind and understanding manner in which he welcomed my researcher Ann Hoffmann on her visits to Oslo in 1983 and 1984. Mr. Bryde gave generously of his time, answering innumerable questions and clarifying many details of his aunt's life and relationships. The considerable Dedichen archive of papers was invaluable not only in my historical research and reconstruction, in fixing dates and places, particularly in the 1930s and 1940s, but also in confirming recollections, conversations and claims made by Ari and many others both in this chapter and throughout the whole book.

65
"It had an odor": Ingeborg Dedichen with Henry Pessar, *Onassis, Mon Amour* (Paris: Editions Pygmalion, 1975), p. 137.

65
"Liked to lick me": Ibid.

75
Fritz Mandl had already acquired a cattle ranch: "Poison from Europe," *The American Mercury,* January 1945.

Among the many publications that contributed to my understanding of the shipping business I am indebted to *Cases on Mercantile Law* by J. Charlesworth (London: Stevens & Sons Ltd., 1951); *Chartering and Shipping Terms* by J. Bes (Netherlands: Uitgeverij V/H C.De Boer Jr., Hilversum, 1951); *Lloyd's List, New York Journal of Commerce, Seatrade* and *Shipping Gazette.*

CHAPTER FIVE

Ari's recollections of this period were extraordinarily accurate. Emotions and thoughts he described to me in conversations that stretched over 1967–68, and lasted through the summer and autumn months of 1974, are repeatedly given affirmation in the letters and cables he exchanged with Ingeborg in 1940. He told me in Paris in the summer of 1974: "I was totally to blame for the bad times [with Ingse]. I was not very smart about some things. I was thinking about business too much. I always thought that there was plenty of time to relax and be happy, and there never is." Nearly thirty years earlier (see p. 79) he had written to her, "I allowed myself to be too absorbed": Undated, no address; DP (Dedichen Papers). An interesting account of the evacuation of the British embassy can be found on pages 232–33 of *The Paris Embassy* by Cynthia Gladwyn (London: Collins, 1976).

83
"My darling darling love": Hotel Tivoli, July 16, 1940; DP.

84
"Please try in friendship": Hotel Tivoli, August 8, 1940; DP.

84
"I can't go on": Hotel Tivoli, August 16, 1940; DP.

85
"An inestimable gift": Hotel Tivoli, September 2, 1940; DP.

85
"Ah mon dieu": Hotel Tivoli, September 3, 1940; DP.

89
It was at about this time that he first met Geraldine Spreckles: I first interviewed Geraldine Spreckles Fuller at her apartment on Park Avenue, New York City, September 21, 1983, and talked with her again when she invited me to lunch, with her husband, Andrew Fuller, at their home in Southampton, Long Island, N.Y., September 22, 1984. She had never talked publicly about her relationship with Ari before, and her personal reminiscences and opinions of the man she almost married in 1942 are in every sense a revelation. Her closeness to Ari at one of the most interesting and least-known periods of his life, and perhaps his most formative years, gave her many remarkable opportunities to observe his unpredictable humor, immense pride and private demons. I am deeply indebted to Geraldine Fuller. Not only was she extraordinarily gracious, kind and helpful at a time, I later learned, when she was recovering from illness, but she made no demands and imposed no restrictions whatsoever.

90
He gave his nationality as Argentine: Information contained in a letter written by J. Edgar Hoover to the head of the Los Angeles Federal Bureau of Investigation and obtained through the Freedom of Information Act.

93
"Nazi agents": Quoted in *Preminger, An Autobiography* (New York: Doubleday, 1977), p. 79. I interviewed Preminger at his apartment in New York on February 16, 1983, but it was shortly after he had had a serious

accident that affected his memory, and he was unable to add anything to his published remark.

96
She wished she were married to Ari now: According to Ingeborg's nephew, Finn Bryde, interviewed in Oslo in September 1983, the tragedy, and the recurring pattern, was that throughout their relationship when Ari wanted marriage, Ingeborg didn't; and when she was ready to marry, he didn't want it.

97
"Black butter": Onassis, *Mon Amour,* p. 201.

98
"From now on": Ibid., p. 215.

CHAPTER SIX

99–100
"Bisto kids, a hungry-looking pair": Heathfield Magazine, January 1939.

100
"We are pleased that she has gained her blue bow": In an interview with my researcher on August 25, 1983, the headmistress's secretary, Mrs. A. Jacot, explained that "bows" are given not necessarily for academic achievement, but for progress generally. She thought Tina had done very well to be given one in only her third term at the school.

Although Mme. Livanos was too unwell to talk with me personally, I am grateful for her permission to pursue my research at Heathfield, and for her blessing for this book.

102
"We never *stop trying":* Ari is reported to have made this remark on a number of occasions, but in Costa Gratsos's opinion this was the first.

103
Diamonds and Rolls-Royces: Time, May 16, 1949.

103
Shipping contracts, loans to buy more ships: Ibid.

104
When the application was turned down: Senate Report on the Sale of Government-Owned Surplus Tanker Vessels, May 29, 1952, p. 21.

105
Six hundred shares of this stock: Ibid.

105
Almost immediately, Dudley paid Admiral Bowen: Ibid.

105
During the following six months: Ibid.

106
Cokkinis (who had been naturalized a United States citizen): FBI memorandum from Allen J. Krause, department attorney in charge of criminal proceedings, to the head of the administrative regulations section, October 31, 1951, p. 6; obtained through the Freedom of Information Act.

107
OPM, he called the formula: Now common usage in financial circles, the OPM abridgement was first used by Tina, whose fondness for cryptic references (VBI's were people she found Very Boring Indeed; TBA's were those To Be Avoided) amused those in on the schoolgirl code.

CHAPTER SEVEN

The History of Modern Whaling by J. N. Tonnessen and A. O. Johnsen (London: C. Hurst & Co., 1982) was a basic source for the whaling material in this and subsequent chapters.

The Jiddah Agreement became the subject of many dispatches and articles in newspapers and magazines around the world. An essential source was the reporting in *Time, Newsweek, Paris Match, The New York Times* and the *International Herald Tribune.* Three volumes were very useful to my understanding of the politics of oil in the Middle East: *Blood, Oil and Sand* by Ray Brock (London: Bodley Head, 1952); *Power Play* by Leonard Mosley (New York: Random House, 1973); and *The Seven Sisters* by Anthony Sampson (New York: Bantam Books, 1976; London: Hodder and Stoughton Ltd., 1975).

111
"Ari was a no-desk executive": Although this was the impression he liked to give to his staff, he spent many hours every day (often in the early morning hours) at his desk.

112
"A new and amazingly prolific source of capital": Department of State Foreign Service documents obtained through the Freedom of Information Act.

114
"Onassis's agent": FBI documents obtained through the FIA.

114

Ari had cause for concern: Senate Interim Report on the Sale of Government-Owned Surplus Tanker Vessels, May 29, 1952.

115

"The New York office should immediately ascertain": FBI memorandum obtained through the FIA.

116

A figure of one million dollars: Time, November 22, 1954.

118

Now specialized in advising countries in the Moslem world: Time, October 6, 1952; *Fortune*, November 1952. I am indebted to Amos E. Simpson's *Hjalmar Schacht in Perspective* (The Hague: Moutan, 1969), and also to Kathleen Brown for her careful translation of so much German material, including the Schacht entry in *Biographisches Worterbuch zur Deutschen Geschichte*, vol. 3, 2d edition, and for her research into Ari's German interests.

CHAPTER EIGHT

120

"He was especially mad about Brownell": Ari was not alone. On February 17, 1954, Washington columnist Drew Pearson noted in his diary, "The Joe Caseys came for dinner. Joe has just been indicted on the sale of surplus tankers. He says [that] Brownell had been his personal attorney and had recommended in favor of the transfer of the tankers. The legal question at issue is whether an American citizen can transfer tankers he purchases from the United States government to foreigners. Brownell apparently O.K.'d such a transfer. Casey says that Onassis the Greek bought up various T-2 tankers which had been anchored in the Hudson and James rivers, where nobody wanted them. He also has been indicted and he also retained Brownell as his legal adviser. He paid Brownell ten thousand dollars personally": *Drew Pearson Diaries 1949–1959* (ed. Tyler Abell; New York: Holt, Rinehart & Winston, 1974; London: Jonathan Cape, 1974).

121

"He was traveling via": FBI documents obtained through the FIA.

125

"Those of us who truly comprehend": Elaine Davenport and Paul Eddy, with Mark Hurwitz, *The Hughes Papers* (London: André Deutsch, 1977).

125

From the beginning the CIA was picking up the tab: Inspector General's Report, 1967; Congressional Document O.C., 5.30.75.

125

Along the way he produced a pornographic movie: Ibid.

125

About two weeks after Ari's arrest: Interim Report of the U.S. Senate Select Committee to Study Governmental Operations with Respect to Intelligence Activities, November 1975.

125

Rome was the center of the CIA's covert political action program: William Colby, with Peter Forbath, *Honorable Men: My Life in the CIA* (New York: Simon and Schuster, 1977; London: Hutchinson, 1978).

125

"I want Onassis brought to heel": Author's interview with Alan Campbell-Johnson, London, January 10, 1983.

126

Maheu lost no time: Congressional Document O.C. 1975.

127

"Nixon gave us the whole bit": Jim Hougan, *Spooks, The Haunting of America: The Private Use of Secret Agents* (New York: Morrow, 1978), pp. 292–93.

127

For Nixon was extremely close to CIA boss Allen Dulles: Leonard Mosley, *Dulles: A Biography of Eleanor, Allen, and John Foster Dulles and Their Family Network* (New York: The Dial Press, 1978; London: Hodder and Stoughton, 1978).

127

The Nixons and Janet and John Foster Dulles became frequent dinner companions: Ibid.

128

"High Saudi circles": Department of State documents obtained through the FIA.

129

"He gave the impression": Parker T. Hart, quoted in *Aristotle Onassis.*

130

On June 12 he was back in Paris: I thank C. L. Sulzberger for permission to use these extracts from *A Long Row of Candles: Memoirs and Diaries 1934–54* (New York: Macmillan, 1969; London: Macdonald, 1969), and for our interesting conversation at his home in Paris on January 13, 1983.

133

"We believe it was a case of a smart Greek": CIA documents obtained through the FIA.

134

"From practical business viewpoint": Department of State documents obtained through the FIA.

135

"Fight fire with fire": Interview with Allen Dulles, "Meet the Press," NBC, December 31, 1961.

135

"Onassis was like a younger brother": Author's interview with Alan Campbell-Johnson, London, January 10, 1983.

137

"Riddled with corruption": Leonard Mosley, *Power Play* (New York: Random House, 1973; London: Weidenfeld and Nicholson Ltd., 1974).

CHAPTER NINE

Material for this chapter comes from various contemporary news accounts together with *Reports of the Whaling Board*, Oslo, 1972; the *Norwegian Whaling Gazette*, Sandefjord; and the *International Whaling Commission Reports* (annual), London and Cambridge. In addition to the invaluable *History of Modern Whaling*, I am also indebted to the Norwegian Whale Board archives. I am especially grateful to Mrs. Emery Reves, whose long interview at La Pausa, Roquebrune, with my researcher Ann Hoffmann over the weekend of November 18–20, 1983, has contributed important new material to the origins of the Churchill-Onassis friendship. Mrs. Reves spoke frankly and in depth for the first time about the years when she and her late husband had known Ari. Not only had she prepared for the interview, collecting her memories and thoughts in sequence, but she was also most patient and cooperative subsequently in answering my many queries.

I also thank Mary Soames for the enlightening conversation she had with Ann Hoffmann in London, February 16, 1984, and acknowledge the quotation from her father's letter from La Pausa, first published in her biography, *Clementine Churchill* (Boston: Houghton Mifflin Co., 1979; London: Cassell, 1979). I am also grateful to Doreen Pugh, Churchill's personal secretary, who had accompanied him to La Pausa on a number of visits; her willingness to check facts, dates and details for me in her diaries, and the conversation she had with Ann Hoffmann in London, January 23, 1984, was of immense help.

144
In 1955 the SBM paid: *London Evening Standard*, September 19, 1955.

145
She was stunned: Margot Fonteyn: Autobiography (New York: Knopf, 1975).

146
"A hundred years ago": Quoted in *Paris Match*, July 16, 1955.

147
"He asked me": Author's interview with Nigel Neilson, London, July 26, 1983; also with my researcher Ann Hoffmann, London, January 24, 1984.

148
"Anxious to plant the Panamanian flag atop the palace": In an interview with *Paris Match* (July 4, 1953), Ari denied any such ambition; he was content to leave the flag of Panama on his ships: "Besides, there's a French-Monaguesque tradition which limits the tonnage of the principality. Would *I* oppose that?" he asked.

150
Philadelphia Social Register: "The stupendous upward mobility of the [Kelly] family did not suffice to get them into the Philadelphia Social Register": Jack Kroll, with Scott Sullivan, *Newsweek*, September 27, 1982.

152
Forty agents had been assigned: FBI documents obtained through the FIA.

158
Returning to the library: It seems that Wendy Russell Reves succeeded completely in changing Churchill's view of Ari. The following day, January 17, 1956, Churchill wrote to his wife in London: "Randolph brought Onassis (the one with the big yacht) to dinner last night. He made a good impression upon me. He is a vy able and masterful man & told us a lot about Whales. He kissed my hand!"

158
Nevertheless, when Ari came down the gangway: An entry in Doreen Pugh diary establishes this as Easter Monday, April 2, 1956.

CHAPTER TEN

The description of Ari's appearance before the congressional subcommittee is based on contemporary newspaper accounts, especially reports in the *New York Times* and the *Washington Post*, together with the recollections of Ari, Costa Gratsos and John Meyer, made during conversations with the author. In an interview in Paris in December 1982, Tom Fabre talked at length with my researcher Jill Ibrahim of his association with Ari. In addition to much valuable information, he gave several useful leads. He has my warm thanks.

159
"With the posturing spirit": Author's interview with a former Monaco officeholder, who asks that he not be named.

159
Ari was extremely conscious: Author's interview with Alan Brien, London, May 13, 1985.

160
"Mr. Onassis, you were badly brought up": London *Daily Mail*, April 17, 1956.

160
On one occasion: Ibid.

164
"Maybe he thought": The Kennedys: An American Drama by Peter Collier and David Horowitz (New York: Summit Books, 1984), p. 196.

165
In May on the BBC: Transmitted May 5, 1958.

165
"He was quite a civilized man": Author's interview with Sir Woodrow Wyatt, London, May 10, 1983.

169
Beaverbrook was delighted: Author's interview with Sam White, Paris, October 7, 1982.

169
Beaverbrook letter: Beaverbrook Papers, House of Lords Record Office.

169
"Together with Lady Churchill": Ibid.

169
"Tied and bound": Ibid.

CHAPTER ELEVEN

The account of the fateful *Christina* cruise in July 1959 comes from several sources, but I am most deeply grateful to Lady Sargant, the former Nonie Montague Browne, who gave two extremely helpful interviews in London, May 5 and August 9, 1983, to my researcher Ann Hoffmann. Lady Sargant, who accompanied Churchill on eight cruises on the *Christina*, and knew Ari for almost twenty years, not only talked at length to Ms. Hoffmann, and took the trouble to read and approve Ms. Hoffmann's notes, but added many additional comments and observations, culled from her diaries; she also gave her own wise and helpful asessments of Ari, his family and many of the people involved in this episode.

170
"One lunch": Author's conversation with Alexander Onassis, in Paris, c. April 1968.

170
In one spectacular temper tantrum: Author's interview with Joseph Bolker in Los Angeles, February 13, 1983.

171
"Almost ashamed": From a friend who asked not to be named, interviewed in France by Ann Hoffmann.

172
Sixty-three dollars: Time, October 29, 1956.

172
In his 1981 biography: My Wife Maria Callas (New York: Farrar, Straus and Giroux, Inc., 1982; London: Bodley Head, 1983; first published in Italian as *Maria Callas mia moglie:* Rusconi Libri S.p.A, Milan, 1981.)

173
He sold his factories: Time, October 29, 1956.

176
"I sometimes wish": William Hickey, *London Daily Express,* June 18, 1959.

176
The fee for her concert: Arianna Stassinopoulos, *Maria Callas* (New York: Simon and Schuster, 1981; London: Weidenfeld & Nicolson Ltd., 1980).

177
She boasted: In her memoirs Maxwell admitted that she had "never had a sexual experience, nor did I ever want one" *(Elsa Maxwell's Own Story:* Boston: Little, Brown, 1954; published in England under the title *I Married the World:* London: Heinemann, Ltd., 1955).

177

Speculative attempts: Lady Sargant politely confined her observations to the fact that Meneghini "had big feet and was always moving them about under the table."

178

Debaucheries and bacchanalia: On July 23, 1984, Anthony Montague Browne won a public apology in the High Court over allegations in Meneghini's book that he and his wife, together with Sir Winston and Lady Churchill, were present during an orgy on this cruise. His counsel called the claim a "gross and inexcusable fiction." The English publishers, Bodley Head, accepted there was no truth in the claim.

179

Putting off the Bellini score: Stassinopoulos, *Maria Callas.*

180

Artemis, Ari's "little sister": Interview with Lady Sargant.

181

He could not rid from his mind: "It seemed almost as if he [the patriarch] were performing a marriage rite," Meneghini recorded in his memoirs.

181

"Don't touch": Ibid.

181

"We're floating in shit": Meneghini, *My Wife Maria Callas.*

182

"You must either wallop a man": Lord Moran, *Churchill: The Struggle for Survival 1940–65* (Boston: Houghton Mifflin, 1966; London: Constable, 1966).

183

"Almost completely naked": Meneghini, *My Wife Maria Callas.*

186

"Of course, how could I help but": London *Daily Mail,* September 9, 1959.

188

Help her over emotional and drug problems: Author's interview with Geraldine Fuller, New York, September 21, 1983.

CHAPTER TWELVE

The story of Maria and Ari's battle with Vergottis (Onassis and Calogeropoulos v. Vergottis) is based on court records (*Lloyd's List Law Reports: Queen's Bench Division Commercial Court* before Mr. Justice Roskill: April 17–28, 1967) with background insights and opinions from three lawyers involved in the case, all of whom asked that they not be named. For material from the Supreme Court of Judicature Court of Appeal (January 23, 1968), I am indebted to the transcript from the shorthand notes of The Association of Official Shorthandwriters, Ltd., Royal Courts of Justice. Of the many books written about Maria Callas the two I found most helpful were John Ardoin's *The Callas Legacy* (New York: Scribner's, c. 1977; London: Duckworth, 1977) and Arianna Stassinopoulos's *Maria Callas*.

189
"Even in love": From a letter Tina wrote to a London friend, who does not wish to be identified.

191
"So absorbed in themselves": Author's conversation with Alexander Onassis, Paris, c. April 1968.

192
"In Greece he behaved like a Greek": Fraser, Jacobson, Ottaway, Chester, *Aristotle Onassis,* p. 215.

194
"Sacra Roman Rota": On February 16, 1964, the Vatican announced the annulment of Lee Radziwill's first marriage. To be successful before this tribunal, a person must prove that the marriage, in effect, never took place; applicants sometimes claim that it was never consummated. "Many Catholics were not pleased with the Vatican's decision and felt that the influence of the Kennedys might have been felt in Rome. A Roman Catholic bishop in Nova Scotia publicly condemned the verdict": From author's profile of Lee Radziwill, *Cosmopolitan,* March 1968.

195
"Just tell her to cool it": Kitty Kelley, *Jackie Oh!* (Secaucus, N.J: L. Stuart, c. 1978; London: Hart-Davis, MacGibbon Ltd., 1978).

196
"Indicated he would like": FBI documents obtained through the FIA.

197
"Guilt feelings": Benjamin Bradlee, *Conversations with Kennedy* (New York: W. W. Norton & Co., 1975).

198
"The center of interest": William Manchester, *The Death of a President* (New York: Harper and Row, 1967; London: Michael Joseph, 1967).

200
"As long as I hear": Time, October 29, 1956.

205
At one point: Stassinopoulos, *Maria Callas.*

CHAPTER THIRTEEN

Jacqueline Onassis's rendezvous with the *Christina* in the Virgin Islands was first described to me by Joan Thring Stafford in London on March 21, 1975. I have met and talked with her many times since. Her stylish, ironic, firsthand descriptions of incidents are difficult to paraphrase with justice, and I trust she will accept my rendering of the material she has generously contributed to this chapter. Press coverage of the wedding ceremony on Skorpios was limited to a small number of cameramen and reporters, who were kept outside the church. They briefed their colleagues on their return to Athens on Sunday evening, under a pool arrangement; the films were also shared. Although the description of the ceremony is based on various newspaper accounts, two sources deserve special mention: Alvin Shuster's report appearing in the *New York Times,* October 21, 1968; and *Newsweek's* cover story, October 28, 1968. My account was amplified with the help of several of the guests, including Alexander Onassis and Artemis Garofalides.

The books that have been of most value to my understanding of the subversion and intrigue of the colonels' regime are John A. Katris's *Eyewitness in Greece* (St. Louis, MO.: New Critics Press Inc., 1971); the pseudonymous Athenian's *Inside the Colonels' Greece* (London: Chatto & Windus, 1972); William H. McNeill's *The Metamorphosis of Greece since World War II* (The University of Chicago, 1978; Basil Blackwell, Oxford, 1978); C. M. Woodhouse's *The Rise and Fall of the Greek Colonels* (London: Granada Publishing, 1985); *Greece under Military Rule,* ed. Richard Clogg and George Yannopoulos (London: Secker & Warburg, 1972).

211
"He's spending an awful lot": Richard Lee, "Ethel Kennedy Today," *Washingtonian,* June 1983.

211
"Do you know what I think": Arthur M. Schlesinger, Jr., *Robert Kennedy and His Times* (New York: Houghton Mifflin, 1978).

212
"I guess you know": Fred Sparks, *The $20,000,000 Honeymoon* (New York: Bernard Geis Associates, 1970), p. 26.

214
"They were certainly not yet lovers": Author's interview with Joan Thring Stafford.

216
"Deeply despised": Bobby Baker, *Wheeling and Dealing* (New York: W. W. Norton & Co., 1978).

216
"Enjoyed reading FBI files": David Halberstam, *The Best and the Brightest* (New York: Random House, 1972).

216
Old friends: Schlesinger, Jr., *Robert Kennedy and His Times*.

216
In his bargaining: "The Death of Dave Karr, and Other Mysteries," *Fortune*, December 3, 1979.

217
"I hate this country": Kitty Kelley, *Jackie Oh!*

217
"As a matter of fact": Schlesinger, Jr., *Robert Kennedy and His Times*.

218
"She was shocked": Author's interview with a confidential source.

219
"Scrunched up": Rose Fitzgerald Kennedy, *Times to Remember* (New York: Doubleday & Co., 1974; London: Collins, 1974).

221
"We love Jackie": Willi Frischauer, *Jackie* (London: Sphere Books, 1977).

221
"This is in accordance": Thomas Wiseman, *The Money Motive: A Study of an Obsession* (New York: Random House, 1974; London: Hutchinson, 1974).

222
"He did not feel": Cary Reich, *Financier: The Biography of André Meyer* (New York: Morrow & Co., Inc., 1983), p. 262.

222
"Where's the bottle": Jack Anderson and Joseph Spear, *Washington Post*, August 26, 1985.

223
Stipulating separate bedrooms: Christian Cafarakis, *The Fabulous Onassis, His Life and Loves* (New York: William Morrow & Co., Inc., 1972).

223
"He could get": Pierre Salinger in an interview with author's researcher Jill Ibrahim, Paris, December 1982.

223
"Stop all this": Cardinal Cushing, Boston, October 1968.

225
"Oh shit!": Cited by Pierre Salinger, Paris, December 1982.

226–7
"Was not a person who would jump rashly": Rose Fitzgerald Kennedy, *Times to Remember.*

227
"Nobody knew": Donald McGregor in an interview with author's aviation researcher, Mike Jerram, in Northamptonshire, England, September 1983.

228
"PT-109 tie clip": New York Times, October 21, 1968.

228
"Billy," she said: Billy Baldwin Remembers (New York: Harcourt Brace Jovanovich, 1974).

230
"With the coming of the Colonels": Helen Vlachos, *House Arrest* (Boston: Gambit, 1971).

231
"Forty dresses": Time, June 11, 1973.

231
Although he never studied economics: Katris, *Eyewitness in Greece*, p. 252.

231
"It was even corroborated by": Solon Grigoriadis, *Istoria tis Diktatorias* (3 vols., Athens, 1976), III, p. 343, quoting interview with Senator Thomas Eagleton in *Acropolis*, August 22, 1975.

232
"No account books": New York Times, September 15, 1968.

233

The law lords upheld: Onassis and Another (feme sole) versus Vergottis et è contra, Vol. 1170, House of Lords Record Office.

235

"As you might have noticed": FBI document obtained through FIA.

237

"Look here, you!": Katris, *Eyewitness in Greece*, p. 254.

CHAPTER FOURTEEN

Fiona Thyssen I did not meet until September 5, 1983, but I have spent many hours with her since, and owe her a debt of gratitude that cannot ever adequately be expressed. This chapter, and much of what follows, could not have been written with so much factual detail and intimate knowledge had it not been for her generosity and exemplary patience in answering my many questions. That in the course of our meetings we became friends is perhaps the most rewarding fringe benefit I have received from the writing of this biography. Her warm sense of humanity, eye for telling detail, and willingness to talk to me with such openness about herself, as well as about many others in this story, make of her almost a collaborator, and have done so much to enrich, explain and throw new light on the Onassis saga. Her approval, in October of 1985, when she read the typescript of these pages, made the long and difficult process of writing a book such as this worthwhile.

I want next to thank Joseph Bolker, Christina's first husband, who agreed to talk to me at his home in Los Angeles, February 13, 1983, and was primed and candid beyond any hopes that a biographer might have. I am grateful to Mr. Bolker not only for giving up hours of a precious weekend with his new wife, Victoria Tatyana, and their young son, but letting me see personal letters supporting his version of events.

249

"Sophists": *Time*, November 1, 1971.

250

"He could make": Author's interview with Willi Frischauer in London, c. June 1974.

250

"What happened I don't know": In interview with author's aviation researcher, Mike Jerram.

253

"Although she wanted": Author's interview with confidential source.

CHAPTER FIFTEEN

The background to the private dramas, the details of the deepening relationship between Alexander and Fiona, the growing gulf between Alexander and his father, the description of the hospital scenes and the family
gathering in Athens, come essentially from Fiona Thyssen. I am indebted
to consultant neurosurgeon Alan E. Richardson, F.R.C.S., who gave generously of his valuable time (London, May 17, 1983) to recollect his part
in the events of January 22–23, 1973; and later to take the trouble to write
a thoughtful answer to my further query. Roy Cohn was similarly kind in
finding time in a busy schedule (New York, February 17, 1983) not only to
talk to me about Ari's plans to divorce Jackie but to detail the timetable
of events that brought his client to that decision. Mr. Cohn's contribution
to my clearer understanding of both Ari's state of mind and his relationship with his wife at this time has been indispensable. Donald McGregor
was immensely kind and helpful in the summer of 1983, both through his
reminiscences and the loan of many important documents, including a
copy of his own handwritten statement made to the Greek authorities on
the accident. The description of the Piaggio crash comes from his recollections and statement, and also from the investigation report of the Greek
air force. I am grateful to Mike Jerram, whose research into the Piaggio
disaster, and all of Ari's aviation ventures, has been meticulous. Once
again I must thank Geraldine Fuller, this time for the story of the Haiti
cruise.

261
"Cool and sharp": Willi Frischauer, *Jackie*.

263
"What does she do": Jack Anderson, *New York Post*, April 16, 1975.

275
He repeatedly played a tape: Author's interview with a confidential source.

CHAPTER SIXTEEN

Many people have helped me piece together the events contained in this
chapter, most of whom are identified in the narrative, including Costa
Konialidis, Hélène Gaillet, Geraldine Fuller, Sir John Russell, Wendy
Russell Reves and several others who have requested to remain anonymous. For facts about the state of the tanker market and the critical
position of Ari's fleet at this time I have gone to contemporary newspaper
accounts, including reports in *Business Week*, the *Wall Street Journal* and
the *London Financial Times*. The Durham Point debacle was covered in
many newspapers, but I am especially indebted to John Kifner's report
("Onassis Refinery Plan Divides New Hampshire Area") in the *New York*

Times, January 27, 1974; and Gerry Nadel's *Esquire* article ("The Score from New Hampshire: Democracy 1, Aristotle Onassis 0") in July 1974.

278
"There were about eight of us": Author's interview with Hélène Gaillet, New York, September 23, 1983.

280
"She always seemed": Author's interview with Sir John Russell, London, April 6, 1983.

280
"Late one night": Author's interview with a source that does not wish to be identified.

282
"State is the pipple": Gerry Nadel.

283
"Final symptom": Author's interview with confidential source.

284
Aristotle Socrates Onassis was drafting: Newsweek, July 28, 1975.

284
Alpha and Beta: New York Times, June 8, 1975.

285
"Period of togetherness": Liz Smith, "Jacqueline Kennedy Onassis: The Ultimate Goddess," *Cosmopolitan,* October 1974.

286
It was Booras: New York Times, January 27, 1974.

287
The umpteenth time: Gerry Nadel.

288
"She had acquired": Author's interview with a confidential source.

CHAPTER SEVENTEEN

The background to the public events described in this chapter, to Christina's suicide bid in London, to Tina's death in Paris, to Ari's flight to Athens to try to save his Olympic airline, and to his final days comes from many published sources in the United States and Europe. For the details I am indebted to a number of people. Peter Stephens's personal recollections have been an invaluable source of new material, and frequently a confirmation of stories and information obtained from others; he drew on his long experience as Paris bureau chief of the *London Daily Mirror* to help me find my way to many of the French bankers, socialites and others who had been close to Ari and Tina.

290
"I think he suddenly": Author's interview with a confidential source.

290
"Perhaps she was simply numb": Ibid.

290–91
"Is she always that aloof?": Author's interview with Nigel Neilson, London, July 26, 1983.

293
"I've never been able to decide": Author's interview with Peter Stephens, Paris, January 13, 1983.

293
"The psychic wounds": Author's interview with a confidential source.

293
"Not a hundred percent": Author's interview with Hélène Gaillet, New York, September 23, 1983.

296
His habit of pressing: Author's interview with Walter G. Conrad, Hyannis, Massachusetts, September 24, 1983.

296
"Promotion campaign rarely equalled": Wall Street Journal, October 21, 1974.

296
"He was so out of touch": Author's interview with confidential source.

297
Jackie was with some of the old JFK team: Time, December 30, 1974.

297
Skiing with her son: Time, January 13, 1975.

298
It was later revealed: "The Reality Behind the Onassis Myth" *by Lewis Beman, Fortune,* October 1975.

300
It was a dry, almost balmy evening: National Meteorological Institute, Paris.

303
"Artists' exit": Author's interview with hospital sources.

304
It rained for twelve hours: National Meteorological Institute, Paris.

304
She called Teddy Kennedy: Kitty Kelley, *Jackie Oh!*

306
"She knew that Teddy": Author's interview with a confidential source.

306
"1900–1975": London Times, March 19, 1975.

306
As the sky darkened: New York Times, March 19, 1975.

EPILOGUE

Once again I am indebted to Roy Cohn for his informed insights into the relationship between Jacqueline Onassis and her stepdaughter after Ari's death. The bizarre manner of Johnny Meyer's death in Florida was described to me by Brian Wells. Of the many gossip writers who have kept assiduous track of Christina's peripatetic engagements, I am especially grateful to Nigel Dempster in London, Suzy and Liz Smith in New York, and the unnumbered Christina specialists on *Paris Match.*

307
Renounced her United States citizenship: New York Times, June 9, 1975.

307
Beneficiary of that trust: Ibid.

308
Devoted essentially to social welfare: New York Daily News, June 6, 1975.

308
Task force: Seatrade, April 1975.

309
Ledgers for one corporation: New York Times, June 15, 1975.

311
Marking the fortieth day: Time, May 5, 1975.

311
"Of course there were business influences": Author's interview with confidential source.

313
Olympic paid out seventeen million dollars: Fortune, October 1975.

313
Olympic Bravery *ran aground: New York Times*, October 9, 1977.

313
"The vicious circle": Cited in an interview with Henri Leridon, *London Daily Mail*, July 28, 1975.

313
A private nurse: Ibid.

314
The lovers had a great deal in common: New York Times, July 23, 1975.

314
The colonels' successors: Ibid.

315
"So loved that child": Ibid.

316
Important Soviet officials: Fortune, December 3, 1979.

316
Faced charges of fraud: UPI agency report, Athens, October 24, 1976.

316
In Paris she was reported: New York Daily News, November 24, 1976.

317
"Who is Dostoyevsky?": *Time*, August 14, 1978.

317
Tanker from D. K. Ludwig: Wall Street Journal, February 22, 1977.

318
"Maria never did get": Author's interview with confidential source.

318
A quick divorce: Jack Anderson, *Parade*, April 29, 1979.

318
The affair was first uncovered: Author's interview with French intelligence source.

318
Christina had access: Author's interview with British intelligence source.

321
"Are you still in love with your wife?": Jack Anderson, *Parade*, April 29, 1979.

322
Poisoned by the Russians: *Fortune*, December 3, 1979.

324
"You dare not admire": Author's interview with Jean-Pierre de Lucovich, Paris, January 16, 1983.

326
She invited Jamie: Nigel Dempster, *London Daily Mail*, August 30, 1983.

326
"White coats, ambulances, the lot": You, *London Mail on Sunday*, July 28, 1985.

327
Late one afternoon: Author's researcher Ann Hoffmann's interview with Finn Bryde, Oslo, September 1983.

INDEX

ABOUT THE AUTHOR

In 1968, British journalist and novelist Peter Evans was called to Paris to meet Aristotle Onassis. Surprised and intrigued, Evans went to the meeting and discovered that Onassis was thinking of "making a book" about his life. Evans was interested, but wary of writing a sanitized biography of the shipping magnate. Onassis assured him that the book would be "a hundred percenter, exactly how it was." He provided Evans with total access to his friends, family, business colleagues, and himself but, after months of conversations, Ari abruptly canceled the project. After Onassis died, Evans set to work again, digging even deeper than his subject may have intended.

Ari is the explosive result.

Peter Evans is also the author of *The Englishman's Daughter*. He lives in London.